SURRENDER UNTO ME

An Overview of the Bhagavad-gītā

SURRENDER UNTO ME

An Overview of the Bhagavad-gītā

Based on the commentaries of
Śrīla Viśvanātha Cakravartī Ṭhākura,
Śrīla Baladeva Vidyābhūṣaṇa,
and His Divine Grace
A. C. Bhaktivedanta Swami Prabhupāda,
Founder-*Ācārya* of the International Society
for Krishna Consciousness

BHŪRIJANA DĀSA

VIHE
PUBLICATIONS

Readers interested in the subject matter of this book are invited to correspond with the publisher at info@vihepublications.com or visit https://vihepublications.com

ISBN: 978-0-9925219-29

Printed in India

Reprinted 2021

To Śrīla Prabhupāda,

who combated illusion
with the fury of Arjuna,
the powerful, victorious,
and ferocious warrior-hero,
but who also embodied
the gentle simplicity of
fearless Prahlāda, a young boy.

Contents

Chapters

Appendixes

Foreword

Only one out of many thousands of people even wants to leave the material world, and of those rare souls, hardly one knows how to do it. By the mercy of Śrīla Prabhupāda, and without deserving it, we have received this most precious knowledge. The key to our release from material entanglement is simply to take advantage of the association of Hari, *guru, Bhāgavata* and *Gītā*. The Supreme Person comes to us in His names, His *mūrtis* and His dearmost devotees, and He gives us the essence of revealed scriptures, specially packaged for our easy consumption in this dull-minded age. Thus He provides us the solid *tattva-jñāna* to understand how to correctly put aside *māyā* and to approach Him.

Śrīmad-Bhāgavatam (1.16.6) explains that for anyone with a sense of his real self-interest, the only discussions worth hearing are those that glorify God and His devotees. *Kim anyair asad-ālāpair āyuṣo yad asad-vyayaḥ:* "What is the use of topics which simply waste one's valuable life?" Śrīla Prabhupāda said that *kṛṣṇa-kathā* comes in two varieties: one spoken by Lord Kṛṣṇa and the other spoken about Him. Of course, *Śrīmad-Bhāgavatam* is not the only book about Kṛṣṇa, and *Bhagavad-gītā* is not the only instruction spoken by Him. Many of the other *Purāṇas* have chapters describing Kṛṣṇa's pastimes in Vṛndāvana, Mathurā, and Dvārakā, and Kṛṣṇa spoke another wonderful *Gītā* to Uddhava. Many Vaiṣṇavas prefer to study Kṛṣṇa indirectly in the *Vedānta-sūtra*. Some persons worship demigods and like to read scriptures such as the *Devī-bhāgavata*, while others prefer *Time* magazine. Therefore those who understand the prime importance of hearing constantly from the *Bhāgavatam* and *Gītā* are especially fortunate. They have received the very uncommon mercy of Lord Śrī Caitanya Mahāprabhu and the *ācāryas* who are His servants. These most fortunate devotees can understand that *Śrīmad-Bhāgavatam* is not just another *Purāṇa* and that what Kṛṣṇa and Arjuna said to each other at Kurukṣetra is unique. *Ekaṁ śāstraṁ devakī-putra-gītam:* In Śaṅkarācārya's opinion, even if all the other scriptures in the world were to disappear, *Bhagavad-gītā* alone would perfectly fulfill the needs in everyone's spiritual education.

What is so special about this one short book? In it Kṛṣṇa does not explicitly reveal that much about Himself. He doesn't describe His intimate pleasure pastimes. He doesn't say anything about His eternal kingdom other than that there is no need of sunlight or electricity, and that whoever goes there never returns. But He does address Himself in His *Gītā* to the conditioned souls in the material world, especially the spiritually unfit souls of the modern age, and tells them what they need to hear. He says in uncomplicated terms why they should not remain entrapped in the bodily concept of life, and how, step by step, they can become free and regain their real life. Anyone who is still a conditioned soul should be glad to hear these instructions on the science of liberation. Because they were spoken by the one person most competent to teach them, they have all potency to transform the life of anyone who hears them with a little faith.

Those who are already liberated also relish the Personality of Godhead's words on these essential topics and refer to them regularly while preaching. I was informed by a predecessor of mine in the BBT Sanskrit department of something that Śrīla Prabhupāda once told him. Śrīla Prabhupāda said that every devotee who wants to be a good preacher should become proficient in *Bhagavad-gītā*. Even in his own morning *Bhāgavatam* classes, Śrīla Prabhupāda noted, most of the verses he cited were from the *Gītā*.

It was *Bhagavad-gītā As It Is,* the perfect instructions of the Supreme passed on to us by His perfect devotee, that made most of us decide to enter the Vaiṣṇava path. Now that we have made a little progress, we shouldn't forget the book's importance; it is not just for beginners. Rather, it is the distilled essence of the *Upaniṣads,* of the exacting philosophy of *Vedānta.* It may have been placed by Śrīla Dvaipāyana Vyāsa within the entertaining *Mahābhārata,* which is designated for the use of women, *śūdras,* and unqualified *brāhmaṇas,* but its being hidden in that fashion does not at all diminish its real glory. Lord Kṛṣṇa also effaces Himself in *Mahābhārata,* taking a secondary role in deference to the Pāṇḍavas; but when he finally reveals Himself fully to Arjuna at a moment of crisis in the *Bhīṣma-parva,* we become freed from doubt as to who Kṛṣṇa really is and who we are in relation to Him.

This new overview of the *Bhagavad-gītā,* by His Grace Bhūrijana Prabhu, is a welcome addition to the shelf of books by Śrīla Prabhupāda's disciples. *Surrender Unto Me* offers valuable guidance in understanding the dynamic logic of the *Gītā,* the thread of the conversation from verse to verse. We hear, from the great Gauḍīya *ācāryas* Śrīla Viśvanātha Cakravartī and Śrīla Baladeva Vidyābhūṣaṇa, elucidations that bring us closer to a full understanding of Śrīla Prabhupāda's explanation. Rather than distracting from the glories of the Bhaktivedanta purports in *Bhagavad-gītā As It Is, Surrender Unto Me* turns on them a spotlight. I have no doubt that after studying *Surrender Unto Me* devotees will better appreciate and understand the *Gītā.*

That Bhūrijana Prabhu has been able to illuminate the *Gītā* and Śrīla Prabhupāda's purports so well is proof that he has satisfied Śrīla Prabhupāda by his devotional service. We can also get that same mercy by giving careful attention to studying *Bhagavad-gītā* and practicing what Kṛṣṇa teaches. One episode in Śrīla Prabhupāda's preaching, about which I once heard, may be spurious but apt: When a proud Indian gentleman announced, "Swamijī, I can recite the *Bhagavad-gītā* in forty-eight minutes," Śrīla Prabhupāda asked, "But can you live the *Bhagavad-gītā* for forty-eight minutes?" Bhūrijana Prabhu has been reading and living the *Bhagavad-gītā* for more than a quarter of a century. Despite what he may say about himself in his humility, this is proof enough to me that he has earned Śrīla Prabhupāda's satisfaction and is fit to comment on these most confidential instructions of the blessed Lord.

His Grace Gopīparāṇadhana Dāsa,
Late BBT Senior Sanskrit Editor

Preface

Some people aren't satisfied unless they understand how a thing works. They must know how its pieces fit together and its parts move, and they question, feel dissatisfied and remain disturbed until they find out. I am one of those people.

As soon as I began studying Śrīla Prabhupāda's *Bhagavad-gītā As It Is*, when the purple-covered, abridged Macmillan edition was published in 1969, I almost immediately began to tinker and fiddle with the verses to discover their philosophical continuity. I began with the assumption that Śrī Kṛṣṇa, the Supreme Personality of Godhead, had spoken His verses both logically and systematically.

Certainly Śrīla Prabhupāda had made Kṛṣṇa's goal ring clear in almost every verse and purport of *Bhagavad-gītā*. No one could misconstrue the universal form or formless Brahman to be the supreme realization. Nor could anyone misunderstand the actual process for advancement which Kṛṣṇa recommended. That process was not altruism, austerity, meditation, charity, *yoga āsanas* or renunciation. It was *bhakti*, His own devotional service. In other words, Śrīla Prabhupāda's *Bhagavad-gītā As It Is* neatly popped every bubble of misconception about Kṛṣṇa's purpose in speaking the *Gītā*.

Kṛṣṇa, Śrīla Prabhupāda transparently revealed, is the Supreme Personality of Godhead, the source of all. The living entities are not God, as I was imagining the first time I read *Bhagavad-gītā*. Rather, hard as it is to swallow, we are simply His insignificant servants, meant to surrender and serve Him under the guidance of His representative, a spiritual master.

Despite personal limitations and my inability to perfectly execute *bhakti-yoga*, all the above-mentioned conclusions became quickly and unavoidably evident through Śrīla Prabhupāda's powerful presentation. Yet I wasn't satisfied. I wanted to understand the *Gītā's* logic. *Surrender Unto Me* is the fruit of twenty-seven years of study. It is my attempt to understand and explain the philosophic progression in *Bhagavad-gītā* – how the verses, sections, and chapters fit together.

While teaching *Bhagavad-gītā* Overview courses in Vṛndāvana and other places around the world, I discovered that devotees not only appreciated the systematic presentation of the *Gītā's* progression but were also practically helped by their study. I've placed into three categories the practical benefits of studying the *Bhagavad-gītā* in overview:

1) A deepened understanding of the *Bhagavad-gītā* increases our ability to apply *śāstra* in our lives and increases our enthusiasm to preach. Generally, after a few years in the Hare Kṛṣṇa movement, devotees consider the *Gītā* a known book. After all, it covers our basic philosophy, the ABCs of spiritual understanding. Yet Śrīla Prabhupāda requested that our understanding be more than basic. He said we should know the *Bhagavad-gītā* backwards and forwards like the Christians know the Bible. Why? For preaching, certainly, but also because practical answers to most of life's questions can be found in *Bhagavad-gītā*.

When I began to assist other devotees in their study – verse by verse and purport by purport – I discovered that we all had many questions. "Oh, I never understood that verse and purport before," was a phrase commonly heard in the class. *Surrender Unto Me,* I hope, will answer unanswered questions and strengthen our philosophical foundation.

The *Gītā,* when thoroughly understood, allows us to observe the modes of nature pushing and pulling everyone. We learn the difference between the unique way Kṛṣṇa cares for His devotees and how He reciprocates with others. We hear Kṛṣṇa's plea for all to come to Him. We learn the gradual steps of elevation on the path of *bhakti;* we learn to recognize one fixed in transcendance; and we learn the qualities a devotee must cultivate to make advancement. Kṛṣṇa explains His laws that govern the transmigration of the soul. He clearly describes how each element within the Vedic culture, when carried to perfection, leads to His service. We hear arguments against atheism, impersonalism, and Māyāvāda philosophy. We encounter stages of doubt. We hear of Kṛṣṇa's opulence and power, and learn various ways of seeing and remembering Him. We learn the essence of *bhakti* and how to act and not act – according to our actual position – so that our advancement in Kṛṣṇa's service is nurtured. And we hear of the protection and deep commitment Kṛṣṇa offers His devotees.

Equipped with answers to our own questions and confident of our ability to answer those of others, our own fresh enthusiasm about the *Gītā* naturally encourages us to apply the teachings to ourselves and to teach them to others.

2) The *Gītā* details progressive stages of advancement in *bhakti*. As our understanding of these stages increases, our ability to practically apply them is enhanced. As a *gurukula* teacher, I learned that effective instruction must necessarily be addressed to a student's actual stage of advancement. Instruction directed to what I wished or imagined to be the student's level, or to the group level of his classmates, proved counter-productive.

But how many devotees thoroughly understand the levels of advancement that Kṛṣṇa describes in *Bhagavad-gītā*? Without rigorous knowledge of those progressions, such as the *yoga* ladder, we can sincerely err in our advice and instructions to others. If our understanding remains general and we prescribe the one medicine, for example, "fully-surrendered temple life" to all, we risk creating havoc and confusion among congregational members and temple devotees, celibates and householders. Or, conversely, if we fail to administer that correct medicine when appropriate, we also blunder into disservice. Having an overview of the levels of progress described in *Bhagavad-gītā* can add śāstric structure to our management, instruction, and counsel. Realization of this knowledge is also most relevant in applying *Bhagavad-gītā* in our own lives.

At this point, I'd like to state the specific goal of my attempt in this book to clarify the steps of the *yoga* ladder. I do not promote a viewpoint that those practicing devotional service on the level of *sākama karma-yoga* and *niṣkāma karma-yoga* are not devotees, nor am I arguing that only full *bhaktas* – those on the platform of pure transcendental service – should be termed devotees. Rather, my aim in delineating the levels of *yoga* practice – supported by Śrīla Prabhupāda's liberal view of all practioners as devotees – is to provide the vocabulary and the definitions to aid devotees in recognizing their own levels of advancement and to increase their ability to serve others. The view of devotional service in this book is that all those desiring to serve Kṛṣṇa and His devotees are devotees, yet all nevertheless practice devotional service, according to their advancement, on different levels.

3) Drawing from the commentaries of great Vaiṣṇava *ācāryas* connects us to our tradition. The Hare Kṛṣṇa movement is not a new religion. Rather, it represents the grand tradition of Madhva-Gauḍīya Vaiṣṇavism. Śrīla Prabhupāda, Śrīla Viśvanātha Cakravartī Ṭhākura, and Śrīla Baladeva Vidyābhūṣaṇa are our heroes, and we should get to know and respect the entirety of our brilliant heritage.

Indeed, it was a *Bhagavad-gītā* commentary by Śrīla Viśvanātha Cakravartī Ṭhākura that struck Śrīla Prabhupāda and further fixed him in his determination to satisfy his spiritual master by preaching Kṛṣṇa consciousness in the West:

> Of all kinds of intelligence, the best is intelligence focused on *bhakti-yoga.* In *bhakti-yoga,* one's intelligence becomes single-pointed, or fixed in determination. One thinks, "The instructions of my spiritual master to worship the Personality of Godhead by chanting, remembering, serving His feet, and so on are my only *sādhana,* my only *sādhya,* my only livelihood. I am incapable of giving up these instructions either in the stage of practice or in the stage of perfection. They alone are my object of desire and my only responsibility. Besides them I can desire no other responsibility, not even in my dreams. It is all the same to me whether I feel happy or unhappy, or whether my material existence is eradicated or not. (commentary on Bg. 2.41)

I recommend keeping the *Bhagavad-gītā As It Is* open for reference while reading *Surrender Unto Me.*

Acknowledgments

This book took years to write and refine, and I do not view it as my work alone. Since its first printing, Surrender Unto Me has been reprinted a number of times – several times with further refinements to the text, and now, with this new edition, an added appendix that defines the terms used in Surrender Unto Me and an updated and expanded index.

I'd like to thank the following devotees for their contributions to each of the printings of Surrender Unto Me, from the first to the present edition. In expressing my appreciation, I am embarrassed by my incapacity to express my actual gratitude.

Not only did Tattvavit Dāsa edit, but he added a mighty, final exertion to organize, clarify, and sharpen the manuscript. He adopted the book and gave it the full attention and care one gives his own beloved child.

Kaiśorī Devī Dāsī edited and proofread the text. She has been connected with this project since its inception several years ago, and she has continuously offered encouragement and seasoned advice. In addition, Kaiśorī, along with Gopīnāth Prasād Dāsa, guided this second edition to completion. Gopīnāth Prasād also refreshed the layout of the book, layed out the new sections of the book, and worked with the printers.

The late Gopīparāṇadhana Dāsa translated and edited the included commentaries by Śrīla Viśvanātha Cakravartī Ṭhākura and Śrīla Baladeva Vidyābhūṣaṇa. He also focused his scrutinizing eye on the entire manuscript for philosophical accuracy and offered solid general advice. He patiently answered almost endless, sometimes picky questions.

Bhakti Caitanya Mahārāja read the typeset manuscript, contributed literary and philosophical refinements, and helped me distill my presentation.

Jayādvaita Swami encouraged me to complete this book, and he edited its introduction. Romapāda Mahārāja also offered encouragement.

Yamarāja Dāsa, our perennial cover designer, designed an attractive cover. Bhakta-rūpa Dāsa inspired the title.

Aniruddha Dāsa helped us communicate with Bhakta Trevor Absalam, who compiled a fine index on short notice for the first edition. The updated and expanded index found in this second edition was written by Ananta Krishna Dāsa (Adrian Eldridge).

The late Śaraṇāgati Devī Dāsī and Bhaktin Penny (later initiated as Prema Latā Devī Dāsī) proofread the first edition, and Pārvatī Devī Dāsī and Bhaktin Vanessa typed the original manuscript long before computers made that an easier task.

Madhusūdhana Dāsa and Nikuñja-vilāsinī Devī Dāsī helped typeset the index of the first edition. Bindu Mādhava Dāsa, the late Jaḍa Bharata Dāsa, Krsnadāsa Kavirāja Dāsa, and Jīva Gosvāmī Dāsa gave computer-related assistance. Pratyatoṣa Dāsa's generous gift of a computer years ago allowed me the distinction of using the first computer in Vṛndāvana. With that computer, this book began its electronic journey to completion.

Lalitā-mañjarī Devī Dāsī, my daughter, years ago transcribed many Bhagavad-gītā Overview lectures that served as the basis of this book. She also layed out the first printing of the book while she was on pilgrimage back home in Vṛndāvana. Despite countless computer-related obstacles in India, she completed her mission.

Braja Bihārī Dāsa managed to manage the first edition of the book to completion. To him and his wife, Ānanda-vṛndāvaneśvarī Devī Dasī, I offer special thanks.

Thank you all.

Bhūrijana Dāsa

First edition completed on February 12, 1997, Vasanta Pañcamī, the appearance anniversary of Śrīla Raghunātha Dāsa Goswāmī and the disappearance anniversary of Śrīla Viśvanātha Cakravartī Ṭhākura.

Second edition completed on February 1, 2017, the same day on the Vaiṣṇava calendar twenty years later.

Introduction

Bhagavad-gītā As It Is, by Śrīla Prabhupāda, with his Bhaktivedanta purports, is so uniquely powerful that thousands and thousands of souls have reached the conclusion of *Bhagavad-gītā* by reading it. Even those without the association of devotees have been touched by Śrīla Prabhupāda's translation and purports and have surrendered at his lotus feet. Thus Śrīla Prabhupāda's *Bhagavad-gītā As It Is,* fully empowered by the disciplic succession, is certainly the prime edition to be read and distributed in the Age of Kali.

Once, however, when asked what he would translate after the *Śrīmad-Bhāgavatam,* Śrīla Prabhupāda responded, "Oh, maybe Jīva Gosvāmī's *Ṣaṭ-sandarbha* or *Vedānta-sūtra* – there are so many – or *Bhagavad-gītā.*"

Pradyumna Dāsa relates, on the video series "Memories of Śrīla Prabhupāda", that a devotee spoke up: "Śrīla Prabhupāda, you've already done the *Bhagavad-gītā.*"

Śrīla Prabhupāda replied, "We did *Bhagavad-gītā,* but there are so many commentaries. Śrīla Rāmānujācārya, Śrīla Madhvācārya – everyone has given his *Gītā*. We could do many *Gītās,* not just one."

This *Bhagavad-gītā* overview is thus drawn from Śrīla Prabhupāda's verse translations and purports and the commentaries of two great Gauḍīya Vaiṣṇava *ācāryas,* Śrī Śrīmad Viśvanātha Cakravartī Ṭhākura, whose commentary is entitled *Sārātha-varṣaṇi,* and Śrī Śrīmad Baladeva Vidyābhūṣaṇa, whose commentary is called *Gītā-bhūṣaṇa*. In writing this overview I also took into account the commentaries of Śrī Śrīmad Śrīdhara Svāmī and Śrī Śrīmad Rāmānujācārya. This book, therefore, is for serious students, especially those who have deeply studied *Bhagavad-gītā As It Is* and want to increase their understanding of its difficult concepts and how its verses, sections and chapters are connected. Śrīla Prabhupāda wrote in his purport to *Śrīmad-Bhāgavatam* 1.1.1: "Within the past five hundred years, many erudite scholars and *ācāryas* like

Jīva Gosvāmī, Sanātana Gosvāmī, Viśvanātha Cakravartī, Vallabhācārya and many other distinguished scholars even after the time of Lord Caitanya made elaborate commentaries on the *Bhāgavatam*. And the serious student would do well to attempt to go through them to better relish the transcendental messages." As with the *Bhāgavatam,* so also with *Bhagavad-gītā*.

My relationship with *Bhagavad-gītā* started before I began chanting Hare Kṛṣṇa. My first reading of the book took place during my student years at the University of Buffalo. It was not Śrīla Prabhupāda's *Bhagavad-gītā;* his first Macmillan edition had not yet been published. I remember being so excited by the book that I not only stayed up all night reading it, I vowed to read it every night thereafter. I appreciated the *Bhagavad-gītā* so much that I even named my cat after it! Yet despite my enthusiasm, I couldn't penetrate even a centimeter into the *Gītā's* purpose. I did not have Śrīla Prabhupāda's translations and commentary. All I could think was that the book was wonderful – and wonder why Kṛṣṇa had to insist that He was God.

Not long after, I met Śrīla Prabhupāda's disciple Rūpānuga Dāsa, and I began to chant Hare Kṛṣṇa. Śrīla Prabhupāda's *Gītā* was published one year later, and I finished the eighteenth chapter in the university's stuffy library hall. Kṛṣṇa's final instructions were so thrilling that my breathing came fast and my hair stood on end. I ran out of the library a new man. My only desire was to surrender to Kṛṣṇa, the Supreme Personality of Godhead, and to share His message with others. When I graduated in January 1969, Śrīla Prabhupāda wrote me a letter:

> I am very pleased that you are graduating from college in a few days and are anxious to engage your labors in spreading this Krishna consciousness movement. Also I request you to study carefully the *Bhagavad-gītā As It Is* because there is so much important service that an intelligent boy such as you can do in preaching work and spreading our movement around the world.

The *Bhagavad-gītā* thus became "my" book. It was practically all I studied from 1969 through 1985. Early in my studies (1969), I decided to write an overview for myself in which I would attempt to trace the flow of philosophy and the connections between the verses. Soon after, when *Back to Godhead* began publishing chapter summaries one by one, I became more inspired, but suspended my work on an overview. Those chapter summaries stopped, however, near the middle of the *Gītā,* so I began again to work on my own overview.

My overview finally neared completion when I moved to Vṛndāvana in 1983. My studies were aided by a computer that Pratyatośa Dāsa kindly donated. I sat hour after hour writing down the connections between the verses and boiling them down into concise chapter summaries. Finally, I wrote an eight-page overview of the eighteen chapters, which is included as an appendix to this book. When the Vṛndāvana Institute for Higher Education held its third semester during Kārtika 1988, I taught my first *Bhagavad-gītā* Overview course. As I taught I continued to study and to further refine my understanding.

Still, the connections between several verses, sections, and even chapters continued to elude me. After teaching and studying further on my own, I had the good fortune to hear the *Bhagavad-gītā* commentaries of Śrīla Viśvanātha Cakravartī Ṭhākura and Śrīla Baladeva Vidyābhūṣaṇa. The gaps in my understanding continued to lessen, as the *ācāryas* often made a point of saying: "The next verses are about such-and-such topic."

I worked still further for years. Sections in chapter two, the *yoga* ladder, elements of chapters three and four, the connection between chapters seven and eight, the opening verses of chapter eight, the final section of chapter nine, the progression in chapter twelve, difficult verses and purports in chapter thirteen, the final section in chapter fifteen, elements and connections in and between chapters sixteen and seventeen, and the summary connections in chapter eighteen continued to evolve and be refined as the book went into production.

While compiling the overview I encountered the fact that Śrīla Viśvanātha Cakravartī Ṭhākura, Śrīla Baladeva Vidyābhūṣaṇa, and Śrīla Prabhupāda sometimes presented differing analyses of verses or sections. In addition, many great Vaiṣṇava *ācāryas,* such as Śrīla Madhvācārya, Śrīla Rāmānujācārya, and Śrīla Śrīdhara Svāmī all wrote unique commentaries on the *Bhagavad-gītā.* Although their explanations in places concurred, in other places they differed.

In a conversation regarding the strong difference of opinion among the five great preachers who appeared in India – Buddha, Śaṅkara, Rāmānuja, Madhva, and Lord Caitanya – Śrīla Prabhupāda explained that no actual contradictions exist. Ultimately, the conclusion expressed by the *ācāryas* is consistent. In the following conversation with disciples on March 9, 1976, Śrīla Prabhupāda explained that seemingly contradictory instructions may be given:

> **Devotee:** In one of your *Bhagavad-gītā* purports you say a *sannyāsī* should never discourage a young man from getting married. But we have understood that a *sannyāsī* should encourage young men to remain *brahmacārīs*. So it seems like some kind of... [contradiction].
>
> **Śrīla Prabhupāda:** Just like Kṛṣṇa says, *niyataṁ kuru karma tvam:* "Always be engaged in your prescribed work." And at last He says, *sarva-dharmān parityajya mām ekaṁ śaraṇaṁ vraja.* ["Abandon all varieties of religion and just surrender unto Me."] Now we have to adjust. That is not contradiction. That is suitable to the time and circumstance.

Not only do the *ācāryas* at times give different translations and meanings to śāstric verses, Śrīla Prabhupāda himself at times gave different translations and purports to the same verses – see, for example, the *catuḥ-ślokī Bhāgavatam* discussed in *Bhāg.* 2.9.32–5 and Cc., *Ādi* 1.53–6.

He also emphasized different aspects of Arjuna's weakness in not wanting to fight (Bg. 1.28–29). Text 28 states, "Arjuna said: My dear Kṛṣṇa, seeing my friends and relatives present before me in such a fighting spirit, I feel the limbs of my body quivering and my mouth drying up." Śrīla Prabhupāda writes in his purport, "Such symptoms in Arjuna were not due to weakness but to his softheartedness, a characteristic of a pure devotee of the Lord." Text 29 states, "My whole body is trembling, my hair is standing on end, my bow Gāṇḍīva is slipping from my hand, and my skin is burning." Śrīla Prabhupāda's purport says, "Arjuna's symptoms in this situation are out of material fear – namely, loss of life... All these are due to a material conception of life."

Are these varying interpretations? Obviously not. Rather, they are relevant to particular contexts, with differing emphases, each meant to carry the reader to the same point: "Surrender unto Me."

Another example is the discussion of the *yoga* ladder in *Bhagavad-gītā*. When Śrīla Prabhupāda describes the *yoga* ladder, which is at times a technical and subtle topic, he often mercifully reveals Kṛṣṇa's ultimate desire that the conditioned soul surrender to Him in *bhakti*. Śrīla Prabhupāda often brings Kṛṣṇa's ultimate desire to the forefront in his purports, while another commentator may describe Kṛṣṇa's words more literally to show how Kṛṣṇa directed Arjuna in a step-by-step fashion.

Śrīla Viśvanātha Cakravartī Ṭhākura distinguishes *karma-yoga* from *bhakti-yoga* and explains quite technically their subtle differences. Śrīla Baladeva Vidyābhūṣaṇa, by contrast, points out that *karma-yoga* and *bhakti-yoga* are the same, because *karma-yoga* leads to *bhakti-yoga*. Śrīla Prabhupāda generally translates *karma-yoga* as *bhakti-yoga* because they are in fact nondifferent. Śrīla Prabhupāda thus usually equates them: "Service for the cause of the Lord is called *karma-yoga* or *buddhi-yoga*, or in plain words, devotional service to the Lord." (Bg. 2.51, purport) Yet in order to understand and present the overview, I found it more convenient to distinguish *karma-yoga* from *bhakti* to emphasize how *karma-yoga* leads to *bhakti*. At times, Śrīla Prabhupāda also makes this distinction:

> When we speak of *yoga* we refer to linking our consciousness with the Supreme Absolute Truth. Such a process is named differently by various practitioners in terms of the particular method adopted. When the linking process is predominantly in fruitive activities it is called *karma-yoga*, when it is predominantly empirical it is called *jñāna-yoga*, and when it is predominantly in a devotional relationship with the Supreme Lord it is called *bhakti-yoga*. *Bhakti-yoga*, or Kṛṣṇa consciousness, is the ultimate perfection of all *yogas*. (Bg. 6.46, purport)

Considering all of the above, in this book I sometimes cite the *ācāryas* even if they have made points different from those made in Śrīla Prabhupāda's purports. I used three criteria in deciding whether to include their comments: 1) if the *ācārya's* comment was especially wonderful and Śrīla Prabhupāda had not included it in *Bhagavad-gītā As It Is;* 2) if the *ācārya's* comment helped to illuminate a verse from a different angle; 3) if the *ācārya's* comment described the connections between verses, sections, or chapters.

So as not to interfere with the readability of the text and make it appear overly academic, I have often incorporated many of the thoughts of Śrīla Prabhupāda, Śrīla Viśvanātha Cakravartī Ṭhākura, and Śrīla Baladeva Vidyābhūṣaṇa directly into my own comments. In general, I have included direct quotations from Śrīla Prabhupāda's purports to indicate how they clarify the more subtle meanings of the verses or express connections needed to understand the overview. In the second half of chapter eighteen, the *ācāryas'* comments were so outstanding that I included as many as was practical.

I pray that Śrīla Prabhupāda will be pleased with me, and I place this book, written in pursuance of his order to me to study and preach *Bhagavad-gītā* around the world, as an offering in his lotus hand. My study of the *Gītā* in overview has increased my appreciation of the verses of the *Bhagavad-gītā* and strengthened my preaching and my ability to apply the *Bhagavad-gītā* in my own life. After having offered *Surrender Unto Me – An Overview of the Bhagavad-gītā* to Śrīla Prabhupāda, I then offer it as *mahā-prasāda* to serious students of the *Bhagavad-gītā* and pray that their reading of it will award them the same benefits. I pray that the merciful devotees, who are always compassionate to fallen souls, will forgive and correct any faults in this overview.

Chapter One

Observing the Armies On the Battlefield of Kurukṣetra

1 Dhṛtarāṣṭra said: O Sañjaya, after my sons and the sons of Pāṇḍu assembled in the place of pilgrimage at Kurukṣetra, desiring to fight, what did they do?

The *Mahābhārata* describes in great detail the political intrigues that led to the Battle of Kurukṣetra, about which blind King Dhṛtarāṣṭra now inquires from his secretary, Sañjaya. At this point in the *Mahābhārata,* the sons of Pāṇḍu are assembled with their allies to fight the sons of Dhṛtarāṣṭra and their allies. Literally hundreds of millions – from powerful generals to common foot soldiers – have gathered with their weapons, horses, and elephants to fight in one of the biggest battles of all time.

The climax of the entire epic is fast approaching. Which valiant soldiers will survive? Which side will win? Will good triumph over evil? Certainly no one's mind at this point is wandering. The battle is about to begin – the first twenty-seven *ślokas* of the *Gītā* set the battlefield scene – and suddenly Kṛṣṇa inserts into our open ears, minds, and hearts philosophy that will awaken us to our immortality.

Śrīla Prabhupāda explains Kṛṣṇa's compassion: "We have taken a very difficult task, to convince people to take to Kṛṣṇa consciousness, but that is the only benefit, or the supreme goal, of life. Kṛṣṇa personally comes to teach this science. Why did Kṛṣṇa leave the *Bhagavad-gītā*? Out of His compassion – so that 'After My disappearance people will take advantage of this *Bhagavad-gītā;* as I instructed My dear friend Arjuna, they will also take advantage and become free from the clutches of death.' This is the purpose of *Bhagavad-gītā.*" (Lecture, September 7, 1975, Vṛndāvana)

Śrīla Prabhupāda writes in his purport that this first verse reveals Dhṛtarāṣṭra's inclinations: "Both the Pāṇḍavas and the sons of Dhṛtarāṣṭra belong to the same family, but Dhṛtarāṣṭra's mind is disclosed herein. He deliberately claimed only his sons as Kurus, and he separated the sons of Pāṇḍu from the family heritage."

Dhṛtarāṣṭra was afraid. His sons' opponents included warriors like Arjuna and Bhīma. Most frightening of all, Kṛṣṇa, the Supreme Personality of Godhead Himself, was on the battlefield, driving Arjuna's chariot.

In addition, the battle would take place in the holy *dhāma* of Kurukṣetra. The Pāṇḍavas were exceedingly pious, and Dhṛtarāṣṭra did not want the favorable influence of the *dhāma* to aid the Pāṇḍavas or to influence his own sons to compromise. He wanted the battle to begin and the Pāṇḍavas dead. He hoped the *dhāma* would influence the Pāṇḍavas to renounce their claim, in order to avoid all bloodshed. Thus Dhṛtarāṣṭra asked Sañjaya, "What did my sons and the sons of Pāṇḍu do?"

2 Sañjaya said: O King, after looking over the army arranged in military formation by the sons of Pāṇḍu, King Duryodhana went to his teacher and spoke the following words.

3 O my teacher, behold the great army of the sons of Pāṇḍu, so expertly arranged by your intelligent disciple the son of Drupada.

Duryodhana was a great politician. He could have mentioned Dhṛṣṭadyumna's name directly, but instead he purposely called him the son of Drupada. Drupada and Droṇa were enemies, and therefore to incite Droṇa's anger, Duryodhana reminded Droṇa that his enemy's son, Dhṛṣṭadyumna, was arranging the armies. Because Droṇa was naturally inclined to the Pāṇḍavas, especially to Arjuna, his greatest student, Duryodhana needed to use whatever ploys he could to ensure that Droṇa would fight to the best of his ability.

Drupada and Droṇa had attended the same *gurukula* even though Droṇa was the son of a poor *brāhmaṇa* and Drupada was a prince. Despite the differences in their backgrounds, the two became intimate friends. In a moment of affection

Drupada told his friend that when he inherited the kingdom, he would give him half of it. Droṇa took his friend's words to heart.

Long after they had graduated and Droṇa had entered *gṛhastha* life, he found his son crying for milk. Droṇa was so poor that he could not afford to buy milk for his child. Then he remembered Drupada's promise and thought, "Let me go to my dear friend Drupada and beg a cow from him."

When Droṇa arrived at Drupada's palace, he was not properly received. Drupada said, *"I* am *your* friend? Friendship can be recognized only among equals. Get out of here immediately!" Droṇa vowed revenge. Later, he trained both the Kuru and Paṇḍava princes in the military arts and then asked for his *guru-dakṣiṇā:* "Capture Drupada and bring him before me."

The Kauravas offered to try first, but Drupada easily defeated them and sent them back to Droṇa in embarrassment. Droṇācārya was mortified. Arjuna then came forward. The other Pāṇḍavas lined up behind him as he attacked Pāñcāla, Drupada's kingdom. After a fierce battle Arjuna captured and bound Drupada in ropes and carried him to Droṇācārya's feet. Droṇācārya then took half of Drupada's kingdom by force and thus made Drupada his enemy.

Drupada then performed a sacrifice to obtain a son who would kill Droṇa. That son was Dhṛṣṭadyumna. Dhṛṣṭadyumna later approached Droṇācārya to study military science, and although Droṇācārya knew that Dhṛṣṭadyumna was specifically empowered to kill him, he did not hesitate to train him. Such is the liberality of a *brāhmaṇa*. The *brāhmaṇa*'s liberal heart is compared to the sun, which does not withhold its light from the courtyard of anyone, even a thief. Similarly, Droṇācārya did not hesitate to impart all his military secrets to Dhṛṣṭadyumna.

4 Here in this army are many heroic bowmen equal in fighting to Bhīma and Arjuna: great fighters like Yuyudhāna, Virāṭa, and Drupada.

Again Duryodhana mentioned Drupada to incite Droṇa's anger. Duryodhana also mentioned Bhīma and Arjuna. Arjuna was a powerful foe. Not only had he studied under Droṇa, but he had gone to the heavenly planets, later fought with Lord Śiva, and been given many celestial weapons.

Duryodhana, however, was especially afraid of Bhīma's fiery temperament and expertise in fighting. Therefore he mentions his name first. Bhīma was furious with Dhṛtarāṣṭra's sons. Before the battle, he took three vows. First, he vowed to kill each of Dhṛtarāṣṭra's one hundred sons. (During the battle Arjuna and the other Pāṇḍavas had opportunities to kill some of Dhṛtarāṣṭra's sons, but they refrained from doing so to allow Bhīma to fulfill his vow. During the battle Bhīma's anger was inflamed. He screamed, jumped up and down, and drank the blood of each son of Dhṛtarāṣṭra he killed. Even the warriors on the Pāṇḍavas' side feared his rage.)

Second, he vowed to break Duryodhana's thigh. When Draupadī was being insulted, Duryodhana had uncovered his thigh and motioned to Draupadī, saying, "Come and sit on my lap! You are fit for my enjoyment." Bhīma burned with anger and hatred. For thirteen years, he had been burning as he waited to destroy the Kauravas.

Third, Bhīma vowed to tear open Duḥśāsana's chest, pry out his heart, and drink his blood. Duḥśāsana had touched and opened Draupadī's tied and sanctified hair. For that, Bhīma also vowed to rip off his arm. Draupadī had promised to keep her hair untied until she had washed it with Duḥśāsana's blood. Bhīma later carried that blood in his hands to Draupadī.

Duryodhana named all these fighters to persuade Droṇācārya to free himself from whatever sentiments he felt for the Pāṇḍavas and to kill them in battle. He then continued to describe the Pāṇḍavas' strength.

5 There are also great heroic, powerful fighters like Dhṛṣṭaketu, Cekitāna, Kāśirāja, Purujit, Kuntibhoja, and Śaibya.

6 There are the mighty Yudhāmanyu, the very powerful Uttamaujā, the son of Subhadrā, and the sons of Draupadī. All these warriors are great chariot fighters.

7 But for your information, O best of the brāhmaṇas, let me tell you about the captains who are especially qualified to lead my military force.

Duryodhana did not want to discourage those listening to his fears about the Pāṇḍavas' strength, so he added, "Let me tell you about the great warriors on my side."

8 There are personalities like you, Bhīṣma, Karṇa, Kṛpa, Aśvatthāmā, Vikarṇa, and the son of Somadatta called Bhūriśravā, who are always victorious in battle.

Duryodhana was speaking to the two great warriors Bhīṣma and Droṇācārya. While the king addressed Droṇācārya, all his other fighters gathered to listen. Therefore, Duryodhana, as an expert diplomat, began to describe the Kauravas' strength with the words *bhavān bhīṣmaś ca karṇaś ca.* Yet before he spoke he was caught in another difficult situation. Facing him were two great warriors: Bhīṣma was the commander-in-chief of the army, and Droṇa was Duryodhana's military *guru.* Whom, then, should he mention first?

Duryodhana was clever. He knew that Bhīṣma was a *kṣatriya* and Droṇa a *brāhmaṇa.* If he mentioned Bhīṣma first, Droṇācārya would be insulted. As a *kṣatriya,* however, Bhīṣma would honor the etiquette of offering the *brāhmaṇa* more respect. Thus Duryodhana said, *bhavān bhīṣmaś:* "There are personalities like you, Droṇācārya, and Bhīṣma."

He next mentioned Karṇa. Bhīṣma and Karṇa were enemies. Because Karṇa thought, "What's the use? I will fight and kill everyone, and this aged general will get all the credit," he had vowed not to fight until Bhīṣma was killed.

Duryodhana next mentioned Kṛpācārya, a relative of Droṇa, then Aśvatthāmā, Droṇa's son. In these ways, he hoped to inspire Droṇa.

Surprisingly, Duryodhana next mentioned his own brother Vikarṇa. Vikarṇa was not of the same caliber as Bhīṣma or Droṇa, but because he was the only brother who had objected to the Kauravas' insult to Draupadī, Duryodhana assumed that he was sympathetic to the Pāṇḍavas and that he might defect from the Kaurava army. Therefore Duryodhana flattered

Vikarṇa by including his name among the more powerful fighters on whom he was relying on.

Defection was always an important concern for military leaders. Although *kṣatriyas* love to fight, they are not always concerned whose side they fight on. Therefore Yudhiṣṭhira announced at the beginning of the war that religious principles allow defection before the battle starts, but once it has begun, warriors must stay on their chosen sides.

Both Kṛṣṇa and Duryodhana were active in recruiting defectors. Kṛṣṇa and Kuntīdevī approached her son Karṇa and invited him to join the Pāṇḍavas' side. Kṛṣṇa told Karṇa that he was actually the eldest Paṇḍava, and He encouraged him to fight alongside his brothers, especially because he wouldn't be joining the battle until after Bhīṣma's death. Karṇa, however, would not abandon his loyalty to Duryodhana.

On his side, Duryodhana both tried to keep Vikarṇa and to win over the Pāṇḍavas' uncle Śalya. Karṇa needed a fit charioteer, and Śalya was both an acclaimed charioteer and a *mahāratha* warrior. As Śalya and his army traveled the long distance to join the Pāṇḍavas' side in the battle, they found pleasant accommodations – that Duryodhana had arranged for them – along the way. Duryodhana's clever ministers encouraged the tired Śalya to make full use of the facilities. They took such good care of him that Śalya said, "Yudhiṣṭhira must have arranged these accommodations. Whoever has arranged this for me – I'll do whatever he wants." Duryodhana then appeared and said, "It was I who made these arrangements, and I want you to fight on my side." Śalya kept his word, fought for Duryodhana, and eventually became the final Kaurava commander-in-chief.

9 There are many other heroes who are prepared to lay down their lives for my sake. All of them are well equipped with different kinds of weapons, and all are experienced in military science.

10 Our strength is immeasurable, and we are perfectly protected by Grandfather Bhīṣma, whereas the strength of the Pāṇḍavas, carefully protected by Bhīma, is limited.

Śrīla Prabhupāda has translated the first Sanskrit word in text 10, *aparyāptam* as "immeasurable," and his purport explains the verse accordingly. Śrīla Baladeva Vidyābhūṣaṇa has also taken the meaning of *aparyāptam* in that way. Śrīla Viśvanātha Cakravartī Ṭhākura, however, has given *aparyāptam* an opposite meaning. Thus, depending on which way the word is taken, the first line of the verse can mean either "Our strength is immeasurable" or "Our strength is insufficient." When the first meaning is used (as it was by Śrīla Prabhupāda), then the sentence continues: "… and we are perfectly protected by Grandfather Bhīṣma." Bhīṣma became encouraged when he heard this meaning.

The second meaning, however, was intended to encourage Droṇācārya: "Our strength is insufficient *because* we are protected by Bhīṣma." Bhīṣma was a formidable warrior, but because he favored the Pāṇḍavas, Duryodhana felt he would not fight to his full capacity. Droṇācārya took the second meaning, and he understood Duryodhana's message to be: "Our strength is insufficient because of Bhīṣma's split loyalties. Therefore, Droṇa, you must fight even harder to make up for Bhīṣma's weakness." Thus the expert diplomat Duryodhana encouraged both Bhīṣma and Droṇa with this one word.

11 All of you must now give full support to Grandfather Bhīṣma, as you stand at your respective strategic points of entrance into the phalanx of the army.

Śrīla Prabhupāda explains this text in his purport: "Duryodhana, after praising the prowess of Bhīṣma, further considered that others might think that they had been considered less important, so in his usual diplomatic way, he tried to adjust the situation in the above words. He emphasized that Bhīṣmadeva was undoubtedly the greatest hero, but he was an old man, so everyone must especially think of his protection from all sides."

12 Then Bhīṣma, the great valiant grandsire of the Kuru dynasty, the grandfather of the fighters, blew his conchshell very loudly, making a sound like the roar of a lion, giving Duryodhana joy.

Bhīṣma did not answer Duryodhana's words. Instead, he replied by blowing his conchshell, which meant: "Despite your heroic words, victory or defeat lies in the Lord's hands. I will do my duty and lay down my life for your sake, but that will not guarantee your victory." The conchshell, being a symbol of Viṣṇu, indicates that Duryodhana had no chance of victory in the battle, because Kṛṣṇa, the origin of Viṣṇu, was present on the opposing side.

13 After that, the conchshells, drums, bugles, trumpets, and horns were all suddenly sounded, and the combined sound was tumultuous.

14 On the other side, both Lord Kṛṣṇa and Arjuna, stationed on a great chariot drawn by white horses, sounded their transcendental conchshells.

15 Lord Kṛṣṇa blew His conchshell, called Pañcajanya; Arjuna blew his, the Devadatta; and Bhīma, the voracious eater and performer of herculean tasks, blew his terrific conchshell, called Pauṇḍra.

Arjuna's position was unique. Kṛṣṇa, the Supreme Personality of Godhead, had agreed to become his charioteer. Agni, the fire god, had donated his chariot. Citraratha, the chief of the Gandharvas, had given him his beautiful white horses. Indra, his father, had given him his conchshell and quiver.

16–18 King Yudhiṣṭhira, the son of Kuntī, blew his conchshell, the Ananta-vijaya, and Nakula and Sahadeva blew the Sughoṣa and Maṇipuṣpaka. That great archer the King of Kāśī, the great fighter Śikhaṇḍī, Dhṛṣṭadyumna, Virāṭa, the unconquerable Sātyakī, Drupada, the sons of Draupadī, and the others, O King, such as the mighty-armed son of Subhadrā, all blew their respective conchshells.

19 The blowing of these different conchshells became uproarious. Vibrating both in the sky and on the earth, it shattered the hearts of the sons of Dhṛtarāṣṭra.

20 At that time Arjuna, the son of Pāṇḍu, seated in the chariot bearing the flag marked with Hanumān, took up his bow and prepared to shoot his arrows. O King, after looking at the sons of Dhṛtarāṣṭra drawn in military array, Arjuna then spoke to Lord Kṛṣṇa these words.

The atmosphere was surcharged. The world's most powerful *kṣatriyas* had gathered to fight and were filled with the spirit of battle. This war differed from the situation Śrīla Prabhupāda criticized in the 1960s, when the United States drafted students, not *kṣatriyas,* and forced them into battle. These men were fighting men; fighting was in their blood. Just as devotees come from around the world to Vṛndāvana or Māyāpur, so these *kṣatriyas* came from all over the world to fight. They had faith that dying on the battlefield would gain them entrance into the heavenly planets.

The two armies were in formation. Conchshells were blowing. The hair of warriors stood on end in anticipation. Kṛṣṇa was with Arjuna on his chariot.

Hanumān, decorating the chariot's flag, was ready to shout his war cries to help Bhīma terrify the enemy. Earlier, the *Mahābhārata* describes a meeting between Hanumān and Bhīma. Once, while Arjuna was seeking celestial weapons, the remaining Pāṇḍavas wandered to Badarikāśrama, high in the Himālayas. Suddenly, the Ālakanandā River carried to Draupadī a beautiful and fragrant thousand-petaled lotus flower. Draupadī was captivated by its beauty and scent. "Bhīma, this lotus flower is so beautiful, I should offer it to Yudhiṣṭhira Mahārāja. Could you get me a few more? We could take some back to our hermitage in Kāmyaka."

Bhīma grabbed his club and charged up a mountainside where no mortals were permitted. As he ran, he bellowed and frightened elephants and lions. He uprooted trees as he pushed them aside. Not caring for the ferocious jungle beasts, he climbed the steep mountain until his progress was blocked by a huge monkey lying across the path.

"Why are you making so much noise and scaring all the animals?" the monkey asked. "Just sit down here and eat some fruit."

"Move aside," ordered Bhīma, for etiquette forbade him to step over the monkey. The monkey's reply?

"I am too old to move. Jump over me."

Bhīma, becoming angry, repeated his order, but the monkey, again pleading the weakness of old age, requested Bhīma to simply move his tail aside. Unlimitedly powerful Bhīma grabbed the tail and tried, but failed. Amazed, he respectfully inquired as to the monkey's identity and was overjoyed to learn that he had met his brother Hanumān, for both Bhīma and Hanumān are sons of Vāyu. Hanumān first embraced Bhīma and then showed him the huge form with which he had leaped to Laṅkā. He then offered Bhīma the following blessings.

"I shall remain present on the flag of your brother Arjuna. When you roar like a lion on the battlefield, my voice will join with yours to strike terror into the hearts of your enemies. You will be victorious and regain your kingdom."

Now Arjuna, his chariot driven by Kṛṣṇa and marked with the flag of Hanumān, picked up his bow. The horses and elephants moved excitedly. The opening arrows of the long awaited battle were now to be released. Arjuna, just on the brink of battle, spoke the following words.

21–22 Arjuna said: O infallible one, please draw my chariot between the two armies so that I may see those present here, who desire to fight, and with whom I must contend in this great trial of arms.

This is Kṛṣṇa's first appearance in *Bhagavad-gītā*. What is He doing? He is driving Arjuna's chariot and accepting his orders. This is glorious: Kṛṣṇa, the supreme controller, is taking orders from His devotee as if He were a menial servant.

Śrīla Prabhupāda writes in his purport: "Although Lord Kṛṣṇa is the Supreme Personality of Godhead, out of His causeless mercy He was engaged in the service of His friend. He never fails in His affection for His devotees, and thus He is addressed herein as infallible. . . The relationship between the Lord and His servitor is very sweet and transcendental. The servitor is always ready to render service to the Lord, and, similarly, the Lord is always seeking an opportunity to render some service to the devotee." Of all Kṛṣṇa's qualities, His *bhakta-vatsala* quality is most endearing.

In text 20, Arjuna picked up his bow, ready to fight. Both

armies are waiting. Arjuna had previously vowed to kill anyone who even suggested he put down his bow. Now, in texts 21–22, Arjuna suddenly says, "O infallible one, please draw my chariot between the two armies so that I may see those present here, who desire to fight, and with whom I must contend in this great trial of arms." Arjuna's request hints that he is already indecisive about taking part in the battle.

23 Let me see those who have come here to fight, wishing to please the evil-minded son of Dhṛtarāṣṭra.

24 Sañjaya said: O descendant of Bharata, having thus been addressed by Arjuna, Lord Kṛṣṇa drew up the fine chariot in the midst of the armies of both parties.

25 In the presence of Bhīṣma, Droṇa, and all the other chieftains of the world, the Lord said, Just behold, Pārtha, all the Kurus assembled here.

Hundreds of millions of warriors were in the Kuru armies, yet Kṛṣṇa drove Arjuna's chariot directly before Bhīṣma and Droṇa (*bhīṣma-droṇa-pramukhataḥ*). In this way Kṛṣṇa forced Arjuna to see that both his grandfather and his *guru* were determined to oppose him in battle. Kṛṣṇa thus drew out Arjuna's familial attachment so He could speak *Bhagavad-gītā*. Kṛṣṇa was teasing Arjuna: "It is only Kurus – on both sides – who are assembled."

Baladeva Vidyābhūṣaṇa adds this explanation of Kṛṣṇa's words: "'Because you are the son of My father's sister, I am going to serve as your chariot driver. But now you are about to abandon your desire to fight.' Thus Kṛṣṇa jokingly implied, 'What's the use of *looking* at the enemy's army?'"

In this way Kṛṣṇa affirmed the thoughts in Arjuna's mind. Sañjaya describes this scene to Dhṛtarāṣṭra and then goes on to name the other family members Arjuna sees before him.

26 There Arjuna could see, within the midst of the armies of both parties, his fathers, grandfathers, teachers, maternal uncles, brothers, sons, grandsons, friends, and also his fathers-in-law and well-wishers.

Śrīla Prabhupāda provides the names of those Arjuna saw: "On the battlefield Arjuna could see all kinds of relatives. He could see persons like Bhūriśravā, who were his father's contemporaries, grandfathers Bhīṣma and Somadatta, teachers like Droṇācārya and Kṛpācārya, maternal uncles like Śalya and Śakuni, brothers like Duryodhana, sons like Lakṣmaṇa, friends like Aśvatthāmā, well-wishers like Kṛtavarmā, etc. He could see also the armies which contained many of his friends."

27 When the son of Kuntī, Arjuna, saw all these different grades of friends and relatives, he became overwhelmed with compassion and spoke thus.

Kṛṣṇa has driven Arjuna's chariot so that Arjuna is face to face with Bhīṣma and Droṇa. Thus we can understand it is by Kṛṣṇa's arrangement that Arjuna, on the verge of fighting with and perhaps even killing his respected grandfather, Bhīṣma, and his military *guru*, Droṇa, is feeling compassion and reverential affection just prior to the Battle of Kurukṣetra.

Beginning with verse 28, Arjuna will describe his reasons for desiring not to fight, and Kṛṣṇa will reject them all. I have analyzed Arjuna's reasons and put them into five categories:

1) *Compassion.* Arjuna has deep compassion for those he is about to kill. He doesn't want to kill his loved ones.

2) *Enjoyment.* This is a less noble reason. Arjuna knows it will be impossible for him to enjoy the kingdom if he wins it at the cost of the lives of his family members.

3) *Destruction of family.* With the death of so many great *kṣatriyas,* irreligion will flourish, and the women will be unprotected and corrupted by unscrupulous men. Therefore society will be overrun by unwanted progeny. The traditional Vedic rituals will no longer be performed because no one will be qualified to perform them, and thus hell will await both the family and the destroyer of the family.

4) *Fear of sinful reactions.* Arjuna thinks that the enjoyment of royal happiness is not worth the suffering he will have to

undergo as a sinful reaction for destroying the family and killing his superiors.

5) *Indecision.* Arjuna is not convinced that conquering his enemies is better than being conquered by them. The kingdom is flourishing under Duryodhana's rule, so why should the Pāṇḍavas fight only to take over the kingdom for themselves? He wonders whether millions of people should die just to enthrone him and his family.

Arjuna is softhearted, compassionate, and logical. He knows *śāstra* and is cultured and intelligent. Because of these qualities, his heart breaks when he sees his friends and relatives ready to fight.

28 Arjuna said: My dear Kṛṣṇa, seeing my friends and relatives present before me in such a fighting spirit, I feel the limbs of my body quivering and my mouth drying up.

Although Duryodhana was prepared to kill in order to keep the kingdom, should a softhearted, compassionate devotee like Arjuna act so foolishly? Is gaining a kingdom, which is, after all, a temporary gain, worth the price of committing unlimited sin? Śrīla Prabhupāda comments that Arjuna's symptoms "are due to softheartedness resulting from his being a great devotee of the Lord." (Bg. 1.45, purport)

29 My whole body is trembling, my hair is standing on end, my bow Gāṇḍīva is slipping from my hand, and my skin is burning.

30 I am now unable to stand here any longer. I am forgetting myself, and my mind is reeling. I see only causes of misfortune, O Kṛṣṇa, killer of the Keśī demon.

The words *nimittāni* and *viparītāni* are significant. Śrīla Prabhupāda translates *nimittāni* as "causes" and *viparītāni* as "just the opposite." Arjuna foresees that the very events he fears will necessarily occur, and he thinks, "This battle will cause just the opposite of my desires."

In his purport to verse 30, Śrīla Prabhupāda summarizes the faults in Arjuna's reasoning as the faults in the reasoning of every conditioned soul: "Arjuna envisioned only painful reverses in the battlefield – he would not be happy even by gaining victory over the foe....When a man sees only frustration in his expectations, he thinks, 'Why am I here?' Everyone is interested in himself and his own welfare. No one is interested in the Supreme Self. Arjuna is showing ignorance of his real self-interest by Kṛṣṇa's will. One's real self-interest lies in Viṣṇu, or Kṛṣṇa. The conditioned soul forgets this, and therefore suffers material pains. Arjuna thought that his victory in the battle would only be a cause of lamentation for him."

We may view Arjuna's lamentation but predict that he will be victorious, as Kṛṣṇa is His chariot driver. Arjuna will not go to the heavenly planets, as will those he kills, but at least he will win the kingdom. Arjuna, however, does not consider a kingdom worth the sinful reaction he will acquire by fighting and killing in the battle. He is considering only how the battle will affect him, and he sees only results opposite to his desires. In this way he loses all will to fight.

31 I do not see how any good can come from killing my own kinsmen in this battle, nor can I, my dear Kṛṣṇa, desire any subsequent victory, kingdom or happiness.

Verses 31–35 describe Arjuna's second reason not to fight. Śrīla Viśvanātha Cakravartī explains Arjuna's thinking as follows: "I will win the battle, but I will suffer greatly. Those I kill will be elevated to the sun planet, but no good reaction will come to me." Arjuna continues to explain the intolerable results he envisions.

32–35 O Govinda, of what avail to us are a kingdom, happiness, or even life itself when all those for whom we may desire them are now arrayed on this battlefield? O Madhusūdana, when teachers, fathers, sons, grandfathers, maternal uncles, fathers-in-law, grandsons, brothers-in-law, and other relatives are ready to give up their lives and properties and are standing before me, why should I wish to kill them, even though they might otherwise kill me? O maintainer of all living entities, I am

not prepared to fight with them even in exchange for the three worlds, let alone this earth. What pleasure will we derive from killing the sons of Dhṛtarāṣṭra?

Arjuna calls Kṛṣṇa "Janārdana," the maintainer of all living entities. He wonders how Kṛṣṇa, everyone's maintainer, can be desiring everyone's death. The word *janārdana* has another meaning. *Jana* means "person," and *ardana* means "killer." Śrīla Baladeva Vidyābhūṣaṇa explains that Arjuna calls Kṛṣṇa "Janārdana" to suggest, "O Janārdana, if they need to be killed, then You, who are the remover of the earth's burden, should kill them. There won't be any trace of sinful reaction for You, the supreme controller." In this way Arjuna hopes to remain free from sinful reaction.

The Pāṇḍavas, of course, won the battle and ascended the throne, yet they remained in power for only thirty-seven years. Arjuna's conviction is that brief, kingly pleasures are not worth the sinful reaction of suffering in hell for millions of years because of killing friends, *guru,* grandfathers, cousins, and other relatives. Arjuna concludes that planning for enjoyment while overlooking future suffering is foolish. He continues this reasoning in verse 36.

36 Sin will overcome us if we slay such aggressors. Therefore it is not proper for us to kill the sons of Dhṛtarāṣṭra and our friends. What should we gain, O Kṛṣṇa, husband of the goddess of fortune, and how could we be happy by killing our own kinsmen?

Here, Arjuna calls Kṛṣṇa "Mādhava," the husband of the goddess of fortune. Arjuna, according to Śrīla Baladeva Vidyābhūṣaṇa, thus asks Kṛṣṇa, "O Mādhava, why are You, the husband of the goddess of fortune, engaging me in this unfortunate battle?"

Arjuna says, "Sin will overcome us if we slay such aggressors." Śrīla Prabhupāda explains in his purport that according to Vedic injunction, no sin occurs if one kills an aggressor. He then lists six types of aggressors: 1) a poison giver, 2) an arsonist, 3) one who attacks with deadly weapons, 4) a thief, 5) one who occupies another's land, and 6) one who kidnaps another's wife.

The Pāṇḍavas suffered each of these forms of aggression at the hands of the Kauravas, who were now poised to attack. Duryodhana fed Bhīma a poisoned cake. He arranged for a house of *lac* to be built for the Pāṇḍavas and conspired to have it set ablaze while they slept. Śakuni cheated in a dice game and plundered all their wealth. The Kauravas then occupied the Pāṇḍavas' land. Finally, they stole Draupadī by foul means, once during the dice game and once when Jayadratha attempted to kidnap her. *Artha-śāstra* allows that such aggressors be killed. Why then does Arjuna say sin will overcome him by killing them? According to Śrīla Viśvanātha Cakravartī Ṭhākura, Arjuna is speaking from the level of *dharma-śāstra,* not *artha-śāstra. Dharma-śāstra,* which is more authoritative, propounds that killing one's friends and relatives is never permitted.

37–38 O Janārdana, although these men, their hearts overtaken by greed, see no fault in killing one's family or quarreling with friends, why should we, who can see the crime in destroying a family, engage in these acts of sin?

Arjuna fears the ensuing horror of two powerful dynasties fighting and destroying each other. (This is Arjuna's third reason not to fight.) *Kṣatriya* spirit engendered family pride. *Kṣatriyas* upheld the pious family traditions and passed them on to future generations. What would happen if all the *kṣatriyas* were killed? The entire society, which depended on the authority of Vedic kings, would fall into disarray. No sacrifices would be performed for the forefathers or future generations. Young men would become unrestrained, frivolous, and impure. Vanquishing a powerful royal dynasty would, in fact, make the future of the entire world dim and bring unlimited misfortune. Arjuna understood all this.

39 With the destruction of dynasty, the eternal family tradition is vanquished, and thus the rest of the family becomes involved in irreligion.

Arjuna fears that if he were to engage in the irreligious killing of his grandfather and *guru,* the women of the family would think, "Our men have become irreligious; let us also act irreligiously."

40 When irreligion is prominent in the family, O Kṛṣṇa, the women of the family become polluted, and from the degradation of womanhood, O descendant of Vṛṣṇi, comes unwanted progeny.

Kṛṣṇa called Arjuna "Pārtha" to remind him of his *kṣatriya* heritage. In this verse, Arjuna calls Kṛṣṇa "Vārṣṇeya," descendant of Vṛṣṇi, because he wants Kṛṣṇa to think how He would feel if the Vṛṣṇi dynasty were on the verge of destruction.

41 An increase of unwanted population certainly causes hellish life both for the family and for those who destroy the family tradition. The ancestors of such corrupt families fall down, because the performances for offering them food and water are entirely stopped.

We can further support Arjuna's argument by saying, "Even Śrī Caitanya Mahāprabhu traveled to Gāyā to offer the *śrāddha* ceremony for His departed father. Are such sacrifices unimportant? Ancestors depend on those ceremonies to attain freedom from suffering. If the offerings to the forefathers are stopped, generations of family members will remain in hell." Again, Arjuna was primarily considering his own sinful reaction by becoming a party to stopping those offerings.

In his purport, Śrīla Prabhupāda answers Arjuna's doubt:

devarṣi-bhūtāpta-nṛṇāṁ pitṝṇāṁ
na kiṅkaro nāyam ṛṇī ca rājan
sarvātmanā yaḥ śaraṇaṁ śaraṇyaṁ
gato mukundaṁ parihṛtya kartam

"Anyone who has taken shelter of the lotus feet of Mukunda, the giver of liberation, giving up all kinds of obligation, and has taken to the path in all seriousness, owes neither duties nor obligations to the demigods, sages, general living entities, family members, humankind, or forefathers." (*Bhāg.* 11.5.41)

Such obligations are automatically fulfilled by performance of devotional service to the Supreme Personality of Godhead.

42 By the evil deeds of those who destroy the family tradition and thus give rise to unwanted children, all kinds of community projects and family welfare activities are devastated.

43 O Kṛṣṇa, maintainer of the people, I have heard by disciplic succession that those who destroy family traditions dwell always in hell.

44 Alas, how strange it is that we are preparing to commit greatly sinful acts. Driven by the desire to enjoy royal happiness, we are intent on killing our own kinsmen.

45 Better for me if the sons of Dhṛtarāṣṭra, weapons in hand, were to kill me unarmed and unresisting on the battlefield.

If Arjuna does not fight, he will become bereft of his occupation and left to beg for his sustenance. Begging, however, is unthinkable for a *kṣatriya*. The following incident illustrates this element of the *kṣatriya* spirit.

After Bhīma met Hanumān, he continued seeking fragrant, thousand-petal lotuses Draupadī had asked for. Finally, he arrived at a lake filled with those lotuses and entered the water. This was Kuvera's lake, and Bhīma did not have permission to enter. Hundreds of Yakṣas and Rākṣasas appeared and challenged Bhīma, saying, "What are you doing here! You are forbidden to enter this lake. Go and ask Kuvera for his permission. If he allows you, you may pick as many flowers as you like. If you try to pick flowers without his permission, you will be destroyed by Kuvera's army."

Bhīma jumped from the water, yelling, "I am a *kṣatriya*! *Kṣatriyas* don't beg favors from anyone!" The Yakṣas and Rākṣasas then attacked Bhīma, and Bhīma destroyed them all.

For a *kṣatriya,* begging is unthinkable. Neither his culture nor his psychology allow it. Therefore Arjuna says that it is better for him to be killed unarmed and unresisting on the battlefield than to incur unlimited sins by fighting or to be forced to live a beggar's life.

46 Sañjaya said: Arjuna, having thus spoken on the battlefield, cast aside his bow and arrows and sat down on the chariot, his mind overwhelmed with grief.

Arjuna had vowed to kill anyone who even suggested he put down his bow. An incident later tested that vow.

During the battle, Karṇa defeated and severely injured Yudhiṣṭhira. Karṇa then taunted Yudhiṣṭhira, saying, "You are not even a *kṣatriya*! You should learn how to fight. See how easily I have defeated you! I'm not even going to bother to kill you."

When Arjuna heard of Yudhiṣṭhira's injury, he immediately left the battlefield and went to Yudhiṣṭhira's tent. Upon hearing that Arjuna had left the battlefield, Yudhiṣṭhira concluded that Arjuna, avenging his honor, had already killed Karṇa and had now come to inform him.

But it wasn't true. Arjuna had left the battlefield only out of concern for Yudhiṣṭhira's injury.

As soon as Yudhiṣṭhira saw Arjuna, he asked, "Have you killed Karṇa and avenged me?"

Arjuna replied, "No, I did not kill Karṇa. I only came to see how badly you were hurt."

Yudhiṣṭhira was furious. He said, "You have left the battlefield without even killing Karṇa? You coward! How could you have done this? It is better that you give up your Gāṇḍīva bow!"

Upon hearing his words, Arjuna became enraged and thought, "How dare Yudhiṣṭhira suggest that I give up my Gāṇḍīva bow, which is more dear to me than my life! I have vowed to kill anyone..."

Arjuna drew his sword to slay his brother. Kṛṣṇa, who was watching, immediately caught Arjuna's arm and said, "All right, you have to kill Yudhiṣṭhira. It is your vow, but kill him by insulting him. For a *kṣatriya,* an insult is worse than death."

As Yudhiṣṭhira sat there regretting his words to Arjuna, Arjuna angrily approached him and said, "You say I am a coward because I left the battlefield without killing Karṇa, but look what *you* have done. You looked on as our wife Draupadī was insulted. I would have alone killed the entire Kaurava army, but you would not allow me. You are not a man. You are not a king!"

Arjuna finished hurling his insults at Yudhiṣṭhira, but then quickly touched Yudhiṣṭhira's feet and begged forgiveness for his words.

Arjuna had not lightly made his "Gāṇḍīva vow." Therefore it is significant that Arjuna – the great son of Pāṇḍu and Indra – himself cast aside his bow and sat down on the chariot, his mind overwhelmed with grief. We can only imagine how disturbed Arjuna must have been about the disaster awaiting him and the entire world.

Chapter Two

Contents of the Gītā Summarized

1 Sañjaya said: Seeing Arjuna full of compassion, his mind depressed, his eyes full of tears, Madhusūdana, Kṛṣṇa, spoke the following words.

By calling Kṛṣṇa "Madhusūdana," Sañjaya informs Dhṛtarāṣṭra that Arjuna's doubts will now be killed by the killer of the Madhu demon. As Śrīla Prabhupāda explains, "The word 'Madhusūdana' is significant in this verse. Lord Kṛṣṇa killed the demon Madhu, and now Arjuna wanted Kṛṣṇa to kill the demon of misunderstanding that had overtaken him in the discharge of his duty."

Dhṛtarāṣṭra was happy to hear of Arjuna's mood of renunciation. Now his sons could be victorious. Sañjaya's words, however, dispel Dhṛtarāṣṭra's happiness.

2 The Supreme Personality of Godhead said: My dear Arjuna, how have these impurities come upon you? They are not at all befitting a man who knows the value of life. They lead not to higher planets but to infamy.

Kṛṣṇa tells Arjuna that his many good arguments are *anārya-juṣṭam,* not befitting an Āryan. Arjuna's impurities will not lead him to Svargaloka (*asvargyam*) and will only cause him infamy (*akīrti-karam*). In other words, Arjuna will become infamous in the present and then at death will not be awarded residence in the higher planets. Therefore Kṛṣṇa does not approve of Arjuna's compassion.

3 O son of Pṛthā, do not yield to this degrading impotence. It does not become you. Give up such petty weakness of heart and arise, O chastiser of the enemy.

Kṛṣṇa immediately decries Arjuna's decision with the word *klaibyam,* impotence. *Kṣatriyas* are by nature proud and virile. By accusing Arjuna of impotence and weakness, Kṛṣṇa slaps him. Simultaneously Kṛṣṇa reminds Arjuna of his great heritage by addressing him as Pārtha. Arjuna is the son of Lord Indra, who is a great warrior and the king of the heavenly planets. Kṛṣṇa wants to know how someone with such a high birth could act more like a *kṣatra-bandhu,* simply a member of a *kṣatriya* family, than an actual *kṣatriya.* Śrīla Prabhupāda says, "If the son of a *kṣatriya* declines to fight, he is a *kṣatriya* in name only."

Kṛṣṇa has not accepted Arjuna's numerous arguments. *Kṣudram* means low-class and petty. Kṛṣṇa directs this insult at Arjuna to challenge him and stir his *kṣatriya* blood. Arjuna responds in the next verse and tries to disprove Kṛṣṇa's analysis.

4 Arjuna said: O killer of enemies, O killer of Madhu, how can I counterattack with arrows in battle men like Bhīṣma and Droṇa, who are worthy of my worship?

Arjuna wants Kṛṣṇa to know that his decision not to fight is due to strong-heartedness, not weak-heartedness. As Śrīla Prabhupāda mentions, offering even a verbal argument to one's superiors transgresses Vedic etiquette, what to speak of fighting and killing them.

According to Śrīla Viśvanātha Cakravartī Ṭhākura, by addressing Kṛṣṇa as Madhusūdana and Arisūdana, Arjuna calls attention to the fact that Kṛṣṇa is the killer of His enemies, not of His *guru* and grandfather. Arjuna would prefer to offer flowers at the feet of Droṇa and Bhīṣma, not arrows.

But how would Arjuna maintain himself if he were to give up his duty as a warrior and not fight?

5 It would be better to live in this world by begging than to live at the cost of the lives of great souls who are my teachers. Even though desiring worldly gain, they are superiors. If they are killed, everything we enjoy will be tainted with blood.

Again, *kṣatriyas* do not beg; they rule. Without a kingdom, Arjuna would have nothing to rule. Arjuna is well aware of this, but he prefers the embarrassment of begging to the sinful reaction for killing his worshipable superiors. Although his present life would be difficult, his future life would not be stained with the sin of killing his *guru.*

Arjuna, strongly justifying his position, continues in the next verse to give his fifth and final reason not to fight (referred to in the comment to Bg. 1.27).

6 Nor do we know which is better – conquering them or being conquered by them. If we killed the sons of Dhṛtarāṣṭra, we should not care to live. Yet they are now standing before us on the battlefield.

Arjuna does not know what to do. If he does not fight, he will have to beg. If he fights and wins, he will kill almost all his friends and relatives. Fighting and losing will mean his death. Therefore he is confused about his duty. Śrīla Prabhupāda writes in his purport, however, that Arjuna has the qualities necessary to receive knowledge. His mind and senses are controlled and he is detached, faithful, and tolerant. Perplexed yet eager for enlightenment, Arjuna recites the following verse.

7 Now I am confused about my duty and have lost all composure because of miserly weakness. In this condition I am asking You to tell me for certain what is best for me. Now I am Your disciple, and a soul surrendered unto You. Please instruct me.

Arjuna has based his reasons not to fight on compassion, logic, and *śāstra,* yet the result of his reasoning has been confusion. Therefore, to remove his confusion, Arjuna surrenders to his *guru*, Śrī Kṛṣṇa. Śrīla Prabhupāda explains that on our own we will always become confused, despite our best endeavors to solve our problems:

> By nature's own way the complete system of material activities is a source of perplexity for everyone. In every step there is perplexity, and therefore it behooves one to approach a bona fide spiritual master who can give one proper guidance for executing the purpose of life. All Vedic literatures advise us to approach

a bona fide spiritual master to get free from the perplexities of life, which happen without our desire. They are like a forest fire that somehow blazes without being set by anyone. Similarly, the world situation is such that perplexities of life automatically appear, without our wanting such confusion. No one wants fire, and yet it takes place, and we become perplexed. The Vedic wisdom therefore advises that in order to solve the perplexities of life and to understand the science of the solution, one must approach a spiritual master who is in the disciplic succession. A person with a bona fide spiritual master is supposed to know everything. One should not, therefore, remain in material perplexities but should approach a spiritual master. This is the purport of this verse.

Because Arjuna surrenders to Kṛṣṇa in text 7, we naturally expect Kṛṣṇa to begin His instructions in text 8. But He doesn't. He has not yet accepted Arjuna as His student.

When Arjuna says, "I am perplexed, confused, and I want to surrender to You," Śrīla Baladeva Vidyābhūṣaṇa gives Kṛṣṇa's reply as follows: "You know *śāstra*. Why not use your own logic and reasoning?" Śrīla Viśvanātha Cakravartī Ṭhākura says that Kṛṣṇa replies: "I'm your friend. I'm not in the mood of being your *guru,* so how can I accept you as my disciple? Because you have a respectful attitude toward Vyāsadeva and others, why not go to them?" Kṛṣṇa's initial reponse thus tests Arjuna's determination, and Arjuna further expresses his desire to surrender to Kṛṣṇa in the next verse.

8 I can find no means to drive away this grief which is drying up my senses. I will not be able to dispel it even if I win a prosperous, unrivaled kingdom on earth with sovereignty like the demigods in heaven.

Again Arjuna asks Kṛṣṇa to enlighten him and dispel his distress. For he knows that even a prosperous kingdom or heavenly pleasures will leave him unsatisfied.

9 Sañjaya said: Having spoken thus, Arjuna, chastiser of enemies, told Kṛṣṇa, "Govinda, I shall not fight," and fell silent.

Srīla Baladeva Vidyābhūṣaṇa comments that Arjuna, by addressing Kṛṣṇa as Hṛṣīkeśa, the master of the senses, indicates: "Because You are the master of my senses, You are going to draw my intelligence into involvement with the fighting. And because You are the knower of the *Vedas*, You are going to make me understand that this fight is my personal *dharma*."

Śrīla Prabhupāda explains the significance of the word *parantapa:* "Dhṛtarāṣṭra must have been very glad to understand that Arjuna was not going to fight and was instead leaving the battlefield for the begging profession. But Sañjaya disappointed him again in relating that Arjuna was competent to kill his enemies (*parantapaḥ*). Although Arjuna was, for the time being, overwhelmed with grief due to family affection, he surrendered unto Kṛṣṇa, the supreme spiritual master, as a disciple."

Sañjaya next tells Dhṛtarāṣṭra Kṛṣṇa's reaction to Arjuna's words.

10 O descendant of Bharata, at that time Kṛṣṇa, smiling, in the midst of both the armies, spoke the following words to the grief-stricken Arjuna.

Prahasan literally means "smiling." Śrīla Prabhupāda explains that Kṛṣṇa is smiling because His friend has become a disciple. Kṛṣṇa's smile gradually changes to a grave expression. He will now act as Arjuna's spiritual master, and talks between the spiritual master and disciple are serious. Therefore Kṛṣṇa smiles as His friendly affection gives way to parental affection, which is similar to the relationship between *guru* and disciple.

Assuming the role of the *guru*, Kṛṣṇa became grave because He was teaching not only Arjuna but all humanity. Śrīla Prabhupāda says, "It appears that the talk between the master and the disciple was openly exchanged in the presence of both armies so that all were benefited." *Bhagavad-gītā* is not intended for any particular person, society or community, but for all people at all times.

11 The Supreme Personality of Godhead said: While speaking learned words, you are mourning for what is not worthy of

grief. Those who are wise lament neither for the living nor for the dead.

Having now accepted Arjuna's surrender, Kṛṣṇa immediately chastises His student. He tells Arjuna that although he spoke with the authority of a wise man, he is lamenting about something for which no wise man would lament. In essence He is calling Arjuna a fool. Although Arjuna's words are true according to *dharma* and *rāja-nīti* (statesmanship), they do not take into consideration the true, basic standard of knowledge: the difference between the body and the soul.

This verse serves as a prelude to text 12, which will further establish spiritual truth by refuting the bodily concept of life.

12 Never was there a time when I did not exist, nor you, nor all these kings; nor in the future shall any of us cease to be.

Kṛṣṇa is saying, "In the past I was Kṛṣṇa, in the present I am Kṛṣṇa, and in the future I will be Kṛṣṇa. In the past you existed, in the present you exist, and in the future you will exist. All these kings assembled here to fight were all individuals in the past, are individuals in the present, and will continue to be individuals in the future. In other words, we are all eternally spiritual individuals."

In this verse Kṛṣṇa immediately defeats the Māyāvāda concept of the oneness of the Supreme and the living entities by identifying Himself as an individual: the Supreme Personality of Godhead. He also identifies Arjuna and all the assembled kings as eternal individuals. He does not say that in the future Arjuna and the kings will become one with Him, nor does he say that He was formless in the past, that He has assumed a form now and in the future He will again become formless. Rather, He states His point clearly: "I was Kṛṣṇa, I am Kṛṣṇa, and I will always be Kṛṣṇa." Similarly, Kṛṣṇa asserts Arjuna's eternal individuality. It is not that Arjuna or the assembled kings were merged into Kṛṣṇa in the past, have now assumed bodily forms because of illusion and in the future will again be merged into Kṛṣṇa. As Śrīla Prabhupāda mentions, Māyāvādīs may argue "...that the plurality mentioned in this verse is conventional and that it refers to the body. But previous to this verse such a bodily conception is already condemned. After condemning the bodily conception of the living entities, how was it possible for Kṛṣṇa to place a conventional proposition on the body again?" On the contrary, Kṛṣṇa clearly stresses spiritual individuality.

This basic understanding of the difference between the individual soul and his temporary body is further stressed in the next verse.

13 As the embodied soul continuously passes, in this body, from boyhood to youth to old age, the soul similarly passes into another body at death. A sober person is not bewildered by such a change.

In response to Arjuna's balking at killing Bhīṣma and Droṇa, Kṛṣṇa has assured Arjuna that Bhīṣma and Droṇa are both souls and cannot die. Death is simply a change of body. Every embodied soul must endure it. Bhīṣma passed through the stages of boyhood (*kaumāram*), then youth (*yauvanam*), and now he is an old man (*jarā*); he has already changed bodies many times. A wise man is not bewildered by these bodily changes. Neither does he lament for them, because such lamentation is based on illusion.

The history of Mahārāja Yayāti provides a graphic example. After growing old, Mahārāja Yayāti traded his old age for his son's youth. Upon his obtaining a youthful body, no one lamented that the king had relinquished his old body. Rather, everyone was happy. Here Kṛṣṇa asks Arjuna, "Why lament if Bhīṣma and Droṇa take on new, young bodies? Do not be bewildered. *Dhīras tatra na muhyati:* a sober person is not bewildered by such a change."

According to both Srīla Viśvanātha Cakravartī Ṭhākura and Srīla Baladeva Vidyābhūṣaṇa, Arjuna agrees with Kṛṣṇa that Bhīṣma and Droṇa would be better off in younger bodies; but, Arjuna explains, his reluctance to fight is due to his current relationship with them, which is based on their present bodies, and he will feel misery in their absence. Śrīla Viśvanātha Cakravartī Ṭhākura comments:

> [One may say:] By connection with the self, even one's body becomes an object of affection. By a connection with one's body, one's children, siblings, and so on also become dear. So when they are destroyed, one naturally experiences unhappiness.
>
> This objection is answered by the verse beginning *dehinaḥ*. The *jīva,* who is the possessor of his body, reaches the stage of childhood. When that boyhood is then "destroyed," he reaches youth, and when his youth is "destroyed," he reaches old age. In the same way one attains another body. So, just as one doesn't lament when his stages of childhood and youth have been "destroyed," even though they are objects of his affection, similarly one should not lament when his body is "destroyed," even though it is an object of affection because of its connection with the self.
>
> Someone may counter-claim that there is indeed unhappiness when one's youth is destroyed and one reaches old age.
>
> But in response we can say that one rejoices when his childhood is destroyed and he reaches youth. Thus we should rejoice that Bhīṣma, Droṇa and others are going to receive new bodies after their old ones are destroyed. Or else we may say that just as one person in the same body achieves all the stages beginning with childhood, similarly the same one *jīva,* who possesses bodies, obtains a whole series of bodies.

Śrīla Baladeva Vidyābhūṣaṇa comments:

> [One may say:] Although the souls who are now conditioned by the bodies of Bhīṣma and so on are eternal, it is natural that there be sorrow upon the destruction of their bodies, which were the facilities for their enjoyment.
>
> [The answer is as follows:] With the destruction of the decrepit bodies of Bhīṣma and so on, they are going to receive new bodies. That should be a cause for rejoicing, just as was Yayāti's regaining his youth.

Text 14 is Kṛṣṇa's reply to Arjuna's specific hesitancy.

14 O son of Kuntī, the nonpermanent appearance of happiness and distress, and their disappearance in due course, are like the appearance and disappearance of winter and summer seasons.

They arise from sense perception, O scion of Bharata, and one must learn to tolerate them without being disturbed.

Kṛṣṇa instructs Arjuna not to lament, but to tolerate. Arjuna should not forsake his duty because of the temporary pains and pleasures that arise.

15 O best among men [Arjuna], the person who is not disturbed by happiness and distress and is steady in both is certainly eligible for liberation.

Kṛṣṇa once more instructs Arjuna to tolerate and to perform his duty and attain liberation. By performing our prescribed duties (*karma*) we obtain knowledge (*jñāna*), which is a prerequisite for liberation.

16 Those who are seers of the truth have concluded that of the nonexistent [the material body] there is no endurance and of the eternal [the soul] there is no change. This they have concluded by studying the nature of both.

Kṛṣṇa again rebukes Arjuna. Seers of the truth recognize the difference between the body and the soul. Indirectly, He tells Arjuna that despite his previous scholarly words, he has not understood things as they are. Kṛṣṇa clarifies the truth by offering two propositions in this verse: 1) *nāsato vidyate bhāvo* and 2) *nābhāvo vidyate sataḥ*. First, the material body and all material situations are temporary; they have no actual existence. Second, only those things that are *sat,* eternal, truly exist.

17 That which pervades the entire body you should know to be indestructible. No one is able to destroy that imperishable soul.

This verse refers to Kṛṣṇa's second point (*nābhāvo vidyate sataḥ*) in text 16. Kṛṣṇa here explains the body-soul duality. After His brief explanation here, He will not mention this most basic point again in *Bhagavad-gītā.* Kṛṣṇa explains His first point (*nāsato vidyate bhāvo*) in text 18.

18 The material body of the indestructible, immeasurable, and eternal living entity is sure to come to an end; therefore, fight, O descendant of Bharata.

This verse reverses Arjuna's argument that by not fighting he will save his family members from harm. Everyone's body must perish, for no material body has true existence. Fearing for the death of others is ignorance. The soul, the real person within the body, is indestructible. Śrīla Prabhupāda writes: "So from both viewpoints there is no cause of lamentation, because the living entity as he is cannot be killed nor can the material body be saved for any length of time or permanently protected."

19 Neither he who thinks the living entity the slayer nor he who thinks it slain is in knowledge, for the self slays not nor is slain.

Śrīla Viśvanātha Cakravartī Ṭhākura comments: "The self is neither the subject of the act of killing nor its object. He who thinks that the soul is the killer (that Arjuna is killing Bhīṣma and others) and he who thinks that the soul is killed (that Bhīṣma and others have been killed by Arjuna) are both ignorant." No one can truly kill or be killed. Kṛṣṇa elaborates on this point in the next verse.

20 For the soul there is neither birth nor death at any time. He has not come into being, does not come into being, and will not come into being. He is unborn, eternal, ever-existing, and primeval. He is not slain when the body is slain.

Kṛṣṇa clearly delineates the eternality of the soul. *Na jāyate mriyate:* the soul is not born and it never dies. The soul is *aja,* unborn in the past, present, or future, and *śāśvataḥ,* deathless. Again Arjuna's fear of killing his *guru* is defeated. In this way Kṛṣṇa continues to dismantle Arjuna's arguments against fighting.

21 O Pārtha, how can a person who knows that the soul is indestructible, eternal, unborn, and immutable kill anyone or cause anyone to kill?

Kṛṣṇa here offers Arjuna *jñāna,* knowledge. With this knowledge he can engage in warfare, yet incur no sinful reaction. Śrīla Prabhupāda describes why Arjuna should fight:

> Although the justice of the peace awards capital punishment to a person condemned for murder, the justice of the peace cannot be blamed, because he orders violence to another person according to the codes of justice....Similarly, when Kṛṣṇa orders fighting, it must be concluded that violence is for supreme justice, and thus Arjuna should follow the instruction, knowing well that such violence, committed in the act of fighting for Kṛṣṇa, is not violence at all because, at any rate, the man, or rather the soul, cannot be killed; so for the administration of justice, so-called violence is permitted.

According to Srīla Baladeva Vidyābhūṣaṇa, Arjuna may think, "Granting that the soul does not die, still the bodies of the men called Bhīṣma and others are going to be destroyed in the battle. That is wrong because it will improperly deprive them of the happiness they derive from their bodies." Kṛṣṇa explains to Arjuna the fault of this logic in the next verse.

22 As a person puts on new garments, giving up old ones, the soul similarly accepts new material bodies, giving up the old and useless ones.

Changing bodies is inevitable. Again, Arjuna's refusal to fight will not protect Bhīṣma, Droṇa, or anyone else on the battlefield from having to change bodies. Thus Arjuna's reasoning is once more defeated by Kṛṣṇa.

23 The soul can never be cut to pieces by any weapon, nor burned by fire, nor moistened by water, nor withered by the wind.

Arjuna is a great *kṣatriya,* and he has an arsenal of powerful weapons. Although he has a hard-tempered sword, that sword cannot cut the soul. Although he possesses a fire weapon, that fire cannot burn the soul. Neither can his water weapon inundate it, nor his wind weapon wither the eternal soul.

24 This individual soul is unbreakable and insoluble, and can be neither burned nor dried. He is everlasting, present everywhere, unchangeable, immovable, and eternally the same.

25 It is said that the soul is invisible, inconceivable, and immutable. Knowing this, you should not grieve for the body.

These *ślokas* reiterate a principle Kṛṣṇa has already established. Generally such repetition is considered improper in Sanskrit literature, but Kṛṣṇa repeats himself to remove all doubts about the soul's eternality.

Kṛṣṇa now begins offering another argument to convince Arjuna to take part in the battle. Verse 26 starts with the words *atha ca,* "if, however," which indicates that Kṛṣṇa will now begin to discuss a new topic. Śrīla Viśvanātha Cakravartī Ṭhākura explains Kṛṣṇa's thinking: "I have thus far explained things to you from the viewpoint of *śāstra.* Now I will explain them from the worldly point of view."

26 If, however, you think that the soul [or the symptoms of life] is always born and dies forever, you still have no reason to lament, O mighty-armed.

Kṛṣṇa first explained the soul's eternality. Now He argues on the basis of principles presented by other philosophers, namely, atheists and Buddhists. Kṛṣṇa thus checkmates Arjuna.

If all the assembled warriors are factually eternal souls, no one will die on the battlefield, and Arjuna should therefore do his duty and fight. If no soul exists and life is simply the result of a chemical combination, then still Arjuna should do his duty and fight. If Arjuna accepts the argument for the nonexistence of the soul, then he should not be afraid to fight. After all, how can he be a killer of a combination of chemicals? Thus whether the soul exists or not, Arjuna should not lament but should fight.

27 One who has taken his birth is sure to die, and after death one is sure to take birth again. Therefore, in the unavoidable discharge of your duty, you should not lament.

Arjuna is wrong if he thinks he will stop the Kauravas' deaths by not fighting. When the eternal soul contacts a temporary material body, birth takes place. When the eternal soul loses contact with that body, death results. This point is again explained in the next verse.

28 All created beings are unmanifest in their beginning, manifest in their interim state, and unmanifest again when annihilated. So what need is there for lamentation?

Kṛṣṇa has just said that Arjuna should fight whether he believes in an eternal soul possessing a material body or that no soul, only a body, exists. This verse explains that whether or not we believe in the soul, the material body was previously unmanifested. Now, for some time, the body is manifest, and in the future it will again become unmanifested. The body must be annihilated. What is the use, therefore, of lamentation? Arjuna should fight, regardless of which knowledge of the soul he accepts as true.

Jñāna describing the difference between the body and soul continues until text 30. Verse 29 is the "amazing" verse.

29 Some look on the soul as amazing, some describe him as amazing, and some hear of him as amazing, while others, even after hearing about him, cannot understand him at all.

Āścarya-vat means "amazing." *Paśyati* means "sees." *Vadati* means "describes." *Śṛṇoti* means "hears." The first line of this verse says *āścarya-vat paśyati:* "Some look on the soul as amazing." The second line says *āścarya-vad vadati:* "Some people speak about the soul as amazing." And the third line says *āścarya-vac…śṛṇoti:* "Some hear about the soul and think of him as amazing."

In the first line of Śrīla Prabhupāda's translation, "Some look on the soul as amazing," *āścarya-vat,* "amazing," is taken to modify "soul," which is the object of the sentence. Śrīla Baladeva Vidyābhūṣaṇa has given two more interpretations, wherein the word *āścarya-vat* additionally modifies the sentence's subject and verb. Thus each line of this verse can be explained in three ways, as the word for "amazing" changes from modifying the object (the soul) to modifying the subject and verb.

Āścarya-vat can modify "people," the subject of the sentence: "Some people, who are amazing, look upon the soul."

If *āścarya-vat* modifies the verb, "look," the sentence reads, "Some people look – amazingly – at the soul."

Depending on how one translates this "amazing" verse, the people who see the soul are amazing, the soul is amazing, or the power to see the soul is amazing.

The second line, "Some people describe the soul as amazing," can also be translated in three ways with *vadati,* "describes," replacing "sees." Similarly, the third line can be translated in three ways by using the word *ṣṛṇoti,* "hears."

Text 30 concludes those verses that have described *jñāna.*

30 O descendant of Bharata, he who dwells in the body can never be slain. Therefore you need not grieve for any living being.

As the best of communicators, Kṛṣṇa has concluded this part of His instruction with a half-verse summary of the soul's eternality. Thus Kṛṣṇa has destroyed Arjuna's illusion with knowledge. Proper knowledge leads to proper action. The following section directly attacks Arjuna's desire, based on ignorance, to neglect his duty out of a sense of compassion for his family members.

In the next group of verses (31–38), Kṛṣṇa continues His attempt to convince Arjuna to fight. The motives He stresses here, however, are not based on knowledge but on fruitive activity and religious duty. In this way Kṛṣṇa attacks another of Arjuna's reasons, that is, that he will not be able to enjoy himself after he engages in the battle.

Therefore, in texts 31–33, Kṛṣṇa presents Arjuna with the argument that dutiful fighting, not fleeing the battlefield, will lead to enjoyment.

31 Considering your specific duty as a kṣatriya, you should know that there is no better engagement for you than fighting on religious principles; and so there is no need for hesitation.

In the previous section Kṛṣṇa used arguments based on *jñāna* to induce Arjuna to fight. Now Kṛṣṇa will use less elevated principles, ones which promise a material reward.

For a *kṣatriya,* fighting is equivalent to a *brāhmaṇa's* performance of fire sacrifices. By performing their duties, neither the *kṣatriya* nor the *brāhmaṇa* incurs sinful reactions. Therefore Kṛṣṇa argues that Arjuna will not suffer sinful reactions in fighting the battle of Kurukṣetra.

32 O Pārtha, happy are the kṣatriyas to whom such fighting opportunities come unsought, opening for them the doors of the heavenly planets.

The heavenly planets are the goal of those following the *karma-kāṇḍa* processes. Kṛṣṇa tells Arjuna, who fears for his relatives' welfare, that he can send them to the heavenly planets by defeating them in battle. Arjuna, too, will gain everything by fighting. If he doesn't fight, he will lose all.

33 If, however, you do not perform your religious duty of fighting, then you will certainly incur sins for neglecting your duties and thus lose your reputation as a fighter.

This verse specifically defeats Arjuna's argument that he will incur sins by fighting. Rather, the opposite is true.

In texts 33–37, Kṛṣṇa describes additional losses Arjuna will suffer if he neglects his duty. Arjuna thinks it will be more noble to leave the battlefield, but Kṛṣṇa argues otherwise.

34 People will always speak of your infamy, and for a respectable person, dishonor is worse than death.

We may question why a devotee like Arjuna should be concerned about honor or dishonor. We should understand that in this section of *Bhagavad-gītā,* Kṛṣṇa is not speaking to Arjuna on the transcendental platform of devotional service. Rather, He is addressing Arjuna's brave *kṣatriya* spirit. The pain of a disgraced life will be more painful than death for a warrior like Arjuna.

Śrīla Prabhupāda paraphrases Kṛṣṇa's admonishments in his purport: "Both as friend and philosopher to Arjuna, Lord Kṛṣṇa now gives His final judgment regarding Arjuna's refusal to fight. The Lord says, 'Arjuna, if you leave the battlefield before the battle even begins, people will call you a coward. And if you think that people may call you bad names but that you will save your life by fleeing the battlefield, then My advice is that you'd do better to die in the battle. For a respectable man like you, ill fame is worse than death. So, you should not flee for fear of your life; better to die in the battle. That will save you from the ill fame of misusing My friendship and from losing your prestige in society.'"

35 The great generals who have highly esteemed your name and fame will think that you have left the battlefield out of fear only, and thus they will consider you insignificant.

Śrīla Prabhupāda elaborates in his purport: "Lord Kṛṣṇa continued to give His verdict to Arjuna: 'Do not think that the great generals like Duryodhana, Karṇa, and other contemporaries will think that you have left the battlefield out of compassion for your brothers and grandfather. They will think that you have left out of fear for your life. And thus their high estimation of your personality will go to hell.'"

For a renowned *kṣatriya* such as Arjuna, the loss of his reputation and others' esteem will be more painful than his enemies' arrows.

36 Your enemies will describe you in many unkind words and scorn your ability. What could be more painful for you?

Arjuna's compassion will be seen as cowardly weakness. The result of his so-called compassion, which is based on illusion, will simply be infamy. Thus Kṛṣṇa again defeats Arjuna's "compassion." Śrīla Prabhupāda writes: "Lord Kṛṣṇa was astonished in the beginning at Arjuna's uncalled-for plea for compassion, and He described his compassion as befitting the non-Āryans. Now in so many words, He has proved His statements against Arjuna's so-called compassion."

Kṛṣṇa gives his final verdict in the next verse.

37 O son of Kuntī, either you will be killed on the battlefield and attain the heavenly planets, or you will conquer and enjoy the earthly kingdom. Therefore, get up with determination and fight.

Arjuna had concluded that fighting would bring him not enjoyment but misery. Kṛṣṇa herein defeats that point. "Winning the battle," Arjuna thought, "will cause the death of those with whom I would have enjoyed the kingdom. Losing will mean my own death." Kṛṣṇa's words reverse Arjuna's plan for attaining happiness: "If you are killed on the battlefield, you will attain the heavenly planets. If you are victorious, you will enjoy the earthly kingdom." Because there is no loss in either event, Kṛṣṇa says, "Get up with determination and fight."

Kṛṣṇa's arguments, meant to inspire Arjuna to fight, are a particular set of instructions that address material enjoyment (based on identifying oneself with one's body) as the motivating force behind Arjuna's performance of duty. Kṛṣṇa ends this section in the next verse and then takes the discussion (in verse 39) to the higher level of working in knowledge.

38 Do thou fight for the sake of fighting, without considering happiness or distress, loss or gain, victory or defeat – and by so doing you shall never incur sin.

Arjuna reasoned earlier that fighting the battle would cause him to suffer prolonged sinful reactions, but here Kṛṣṇa explains that no sin will be incurred by one who executes his duty in the proper consciousness.

Previously (in verses 11–30), to remove Arjuna's arguments against fighting, Kṛṣṇa presented *jñāna,* the difference between the body and the soul: Because Arjuna and the other warriors are eternal souls, no one would die; only the body, which unavoidably perishes, can be slain. After presenting those arguments, Kṛṣṇa encouraged Arjuna to fight based on fruitive considerations (*karma*) to gain pleasure and to avoid suffering. Now Kṛṣṇa instructs Arjuna to combine both – *jñāna* (knowledge) and *karma* (activity) – and to fight with detachment. Working in this consciousness is technically called *niṣkāma karma-yoga* or *buddhi-yoga,* detached work on the platform of knowledge. Śrīla Baladeva Vidyābhūṣaṇa defines *buddhi-yoga* as "*niṣkāma karma-yoga* incorporating *jñāna* within itself."*

One can perform *niṣkāma karma-yoga* on one of two levels depending on the advancement of one's transcendental knowledge. One who simply has *jñāna,* knowledge that he is not his body, performs *niṣkāma karma,* detached work. Such a person receives no reactions for his work because his knowledge has fostered his detachment from the work's results.

However, one who has actual knowledge of Kṛṣṇa possesses superior knowledge. He not only knows of his spiritual identity beyond his body, but he also knows that he is Kṛṣṇa's eternal servant. Such a person also performs *niṣkāma karma,* but he receives no reactions for his work because he offers the fruits of his work to Kṛṣṇa.

Both *niṣkāma karma-yogīs* are free from reaction because they practice detachment in knowledge, but the *niṣkāma karma-yogī* who aspires for Kṛṣṇa's loving service is far superior. He may not yet be on the level of transcendental devotional service, but his activities will one day lead him to Kṛṣṇa's lotus feet. The *niṣkāma karma-yogī* who knows only that he is not his body may, if he desires *brahmavāda* liberation, gradually attain *mukti.* Or, if his transcendental knowledge increases because he associates with Vaiṣṇavas, he may elevate his desire and attain Kṛṣṇa's service.

Śrīla Prabhupāda's purport brings this verse to the level of *bhakti:* "Lord Kṛṣṇa now directly says that Arjuna should fight for the sake of fighting because He desires the battle. There is no consideration of happiness or distress, profit or gain, victory or defeat in the activities of Kṛṣṇa consciousness. That everything should be performed for the sake of Kṛṣṇa is transcendental consciousness; so there is no reaction to material activities."

---

* My description of the *yoga* ladder splits *karma-yoga* into two divisions: *sakāma karma-yoga,* where one offers Kṛṣṇa a portion of the fruits of one's work, and *niṣkāma karma-yoga,* where one offers the complete fruit of his works. As one begins to advance spiritually, one generally passes through the *sakāma* stage on the way through the *niṣkāma* stage as he moves toward the fully surrendered practice of pure *bhakti*. For a more complete explanation of these and other terms, see Appendix 1.

Kṛṣṇa, in this verse, has directly instructed Arjuna to fight, though His order is in the form of requesting Arjuna to fight dutifully "for the sake of fighting." Actually, Arjuna's fighting *will* ultimately be impelled by his desire to fulfill this order of Kṛṣṇa's. That is *bhakti.* Kṛṣṇa wants Arjuna to fight on His order, as His surrendered servant, with *bhakti,* detached from the results. In this way Arjuna will remain sinless.

39 Thus far I have described this knowledge to you through analytical study. Now listen as I explain it in terms of working without fruitive results. O son of Pṛthā, when you act in such knowledge you can free yourself from the bondage of works.

In texts 11–30, Kṛṣṇa described *jñāna,* knowledge, as the difference between spirit and matter or the soul and the body. The activities of *jñāna-yoga* are basically the same as those of *sāṅkhya-yoga,* the analytical study of matter and spirit. To practice either, one must renounce all activities and practice meditation. Kṛṣṇa, however, has consistently instructed Arjuna in another way. He has told him to work in a renounced spirit, not to renounce activity.

Verse 39 hints that analytical study (*sāṅkhya*) means the renunciation of activity, which, if successfully performed, elevates one in *jñāna*. But Kṛṣṇa does not recommend that Arjuna renounce his activities. He therefore explains the benefits of action, not renunciation of activity, and says that action should be executed in knowledge with the understanding (*jñāna*) that one is not his body. Kṛṣṇa encourages Arjuna to listen attentively and to hear how to become free from sinful reactions. Śrīla Prabhupāda explains in his purport:

> Arjuna has already accepted Kṛṣṇa as his spiritual master by surrendering himself unto Him: *śiṣyas te 'haṁ śādhi māṁ tvāṁ prapannam.* Consequently, Kṛṣṇa will now tell him about the working process in *buddhi-yoga,* or *karma-yoga,* or in other words, the practice of devotional service only for the sense gratification of the Lord. This *buddhi-yoga* is clearly explained in chapter ten, verse ten, as being direct communion with the Lord, who is sitting as Paramātmā in everyone's heart. But such

> communion does not take place without devotional service. One who is therefore situated in devotional or transcendental loving service to the Lord, or, in other words, in Kṛṣṇa consciousness, attains to this stage of *buddhi-yoga* by the special grace of the Lord. The Lord says, therefore, that only to those who are always engaged in devotional service out of transcendental love does He award the pure knowledge of devotion in love. In that way the devotee can reach Him easily in the ever-blissful kingdom of God.

Buddhi-yoga or *karma-yoga* may be practiced at different stages. The topmost stage, as Śrīla Prabhupāda mentions above, is when Kṛṣṇa blesses the devotee and inspires him with full *buddhi,* and thus one effortlessly becomes fully absorbed in Kṛṣṇa consciousness. That is called love of God.

40 In this endeavor there is no loss or diminution, and a little advancement on this path can protect one from the most dangerous type of fear.

Endeavor in Kṛṣṇa consciousness (*buddhi-yoga*) saves us from rebirth in a lower species and from remaining trapped in the wheel of *saṁsāra*. There is no loss or diminution because all advancement is eternal. Material advancement, of course, is always temporary.

Kṛṣṇa continues encouraging Arjuna to hear about *buddhi-yoga*. Verse 41 has special significance for ISKCON devotees.

41 Those who are on this path are resolute in purpose, and their aim is one. O beloved child of the Kurus, the intelligence of those who are irresolute is many-branched.

Vyavasāyātmikā buddhiḥ, one-pointed intelligence, is required for success. Śrīla Prabhupāda once told his disciples that in the 1950s, before he spread Kṛṣṇa consciousness throughout the world, he read the commentary on this verse written by Śrīla Viśvanātha Cakravartī Ṭhākura. He said he was struck by the commentary, which further fixed him in his resolve to follow Śrīla Bhaktisiddhānta Sarasvatī Ṭhākura's order to preach Kṛṣṇa consciousness in English.

Śrīla Viśvanātha Cakravartī Ṭhākura writes:

> Of all kinds of intelligence, the best is intelligence focused on *bhakti-yoga.* In *bhakti-yoga*, one's intelligence becomes single-pointed, or fixed in determination. One thinks, "The instructions of my spiritual master to worship the Personality of Godhead by chanting, remembering, serving His feet, and so on are my only *sādhana,* my only *sādhya,* my only livelihood. I am incapable of giving up these instructions either in the stage of practice or in the stage of perfection. They alone are my object of desire and my only responsibility. Besides them I can desire no other responsibility, not even in my dreams. It is all the same to me whether I feel happy or unhappy, or whether my material existence is eradicated or not."

Śrīla Prabhupāda comments further on this verse in his purport to *Śrīmad-Bhāgavatam* 2.4.3–4: "The whole matter is concluded in the *Bhagavad-gītā* (2.41) as *vyavasāyātmikā buddhiḥ,* or the absolute path of perfection. Śrī Baladeva Vidyābhūṣaṇa defines this as *bhagavad-arcanā-rūpaika-niṣkāma-karmabhir viśuddha-cittaḥ* – accepting transcendental loving service to the Lord as the prime duty, free from fruitive reaction."

42–43 Men of small knowledge are very much attached to the flowery words of the Vedas, which recommend various fruitive activities for elevation to heavenly planets, resultant good birth, power, and so forth. Being desirous of sense gratification and opulent life, they say that there is nothing more than this.

Here, for the first time, Kṛṣṇa mentions the *Vedas* to Arjuna. He tells Arjuna to give up his *karma-kāṇḍa* mentality, or the idea of using the *Vedas* for many sacrifices aimed at pleasing various demigods to gain temporary fruits and benedictions such as sons, health, power, wealth, longevity, a bountiful harvest or heavenly pleasures. It should be noted that in the previous section, Kṛṣṇa encouraged Arjuna to fight by appealing to the same mentality in Arjuna that He now condemns. Although previously encouraging Arjuna to fight to obtain heaven, Kṛṣṇa now speaks on a higher level, the level of *buddhi-yoga.*

44 In the minds of those who are too attached to sense enjoyment and material opulence, and who are bewildered by such things, the resolute determination for devotional service to the Supreme Lord does not take place.

The result of being attracted to the flowery words of the *Vedas* without knowing their actual purpose is bewilderment. Owing to ignorance and material attachment, *karma-kāṇḍīs* cannot fix their minds on the Supreme. Instead they use the *Vedas* as an excuse to avoid the Vedic purpose: surrender to the Supreme Personality of Godhead. Kṛṣṇa next prescribes how one can overcome this mentality.

45 The Vedas deal mainly with the subject of the three modes of material nature. O Arjuna, become transcendental to these three modes. Be free from all dualities and from all anxieties for gain and safety, and be established in the self.

Kṛṣṇa instructs Arjuna to rise above the fruitive performance of duty. Rather than fighting to gain heavenly pleasures or to avoid infamy, he should be established in self-realization. Arjuna previously reasoned that destroying the family traditions would end the performance of *karma-kāṇḍa* rituals. Kṛṣṇa now defeats that argument by telling Arjuna to rise above those rituals, which are contaminated by the modes of material nature.

In his purport, Śrīla Prabhupāda comments on Kṛṣṇa's first mention of the three modes of material nature and summarizes the process of transcending the modes: "As long as the material body exists, there are actions and reactions in the material modes. One has to learn tolerance in the face of dualities such as happiness and distress, or cold and warmth, and by tolerating such dualities become free from anxieties regarding gain and loss. This transcendental position is achieved in full Kṛṣṇa consciousness when one is fully dependent on the good will of Kṛṣṇa."

Kṛṣṇa concludes His argument in verse 46.

46 All purposes served by a small well can at once be served by a great reservoir of water. Similarly, all the purposes of the Vedas can be served to one who knows the purpose behind them.

Śrīla Viśvanātha Cakravartī Ṭhākura comments that in India, each well is used for only a specific purpose: for drinking water, for washing clothes, for cleaning utensils, or for bathing. All those activities, however, can be performed simultaneously on the shore of a lake or a river. Where a source of fresh water is available, we do not need to go from well to well to fulfill our purposes. Similarly, one who is *vijānataḥ,* in complete knowledge of the Vedic purpose, need only perform *buddhi-yoga* for the Lord's pleasure. The performance of *buddhi-yoga* satisfies the purpose behind the *Vedas*. *Karma-kāṇḍa* rituals then become unnecessary. Even one who has material desires, but who performs *buddhi-yoga,* will become purified, because he is fixed in transcendental knowledge.

Because Kṛṣṇa has explained several alternative levels of activity to Arjuna, He next explains the specific level on which Arjuna is qualified to act.

47 You have a right to perform your prescribed duty, but you are not entitled to the fruits of action. Never consider yourself the cause of the results of your activities, and never be attached to not doing your duty.

This important verse, in which the Lord chooses to instruct Arjuna to perform *niṣkāma karma-yoga,* begins, *karmaṇy evādhikāras te*. Arjuna's *adhikāra,* his personal eligibility, is *eva,* "certainly," for *karma* (work). While working, however, he should not create further reactions by desiring to enjoy the fruits of his work. The concept of duty – dispassionate, proper actions whose performance is its own reward – is becoming increasingly foreign to modern society.

Śrīla Prabhupāda describes this proper approach to work in his purport: "Arjuna was therefore advised by the Lord to fight as a matter of duty without attachment to the result. His non-participation in the battle is another side of attachment. Such attachment never leads one to the path of salvation. Any attachment, positive or negative, is cause for bondage. Inaction is sinful. Therefore, fighting as a matter of duty was the only auspicious path of salvation for Arjuna."

Kṛṣṇa explains the proper consciousness in which to work in the following *śloka*.

48 Perform your duty equipoised, O Arjuna, abandoning all attachment to success or failure. Such equanimity is called yoga.

When one works and is unattached to the fruits of such work, he is performing *karma-yoga.* Detachment is then perfected when he offers the fruits of his work to Kṛṣṇa. Therefore Kṛṣṇa tells Arjuna not to renounce work, but to renounce the fruits of work.

The next verse should be noted because it is connected to the question Arjuna will ask Kṛṣṇa at the opening of chapter three.

49 O Dhanañjaya, keep all abominable activities far distant by devotional service, and in that consciousness surrender unto the Lord. Those who want to enjoy the fruits of their work are misers.

What fruits does one attain who tries to enjoy the results of his work? Only birth and death. Kṛṣṇa criticizes fruitive desires and glorifies *buddhi-yoga* (which Śrīla Prabhupāda translates as "devotional service"). The living entity should work hard to escape suffering, and he should not become further entangled in it. *Buddhi-yoga* liberates one, and the effects of its practice are described as follows.

50 A man engaged in devotional service rids himself of both good and bad actions even in this life. Therefore strive for yoga, which is the art of all work.

The art of work is to act in such a way that we become free from both good and bad reactions. Arjuna fears the sinful reactions from killing his kinsmen, but dutiful, detached work in knowledge will protect him from the fruits stemming from his activities. We must work, but we should be detached from the results.

Jñānīs desire to become free of reactions by renouncing all activities. The same effect can be more easily achieved by acting with detachment. For example, mercury is poisonous, but in the hands of an Āyurvedic doctor, mercury becomes a powerful medicine. Similarly, while regular, attached work entangles the soul in the material world, detached, dutiful work, performed in knowledge and aimed at pleasing the Supreme, leads him to liberation.

51 By thus engaging in devotional service to the Lord, great sages or devotees free themselves from the results of work in the material world. In this way they become free from the cycle of birth and death and attain the state beyond all miseries [by going back to Godhead].

Śrīla Viśvanātha Cakravartī Ṭhākura explains that detached work leads to realized knowledge of the soul. When one thus becomes self-realized, he can gradually become blessed with knowledge of the Lord and can surrender to Him. Such surrender frees him from the material world, and after liberation he becomes eligible to attain Vaikuṇṭha. This progression is known as "the *yoga* ladder." The *yoga* ladder is detailed in the first six chapters of *Bhagavad-gītā.*

52 When your intelligence has passed out of the dense forest of delusion, you shall become indifferent to all that has been heard and all that is to be heard.

How we attain fruitive benefits is described in the *karma-kāṇḍa* section of the *Vedas*. Kṛṣṇa here compares it to a dense forest of material illusion. Arjuna is preoccupied with a fruitive mentality. He thinks that happiness is impossible to obtain and misery is certain if he performs his duty of fighting. Kṛṣṇa tells him, however, that by fighting with *buddhi* he will achieve fixed intelligence (*vyavasāyātmikā-buddhi*) and become indifferent to happiness and distress.

In the next verse, Kṛṣṇa further describes the indifference to Vedic rituals required to achieve the true Vedic goal.

53 When your mind is no longer disturbed by the flowery language of the Vedas, and when it remains fixed in the trance of self-realization, then you will have attained the divine consciousness.

Arjuna must transcend fruitive desires and become fixed in *buddhi-yoga* to achieve success. Desires to perform the prescribed Vedic duties – this sacrifice, that ritual – must no longer disturb the candidate attempting to attain *samādhi,* consciousness that is fixed on the Supreme.

But will a devotee who neglects Vedic verses be lacking instruction? Śrīla Prabhupāda's purport describes the instructing that occurs on different levels of *buddhi-yoga:* "In Kṛṣṇa consciousness, one comes directly into communion with Kṛṣṇa, and thus all directions from Kṛṣṇa may be understood in that transcendental state. One is sure to achieve results by such activities and attain conclusive knowledge. One has only to carry out the orders of Kṛṣṇa or His representative, the spiritual master."

Kṛṣṇa has for the time being finished describing *buddhi-yoga.* Arjuna now asks four questions, in text 54, about the divine consciousness that Kṛṣṇa has just mentioned. Kṛṣṇa answers those questions one by one, beginning with text 55.

54 Arjuna said: O Kṛṣṇa, what are the symptoms of one whose consciousness is thus merged in transcendence? How does he speak, and what is his language? How does he sit, and how does he walk?

Arjuna wants to know how to recognize the *sthita-prajña,* the one in divine consciousness. He therefore asks: "What are his symptoms? How does he speak? How does he sit? How does he walk?" Śrīla Viśvanātha Cakravartī Ṭhākura explains that Arjuna's first question asks: "How is one who is transcendentally situated (*sthita-prajña*) described? What are his characteristics?" Kṛṣṇa answers this first question in text 55. Although these questions seem to deal only with such a person's external behavior, Śrīla Viśvanātha Cakravartī Ṭhākura reveals each question's internal meaning.

55 The Supreme Personality of Godhead said: O Pārtha, when a man gives up all varieties of desire for sense gratification, which arise from mental concoction, and when his mind, thus purified, finds satisfaction in the self alone, then he is said to be in pure transcendental consciousness.

The *sthita-prajña* reveals his position by having no material affection. He is detached from both happiness and misery. Rather, he is fully satisfied by fixing his consciousness on the self.

In texts 56–57 Kṛṣṇa answers Arjuna's second question: "How does he speak?" This question means: "How are his intelligence and words affected by another's affection, anger, or neutrality? In other words, how does he respond?"

56–57 One who is not disturbed in mind even amidst the threefold miseries or elated when there is happiness, and who is free from attachment, fear, and anger, is called a sage of steady mind. In the material world, one who is unaffected by whatever good or evil he may obtain, neither praising it nor despising it, is firmly fixed in perfect knowledge.

A *sthita-dhīr-muni* is both fixed in knowledge and aloof from the material world. He lives on the transcendental platform, and therefore his mind cannot be materially disturbed. Śrīla Prabhupāda writes: "Such a fully Kṛṣṇa conscious person is not at all disturbed by the onslaughts of the threefold miseries, for he accepts all miseries as the mercy of the Lord, thinking himself only worthy of more trouble due to his past misdeeds; and he sees that his miseries, by the Lord's grace, are minimized to the lowest. Similarly, when he is happy he gives credit to the Lord, thinking himself unworthy of the happiness…"

These symptoms describe a Kṛṣṇa conscious person, but they may also describe one who is liberated but not Kṛṣṇa conscious. An exalted devotee is unaffected by material happiness or distress because his consciousness has nothing to do with matter, but one who is simply liberated in Brahman may be neutral in relation to the material world, while having no positive engagement in Kṛṣṇa consciousness. Thus these symptoms are applicable to both personalists and impersonalists, though Śrīla Prabhupāda emphasizes how they apply to personalists.

The next question – "How does he sit?" – means: "How does he *not* engage his senses? What is his mentality when his senses are restrained from their objects?" Kṛṣṇa answers in the next two verses.

58 One who is able to withdraw his senses from sense objects, as the tortoise draws its limbs within the shell, is firmly fixed in perfect consciousness.

Such a person uses his senses only when required. Whether or not that restraint is difficult for him is described in the next verse.

59 The embodied soul may be restricted from sense enjoyment, though the taste for sense objects remains. But, ceasing such engagements by experiencing a higher taste, he is fixed in consciousness.

A transcendentalist's renunciation is not difficult because he has a higher taste. This is especially true of Vaiṣṇavas. As a tortoise naturally draws its limbs into its shell, devotees naturally and fully withdraw their senses from matter by engaging them in Kṛṣṇa's service.

In texts 60–63, Kṛṣṇa explains the danger of Arjuna's plan to renounce work and go to the forest to "gain knowledge" and avoid sinful reaction.

60 The senses are so strong and impetuous, O Arjuna, that they forcibly carry away the mind even of a man of discrimination who is endeavoring to control them.

Kṛṣṇa is telling Arjuna, "Do not give up work. Do not become a *jñānī,* a man who simply discriminates between matter and spirit. Perform your duty in *buddhi-yoga.*" Kṛṣṇa is showing Arjuna the defect of *jñāna* in order to propose the superiority of *bhakti-yoga.*

61 One who restrains his senses, keeping them under full control, and fixes his consciousness upon Me, is known as a man of steady intelligence.

The key words in this verse are *mat-paraḥ,* "in relationship with Me." Thus Kṛṣṇa, directly referring to Himself for the first time as the object of devotion, stresses *bhakti.* We can control the senses only by engaging them in relation to Kṛṣṇa. When our senses are subjugated – fully engaged in Kṛṣṇa's service – our consciousness is called *pratiṣṭhitā,* fixed.

The first half of the process described in this verse is restraint of the senses. Kṛṣṇa then directs one to fix his consciousness on Him. He says that one who has succeeded in both is "known as a man of steady intelligence." But what if, when trying to reach this stage, one fixes his senses on an object of enjoyment and views it as separate from Kṛṣṇa's service?

62–63 While contemplating the objects of the senses, a person develops attachment for them, and from such attachment lust develops, and from lust anger arises. From anger, complete delusion arises, and from delusion bewilderment of memory. When memory is bewildered, intelligence is lost, and when intelligence is lost one falls down again into the material pool.

The mind must be fixed on something. If we don't fix it on Kṛṣṇa, then we get the alternative result herein described.

Beginning with text 64 and continuing almost until the end of chapter two, Kṛṣṇa answers Arjuna's last question: "How does he walk?" The purport of this question is: "How does a man in transcendence engage his senses?"

64 But a person free from all attachment and aversion and able to control his senses through regulative principles of freedom can obtain the complete mercy of the Lord.

With a controlled mind and fixed intelligence, a man in transcendence remains disinterested in combining the senses with their objects. Everything such a great soul does is auspicious, and he experiences full satisfaction.

65 For one thus satisfied [in Kṛṣṇa consciousness], the threefold miseries of material existence exist no longer; in such satisfied consciousness, one's intelligence is soon well established.

A soul connected to Kṛṣṇa through Kṛṣṇa consciousness is free from material attractions and aversions and is fully satisfied. He experiences no misery, for his intelligence, being "well-established," is fixed on Kṛṣṇa (*mat-paraḥ*). Without *bhakti,* regardless of what one possesses or what one does, one cannot be is satisfied, as we see in the example of Śrīla Vyāsadeva's lamentation in the First Canto of *Śrīmad-Bhāgavatam.* Vyāsadeva had compiled the *Vedas,* added the *Purāṇas,* and composed the *Mahābhārata,* yet because he had not emphasized *bhakti,* he remained dissatisfied in mind.

He reflected, "I have, under strict disciplinary vows, unpretentiously worshiped the *Vedas,* the spiritual master, and the altar of sacrifice. I have also abided by the rulings and have shown the import of disciplic succession through the explanation of the *Mahābhārata,* by which even women, *śūdras,* and others [friends of the twice-born] can see the path of religion. I am feeling incomplete, though I myself am fully equipped with everything required by the *Vedas.* This may be because I did not specifically point out the devotional service of the Lord, which is dear both to perfect beings and to the infallible Lord." (*Bhāg.* 1.4.28–31)

What takes place when one lacks satisfaction in Kṛṣṇa consciousness?

66 One who is not connected with the Supreme [in Kṛṣṇa consciousness] can have neither transcendental intelligence nor a steady mind, without which there is no possibility of peace. And how can there be any happiness without peace?

The contrast between this verse and the previous one strengthens Kṛṣṇa's argument. If the mind and intelligence deviate from meditation on Kṛṣṇa, there can be no question of happiness. Deviating from thoughts of Kṛṣṇa and contemplating sense objects results in becoming overwhelmed by desires for material enjoyment.

67 As a boat on the water is swept away by a strong wind, even one of the roaming senses on which the mind focuses can carry away a man's intelligence.

A mind surrendered to the urges of the senses carries away a man's discrimination. His intelligence will thus be stolen by the unfavorable winds of his uncontrolled senses. The senses, however, once subdued, create favorable breezes.

68 Therefore, O mighty-armed, one whose senses are restrained from their objects is certainly of steady intelligence.

Śrīla Viśvanātha Cakravartī Ṭhākura says that *mahā-bāho* implies: "Just as you subdue your enemies, O mighty-armed one, in the same way you should subdue your mind."

69 What is night for all beings is the time of awakening for the self-controlled; and the time of awakening for all beings is night for the introspective sage.

The attached person and the detached person are as different as night and day. The *sthita-prajña* is as unaffected by a mood of sense enjoyment as a sleeping man is unaffected by his surroundings. He is neutral to the happiness and distress that come from his *karma* and is undistracted by viewing objects as sources of sense pleasure.

Kṛṣṇa now gives an example to illustrate the *sthita-prajña's* nature.

70 A person who is not disturbed by the incessant flow of desires – that enter like rivers into the ocean, which is ever being filled but is always still – can alone achieve peace, and not the man who strives to satisfy such desires.

He is unwavering. He does not chase after sense gratification. Kṛṣṇa explains his determination next.

71 A person who has given up all desires for sense gratification, who lives free from desires, who has given up all sense of proprietorship and is devoid of false ego – he alone can attain real peace.

Mahārāja Priyavrata is an excellent example of the person herein described. Although he behaved as a pious but worldly king, he was internally renounced and peaceful because his mind was fixed on the Supreme Personality of Godhead.

This verse ends Kṛṣṇa's answer to the question: "How does he walk?" Kṛṣṇa concludes chapter two with a brief summary.

72 That is the way of the spiritual and godly life, after attaining which a man is not bewildered. If one is thus situated even at the hour of death, one can enter into the kingdom of God.

Kṛṣṇa glorifies the position of the *sthita-prajña.*

Many topics have been discussed in this chapter: the *Vedas,* the modes of material nature, *karma-yoga, karma-kāṇḍa, jñāna, sāṅkhya, buddhi-yoga, vedānta,* the *ātmā,* detachment, *samādhi, sannyāsa,* and *bhakti-yoga.*

Śrīla Prabhupāda writes: "Śrīla Bhaktivinoda Ṭhākura has summarized this second chapter of the *Bhagavad-gītā* as being the contents for the whole text. In *Bhagavad-gītā,* the subject matters are *karma-yoga, jñāna-yoga,* and *bhakti-yoga.* In the second chapter, *karma-yoga* and *jñāna-yoga* have been clearly discussed, and a glimpse of *bhakti-yoga* has also been given, as the contents for the complete text."

Chapter Three

Karma-Yoga

In *Bhagavad-gītā* 2.49 Kṛṣṇa said, *dūreṇa hy avaraṁ karma buddhi-yogād dhanañjaya:* "Keep all abominable activities far distant by devotional service (*buddhi-yoga*)." This instruction has confused Arjuna.

"*Buddhi-yoga*" is *bhakti-yoga,* but it literally means the *yoga* of *buddhi,* intelligence. Taking the meaning of *buddhi* as intelligence, Kṛṣṇa's order would mean that Arjuna, by the use of his intelligence, should avoid all abominable activities. Kṛṣṇa has even emphasized intelligence by using the word *buddhi* ten times in the final thirty-three verses of the second chapter.

We can thus easily imagine Arjuna concluding that he should renounce fighting and thus keep the abominable activity of killing his kinsmen far distant by *buddhi-yoga,* or linking his intelligence to the Supreme. "But why then," thinks Arjuna, "is Kṛṣṇa still urging me to fight?"

Thus Arjuna, in the first two verses of chapter three, asks Kṛṣṇa to clarify His apparently contradictory instructions.

1 Arjuna said: O Janārdana, O Keśava, why do You want to engage me in this ghastly warfare, if You think that intelligence is better than fruitive work?

Śrīla Prabhupāda states in his purport: "Arjuna also thought of Kṛṣṇa consciousness or *buddhi-yoga,* or intelligence in spiritual advancement of knowledge, as something like retirement from active life and the practice of penance and austerity at a secluded place. In other words, he wanted to skillfully avoid the fighting by using Kṛṣṇa consciousness as an excuse. But as a sincere student, he placed the matter before his master and questioned Kṛṣṇa as to his best course of action. In answer, Lord Kṛṣṇa elaborately explained *karma-yoga,* or work in Kṛṣṇa consciousness, in this third chapter."

2 My intelligence is bewildered by Your equivocal instructions. Therefore, please tell me decisively which will be most beneficial for me.

Arjuna, misunderstanding as incompatible the paths of *karma* (spiritual advancement through work) and *jñāna* (the attempt usually through renounced, secluded meditation, to discern oneself as an eternal soul, different from the body), requests, *tad ekaṁ vada:* "Please tell me only one thing."

Śrīla Prabhupāda's purport explains: "Although Kṛṣṇa had no intention of confusing Arjuna by any jugglery of words, Arjuna could not follow the process of Kṛṣṇa consciousness – either by inertia or by active service. In other words, by his questions he is clearing the path of Kṛṣṇa consciousness for all students who seriously want to understand the mystery of the *Bhagavad-gītā*."

Kṛṣṇa will begin answering Arjuna's question by explaining in the following seven verses (3–9), the defect in his desire to renounce his duty.

3 The Supreme Personality of Godhead said: O sinless Arjuna, I have already explained that there are two classes of men who try to realize the self. Some are inclined to understand it by empirical, philosophical speculation, and others by devotional service.

Śrīla Viśvanatha Cakravartī Ṭhākura explains that the word *niṣṭhā* ("faith" or "platform") is significant. *Karma* and *jñāna* are two platforms or stages on the path to transcendental consciousness. The *karma* stage is the platform on which work is recommended, and the *jñāna* stage is the platform on which one is sufficiently purified and detached to renounce work. They are not separate processes, but two rungs, one above the other, on the *yoga* ladder. Depending on one's *niṣṭhā* (his position, faith, or purity of heart), one is recommended to act either on the platform of *karma* or *jñāna*. Arjuna has misunderstood this point and is thinking of *jñāna* and *karma* as two processes leading in different directions.

Kṛṣṇa will now explain that premature renunciation –

renunciation of work accepted before one is sufficiently purified and detached – will bring neither purification nor liberation.

4 Not by merely abstaining from work can one achieve freedom from reaction, nor by renunciation alone can one attain perfection.

Śrīla Prabhupāda's purport states: "The renounced order of life can be accepted when one has been purified by the discharge of the prescribed form of duties which are laid down just to purify the hearts of materialistic men.... Without purification of heart, *sannyāsa* is simply a disturbance to the social order. On the other hand, if someone takes to the transcendental service of the Lord, even without discharging his prescribed duties, whatever he may be able to advance in the cause is accepted by the Lord (*buddhi-yoga*).... Even a slight performance of such a principle enables one to overcome great difficulties."

From text 4 to text 9, Kṛṣṇa describes the active nature of the soul. Inactivity is not an option. One's activities must therefore be directed toward self-purification and self-realization, which are the purposes of performing prescribed duties.

5 Everyone is forced to act helplessly according to the qualities he has acquired from the modes of material nature; therefore no one can refrain from doing something, not even for a moment.

Śrīla Prabhupāda explains in his purport: "It is not a question of embodied life, but it is the nature of the soul to be always active. Without the presence of the spirit soul, the material body cannot move.... As such, the spirit soul has to be engaged in the good work of Kṛṣṇa consciousness; otherwise, it will be engaged in occupations dictated by the illusory energy."

In chapter two, Kṛṣṇa told Arjuna, *karmaṇy evādhikāras te:* your eligibility (*adhikāra*) on the *yoga* ladder is not renunciation of work but action. Because the soul must act, the *Vedas* prescribe duties to purify the living entities. Thus by acting according to *śāstra*, in a detached mood, in knowledge of the difference between the self (the eternal soul) and the body (matter), one becomes elevated to the *jñāna* platform. Only then does one have the option to give up prescribed duties and take *sannyāsa*. If such a person renounces prescribed duties and accepts *sannyāsa,* though his heart is still not purified, he will find himself in difficulty. Kṛṣṇa next describes such an unfortunate renunciant.

6 One who restrains the senses of action but whose mind dwells on sense objects certainly deludes himself and is called a pretender.

Kṛṣṇa tells Arjuna that if work is renounced without *adhikāra* (the qualification or requisite purity of heart), his mind will dwell on sense objects because his heart is not yet pure. He will delude himself, thinking, "I am a renunciant." The Sanskrit word for false actor is *mithyācāra. Mithyā* means "false" and *ācāra* means "activities." Kṛṣṇa is saying, "Your activities will not match your renounced dress, and you will be a pretender." Such a person is not qualified to receive the Lord's mercy. Not only Arjuna but all of us should act according to our eligibility. As Arjuna learned of his eligibility from his spiritual master, we should similarly understand our own eligibility from our *guru*. Kṛṣṇa next compares an attached "*sannyāsī*" and a detached householder.

7 On the other hand, if a sincere person tries to control the active senses by the mind and begins karma-yoga [in Kṛṣṇa consciousness] without attachment, he is by far superior.

This verse describes the dutiful householder as being better situated than the *mithyācāra sannyāsī*. In his purport Śrīla Prabhupāda glorifies the *varṇāśrama* system because it leads a conditioned soul gradually toward self-realization.

8 Perform your prescribed duty, for doing so is better than not working. One cannot even maintain one's physical body without work.

Kṛṣṇa is telling Arjuna, "Work for you, with your *adhikāra* for *karma*, is better than renunciation. You are not on the *jñāna* platform on which you can effectively renounce your prescribed duties." Arjuna is concerned that by working, he will develop material attachments and desires. Just prior to this great battle, he especially fears the reactions that will follow such work. To differentiate ordinary work, which entangles one in the material world, from *karma-yoga,* work that carries one toward liberation, Kṛṣṇa speaks the next verse.

9 Work done as a sacrifice for Viṣṇu has to be performed, otherwise work causes bondage in this material world. Therefore, O son of Kuntī, perform your prescribed duties for His satisfaction, and in that way you will always remain free from bondage.

Verses 3–8 have hinted at *niṣkāma karma,* work with both knowledge and detachment. In other words, *Niṣkāma karma* combines *karma* and *jñāna* and allows a soul to be active, but in a detached way, so that he is protected from material entanglement. Higher still, as stated in text 9, is when one's knowledge increases to include knowledge of Viṣṇu, and the detached activities one then performs are offered to Him with devotion. *Niṣkāma karma* is meant to lead to *bhakti.*

The question arises: "What if a person is overly attached to material life and cannot perform *niṣkāma karma-yoga*?" To explain this Kṛṣṇa now describes the *yoga* ladder, beginning with the lowest rung and gradually moving higher. The next seven verses (10–16) describe the progressive stages of the *yoga* ladder from *karma-kāṇḍa* to *karma-yoga.*

Every soul in the material world attempts (either subtly or grossly) to position himself – not Kṛṣṇa – as the enjoyer and controller. This is true regardless of the body the soul inhabits. The striving of ignorant animals for pleasure, according to their limited capacity, is the same as that of spiritually undeveloped humans, who, in their attempt to taste sensual pleasure, act in ignorance.

The *Vedas* and their supplements contain 100,000 *lakhs* of verses (one *lakh* equals 100,000); of these, a great majority discuss fruitive activities, and only a small percentage discuss *jñāna,* which leads the living entity toward transcendental knowledge and ultimately to an understanding of the Supreme Personality of Godhead. The Vedic culture provides a system by which the materially attached person can satisfy his material desires yet gradually become purified. Therefore such a high percentage of Vedic information centers on *karma-kāṇḍa,* the performance of sacrifices to reach higher planets and to satisfy superior beings, the demigods.

To become situated under the protection of such a system, one must agree to regulate his enjoyment by the descending authority of Vedic formulas. One following that system does not act simply as he desires. His mood of subservience to God's order in the form of the *Vedas* – even though his purpose is to attain sense pleasures – is purifying, for he is following Kṛṣṇa's system. By following this Vedic system of sacrifice, one also implicitly accepts the principle that he is not independent; rather, his enjoyment depends on the satisfaction of higher authorities. Śrīla Prabhupāda confirms this in his purport to *Śrīmad-Bhāgavatam* 2.7.32: "Sacrifices recommended in the Vedic literature for satisfaction of the demigods are a sort of inducement to the sacrificers to realize the existence of higher authorities." Such followers of the *Vedas* are called *karma-kāṇḍīs*.

Gradually, by following the Vedic system, one may accept an eternal, transcendental objective to replace his temporary, fruitive goals. With that acceptance, one abandons the designation of *karma-kāṇḍī* and becomes a *karma-yogī.* By properly performing his appropriate duties, the *karma-yogī* will gradually move from *sakāma karma-yoga* (attached work) to *niṣkāma karma-yoga* (detached work on the platform of *jñāna,* knowledge). He can then follow the *yoga* ladder upward toward liberation, Paramātmā realization and finally devotional service to Kṛṣṇa. His association and desires will dictate how far he actually climbs on his step-by-step ascension of the *yoga* ladder. The *Bhagavad-gītā* describes this gradual ascension in chapters three through six.

In addition to the step-by-step process, Kṛṣṇa explains what takes place when, either from the beginning of one's practices or on any rung of the ladder, one attains the association of a devotee and comes to accept Kṛṣṇa as the Supreme Personality of Godhead and oneself as Kṛṣṇa's servant.

Śrīla Prabhupāda describes this in relationship to Mahārāja Parīkṣit's meeting with Śukadeva Gosvāmī, in his purport to *Śrīmad Bhāgavatam* 2.4.3–4:

> The three activities of religion, economic development and sense gratification are generally attractive for conditioned souls struggling for existence in the material world. Such regulated activities prescribed in the *Vedas* are called the *karma-kāṇḍīya* conception of life, and householders are generally recommended to follow the rules just to enjoy material prosperity both in this life and in the next. Most people are attracted by such activities. . . .As a great emperor of the world, Mahārāja Parīkṣit had to observe such regulations of the Vedic *karma-kāṇḍīya* section, but by his slight association with Śukadeva Gosvāmī he could perfectly understand that Lord Kṛṣṇa, the Absolute Personality of Godhead (Vāsudeva), for whom he had a natural love since his birth, is everything, and thus he fixed his mind firmly upon Him, renouncing all modes of Vedic *karma-kāṇḍīya* activities. This perfectional stage is attained by a *jñānī* after many, many births. The *jñānīs,* or the empiric philosophers endeavoring for liberation, are thousands of times better than the fruitive workers, and out of hundreds of thousands of such *jñānīs* one is liberated factually. And out of hundreds of thousands of such liberated persons, even one person is rarely found who can firmly fix his mind unto the lotus feet of Lord Śrī Kṛṣṇa.

As soon as a person accepts his position as a servant of Kṛṣṇa, though he may be practicing either *sakāma karma-yoga* or *niṣkāma karma-yoga,* he is no longer on the same step-by-step path as other practitioners. Although he may not be fully realized and may still have material attachments, nevertheless, he is more fortunate because he has acknowledged the ultimate goal and will, by steady and appropriate practice, gradually advance in a way that appears parallel to other practitioners but in fact is not.

A devotee who practices *sakāma karma-yoga,* for example, will gradually have his material attachments loosened by his performance of appropriate practices. This is also true of the nondevotee *sakāma karma-yogī.* The devotee *sakāma karma-*

yogī, however, is far superior because he has already begun to aspire for the highest goal. The nondevotee *sakāma karma-yogī* is on the transcendental path but may never reach an understanding of the highest goal. Therefore he may never reach the highest rung of the *yoga* ladder.

Additionally, when one proceeds in a step-by-step fashion, his advancement is limited by his own capabilities, but one who sets Kṛṣṇa's service as his goal attains the mercy of Kṛṣṇa and the Vaiṣṇavas. They act as his supports throughout his spiritual journey. The nondevotee faces these two difficulties: he may never understand that the highest rung of the *yoga* ladder is to attain Kṛṣṇa's service, and he is limited by his own detachment, purity, and power to advance. He does not gain the assistance of Kṛṣṇa's descending mercy.

Actually, as Śrīla Prabhupāda explains in his purport to *Śrī Caitanya-caritāmṛta, Madhya-līlā* 19.149, only a devotee can become *niṣkāma,* desireless:

> If one understands Kṛṣṇa, he immediately becomes desireless (*niṣkāma*) because a *kṛṣṇa-bhakta* knows that his friend and protector in all respects is Kṛṣṇa, who is able to do anything for His devotee. Kṛṣṇa says, *kaunteya pratijānīhi na me bhaktaḥ praṇaśyati:* "O son of Kuntī, declare it boldly that My devotee never perishes." Since Kṛṣṇa gives this assurance, the devotee lives in Kṛṣṇa and has no desire for personal benefit. The background for the devotee is the all-good Himself. Why should the devotee aspire for something good for himself? His only business is to please the Supreme by rendering service as much as possible. A *kṛṣṇa-bhakta* has no desire for his own personal benefit. He is completely protected by the Supreme. *Avaśya rakṣibe kṛṣṇa viśvāsa pālana.* Bhaktivinoda Ṭhākura says that he is desireless because Kṛṣṇa will give him protection in all circumstances. It is not that he expects any assistance from Kṛṣṇa; he simply depends on Kṛṣṇa just as a child depends on his parents. The child does not know how to expect service from his parents, but he is always protected nevertheless. This is called *niṣkāma* (desirelessness).

Although *karmīs, jñānīs,* and *yogīs* fulfill their desires by performing various activities, they are never satisfied. A *karmī* may work very hard to acquire a million dollars, but as soon as he gets a million dollars he desires another million. For the *karmīs,* there is no end of desire. The more the *karmī* gets, the more he desires. The *jñānīs* cannot be desireless because their intelligence is unsound. They want to merge into the Brahman effulgence, but even though they may be raised to that platform, they cannot be satisfied there. There are many *jñānīs* or *sannyāsīs* who give up the world as false, but after taking *sannyāsa* they return to the world to engage in politics or philanthropy or to open schools and hospitals. This means that they could not attain the real Brahman (*brahma satyam*). They have to come down to the material platform to engage in philanthropic activity. Thus they again cultivate desires, and when these desires are exhausted, they desire something different. Therefore the *jñānī* cannot be *niṣkāma,* desireless. Nor can the *yogīs* be desireless, for they desire yogic perfections in order to exhibit some magical feats and gain popularity. People gather around these *yogīs,* and the *yogīs* desire more and more adulation. Because they misuse their mystic power, they fall down again onto the material platform. It is not possible for them to become *niṣkāma,* desireless.

The conclusion is that only the devotees who are simply satisfied in serving the Lord can actually become desireless. Therefore it is written: *kṛṣṇa-bhakta niṣkāma.* Since the *kṛṣṇa-bhakta,* the devotee of Kṛṣṇa, is satisfied with Kṛṣṇa, there is no possibility of falldown.

Thus by studying Śrīla Prabhupāda's *Bhagavad-gītā As It Is,* no one can become bewildered and mistake a rung on the *yoga* ladder as the goal. Śrīla Prabhupāda mercifully reveals Kṛṣṇa's ultimate desire for the conditioned soul – *sarva-dharmān parityajya:* that he abandon all forms of religion and surrender to Him. Why should we remain incomplete, fixed at one level of the elaborate Vedic system, when we can achieve the system's full purpose by the simple, easy step of surrender to Kṛṣṇa? By writing *Bhagavad-gītā As It Is,* Śrīla Prabhupāda clearly proved that the Lord's devotee is even more merciful than the Lord.

10 In the beginning of creation, the Lord of all creatures sent forth generations of men and demigods, along with sacrifices for Viṣṇu, and blessed them by saying, "Be thou happy

by this yajña [sacrifice] because its performance will bestow upon you everything desirable for living happily and achieving liberation."

Kṛṣṇa now begins to explain the Vedic *karma-kāṇḍa* system: live happily and ultimately, gradually, achieve liberation. How can a follower of this system satisfy his desires?

11 The demigods, being pleased by sacrifices, will also please you, and thus, by cooperation between men and demigods, prosperity will reign for all.

12 In charge of the various necessities of life, the demigods, being satisfied by the performance of yajña [sacrifice], will supply all necessities to you. But he who enjoys such gifts without offering them to the demigods in return is certainly a thief.

A thief is punished by the state. The thieves who live within this world without repaying the demigods for the amenities they have used are punished by Yamarāja. Followers of the Vedic system, even though they have material desires, are not punished. Rather, they are elevated by their submission to the Vedic system. The Vedic system limits sense enjoyment to that which is attained through Vedic formulas. Despite a follower's selfish desires, his adherence to Vedic injunctions is a step toward giving up his envy of Kṛṣṇa and his sense of being independent of Him.

Arjuna, however, could think, "I don't need *yajñas,* demigods, and opulent necessities of life. Nor must I perform *yajñas* to live. I will go to the forest and live by begging. I won't take from the demigods, so I won't be sinful by not offering *yajñas* to them. Not only won't I be a thief, but I won't take part in this ghastly, sinful warfare."

Kṛṣṇa replies in the next two verses.

13 The devotees of the Lord are released from all kinds of sins because they eat food which is offered first for sacrifice. Others, who prepare food for personal sense enjoyment, verily eat only sin.

14 All living bodies subsist on food grains, which are produced from rains. Rains are produced by performance of yajña [sacrifice], and yajña is born of prescribed duties.

Kṛṣṇa herein warns Arjuna that even in the forest, all food is nurtured by rain coming from the demigods. Therefore he cannot avoid his obligation to perform the sacrifices born of his prescribed duty.

15 Regulated activities are prescribed in the Vedas, and the Vedas are directly manifested from the Supreme Personality of Godhead. Consequently the all-pervading Transcendence is eternally situated in acts of sacrifice.

Everyone is dependent on food grains. Grains grow from the earth, but their growth is dependent on rain. Rain comes from the performance of *yajñas* offered to Indra. The inspiration and direction to perform such *yajña* comes from the *Vedas* because the *Vedas* describe one's prescribed duties. The followers of the Vedic system, therefore, perform sacrifices to Indra, which result in rain, which produces the grains that we all depend on. The *Vedas* come directly from Lord Viṣṇu's breathing. Thus the link is established for an attached materialist – dependence on food ultimately means dependence on Viṣṇu.

The all-pervading Transcendence, the Personality of Godhead, being absolute, is nondifferent from the act of sacrifice. Gradually, the follower of the *Vedas* understands that Viṣṇu is above the demigods because He is the one who empowers the demigods worshiped in the sacrificial process. In other words, Indra's power to provide rain is supplied by the Personality of Godhead. This understanding gradually blossoms into the realization that Viṣṇu is the only true object of worship.

Kṛṣṇa ends His description of *karma-kāṇḍa* in the next verse.

16 My dear Arjuna, one who does not follow in human life the cycle of sacrifice thus established by the Vedas certainly leads a life full of sin. Living only for the satisfaction of the senses, such a person lives in vain.

He lives in vain because human life is meant for spiritual elevation and he has wasted that opportunity. His engaging solely in animalistic endeavors ensures his taking a lower birth. The performance of *karma-kāṇḍa* sacrifices, however, would gradually purify him by redirecting his desires from concentration on the temporal to concentration on the eternal.

Here is how a follower of the Vedic system progresses: Instead of trying to enjoy his senses unrestrictedly, a follower of the *Vedas* surrenders to Vedic authority, which then regulates his actions and engages him in *karma-kāṇḍa* sacrifices. The goal of those sacrifices is to attain prosperity, either in this life or a future life. Desiring abundance, he may perform a sacrifice to give birth to a son, to reap a bountiful harvest, or to overcome a disease. Those are considered low-level sacrifices because their fruits are limited to this life.

Gradually, however, by associating with *brāhmaṇa* priests, he hears about sacrifices that will award him birth on the higher, heavenly planets. Simultaneously, as he lives in this world, he inevitably experiences a variety of miseries. Family members die, droughts occur, his riches are plundered – difficulties must over time arise because that is the nature of the material world. He is pushed to seriously contemplate Svargaloka: "Why be satisfied with wealth, a son, or health in this life? I can go to Svarga, drink *soma-rasa,* dance with beautiful women, and wander blissfully through the Nanda-kanana gardens. Why live for a hundred years when I can live for thousands?"

Karma-kāṇḍa sacrifices meant to attain either short-term or long-term results are born of the mode of passion. They are performed for selfish, sensual enjoyment. Long-term sacrifices, however, are a step further on the path because they are based on the implicit acceptance of the soul's eternality. The performer of the sacrifice will think, "I am not this body. Therefore I will perform opulent sacrifices, leave this body behind, and attain heaven." Within that thought is the seed of eternal spiritual life.

Then he hears from his priests that there is distress even in heaven. Indra fears attacks on his kingdom. Thus he realizes that he too will experience fear even in Svargaloka. Despite having fulfilled his material desires, he recognizes that his heart is still devoid of true satisfaction. Gradually the truth of material reality dawns on him: Birth and death are everywhere, and the material world is temporary, frustrating, and miserable.

Over time, he becomes receptive to the philosophy of transcendence. Having heard from his priests about sacrifices, and having experienced their results, he has become more trusting of the priests and the *śāstras*. He has also become more detached from material life, because performing sacrifices has allowed him to taste the happiness of sacrificing the hard-earned results of his work. His goal slowly evolves. He no longer thinks of attaining more material happiness but of leaving the material world. Now, after having heard countless verses glorifying *karma-kāṇḍa* sacrifices and their heavenly results, he is ready to consider the *jñāna-kāṇḍa* section of the *Vedas* and to contemplate a nonmaterial, spiritual life based on the soul's eternality. Thus he is no longer a *karma-kāṇḍī* but a *karma-yogī*.

A *karma-yogī* is someone who has accepted transcendence as his objective. There are two types of *karma-yogīs:* Brahmavādīs (impersonalists) and devotees. Each may be on one of two levels: *sakāma* (with material desires) or *niṣkāma* (free from material desires). If a Brahmavādī associates with merciful and powerful devotees, he can abandon his attempts to reach the Brahman and aspire for loving service at Kṛṣṇa's lotus feet.

Both types of *karma-yogīs* progress gradually from *sakāma* to *niṣkāma* by dutifully performing their prescribed duties. As their realizations increase, they also become more detached from matter. Thus they leave their performance of *sakāma karma-yoga* and climb to the next rung of the *yoga* ladder to become *niṣkāma karma-yogīs,* performers of dutiful, detached work. Their work is no longer motivated by fruitive desire, and they perform their work on the platform of *jñāna*.

While progressing in this way, however, the *niṣkāma karma-yogī* may conclude: "My prescribed duties are meant to bring me material rewards. I no longer have material desires. I don't want a son or money or a nice house. I have no desire to go to Svargaloka. I know I am not my body. Because I no longer have material desires, I do not need to perform my prescribed duties."

In the following verses (17–32), Kṛṣṇa explains why one freed from material desires should nevertheless perform his prescribed duties.

17–18 But for one who takes pleasure in the self, whose human life is one of self-realization, and who is satisfied in the self only, fully satiated – for him there is no duty. A self-realized man has no purpose to fulfill in the discharge of his prescribed duties, nor has he any reason not to perform such work. Nor has he any need to depend on any other living being.

These verses describe an *ātma-ratiḥ,* one who takes pleasure in the self. Such a person is not concerned with loss or gain while performing his duty. Nor is he disturbed by obstacles. The next verse explains whether or not such a person should work.

19 Therefore, without being attached to the fruits of activities, one should act as a matter of duty, for by working without attachment one attains the Supreme.

Working without attachment is renunciation – renunciation caused by knowledge. Kṛṣṇa now gives an example of one elevated to perfection by working without attachment.

20 Kings such as Janaka attained perfection solely by performance of prescribed duties. Therefore, just for the sake of educating the people in general, you should perform your work.

If Arjuna renounces work and goes to the forest, as he is suggesting, people will follow his example. What will happen to them? They will find themselves in difficulty because they will be externally renounced but internally absorbed in their material desires. Kṛṣṇa next confirms the importance of setting a proper example.

21 Whatever action a great man performs, common men follow. And whatever standards he sets by exemplary acts, all the world pursues.

Few people consider their own disqualification: "He is more qualified than me, so I should be wary of my tendency to imitate him." If we see another's activities and they seem pleasurable, we immediately want to join in. We do not stop to consider whether such activities will uplift or degrade us. Kṛṣṇa's instructions to Arjuna are meant to uplift humanity. Even though Arjuna, being highly qualified, might do well by going to the forest and begging, others who are less qualified will become degraded because they will imitate Arjuna without considering their own disqualification for renunciation.

Kṛṣṇa now uses Himself as an example.

22 O son of Pṛthā, there is no work prescribed for Me within all the three planetary systems. Nor am I in want of anything, nor have I a need to obtain anything – and yet I am engaged in prescribed duties.

Kṛṣṇa offers two examples: Janaka Mahārāja, who attained perfection by performing his prescribed duties, and now Himself. Certainly Kṛṣṇa, the Supreme Personality of Godhead, needs nothing. He is God, the source of all. An entire universe can be created or destroyed by His will. Although He has no needs, Kṛṣṇa acts according to the scriptures. Why?

23 For if I ever failed to engage in carefully performing prescribed duties, O Pārtha, certainly all men would follow My path.

Śrīla Prabhupāda writes in his purport: "Although such rules and regulations are for the conditioned souls and not Lord Kṛṣṇa, because He descended to establish the principles of religion He followed the prescribed rules. Otherwise, common men would follow in His footsteps, because He is the greatest authority."

One might argue that some of Kṛṣṇa's actions on the battlefield and His behavior in Vṛndāvana with the *gopīs* do not conform to the recommended śāstric path. That is true. Although Kṛṣṇa generally does not transgress scriptural injunctions, He occasionally does so to please His devotees and to exhibit His supreme, independent position. If, therefore, a discrepancy exists between Kṛṣṇa's words and His actions, His words should be followed. No one should imitate Kṛṣṇa, the Supreme Personality of Godhead, and act in opposition to *śāstra.*

Kṛṣṇa continues speaking about Himself.

24 If I did not perform prescribed duties, all these worlds would be put to ruination. I would be the cause of creating unwanted population, and I would thereby destroy the peace of all living beings.

Arjuna said in the first chapter, "If I fight, I'll be the cause of the women being left unprotected, and that will result in unwanted population, *varṇa-saṅkara.*" Here Kṛṣṇa counters that argument and again defeats Arjuna's reasoning by indirectly saying, "If you neglect your duty and decline to fight, *then* you will be the cause of *varṇa-saṅkara.*"

Kṛṣṇa will next compare the attached worker and the detached worker. Then He will describe how a detached man of knowledge should relate to one in ignorance. That description continues until text 32.

25 As the ignorant perform their duties with attachment to results, the learned may similarly act, but without attachment, for the sake of leading people on the right path.

Even a perfect person should perform his duties.

26 So as not to disrupt the minds of ignorant men attached to the fruitive results of prescribed duties, a learned person should not induce them to stop work. Rather, by working in the spirit of devotion, he should engage them in all sorts of activities [for the gradual development of Kṛṣṇa consciousness].

We may preach to an attached materialist: "It's no use working for *māyā*. You can't take your gains with you when you die. What will you eternally gain by such work?" Obviously that is true, but Kṛṣṇa herein recommends an additional strategy: encouraging those who are attached to use their work and its fruits for devotional service. Kṛṣṇa again says that premature renunciation, without spiritual realization, leads to degradation.

This verse describes how those with knowledge should relate to those without knowledge. A person with knowledge should, by his example and words, encourage those who are attached to the results of their work to engage them in Kṛṣṇa's service. This is practical. The third line, *joṣayet sarva-karmāṇi,* indicates that we should first work ourselves, and then (as said in the fourth line) engage others in devotional work.

We have already discussed three levels of work: 1) working only for the fruits (*karma-kāṇḍa*), 2) establishing Kṛṣṇa as the goal yet remaining attached to the fruits (*sakāma karma-yoga*), and 3) being completely detached from the fruits of work (*niṣkāma karma-yoga*). In the second form of work, though the mode of passion is still present, one advances from passion to goodness by renouncing a portion of the results of one's work. A person working in this way will gradually become detached, attain transcendental knowledge, and advance toward the transcendental platform.

Two men may be doing similar work, but each may be working with a different consciousness. Superficially it may appear that their work is the same, but a *sakāma* worker is attached to the fruits of his work *and* to the specific nature of the work he does. The *niṣkāma* worker is detached from the fruits of his work, but remains attached to the work itself. The quality of the work is measured by their attachments.

The highest stage of work occurs when one is detached from the fruits of his work and from the work itself. He continues to work, but his impetus is simply devotional surrender to the order of *guru* and Kṛṣṇa.

Kṛṣṇa next describes the thinking of the ignorant, attached person.

27 The spirit soul bewildered by the influence of false ego thinks himself the doer of activities that are in actuality carried out by the three modes of material nature.

This verse is one of several in the *Gītā* that discuss the doer (*kartā*). Here Kṛṣṇa explains that while the foolish conditioned soul thinks himself the doer (the one accomplishing his work), the work is actually being carried out by the three modes of material nature (*guṇas*). Śrīla Prabhupāda, however, refers to an ultimate doer in his purport: "The materialistic person has no knowledge that ultimately he is under the control of Kṛṣṇa." That topic will be discussed again in chapter four.

Kṛṣṇa next explains the difference between the attached worker and the devotional worker.

28 One who is in knowledge of the Absolute Truth, O mighty-armed, does not engage himself in the senses and sense gratification, knowing well the differences between work in devotion and work for fruitive results.

Śrīla Prabhupāda writes in his purport: "The knower of the Absolute Truth is convinced of his awkward position in material association. He knows that he is part and parcel of the Supreme Personality of Godhead, Kṛṣṇa, and that his position should not be in the material creation. He knows his real identity as part and parcel of the Supreme, who is eternal bliss and knowledge, and he realizes that somehow or other he is entrapped in the material conception of life. In his pure state of existence he is meant to dovetail his activities in devotional service to the Supreme Personality of Godhead, Kṛṣṇa. He therefore engages himself in the activities of Kṛṣṇa consciousness and becomes naturally unattached to the activities of the material senses, which are all circumstantial and temporary. He knows that his material condition of life is under the supreme control of the Lord; consequently he is not disturbed by all kinds of material reactions, which he considers to be the mercy of the Lord. According to *Śrīmad-Bhāgavatam,* one who knows the Absolute Truth in three different features – namely Brahman, Paramātmā, and the Supreme Personality of Godhead – is called *tattva-vit,* for he knows also his own factual position in relationship with the Supreme."

What makes the difference between work in devotion and work for fruitive results is knowledge. The *tattva-vit,* or knower of the Absolute Truth, according to Śrīla Viśvanatha Cakravartī Ṭhākura, thinks, "I am not a *guṇa* [a quality or mode of nature] nor any product of a *guṇa,* nor do I have any connection with any of the *guṇas* or the products of the *guṇas.*" He is, as Śrīla Prabhupāda states, "convinced of his awkward position in material association."

29 Bewildered by the modes of material nature, the ignorant fully engage themselves in material activities and become attached. But the wise should not unsettle them, although these duties are inferior due to the performers' lack of knowledge.

Rather than pushing one who lacks knowledge to renounce his false activities, the wise will engage him in activities that will lead to knowledge. Indeed, a devotee's mood in approaching such persons is self-sacrificing and compassionate, as Śrīla Prabhupāda reveals in his purport: "Men who are ignorant cannot appreciate activities in Kṛṣṇa consciousness, and therefore Lord Kṛṣṇa advises us not to disturb them and simply waste valuable time. But the devotees of the Lord are more kind than the Lord because they understand the purpose of the Lord. Consequently they undertake all kinds of risks, even to the point of approaching ignorant men to try to engage them in the acts of Kṛṣṇa consciousness, which are absolutely necessary for the human being."

Emphasizing detachment for an unqualified person may lead him to a worse condition if he is without positive work in Kṛṣṇa consciousness.

While the past several verses have stressed *niṣkāma karma-yoga* (detached work), the next verse describes *bhakti.*

30 Therefore, O Arjuna, surrendering all your works unto Me, with full knowledge of Me, without desires for profit, with no claims to proprietorship, and free from lethargy, fight.

Kṛṣṇa orders Arjuna to fight, but He also describes the consciousness in which Arjuna should perform that duty. "Without desires for profit" and "with no claims to proprietorship" indicate freedom from the mode of passion. "Freed from lethargy" hints at freedom from ignorance. Knowledge of the difference between the soul and the body is simply born of the mode of goodness (*sattvāt sañjāyate jñānaṁ* – Bg. 14.17). But "full knowledge" is beyond goodness and is transcendental, as it indicates knowledge of the soul's eternal relationship with Kṛṣṇa. When "surrendering all your works unto Me" (*mayi sarvāṇi karmāṇi*) is added to the other above-mentioned requirements, Arjuna's *niṣkāma karma,* fighting in goodness, becomes *bhakti-yoga,* detached work done in devotion for Kṛṣṇa's pleasure. Although Kṛṣṇa has often requested Arjuna to act on the platform of detachment and duty, He now reveals His actual desire that Arjuna fight with devotion.

Śrīla Prabhupāda explains further: "This verse clearly indicates the purpose of the *Bhagavad-gītā*. The Lord instructs that one has to become fully Kṛṣṇa conscious to discharge duties, as if in military discipline....Arjuna was therefore ordered by Śrī Kṛṣṇa to fight as if the Lord were his military commander. One has to sacrifice everything for the good will of the Supreme Lord, and at the same time discharge prescribed duties without claiming proprietorship. Arjuna did not have to consider the order of the Lord; he had only to execute His order."

The next verse describes the result of acting in this way.

31 Those persons who execute their duties according to My injunctions and who follow this teaching faithfully, without envy, become free from the bondage of fruitive actions.

Śrīla Prabhupāda explains: "The injunction of the Supreme Personality of Godhead, Kṛṣṇa, is the essence of all Vedic wisdom and therefore is eternally true without exception. As the *Vedas* are eternal, so this truth of Kṛṣṇa consciousness is also eternal. One should have firm faith in this injunction, without envying the Lord. There are many philosophers who write comments on the *Bhagavad-gītā* but have no faith in Kṛṣṇa. They will never be liberated from the bondage of fruitive action. But an ordinary man with firm faith in the eternal injunctions of the Lord, even though unable to execute such orders, becomes liberated from the bondage of the law of *karma*. In the beginning of Kṛṣṇa consciousness, one may not fully discharge the injunctions of the Lord, but because one is not resentful of this principle and works sincerely without consideration of defeat and hopelessness, he will surely be promoted to the stage of pure Kṛṣṇa consciousness."

In this verse, Kṛṣṇa spoke of the faithful, knowledgeable, nonenvious person. In text 32 we hear the defect of not developing those qualities.

32 But those who, out of envy, disregard these teachings and do not follow them are to be considered bereft of all knowledge, befooled, and ruined in their endeavors for perfection.

On the one hand, success; on the other, ruination – that is Arjuna's choice.

The question arises, according to Śrīla Baladeva Vidyābhūṣaṇa, "Why do people who transgress Your desire not fear punishment from You, as criminals should fear punishment from a king?" Kṛṣṇa's answer follows.

33 Even a man of knowledge acts according to his own nature, for everyone follows the nature he has acquired from the three modes. What can repression accomplish?

Māyā, despite one's intelligence, is invested with the potency to push a conditioned soul away from Kṛṣṇa consciousness. The next *śloka* answers the question, "If we all are helplessly forced to act according to our natures, what is the use of so many rules in the *śāstra* to regulate our activities?"

34 There are principles to regulate attachment and aversion pertaining to the senses and their objects. One should not come under the control of such attachment and aversion, because they are stumbling blocks on the path of self-realization.

According to the dictates of the modes of nature, the conditioned living entity does whatever his mind suggests. Because the mind is surrendered to the senses, whatever we are attached to (*rāga*) we do, and whatever we are averse to (*dveṣa*) we avoid. Kṛṣṇa here instructs us that our actions should not be based on attachment and aversion, which are stumbling blocks on the path of self-realization.

The senses are attracted to the pleasures of this world, especially sex and those bought by wealth. They are repulsed by holy places, fasting, selflessly following our spiritual master and other items that limit sense enjoyment. *Śāstra* directs us to shift our *rāga* and *dveṣa* away from sense gratification by encouraging us to perform our duty with the ultimate aim of acting only for Kṛṣṇa's pleasure. The next verse, therefore, again stresses that we should perform our prescribed duties.

35 It is far better to discharge one's prescribed duties, even though faultily, than another's duties perfectly. Destruction in the course of performing one's own duty is better than engaging in another's duties, for to follow another's path is dangerous.

As Śrīla Prabhupāda explains in his purport, we have both material and spiritual prescribed duties: "But whether material or spiritual, one should stick to his prescribed duties even up to death, rather than imitate another's prescribed duties."

We should be careful to do our own duty and not the duty of another. Duty, like medicine prescribed by a physician, has its proper, curative effect only upon the patient to whom it has been prescribed. A spiritual master prescribes different duties for different individuals according to their natures.

Next, Arjuna asks an important question. After hearing text 34, one may determinedly think, "Yes, from today onward I will steadily do my duty and control my attachments and aversions. I will act only according to *śāstra*." Experience teaches, however, that such immediate inspirations may prove difficult to adhere to over time. Arjuna, being aware of reality, asks the following question.

36 Arjuna said: O descendant of Vṛṣṇi, by what is one impelled to sinful acts, even unwillingly, as if engaged by force?

In the Vedic system, to act contrary to one's prescribed duties is a sinful act. Śrīla Prabhupāda writes, "Sinful actions are not, however, impelled by the Supersoul within, but are due to another cause, as the Lord explains in the next verse."

37 The Supreme Personality of Godhead said: It is lust only, Arjuna, which is born of contact with the material mode of passion and later transformed into wrath, and which is the all-devouring sinful enemy of this world.

Lust is more subtle than wrath. A man of lusty intentions may go undetected. An angry person, however, is easily noticed. Lust inevitably turns to wrath because it cannot be satisfied. Lust burns like fire, and like fire, it is all-devouring. If fuel is added to a fire, rather than satisfying the fire, it makes the fire burn more fiercely. In *rāja-nīti* (instructions for *kṣatriyas* on diplomacy) it is said that an enemy is controlled with words, gifts, a position, or finally, punishment. Lust, however, is *mahā-pāpām,* the mightiest enemy, and most of these ordinary methods will not defeat it. Śrīla Baladeva Vidyābhūṣaṇa comments that *daṇḍa,* punishment, is the only way to deal with lust.

Lust arises from the mode of passion. We should meticulously avoid *rajo-guṇa* if we wish to be free of lusty desires.

Śrīla Prabhupāda explains: "If, therefore, the mode of passion, instead of being degraded into the mode of ignorance, is elevated to the mode of goodness by the prescribed method of living and acting, then one can be saved from the degradation of wrath by spiritual attachment."

Kṛṣṇa explains lust further in the next verse.

38 As fire is covered by smoke, as a mirror is covered by dust, or as the embryo is covered by the womb, the living entity is similarly covered by different degrees of this lust.

Three examples are given here in order of increasing degrees of covering. The first, "as fire is covered by smoke," indicates a thin covering, because the heat and light may still be usable. When a mirror is covered by dust, the covering is thicker. We cannot see the reflection, but at least we can see the mirror. The thickest of coverings is around the embryo covered by the womb. The child in the womb can neither move nor be seen. Śrīla Prabhupāda compares that to the nonmoving entities such as trees; the dust-covered mirror to birds and beasts; and the smoke-covered fire to those in the human form. He concludes by saying, "In the human form of life, one can conquer the enemy, lust, by cultivation of Kṛṣṇa consciousness under able guidance."

The enemy is further described in the next verse.

39 Thus the wise living entity's pure consciousness becomes covered by his eternal enemy in the form of lust, which is never satisfied and which burns like fire.

When one fears his enemy, he must discover where he is situated. Kṛṣṇa next explains where to find lust and why it is so dangerous.

40 The senses, the mind, and the intelligence are the sitting places of this lust. Through them lust covers the real knowledge of the living entity and bewilders him.

Lust is the greatest enemy because it covers our knowledge of the Absolute Truth. And, as it has already been explained in verse 28 of this chapter, it is *that* knowledge which makes the difference between working for Kṛṣṇa and working for fruitive results.

Śrīla Prabhupāda explains in the purport to text 40: "The enemy has captured different strategic positions in the body of the conditioned soul, and therefore Lord Kṛṣṇa is giving hints about those places, so that one who wants to conquer the enemy may know where he can be found."

Before a battle, we should know where to find our enemy. Kṛṣṇa will therefore explain where and how to attack lust in our attempts to overcome its power.

41 Therefore, O Arjuna, best of the Bhāratas, in the very beginning curb this great symbol of sin [lust] by regulating the senses, and slay this destroyer of knowledge and self-realization.

Of the senses, mind, and intelligence, the senses are the grossest. Being gross, they are the easiest to control. Kṛṣṇa therefore recommends that we begin to bring lust under control by regulating the senses. This is automatically done through the *vaidhi-bhakti* process.

While controlling our senses, however, we should not neglect our intelligence. The intelligence, like a guard, is the next-door neighbor of the soul, and its business is to protect us from *māyā*. If the guard has been corrupted by lust, the situation is as dangerous as when a bodyguard is bribed by the enemy. Thus the materially contaminated intelligence, which works in the service of our enemy, should be neglected. We should instead accept the intelligence of *guru*, *sādhu,* and *śāstra*.

42 The working senses are superior to dull matter; mind is higher than the senses; intelligence is still higher than the mind; and he [the soul] is even higher than the intelligence.

Śrīla Prabhupāda writes: "With intelligence one has to seek out the constitutional position of the soul and then engage the mind always in Kṛṣṇa consciousness. That solves the whole problem. A neophyte spiritualist is generally advised to keep aloof from the objects of the senses. But aside from that, one has to strengthen the mind by use of intelligence. If by intelligence one engages one's mind in Kṛṣṇa consciousness, by complete surrender to the Supreme Personality of Godhead, then, automatically, the mind becomes stronger, and even though the senses are very strong, like serpents, they will be no more effective than serpents with broken fangs. But even though the soul is the master of the intelligence and mind, and the senses also, still, unless it is strengthened by association with Kṛṣṇa in Kṛṣṇa consciousness, there is every chance of falling down due to the agitated mind."

The soul is the highest and can control all – the intelligence, the mind, and the senses.

43 Thus knowing oneself to be transcendental to the material senses, mind, and intelligence, O mighty-armed Arjuna, one should steady the mind by deliberate spiritual intelligence [Kṛṣṇa consciousness] and thus – by spiritual strength – conquer this insatiable enemy known as lust.

We should use the strength of our trained intelligence, which should be fixed in transcendental knowledge, to protect us from falling victim to inappropriate actions impelled by passion (*rajo-guṇa*).

In this chapter, Kṛṣṇa has glorified transcendental knowledge as that which elevates us from *sakāma karma-yoga* to *niṣkāma karma-yoga,* from the platform on which we perform our duty with attachment to the platform of detached action. Transcendental knowledge has been described as having the power to purify our consciousness of passion and raise it to goodness. Now, in the final verse of this chapter, Kṛṣṇa has certified transcendental knowledge as being able to award our intelligence the strength to overcome lusty desires. After describing so many of the benefits of transcendental knowledge, Kṛṣṇa will further glorify it in chapter four.

Śrīla Prabhupāda summarizes this chapter as follows: "This third chapter of the *Bhagavad-gītā* is conclusively directive to Kṛṣṇa consciousness by knowing oneself as the eternal servitor of the Supreme Personality of Godhead, without considering impersonal voidness the ultimate end. In the material existence of life, one is certainly influenced by propensities for lust and desire for dominating the resources of material nature. Desires for overlording and sense gratification are the greatest enemies of the conditioned soul; but by the strength of Kṛṣṇa consciousness, one can control the material senses, the mind, and the intelligence. One may not give up work and prescribed duties all of a sudden; but by gradually developing Kṛṣṇa consciousness, one can be situated in a transcendental position without being influenced by the material senses and the mind – by steady intelligence directed toward one's pure identity. This is the sum total of this chapter."

Chapter Four

Transcendental Knowledge

Chapter three discussed how lust covers knowledge and how ignorance binds us with our own attachments. Kṛṣṇa recommended dutiful, detached work (*niṣkāma karma*) as the means to attain transcendental knowledge. In the first two verses, Kṛṣṇa will describe how transcendental knowledge is received.

1 The Personality of Godhead, Lord Śrī Kṛṣṇa, said: I instructed this imperishable science of yoga to the sun god, Vivasvān, and Vivasvān instructed it to Manu, the father of mankind, and Manu in turn instructed it to Ikṣvāku.

Kṛṣṇa first explains that Vivasvān, the root of the Sūrya *kṣatriya* dynasty and a great authority, received this knowledge and attained perfection.

2 This supreme science was thus received through the chain of disciplic succession, and the saintly kings understood it in that way. But in course of time the succession was broken, and therefore the science as it is appears to be lost.

Why does Kṛṣṇa speak this science specifically to Arjuna? The next verse describes Arjuna's qualification.

3 That very ancient science of the relationship with the Supreme is today told by Me to you because you are My devotee as well as My friend and can therefore understand the transcendental mystery of this science.

Only a devotee can understand Kṛṣṇa. Others cannot, because one's relationship with Kṛṣṇa is *rahasya,* or secret, confidential, and mysterious. *Māyā* has covered the living entity's real identity, and Kṛṣṇa has no inclination to remove the covering for anyone other than His devotee.

Arjuna next presents a doubt.

4 Arjuna said: The sun god Vivasvān is senior by birth to You. How am I to understand that in the beginning You instructed this science to him?

Kṛṣṇa explained that one receives transcendental knowledge through disciplic succession. Because Vivasvān is thousands of years old and Kṛṣṇa is Arjuna's contemporary, how could Kṛṣṇa have possibly instructed this science to Vivasvān many thousands of years before? This question, asked for the benefit of others, gives Kṛṣṇa the opportunity to speak directly about Himself.

5 The Personality of Godhead said: Many, many births both you and I have passed. I can remember all of them, but you cannot, O subduer of the enemy!

Both Kṛṣṇa and Arjuna have had many, many births, but because Kṛṣṇa's transcendental body is fully spiritual – different from that of any *jīva* – He never changes His body. Kṛṣṇa can thus remember His many births while Arjuna cannot.

Kṛṣṇa continues to describe transcendental knowledge by explaining His birth and His spiritual form.

6 Although I am unborn and My transcendental body never deteriorates, and although I am the Lord of all living entities, I still appear in every millennium in My original transcendental form.

Kṛṣṇa uses the term *ātma-māyayā* to explain His appearance. *Ātma-māyayā* means "by My internal energy." Kṛṣṇa's birth is extraordinary. He does not appear by force, nor is He subject to the modes of material nature.

In addition, *ātma-māyayā* means that Kṛṣṇa descends to this world by His causeless mercy. Śrīla Prabhupāda explains: "His appearance in His original eternal form is His causeless mercy, bestowed on the living entities so that they can concentrate on the Supreme Lord as He is, and not on mental concoctions or imaginations, which the impersonalist wrongly thinks the Lord's forms to be. The word *māyā,* or *ātma-māyā,* refers to the Lord's causeless mercy, according to the *Viśva-kośa* dictionary." Thus Kṛṣṇa appears by His mercy to fulfill His own desire and to uplift others.

Kṛṣṇa, like the sun, exists before He becomes visible on earth, and, again, like the sun, Kṛṣṇa manifests Himself to our vision on schedule. Kṛṣṇa's body is *aja*, unborn, and *avyaya,* without deterioration. His birth, unlike ours, is not *forced* on Him by pious and impious *karma*. He is the *īśvara,* the controller of the laws of *karma,* and He appears by His internal *prakṛti* (*prākṛtiṁ svām*), not by His external, material energy.

To defeat the Māyāvādī teaching that Kṛṣṇa is in contact with the modes of nature, Śrīla Prabhupāda describes the transcendental nature of Kṛṣṇa's body: "Kṛṣṇa appears in this material world in His original eternal form, with two hands, holding a flute. He appears exactly in His eternal body, uncontaminated by this material world."

Kṛṣṇa next explains the reasons for His appearance.

7 Whenever and wherever there is a decline in religious practice, O descendant of Bharata, and a predominant rise of irreligion – at that time I descend Myself.

Kṛṣṇa appears, or advents. He is not born. He only seems to take birth. Both *bhavati* and *sṛjāmi* mean that Kṛṣṇa becomes manifest. Śrīla Prabhupāda writes: "The word *sṛjāmi* is significant herein. *Sṛjāmi* cannot be used in the sense of creation, because, according to the previous verse, there is no creation of the Lord's form or body, since all of the forms are eternally existent. Therefore, *sṛjāmi* means that the Lord manifests Himself as He is."

Kṛṣṇa next answers two questions: "Why does He come?" and "What does He do?"

8 To deliver the pious and to annihilate the miscreants, as well as to reestablish the principles of religion, I Myself appear, millennium after millennium.

Śrīla Prabhupāda mentions in his purport that the Lord comes to deliver the devotees, but Bg. 14.26 clearly states that a devotee is already beyond the material qualities and is in a transcendental position. If the devotee is already delivered, what need is there for Kṛṣṇa to come and deliver him? Both Śrīla Viśvanātha Cakravartī Ṭhākura and Śrīla Baladeva Vidyābhūṣaṇa answer this question in the same way. They say: "[I manifest Myself] to deliver the pious, who are attracted by My beauty and qualities and who hanker to see Me in person, and to save My exclusive devotees from the misery of their mental agitation. Their hearts are shattering out of eagerness to see Me." Śrīla Prabhupāda confirms this in his purport: "Lord Śrī Kṛṣṇa descends for the specific purpose of mitigating the anxieties of the pure devotees, who are very anxious to see Him in His original Vṛndāvana pastimes. Therefore, the prime purpose of the Kṛṣṇa *avatāra* is to satisfy His unalloyed devotees."

9 One who knows the transcendental nature of My appearance and activities does not, upon leaving the body, take his birth again in this material world, but attains My eternal abode, O Arjuna.

Kṛṣṇa describes the result of realizing transcendental knowledge: A devotee achieves liberation and never has to take birth again in this material world. Śrīla Viśvanātha Cakravartī Ṭhākura comments that such a devotee becomes free from matter even before leaving his body.

The result of going beyond knowledge of Kṛṣṇa to a state of absorption in Kṛṣṇa is given in text 10.

10 Being freed from attachment, fear, and anger, being fully absorbed in Me and taking refuge in Me, many, many persons in the past became purified by knowledge of Me – and thus they all attained transcendental love for Me.

Beyond liberation is the stage of attaining transcendental love for Kṛṣṇa. *Pūtā mad-bhāvam āgatāḥ:* without being purified by knowledge of Kṛṣṇa, how can we become absorbed in Him? We must hear about Him. Transcendental knowledge about

Him is far superior to knowledge that we are souls and not our material bodies. By understanding Kṛṣṇa, we become further purified and attain love for Him.

This verse describes being freed from attachment, fear, and anger. The third chapter listed these items as the coverings of the soul. When our assimilation of transcendental knowledge frees us from attachment, fear, and anger, we can become fully absorbed in Kṛṣṇa consciousness. Then, always thinking of Kṛṣṇa, we can take full shelter of Him and attain transcendental love.

By hearing about Kṛṣṇa, many, many persons in the past became purified and attained love for Kṛṣṇa. They attained love for Kṛṣṇa because this was their desire, and Kṛṣṇa fulfilled it. What, then, occurs when someone takes shelter of Kṛṣṇa with something other than a desire to achieve transcendental love for Him? What if someone is not interested in Kṛṣṇa's eternal service? What if someone wants knowledge of Brahman and takes shelter of Kṛṣṇa to obtain it? The next verse explains how Kṛṣṇa reciprocates with such souls.

11 As all surrender unto Me, I reward them accordingly. Everyone follows My path in all respects, O son of Pṛthā.

Devotees who worship Kṛṣṇa in love go to Goloka Vṛndāvana. The Brahmavādīs who worship Kṛṣṇa to merge into Brahman are awarded their desired result. Śrīla Prabhupāda, therefore, writes in his purport about the *brahmajyoti* and going to Brahman. Śrīla Viśvanātha Cakravartī Ṭhākura comments:

> [One may say:] "Certainly Your exclusive devotees consider Your birth and activities to be eternal. Others, however, don't. In that category are *jñānīs* and others who approach You to perfect their own processes of *jñāna* and so on, and they do not consider Your birth and activities eternal."
>
> Kṛṣṇa responds to this consideration in the verse beginning *ye:* "In whatever manner persons approach Me (*bhajanti*), I reciprocate with them by giving them the fruits of their service. To those who think, 'My Lord's birth and activities are eternal,' and who worship Me with desires centered on My personal pastimes, and in this way experience great happiness, I

reciprocate in kind. Being the Supreme Lord, capable of doing anything, undoing anything, or making anything otherwise, I make such devotees My own *pārṣadas,* or perfect devotees, in order to make *their* birth and activities eternal.

"Descending to this world at suitable times along with these devotees and subsequently disappearing, I thus show My favor to them at every moment. I bestow on them pure love of God as the fruit of their reciprocation with Me.

"To those *jñānīs* and others who consider My birth and activities temporary and My personal form a product of *māyā,* yet still try to reciprocate with Me, I respond in kind by making them accept temporary births and activities again and again. I cause them to fall into the noose of *māyā's* illusion. In this way I give them the reward they deserve: the miseries of birth and death.

"Different are those *jñānīs,* however, who consider My birth and activities eternal and My personal form a manifestation of perfect eternity, knowledge, and bliss, and who approach Me to worship Me for the sake of perfecting their own process of *jñāna.* Those persons simply want to destroy their gross and subtle bodies and obtain liberation. I thus arrange for their attainment of eternal *brahmānanda* and bestow on them as the fruit of their worship an end to birth and death in the realm of ignorance.

"Thus not only My devotees reciprocate with Me, but in all different ways all kinds of human beings follow My path – *jñānīs, karmīs, yogīs,* and worshipers of demigods. In other words, because I incorporate in Myself all identities, all the processes of *jñāna, karma,* and so on constitute the path toward Me."

One could then ask: "If Kṛṣṇa, the Supreme Lord, gives a soul whatever he wants, why don't more persons surrender to Him? Why do they worship others to fulfill their desires?"

Kṛṣṇa answers this question in text 12.

12 Men in this world desire success in fruitive activities, and therefore they worship the demigods. Quickly, of course, men get results from fruitive work in this world.

One who worships Kṛṣṇa for material benefits obtains his desires, but Kṛṣṇa first purifies his heart. The purification may take time, and therefore the material reward may be delayed. Once the reward is achieved, however, the devotee usually no longer wants it. That was true in the case of Dhruva Mahārāja and others. Therefore, greedy people who want material benefits worship the demigods, who are Kṛṣṇa's servants, to get quick results.

One person worships the demigods for fruitive results, another worships Brahman, and yet another worships Kṛṣṇa with devotion. Does Kṛṣṇa, the supreme *īśvara*, control everyone's desires? Is it He who decides that one person will be a materialist and another a devotee and yet another a struggling spiritual aspirant? Is Kṛṣṇa, the supreme controller, responsible for the suffering and enjoyment, pain and pleasure of everyone in this world?

13 According to the three modes of material nature and the work associated with them, the four divisions of human society are created by Me. And although I am the creator of this system, you should know that I am yet the nondoer, being unchangeable.

The *varṇāśrama* system's purpose is to assist in elevating everyone from material consciousness to Kṛṣṇa consciousness. Although the *varṇāśrama* system was created by Kṛṣṇa, it is not He who placed the *jīvas* within that system. This fact was mentioned in text 11 – *ye yathā māṁ prapadyante:* Kṛṣṇa, as the impartial Supersoul, reciprocates with the desires of the living entities. He always remains the nondoer, and He does not directly reward anyone the fruits of work. In addition, Kṛṣṇa Himself is always transcendental to the *varṇāśrama* system despite the fact that He, while in this world, follows the prescribed duties of His *varṇa* and *āśrama*. Even while acting as though He is under *varṇāśrama,* He does not act within it. In that sense, Kṛṣṇa is also the nondoer or nonactor in relationship to *varṇāśrama*. As He is already transcendental and therefore is not elevated by following the system, He is also unchangeable. Śrīla Prabhupāda confirms this by saying, "In spite of His creating the four divisions of human society, Lord Kṛṣṇa does not belong to any of these divisions."

Logically, if I were to award you the fruits of your work, I must be transformed, at least on some level, because I have reacted to what you have done. Kṛṣṇa directly says that He is "the nondoer" and "unchangeable" to show that He, the Absolute Truth, is aloof. Although He is the creator of the *varṇāśrama* system, He awards neither results nor reactions. Thus He is neither contaminated nor transformed.

This is inconceivable. Kṛṣṇa is the Supreme Personality of Godhead, the supreme controller, and the cause of all causes, yet He will not accept responsibility for everything that happens to the *jīvas*. We each must take responsibility for what happens to us, even though everything ultimately depends on Kṛṣṇa. Kṛṣṇa only sanctions – against His own desires – our wayward and rebellious activities and their subsequent results because those activities are products of the expression of our free will. Kṛṣṇa is undoubtedly the cause of all causes – nothing happens without His sanction – yet for our rectification He allows us to act as we like. In the meantime, He awaits the time we will turn to Him and offer Him loving service. Material nature awards to those who do not turn to Him the pious and impious fruits of their activities.

In this verse, Kṛṣṇa explains that He is *akartā,* the nondoer. Kṛṣṇa has previously explained, *prakṛteḥ kriyamāṇāni guṇaiḥ karmāṇi sarvaśaḥ/ ahaṅkāra-vimūḍhātmā kartāham iti manyate:* "The spirit soul bewildered by the influence of false ego thinks himself the doer of activities that are in actuality carried out by the three modes of material nature." (Bg. 3.27)

Our thinking of ourselves as the cause of the results of our activities, Kṛṣṇa said, indicates that we are bewildered. Now Kṛṣṇa tells us not only that we are not the doer, but that He is not the doer either. Who, then, is doing everything?

Kṛṣṇa sometimes takes one side of this issue and sometimes the other. At times He wants to emphasize our position as tiny souls who should not be falsely proud of our prowess or think ourselves rightfully attached to the fruits of our activities. At such times, He emphasizes that we are not the doer, that we do not cause the fruits of our activities, and that the results of our activities are awarded to us by material nature. At other times, He emphasizes our culpability. He then wants us to take full responsibility for our actions and their reactions. Thus, at those times, Kṛṣṇa stresses Himself also as the nondoer.

Kṛṣṇa, the material nature and the living entities are all doers. The living entity desires to act, Kṛṣṇa (as the Supersoul) sanctions it, and the material nature facilitates the activity. Yet the weight of responsibility for the action rests solely on the living entity. Although the living entity has no independent power to act, he initiates actions by his desires, while both the Supersoul and the material nature, being neutral, facilitate their fulfillment.

In the next verse, Kṛṣṇa will further explain how He is the nondoer, or how He acts but does not act, and the value of thoroughly understanding these subtle truths.

14 There is no work that affects Me; nor do I aspire for the fruits of action. One who understands this truth about Me also does not become entangled in the fruitive reactions of work.

Conditioned souls, bound by their independent desires for pleasure, try to act based on those desires. Their attempts cause the modes of material nature to react, which results in activity and its reactions. Kṛṣṇa's own actions are different. Kṛṣṇa engages in many activities, but while acting, He is materially aloof and materially desireless, because His activities are within the internal energy and are free from the modes of material nature. Because His work is materially desireless, no reactions attach themselves to His work. As both He and His devotees are transcendental to material control, neither falls within the *varṇāśrama* system despite their willingly following the strictures of prescribed duties.

As will be mentioned in the next verse, when the *jīva* understands these facts about Kṛṣṇa and applies this transcendental knowledge to his own work and becomes a servant of Kṛṣṇa, he also becomes aloof from the material whirlpool of action and reaction.

15 All the liberated souls in ancient times acted with this understanding of My transcendental nature. Therefore you should perform your duty, following in their footsteps.

Kṛṣṇa has no attachment for the fruits of work. Knowing this, Arjuna should fight with faith, for Kṛṣṇa's pleasure, if he desires to become liberated. Kṛṣṇa wants Arjuna to fight in knowledge of Kṛṣṇa's position and as an offering to Him. In this way Arjuna should follow the example of previous great devotees.

In the next nine verses (16–24), in pursuance of Kṛṣṇa's description of His own work, Kṛṣṇa will explain how work (*karma*) can be seen as inactivity (*akarma*). Arjuna previously said he wished to leave the battlefield and avoid the results of his *karma*, like a *jñānī,* through inactivity. Kṛṣṇa will show him that no *karma* accrues to one who works in transcendental knowledge and that properly performed *karma* can thus be seen as nondifferent from the process of *jñāna*.

16 Even the intelligent are bewildered in determining what is action and what is inaction. Now I shall explain to you what action is, knowing which you shall be liberated from all misfortune.

In the next verse Kṛṣṇa adds the principle of *vikarma,* or forbidden action, to His presentation of *karma* and *akarma*.

17 The intricacies of action are very hard to understand. Therefore one should know properly what action is, what forbidden action is, and what inaction is.

"*Karma*" refers to activities done according to Vedic injunction. Such activities are generally referred to as *karma-kāṇḍa.* Owing to the performer's material desires, *karma-kāṇḍa* yields reactions, albeit good ones.

"*Vikarma*" means activities prohibited in the *Vedas*. Such prohibited actions produce bad reactions.

"*Akarma*" refers to work performed for Kṛṣṇa's pleasure. Such work brings no material reaction, good or bad. In his purport, Śrīla Prabhupāda classifies *vikarma* and *karma* together under the category of *vikarma:*

> To understand Kṛṣṇa consciousness and action according to its modes, one has to learn one's relationship with the Supreme; i.e., one who has learned perfectly knows that every living entity is an eternal servitor of the Lord and that consequently one has to act in Kṛṣṇa consciousness. The entire *Bhagavad-gītā* is

directed toward this conclusion. Any other conclusions, against this consciousness and its attendant actions, are *vikarmas,* or prohibited actions. To understand all this one has to associate with authorities in Kṛṣṇa consciousness and learn the secret from them; this is as good as learning from the Lord directly. Otherwise, even the most intelligent persons will be bewildered.

Having introduced the term *vikarma,* Kṛṣṇa returns to the distinction between *karma* and *akarma.*

18 One who sees inaction in action, and action in inaction, is intelligent among men, and he is in the transcendental position, although engaged in all sorts of activities.

"Inaction in action" refers to devotional service, or activities performed only for Kṛṣṇa's pleasure. Kṛṣṇa's servants receive no material reactions for their service because they act as Kṛṣṇa acts, without the contamination of seeking a reward for their work.

"Action in inaction" is the opposite. A *sannyāsī* without transcendental knowledge of Kṛṣṇa may appear not to be performing work, but as a soul, he can't avoid either activity or the entangling results of that activity. Devoid of transcendental knowledge about Kṛṣṇa, he must act, but he cannot act in Kṛṣṇa's service, for he has no knowledge of Kṛṣṇa. He is thus liable to all reactions.

For example, the *sannyāsī* must breathe. He must also eat. He steps on living entities as he walks. All these activities have no transcendental basis for him, and thus reactions accrue to him.

Every soul is unavoidably active. Artificial attempts at inactivity lead to a further danger, that of unengaged senses coupled with an impure mind. Anyone who attempts spiritual practices while the mind meditates on sense enjoyment will fall down, even if such an unfortunate "renunciant" appears to be less involved in the world than a devotee.

Kṛṣṇa explains this verse further in text 19.

19 One is understood to be in full knowledge whose every endeavor is devoid of desire for sense gratification. He is said

by sages to be a worker for whom the reactions of work have been burned up by the fire of perfect knowledge.

Śrīla Prabhupāda comments: "Only a person in full knowledge can understand the activities of a person in Kṛṣṇa consciousness. Because the person in Kṛṣṇa consciousness is devoid of all kinds of sense-gratificatory propensities, it is to be understood that he has burned up the reactions of his work by perfect knowledge of his constitutional position as the eternal servitor of the Supreme Personality of Godhead. He is actually learned who has attained to such perfection of knowledge."

A devotee in transcendental knowledge never desires sense enjoyment because He knows Kṛṣṇa as his Lord and master and himself as Kṛṣṇa's servant. He is thus freed from material desires, and his actions (*akarma*) produce no reactions.

20 Abandoning all attachment to the results of his activities, ever satisfied and independent, he performs no fruitive action, although engaged in all kinds of undertakings.

We should not give up work; we should be satisfied by dutiful work. We should give up attachment to the fruits of work. This verse describes a *sādhaka,* one endeavoring for perfection. The perfection of this consciousness (*siddha*) is explained in verses 21 and 22.

21 Such a man of understanding acts with mind and intelligence perfectly controlled, gives up all sense of proprietorship over his possessions, and acts only for the bare necessities of life. Thus working, he is not affected by sinful reactions.

Śrīla Prabhupāda explains the understanding of a Kṛṣṇa conscious person:

> He moves exactly like a part of a machine. As a machine part requires oiling and cleaning for maintenance, so a Kṛṣṇa conscious man maintains himself by his work just to remain fit for action in the transcendental loving service of the Lord. He is therefore immune to all the reactions of his endeavors. Like

> an animal, he has no proprietorship even over his own body. A cruel proprietor of an animal sometimes kills the animal in his possession, yet the animal does not protest. Nor does it have any real independence. A Kṛṣṇa conscious person, fully engaged in self-realization, has very little time to falsely possess any material object. For maintaining body and soul, he does not require unfair means of accumulating money. He does not, therefore, become contaminated by such material sins. He is free from all reactions to his actions.

This verse speaks of a highly advanced, perfected devotee who is constantly greedy for Kṛṣṇa's service. He considers himself insignificant and gives no importance to anything outside that service. His qualities will now be further described.

22 He who is satisfied with gain which comes of its own accord, who is free from duality and does not envy, who is steady in both success and failure, is never entangled, although performing actions.

A devotee on this platform does not even endeavor to beg for his sustenance. He depends on Kṛṣṇa, who looks upon such an exalted soul with great affection. Śrīpada Mādhavendra Purī is an example of a devotee on this level. Mādhavendra Purī neither worked nor begged for his food. He ate only when someone was prompted by Kṛṣṇa from within to offer him food.

When Mādhavendra Purī traveled in Vraja-dhāma, he refrained from begging. One day, Kṛṣṇa saw his faith, affection, and detachment and personally brought Mādhavendra Purī milk, as the saint sat at Govinda-kuṇḍa near Govardhana Hill. The devotional consciousness of such a materially detached, spiritually attached soul is so sweet that it even attracts Kṛṣṇa.

Endowed with this consciousness, the devotee's mind is freed from the dualities of the material world. All day the conditioned soul sees good and bad. He yearns for pleasure and tries to avoid distress. The devotee is above such considerations because he sees Kṛṣṇa's hand in everything that occurs.

The next verse introduces *yajña.* This topic will be expanded on in verses 25–33.

23 The work of a man who is unattached to the modes of material nature and who is fully situated in transcendental knowledge merges entirely into transcendence.

Here Śrīla Prabhupāda translates *yajñāya* as "for the sake of Yajña (Kṛṣṇa)." Our work is automatically situated in transcendence when it is performed as a sacrifice for Kṛṣṇa's pleasure.

Kṛṣṇa will describe a variety of sacrifices in the following verses because these sacrifices have transcendental knowledge, the theme of this chapter, as their ultimate goal.

We should not underestimate the importance of acquiring transcendental knowledge. Knowledge about Kṛṣṇa, the *jīvātma,* the material world, and the process of devotional service solidifies our devotional practices. *Tāhāṅ vistārita hañā phale prema-phala ihāṅ mālī sece nitya śravaṇādi jala:* "The [devotional] creeper greatly expands in the Goloka Vṛndāvana planet, and there it produces the fruit of love for Kṛṣṇa. Although remaining in the material world, the gardener regularly sprinkles the creeper with the water of hearing and chanting." (Cc., *Madhya* 19. 155) Śrīla Prabhupāda writes in his purport to this verse:

> Every living entity is wandering within this universe in different species and on different planetary systems according to his fruitive activities. Out of many millions of living entities, one may be fortunate enough to receive the seed of *bhakti-latā,* the creeper of devotional service. By the grace of the spiritual master and Kṛṣṇa, one nourishes the *bhakti-latā* by regularly sprinkling it with the water of *śravaṇa-kīrtana,* hearing and chanting. In this way the seed of *bhakti-latā* sprouts and grows up and up through the whole universe until it penetrates the covering of the material universe and reaches the spiritual world. The *bhakti-latā* continues to grow until it reaches the topmost planetary system, Goloka Vṛndāvana, where Kṛṣṇa lives. There the creeper takes shelter at the lotus feet of the Lord, and that is its final destination. At that time the creeper begins to grow the fruits of ecstatic love of God. It is the duty of the devotee who nourishes the creeper to be very careful. It is said that the watering of the creeper must continue: *ihāṅ mālī sece nitya śravaṇādi jala.* It is

> not that at a certain stage one can stop chanting and hearing and become a mature devotee. If one stops, one certainly falls down from devotional service. Although one may be very exalted in devotional service, he should not give up the watering process of *śravaṇa-kīrtana.* If one gives up that process, it is due to an offense.

Cultivating Kṛṣṇa conscious knowledge is, therefore, essential. Only then can knowledge and work be combined so that one's work becomes a sacrifice to Kṛṣṇa.

Kṛṣṇa summarizes his teachings on *akarma* by next describing the absolute quality of a sacrifice performed in spiritual consciousness.

24 A person who is fully absorbed in Kṛṣṇa consciousness is sure to attain the spiritual kingdom because of his full contribution to spiritual activities, in which the consummation is absolute and that which is offered is of the same spiritual nature.

Work done in transcendental knowledge and performed as a sacrifice is, along with its results, absolute, because all work done for Kṛṣṇa's pleasure produces no *karma* and is therefore transcendental.

Śrīla Prabhupāda explains the sacrifices that will now be described:

> The word *brahma* (Brahman) means "spiritual." The Lord is spiritual, and the rays of His transcendental body are called *brahmajyoti,* His spiritual effulgence. Everything that exists is situated in that *brahmajyoti,* but when the *jyoti* is covered by illusion (*māyā*) or sense gratification, it is called material. This material veil can be removed at once by Kṛṣṇa consciousness; thus the offering for the sake of Kṛṣṇa consciousness, the consuming agent of such an offering or contribution, the process of consumption, the contributor, and the result are – all combined together – Brahman, or the Absolute Truth....When the mind is fully absorbed in Kṛṣṇa consciousness, it is said to be in *samādhi,* or trance. Anything done in such transcendental consciousness is called *yajña,* or sacrifice for the Absolute.

The "contribution, the process of consumption, the contributor, and the result" are all necessary aspects of any sacrifice. The ultimate goal of all the sacrifices that Kṛṣṇa will now list is the pleasure of the Absolute Truth. They all advance a practitioner in transcendental knowledge. In the next nine verses, (25–33) Kṛṣṇa will explain to Arjuna that transcendental knowledge – ultimately about Kṛṣṇa – is to be obtained through these sacrifices and austerities, all of which are typical of Vedic culture.

25 Some yogīs perfectly worship the demigods by offering different sacrifices to them, and some of them offer sacrifices in the fire of the Supreme Brahman.

Kṛṣṇa will later explain that only those who are "less intelligent" worship demigods as if they were supreme or independently able to supply life's necessities. Demigods are empowered by Kṛṣṇa to fulfill a worshiper's desires. Demigod worship will be discussed in more detail in chapters seven and nine.

We can worship the demigods properly by understanding them as agents of Viṣṇu. Mahārāja Bharata, as described in *Bhāg.* 5.7.5–7, provides a proper example of demigod worship. He worshiped the demigods, considering them as parts of the universal body of Lord Viṣṇu, not for material rewards, but to please Lord Viṣṇu.

Next, Kṛṣṇa explains sacrifices according to one's position in *varṇāśrama*.

26 Some [the unadulterated brahmacārīs] sacrifice the hearing process and the senses in the fire of mental control, and others [the regulated householders] sacrifice the objects of the senses in the fire of the senses.

A *brahmacārī's* mind is controlled when he engages it solely in hearing about Kṛṣṇa. The *gṛhastha* performs his sacrifice by restricting sex according to śāstric injunctions.

Kṛṣṇa next discusses *aṣṭāṅga-yoga*.

27 Others, who are interested in achieving self-realization through control of the mind and senses, offer the functions of

all the senses, and of the life breath, as oblations into the fire of the controlled mind.

In the body circulate ten kinds of air, five major and five minor. Controlling them controls the mind, which is the point of this verse. Kṛṣṇa will speak about *aṣṭāṅga-yoga* in detail in chapter six.

Verse 28 mentions four more *yajñas*.

28 Having accepted strict vows, some become enlightened by sacrificing their possessions, and others by performing severe austerities, by practicing the yoga of eightfold mysticism, or by studying the Vedas to advance in transcendental knowledge.

All these sacrifices elevate the participants. Yet pure Kṛṣṇa consciousness is far above these *yajñas,* as Śrīla Prabhupāda reminds us: "Kṛṣṇa consciousness cannot be attained by any one of the above-mentioned types of sacrifice but can be attained only by the mercy of the Lord and His bona fide devotees." Still, these *yajñas* provide gradual upliftment and can be stepping-stones to devotional service.

The following verse again speaks of *prāṇāyāma* (yogic breath control), a part of the *aṣṭāṅga-yoga* practices.

29 Still others, who are inclined to the process of breath restraint to remain in trance, practice by offering the movement of the outgoing breath into the incoming, and the incoming breath into the outgoing, and thus at last remain in trance, stopping all breathing. Others, curtailing the eating process, offer the outgoing breath into itself as a sacrifice.

Kṛṣṇa begins to sum up the purpose of all these sacrifices in the next verse.

30 All these performers who know the meaning of sacrifice become cleansed of sinful reactions, and, having tasted the nectar of the results of sacrifices, they advance toward the supreme eternal atmosphere.

In his purport, Śrīla Prabhupāda explains that sacrifices are meant to award sense control and to free the performer from sinful reactions.

31 O best of the Kuru dynasty, without sacrifice one can never live happily on this planet or in this life: what then of the next?

32 All these different types of sacrifice are approved by the Vedas, and all of them are born of different types of work. Knowing them as such, you will become liberated.

Śrīla Prabhupāda explains: "Different types of sacrifice as discussed above, are mentioned in the *Vedas* to suit the different types of workers. Because men are so deeply absorbed in the bodily concept, these sacrifices are so arranged that one can work either with the body, with the mind, or with the intelligence. But all of them are recommended for ultimately bringing about liberation from the body. This is confirmed by the Lord herewith from His own mouth."

One's position in the modes of material nature dictates his tendency and ability to perform sacrifice. One person, influenced by the modes of material nature and his impressions from previous lives, chooses to perform a sacrifice of breath control. Another performs sacrifice through *yajñas*. Yet another sacrifices material wealth. Superficially these sacrifices appear different. Although born of varieties of consciousness they lead to the same goal. That goal – transcendental knowledge – brings freedom from material life.

Human life is meant for advancing in spiritual life, and the process of advancing is sacrifice. A man works and achieves results as the fruits of his work and should offer at least some of those results in sacrifice to Viṣṇu. One who makes no offering – money, ability, intelligence, mind, or body – simply lives selfishly, in vain, for he has not advanced toward the supreme objective.

Modern man attempts to find happiness without performing sacrifice. His sense enjoyment may increase, but happiness eludes him. Being devoid of transcendental knowledge and condemned as a thief by the law of *karma,* he also suffers in his next life.

The next text establishes transcendental knowledge as the desired result of performing sacrifice.

33 O chastiser of the enemy, the sacrifice performed in knowledge is better than the mere sacrifice of material possessions. After all, O son of Pṛthā, all sacrifices of work culminate in transcendental knowledge.

We may perform a *karma-kāṇḍa* sacrifice and give up limited amounts of sense gratification so that we can increase it later tenfold. This is a sacrifice performed within the material realm. Such a sacrifice is performed with meager knowledge of the difference between body and soul, and with no factual knowledge of Kṛṣṇa's position. Thus that sacrifice is inferior to the sacrifice performed in knowledge. Sacrifices performed in knowledge lead one to higher platforms of transcendental knowledge.

Concluding His discussion of sacrifices, Kṛṣṇa now begins His summary of transcendental knowledge by again describing how it may be directly attained.

34 Just try to learn the truth by approaching a spiritual master. Inquire from him submissively and render service unto him. The self-realized souls can impart knowledge unto you because they have seen the truth.

Śrīla Prabhupāda's purport reveals:

> The path of spiritual realization is undoubtedly difficult. The Lord therefore advises us to approach a bona fide spiritual master in the line of disciplic succession from the Lord Himself. No one can be a bona fide spiritual master without following this principle of disciplic succession. The Lord is the original spiritual master, and a person in the disciplic succession can convey the message of the Lord as it is to his disciple. No one can be spiritually realized by manufacturing his own process, as is the fashion of the foolish pretenders. The *Bhāgavatam* (6.3.19) says, *dharmaṁ tu sākṣād bhagavat-praṇītam:* the path of religion is

> directly enunciated by the Lord. Therefore, mental speculation or dry arguments cannot help lead one to the right path. Nor by independent study of books of knowledge can one progress in spiritual life. One has to approach a bona fide spiritual master to receive the knowledge. Such a spiritual master should be accepted in full surrender, and one should serve the spiritual master like a menial servant, without false prestige. Satisfaction of the self-realized spiritual master is the secret of advancement in spiritual life. Inquiries and submission constitute the proper combination for spiritual understanding. Unless there is submission and service, inquiries from the learned spiritual master will not be effective. One must be able to pass the test of the spiritual master, and when he sees the genuine desire of the disciple, he automatically blesses the disciple with genuine spiritual understanding. In this verse, both blind following and absurd inquiries are condemned. Not only should one hear submissively from the spiritual master, but one must also get a clear understanding from him, in submission and service and inquiries. A bona fide spiritual master is by nature very kind toward the disciple. Therefore when the student is submissive and is always ready to render service, the reciprocation of knowledge and inquiries becomes perfect.

Śrīla Rūpa Gosvāmī explains that accepting the shelter of the lotus feet of a spiritual master is the first item of devotional service (*adau gurupādāśraya*). The knowledge one receives from his spiritual master will now be described.

35 Having obtained real knowledge from a self-realized soul, you will never fall again into such illusion, for by this knowledge you will see that all living beings are but part of the Supreme, or, in other words, that they are Mine.

Śrīla Baladeva Vidyābhūṣaṇa comments that one result of knowledge is that we no longer fall into illusion. Arjuna should not think that his relatives will die. He should understand that all living entities, whether animal or demigod or human, are different from their bodies. In addition, he should understand that all living entities are nondifferent from Kṛṣṇa and situated within Him.

Śrīla Prabhupāda writes: "The result of receiving knowledge from a self-realized soul, or one who knows things as they are, is learning that all living beings are parts and parcels of the Supreme Personality of Godhead, Lord Śrī Kṛṣṇa. The sense of an existence separate from Kṛṣṇa is called *māyā*."

Māyā turns us away from Kṛṣṇa, and then we consider ourselves independent of Him. We are, however, eternally Kṛṣṇa's "part and parcels." We come from Kṛṣṇa (part), yet we are eternally individual units (parcels). We need His shelter and His service. Thus an elevated soul thinks, "I am Kṛṣṇa's, and Kṛṣṇa is mine."

The next verse describes another fruit of transcendental knowledge: going beyond sin.

36 Even if you are considered to be the most sinful of all sinners, when you are situated in the boat of transcendental knowledge you will be able to cross over the ocean of miseries.

In chapter one, Arjuna feared sin and its resultant suffering. Kṛṣṇa herein tells Arjuna the cure is transcendental knowledge, not fleeing the battlefield.

The words *api cet* ("even if") are used when one accepts the occurrence of an unlikely or apparently self-contradictory event. Three questions could be asked, as posed by Śrīla Viśvanātha Cakravartī Ṭhākura: If someone is acting sinfully, how can his heart become purified? And without such purification, how can he develop knowledge? And if he has developed knowledge, how can he act with such impropriety?

Kṛṣṇa is thus describing this "*api cet*" situation to glorify the purifying effects of transcendental knowledge.

37 As a blazing fire turns firewood to ashes, O Arjuna, so does the fire of knowledge burn to ashes all reactions to material activities.

Śrīla Viśvanātha Cakravartī Ṭhākura comments: "Kṛṣṇa says, 'For one whose heart has become purified, I destroy completely whatever *karma* has already been generated with the exception of his *pārabdha-karma.*'" Transcendental knowledge thus destroys all reactions, both pious and sinful; all, that is, except *pārabdha-karma,* or matured reactions, such as one's present material body.

Kṛṣṇa now further glorifies transcendental knowledge.

38 In this world, there is nothing so sublime and pure as transcendental knowledge. Such knowledge is the mature fruit of all mysticism. And one who has become accomplished in the practice of devotional service enjoys this knowledge within himself in due course of time.

Kālena means "in course of time." Kṛṣṇa uses the word *kālena* to warn against premature renunciation – simply adopting the outer garb of a *sannyāsī,* as is sometimes done by Māyāvādīs – as if that will automatically fix us in knowledge and free us of sin. Kṛṣṇa also uses the term *kālena* to encourage detached work, which truly bestows transcendental knowledge. "In course of time" indicates that transcendental knowledge is gradually revealed in the heart of one practicing *niṣkāma karma-yoga.* By work, not by renouncing work, it manifests.

Kṛṣṇa explains the role of faith in acquiring knowledge.

39 A faithful man who is dedicated to transcendental knowledge and who subdues his senses is eligible to achieve such knowledge, and having achieved it he quickly attains the supreme spiritual peace.

Here Kṛṣṇa explains the qualifications a man needs to obtain transcendental knowledge. He must be faithful, dedicated, and sense-controlled. He works faithfully and knows that his detached work will bring transcendental knowledge and "the supreme, spiritual peace" (liberation). Without faith, as Kṛṣṇa explains below, peace is unobtainable.

40 But ignorant and faithless persons who doubt the revealed scriptures do not attain God consciousness; they fall down. For the doubting soul there is happiness neither in this world nor in the next.

Śrīla Viśvanātha Cakravartī Ṭhākura differentiates between the faithless and the doubters. He explains that Kṛṣṇa has mentioned three classes of people who fail: the ignorant (*ajñaḥ*), the faithless (*aśraddadhānaḥ*) and the doubters (*saṁśayātmanaḥ*). "The *ajña* is foolish like the animals. The *aśraddadhāna* has knowledge of *śāstra,* but having seen the mutual disagreements of proponents of various theories, he has no trust in any of them. Although the *saṁśayātmā* has faith, he is swayed by the doubt, 'I don't know whether this process will be effective in my case.'"

Doubters have some faith, but they nevertheless doubt that following *śāstra* will truly award results. They thus follow, but without full faith, hope, and optimism. Such doubters achieve happiness neither in this world nor the next. Even fools attain some material happiness. Doubters attain none.

Kṛṣṇa next reveals how to destroy doubts.

41 One who acts in devotional service, renouncing the fruits of his actions, and whose doubts have been destroyed by transcendental knowledge, is situated factually in the self. Thus he is not bound by the reactions of work, O conqueror of riches.

When a person applies transcendental knowledge to work, he will both act dutifully and renounce the fruits of his actions. Such a person is actually situated in the self. He knows he is not the body. He knows that work performed for Kṛṣṇa's pleasure will not bind him with reactions. His transcendental knowledge has removed his doubts.

In the final verse of this chapter, Kṛṣṇa speaks to impel Arjuna to act in knowledge.

42 Therefore the doubts which have arisen in your heart out of ignorance should be slashed by the weapon of knowledge. Armed with yoga, O Bhārata, stand and fight.

Arjuna, sitting on his chariot, is determined not to fight. Kṛṣṇa wants him to stand, fixed in transcendental knowledge, detached from all results, and fight. Work and knowledge combined will free Arjuna from the sinful reactions he fears.

Śrīla Prabhupāda's purport to this verse summarizes the chapter. I have divided the purport into sections and added headings to categorize the different topics:

The goal of sacrifice (part one)

"The *yoga* system instructed in this chapter is called *sanātana-yoga,* or eternal activities performed by the living entity. This *yoga* has two divisions of sacrificial actions: one is called sacrifice of one's material possessions, and the other is called knowledge of self, which is pure spiritual activity. If sacrifice of one's material possessions is not dovetailed for spiritual realization, then such sacrifice becomes material. But one who performs such sacrifices with a spiritual objective, or in devotional service, makes a perfect sacrifice."

The two levels of spiritual knowledge

"When we come to spiritual activities, we find that these are also divided into two: namely, understanding of one's own self (or one's constitutional position), and the truth regarding the Supreme Personality of Godhead. One who follows the path of *Bhagavad-gītā* as it is can very easily understand these two important divisions of spiritual knowledge. For him there is no difficulty in obtaining perfect knowledge of the self as part and parcel of the Lord. And such understanding is beneficial, for such a person can easily understand the transcendental activities of the Lord."

Learning of the Lord's transcendental activities

"In the beginning of this chapter, the transcendental activities of the Lord were discussed by the Supreme Lord Himself. One who does not understand the instructions of the *Gītā* is faithless and is to be considered to be misusing the fragmental independence awarded to him by the Lord. In spite of such instructions, one who does not understand the real nature of the Lord as the eternal, blissful, all-knowing Personality of Godhead is certainly fool number one."

The goal of sacrifice (part two)

"Ignorance can be removed by gradual acceptance of the principles of Kṛṣṇa consciousness. Kṛṣṇa consciousness is awakened by different types of sacrifices to the demigods, sacrifice to Brahman, sacrifice in celibacy, in household life, in controlling the senses, in practicing mystic *yoga,* in penance, in foregoing material possessions, in studying the *Vedas,* and in partaking of the social institution called *varṇāśrama-dharma.* All of these are known as sacrifice, and all of them are based on regulated action. But within all these activities, the important factor is self-realization. One who seeks *that* objective is the real student of *Bhagavad-gītā,* but one who doubts the authority of Kṛṣṇa falls back."

Properly learning transcendental knowledge

"One is therefore advised to study *Bhagavad-gītā*, or any other scripture, under a bona fide spiritual master, with service and surrender. A bona fide spiritual master is in the disciplic succession from time eternal, and he does not deviate at all from the instructions of the Supreme Lord as they were imparted millions of years ago to the sun god, from whom the instructions of *Bhagavad-gītā* have come down to the earthly kingdom. One should, therefore, follow the path of *Bhagavad-gītā* as it is expressed in the *Gītā* itself and beware of self-interested people after personal aggrandizement who deviate others from the actual path. The Lord is definitely the supreme person, and His activities are transcendental. One who understands this is a liberated person from the very beginning of his study of *Bhagavad-gītā*."

Chapter Five

Karma-yoga – Action in Kṛṣṇa Consciousness

Arjuna is still confused, though he has heard transcendental knowledge from Kṛṣṇa. In texts 16–18 of the fourth chapter, Kṛṣṇa glorified *jñāna* and spoke of action in inaction and inaction in action. In text 41, Kṛṣṇa glorified both *jñāna* and renunciation. Then in text 42, He again ordered Arjuna to fight. Therefore chapter five opens with a question similar to the one Arjuna asked at the beginning of chapter three: "Which is better – work or renunciation of work?"

1 Arjuna said: O Kṛṣṇa, first of all You ask me to renounce work, and then again You recommend work with devotion. Now will You kindly tell me definitely which of the two is more beneficial?

Śrīla Prabhupāda explains in his purport:

> In the fourth chapter the Lord told Arjuna that all kinds of sacrificial work culminate in knowledge. However, at the end of the fourth chapter, the Lord advised Arjuna to wake up and fight, being situated in perfect knowledge. Therefore, by simultaneously stressing the importance of both work in devotion and inaction in knowledge, Kṛṣṇa has perplexed Arjuna and confused his determination. Arjuna understands that renunciation in knowledge involves cessation of all kinds of work performed as sense activities. But if one performs work in devotional service, then how is work stopped? In other words, he thinks that *sannyāsa,* or renunciation in knowledge, should be altogether free from all kinds of activity, because work and renunciation appear to him to be incompatible. He appears not to have understood that work in full knowledge is nonreactive and is therefore the same as inaction. He inquires, therefore, whether he should cease work altogether or work with full knowledge.

It is Kṛṣṇa's plan that Arjuna remain confused, because their dialogue is actually taking place for our benefit, not Arjuna's. Arjuna's perplexity gives Kṛṣṇa the chance to stress further that work and renunciation are not opposed to each other. Rather, one must learn to work in a renounced spirit. Arjuna thinks that *jñāna* implies the renunciation of work, and that knowledge and work, like light and dark, are contradictory. Kṛṣṇa emphasizes, however, that one in knowledge should also work.

2 The Personality of Godhead replied: The renunciation of work and work in devotion are both good for liberation. But, of the two, work in devotional service is better than renunciation of work.

This is the second time Kṛṣṇa has directly rejected seeking perfection through dry renunciation and *jñāna* and has instead recommended work. Both work and renunciation have the same goal, but of the two, detached work is safer, easier, and more practical. Working in knowledge purifies our hearts and solidifies whatever realization we attain. The *karma-sannyāsī* is one who renounces work. If material desires arise, he cannot take shelter of using his senses in work that will purify him; for as a foundational principle, he has renounced all sense interactions. His choice, for his senses, is either mundane action or inaction, as his senses have no legitimate engagement. Detached work is a more practical path of renunciation, for, as Śrīla Baladeva Vidyābhūṣaṇa comments, "Working in renunciation strengthens one's knowledge."

3 One who neither hates nor desires the fruits of his activities is known to be always renounced. Such a person, free from all dualities, easily overcomes material bondage and is completely liberated, O mighty-armed Arjuna.

Such a worker is called a *nitya-sannyāsī*. A *sannyāsī* is meant to achieve liberation, and one who renounces the fruits of his activities will attain it. Such detachment – feeling neither hatred nor desire for the fruits of work – is the mark of a true *sannyāsī*.

4 Only the ignorant speak of devotional service [karma-yoga] as being different from the analytical study of the material world [sāṅkhya]. Those who are actually learned say that he who applies himself well to one of these paths achieves the results of both.

Both *karma-yoga* and *sāṅkhya-yoga* (*jñāna*) involve renunciation. But what is it better to renounce? Should one work with detachment or renounce work altogether?

Kṛṣṇa's answer is clear and consistent: These are not two different paths with separate goals, but aspects of the same path with the same goal.

How are work and renunciation the same? If I am holding a rock in my hand and I want to pick up my ax, I drop the rock to free my hand. Then I can pick up the ax. Similarly, someone with material desires must first drop his material attachment before acquiring a spiritual taste.

However, these two steps can also be performed as one step. By picking up one object I will automatically drop the other. *Karma-yoga* done with detachment allows us to become materially detached and spiritually attached at the same time. This topic will now be further discussed.

5 One who knows that the position reached by means of analytical study can also be attained by devotional service, and who therefore sees analytical study and devotional service to be on the same level, sees things as they are.

Kṛṣṇa repeats His point from text 4 for emphasis. Describing these two processes and how they are related, Śrīla Prabhupāda says:

> The real purpose of philosophical research is to find the ultimate goal of life. Since the ultimate goal of life is self-realization, there is no difference between the conclusions reached by the two processes. By Sāṅkhya philosophical research one comes to the conclusion that a living entity is not a part and parcel of the material world but of the supreme spirit whole. Consequently, the spirit soul has nothing to do with the material world; his actions must be in some relation with the Supreme.

> When he acts in Kṛṣṇa consciousness, he is actually in his constitutional position. In the first process, Sāṅkhya, one has to become detached from matter, and in the devotional *yoga* process one has to attach himself to the work of Kṛṣṇa consciousness. Factually, both processes are the same, although superficially one process appears to involve detachment and the other process appears to involve attachment. Detachment from matter and attachment to Kṛṣṇa are one and the same. One who can see this sees things as they are.

This verse begins, *sāṅkhya-yogau.* Here *sāṅkhya* refers to *jñāna,* and *yoga* refers to *niṣkāma karma-yoga.* Kṛṣṇa clearly recommends devotional service (*karma-yoga*) as the better means to achieve the goal, even though both *jñāna* and *karma-yoga* lead to *sthānam śāśvatam,* "the supreme, eternal abode" (Bg. 18.62).

It is important to understand that Kṛṣṇa is not speaking about a variety of paths leading to a variety of inferior or superior destinations. Rather, He is describing two aspects of a path – one easy and one difficult – with the same goal. (These verses are applicable to anyone trying to attain Brahman, Paramātmā, or Bhagavān realization, but Śrīla Prabhupāda translated *yoga* as "devotional service" to highlight Kṛṣṇa's actual desire and purpose.)

If we renounce activities before our hearts are clean, we will be forced by our unclean hearts to engage in improper activities. The senses will demand engagement, but the *jñāna-yoga* process forbids sense activity. Unless the senses are engaged in good work, it will be difficult to stop improper work. Kṛṣṇa therefore recommends keeping the senses always engaged while simultaneously purifying the heart by working with detachment. This is the more practical and, therefore, superior path. The comparison between the two paths continues in the following verse.

6 Merely renouncing all activities yet not engaging in the devotional service of the Lord cannot make one happy. But a thoughtful person engaged in devotional service can achieve the Supreme without delay.

In texts 7–12, Kṛṣṇa describes how to practice *niṣkāma karma-yoga.*

7 One who works in devotion, who is a pure soul, and who controls his mind and senses is dear to everyone, and everyone is dear to him. Though always working, such a man is never entangled.

In his purport, Śrīla Prabhupāda paraphrases Bg. 2.12, which describes the individuality of the soul. Śrīla Prabhupāda does this because *sarva-bhūtātma-bhūtātmā,* "compassion to all souls," has been taken by Māyāvādīs to mean that a soul becomes the soul of all living entities. Clearly, Kṛṣṇa is not saying that. Instead, He uses the words *sarva-bhūtātma-bhūtātmā* to refer to the compassion of a devotee with three symptoms of advancement, which Śrīla Viśvanātha Cakravartī Ṭhākura defines as: *viśuddhātmā* (a soul with purified intelligence), *vijitātmā* (one who is self-controlled), and *jitendriya* (one who has conquered his senses). A person who possesses these three qualities has not become one with everyone, as the Māyāvādīs say, but feels that everyone is dear to him.

How can everyone be dear to Arjuna as he stands on the battlefield ready to kill his enemies? Śrīla Prabhupāda writes: "Arjuna was only superficially offensive because (as has already been explained in the second chapter) all the assembled persons on the battlefield would continue to live individually, as the soul cannot be slain. So, spiritually, no one was killed on the Battlefield of Kurukṣetra. Only their dresses were changed by the order of Kṛṣṇa, who was personally present. Therefore Arjuna, while fighting on the Battlefield of Kurukṣetra, was not really fighting at all; he was simply carrying out the orders of Kṛṣṇa in full Kṛṣṇa consciousness. Such a person is never entangled in the reactions of work."

In the next two verses, Kṛṣṇa describes the *jitendriya,* the renounced, sense-controlled worker, as he goes about his activities.

8–9 A person in the divine consciousness, although engaged in seeing, hearing, touching, smelling, eating, moving about, sleeping, and breathing, always knows within himself that he

actually does nothing at all. Because while speaking, evacuating, receiving, or opening or closing his eyes, he always knows that only the material senses are engaged with their objects and that he is aloof from them.

Kṛṣṇa now describes how the transcendental knowledge that we are not our bodies should be expressed through work. This knowledge allows us to remain aloof from the body as we work. We see our bodies acting, but we have no interest in the fruits of our actions. Śrīla Viśvanātha Cakravartī Ṭhākura explains that the *niṣkāma karmī,* even while acting with his body, senses, and so on, is a *tattva-vit;* he realizes the self is separate from the body.

Does the work of such a detached person result in any sinful reactions?

10 One who performs his duty without attachment, surrendering the results unto the Supreme Lord, is unaffected by sinful action, as the lotus leaf is untouched by water.

One should be situated in knowledge and then do one's duty with detachment. Such a person will perceive the body's actions – it works, it touches, it moves, it does so many things – but he thinks, "I do nothing. I am a soul and I am aloof." With this realization one can perform his duty without attachment and then surrender all the results to Kṛṣṇa. Thus work remains free from sinful reactions, just as "the lotus leaf is untouched by water." Lotus leaves have a waxy surface, and water immediately glides off them. In the same way, reactions "glide off" one performing *niṣkāma karma-yoga.*

The question can be raised, "If someone is detached from work because he knows that he is a spirit soul and not his body, what is his purpose in working?"

11 The yogīs, abandoning attachment, act with body, mind, intelligence, and even with the senses, only for the purpose of purification.

"*Kaivalya*" comes from the root *kevala,* which in this verse is defined as "purified." One becomes purified by his detached work. Śrīla Viśvanātha Cakravartī Ṭhākura explains: "Although one's mind may sometimes be distracted while making offerings of oblations such as *indrīya svāhā,* still, such a person's senses are *kevala,* acting for the purification of the *ātmā,* or for the sake of purifying the mind."

Śrīla Baladeva Vidyābhūṣaṇa explains this verse as follows: "Citing the behavior of saintly persons as evidence, Kṛṣṇa elaborates on the previous verse with this verse beginning *kāyena*. *Yogīs* carry out work that has to be executed with the body, mind, senses, and so on, without any false identification of the self with the body and so on. *Kevala* means 'fully purified' (*viśuddha*). In the phrase beginning 'abandoning attachment,' the words 'for the purpose of purification of the self' mean 'for the sake of giving up one's false identification with the body as the self, which one has maintained since time immemorial.' "

Śrīla Prabhupāda writes, "This is the perfect stage of Kṛṣṇa consciousness."

Kṛṣṇa next compares the attached with the unattached.

12 The steadily devoted soul attains unadulterated peace because he offers the result of all activities to Me; whereas a person who is not in union with the Divine, who is greedy for the fruits of his labor, becomes entangled.

This is a summary of the previous five verses.

The next four verses answer a question Kṛṣṇa already discussed in the third and fourth chapters, namely, who is the doer – the living entity, material nature, or Kṛṣṇa as Paramātmā? In the first of these four verses, Kṛṣṇa describes the *jīvātmā's* role.

13 When the embodied living being controls his nature and mentally renounces all actions, he resides happily in the city of nine gates [the material body], neither working nor causing work to be done.

No one thinks, "Because I live in a city, I *am* the city." A *sannyāsī* does not identify himself with the city of his material body. Neither does he think of himself as doing nothing. He endeavors, but knows that success ultimately depends on powers beyond him. He thus offers the results of his activities to the Supreme.

What result does he achieve in such consciousness?

14 The embodied spirit, master of the city of his body, does not create activities, nor does he induce people to act, nor does he create the fruits of action. All this is enacted by the modes of material nature.

Śrīla Prabhupāda explains: "The temporary body or material dwelling place which he obtains is the cause of varieties of activities and their resultant reactions. Living in such a conditioned atmosphere, one suffers the results of the activities of the body by identifying himself (in ignorance) with the body. It is ignorance acquired from time immemorial that is the cause of bodily suffering and distress. As soon as the living entity becomes aloof from the activities of the body, he becomes free from the reactions as well. As long as he is in the city of the body, he appears to be the master of it, but actually he is neither its proprietor nor the controller of its actions and reactions."

The living entity within the body does nothing. Kṛṣṇa, in the Sanskrit of this verse, even repeats the word "*na*" three times (*na kartṛtvaṁ na karmāṇi... na karma-phala-saṁyogam*). The conditioned soul does not create activities, nor does he induce people to act, nor does he control the fruits of even his own activities. All this happens by the modes of material nature.

Who, then, controls the modes of material nature? It is the Supersoul. Often, though, after understanding the omnipotence of the Supreme, people wrongly conclude that the responsibility for all actions and all reactions falls on Him: "Because the Supersoul is the doer, He must also be responsible for my sinful actions. Why then should I receive the reactions for what is being caused by the Supersoul?" To remove this misconception, Kṛṣṇa speaks the next verse.

15 Nor does the Supreme Lord assume anyone's sinful or pious activities. Embodied beings, however, are bewildered because of the ignorance which covers their real knowledge.

Kṛṣṇa is advancing His description of the progression of transcendental knowledge, which will take us from knowing ourselves as souls to being liberated by becoming fixed upon the Supersoul.

Basic transcendental knowledge allows us to understand that we are not our bodies. Now we understand that the modes of material nature control our bodies. Both the modes and the living entities are controlled by the Supersoul. Although the Supersoul is the ultimate controller, He is not responsible for the living entity's activities or the reactions to them.

The fault in arguing that "Because the living entity is not the doer, he must not be responsible for his actions and their reactions" is that the living entity, though not the doer, is also not completely aloof. Śrīla Prabhupāda writes: "[The Supreme Lord] does not create a particular situation for any living entity, but the living entity, bewildered by ignorance, desires to be put into certain conditions of life, and thereby his chain of action and reaction begins. A living entity is, by superior nature, full of knowledge. Nevertheless, he is prone to be influenced by ignorance due to his limited power." The living entity must accept responsibility for his own actions.

The *Śrīmad-Bhāgavatam* purport to 10.87.25 states:

> Although the soul is in truth both conscious and active, the proponents of Sāṅkhya philosophy wrongly separate these two functions of the living force (*ātmani ye ca bhidām*), ascribing consciousness to the soul (*puruṣa*) and activity to material nature (*prakṛti*). According to the *Sāṅkhya-kārikā* (19–20),
>
> *tasmāc ca viparyāsāt*
> *siddhaṁ sākṣitvaṁ puruṣasya*
> *kaivalyaṁ mādhya-sthyaṁ*
> *draṣṭṛtvam akartṛ-bhāvaś ca*
>
> "Thus, since the apparent differences between *puruṣas* are only superficial (being due to the various modes of nature that cover them), the *puruṣa's* true status is proven to be that of a witness, characterized by his separateness, his passive indifference, his status of being an observer, and his inactivity."

tasmāt tat-saṁyogād
acetanaṁ cetanā-vad iva liṅgam
guṇa-kartṛtve 'pi tathā
karteva bhavaty udāsīnaḥ

"Thus, by contact with the soul, the unconscious subtle body seems to be conscious, while the soul appears to be the doer although he is aloof from the activity of nature's modes."

Śrīla Vyāsadeva refutes this idea in the section of *Vedānta-sūtra* (2.3.31–39) that begins, *kartā śāstrārtha-vattvāt:* "The *jīva* soul must be a performer of actions, because the injunctions of scripture must have some purpose." Śrīla Baladeva Vidyābhūṣaṇa, in his *Govinda-bhāṣya,* explains: "The *jīva,* not the modes of nature, is the doer. Why? Because the injunctions of scripture must have some purpose (*śāstrārtha-vattvāt*). For example, such scriptural injunctions as *svarga-kāmo yajeta* ('One who desires to attain to heaven should perform ritual sacrifice') and *ātmānam eva lokam upāsīta* ('One should worship with the aim of attaining the spiritual kingdom' – *Bṛhad-āraṇyaka Upaniṣad* 1.4.15) are meaningful only if a conscious doer exists. If the modes of nature were the doer, these statements would serve no purpose. After all, scriptural injunctions engage the living entity in performing prescribed actions by convincing him that he can act to bring about certain enjoyable results. Such a mentality cannot be aroused in the inert modes of nature."

How the living entity in the tight grip of material nature is the doer can be compared to the attempt of a small boy to lift a weight he has just seen his father lift. The boy first desires to lift the weight and then tries. He cannot possibly succeed, but his father sees his small son's desire, stands above him, and out of affection does the actual lifting. Thus the father has actually lifted the weight, but he cannot be considered the only lifter. Unless the desire had been expressed and the attempt made by the child, the father never would have helped and the weight would not have been lifted.

The living entity should not, like the child, become bewildered by false ego and pride and consider himself the doer of activities that he has no ability to perform. That does not mean, however, that the living entity can avoid the responsibility of having performed the activity, because it was he who expressed the desire, he who made the attempt, and he who wants to enjoy the fruit.

When the living entity is ignorant of his eternal relationship with Kṛṣṇa, he chooses his position as an independent enjoyer, which in turn welds him to material nature and places him under its control. Thus he is responsible for his own reactions.

Śrīla Prabhupāda writes in his purport:

> The Lord is *vibhu,* or omniscient, but the living entity is *aṇu,* or atomic. Because he is a living soul, he has the capacity to desire by his free will. Such desire is fulfilled only by the omnipotent Lord. And so, when the living entity is bewildered in his desires, the Lord allows him to fulfill those desires, but the Lord is never responsible for the actions and reactions of the particular situation which may be desired. Being in a bewildered condition, therefore, the embodied soul identifies himself with the circumstantial material body and becomes subjected to the temporary misery and happiness of life. The Lord is the constant companion of the living entity as Paramātmā, or the Supersoul, and therefore He can understand the desires of the individual soul, as one can smell the flavor of a flower by being near it. Desire is a subtle form of conditioning for the living entity. The Lord fulfills his desire as he deserves: Man proposes and God disposes. The individual is not, therefore, omnipotent in fulfilling his desires. The Lord, however, can fulfill all desires, and the Lord, being neutral to everyone, does not interfere with the desires of the minute independent living entities. However, when one desires Kṛṣṇa, the Lord takes special care and encourages one to desire in such a way that one can attain to Him and be eternally happy.

Although the living entity is not the ultimate doer, he still remains responsible for his actions and their results as long as his actions spring from his desire to turn away from Kṛṣṇa. The Supersoul acts as the living entity's best friend and fulfills his desires. Even though He is the supreme controller, He cannot be held accountable for the living entity's choices, for He acts only as sanctioner. The Supersoul, being neutral, is neither responsible for anyone's actions nor is He liable to accept the living entity's good and bad reactions. This is knowledge. Kṛṣṇa describes the results of understanding this in the next verse.

16 When, however, one is enlightened with the knowledge by which nescience is destroyed, then his knowledge reveals everything, as the sun lights up everything in the daytime.

Another way to analyze how knowledge leads to liberation is as follows. There are three doers. The living entity is doer No. 1. If he has knowledge, he realizes that all bodily activities are automatically carried out by the three modes of material nature. Therefore, the modes are doer No. 2. The modes consist of inert matter, however. Thus they simply carry out activities which are desired by the living entity and sanctioned by the Supersoul. Therefore the Supersoul, who only sanctions, can be called doer No. 3.

We become enlightened by accurately understanding the interrelations between the living entity, the three modes of nature, and the Supersoul. This knowledge removes ignorance. When ignorance is removed, the living entity takes shelter of the Supersoul and attains liberation.

17 When one's intelligence, mind, faith, and refuge are all fixed in the Supreme, then one becomes fully cleansed of misgivings through complete knowledge and thus proceeds straight on the path of liberation.

As described in this verse, after one achieves knowledge that he is different from his body – knowledge which is born of the mode of goodness (*sattvāt sañjāyate jñānam*) – to achieve liberation he must become "fixed in the Supreme." When we learn that the Lord is impartial and we fix our intelligence on that quality of the Supersoul, then our sins are destroyed, we become purified, and ultimately we transcend the material world.

And what of the impartiality of those who transcend the material world in this way?

18 The humble sages, by virtue of true knowledge, see with equal vision a learned and gentle brāhmaṇa, a cow, an elephant, a dog, and a dog-eater [outcaste].

True knowledge refers not only to knowing the difference between matter and spirit but to knowing the Supersoul. The learned person sees that the Supersoul has impartially sanctioned the desires of all living entities, regardless of their present karmic positions.

19 Those whose minds are established in sameness and equanimity have already conquered the conditions of birth and death. They are flawless like Brahman, and thus they are already situated in Brahman.

Sameness and equanimity can be experienced on the platforms of Brahman and Paramātmā realization, or Kṛṣṇa consciousness. The Brahmavādī sees everything as situated in Brahman. The Paramātmāvādī sees the Supersoul at work, impartially sanctioning the karmic reactions of all living entities. The Paramātmāvādī is undisturbed because he understands that everything is occurring by the Lord's will. Thus he remains calm even in an ocean of material turbulence. A devotee of Kṛṣṇa recognizes everything that happens to him as Kṛṣṇa's kindness, and everything therefore increases his devotion.

The *Śrīmad-Bhāgavatam* says:

tat te 'nukampāṁ su-samīkṣamāṇo
bhuñjāna evātma-kṛtaṁ vipākam
hṛd-vāg-vapurbhir vidadhan namas te
jīveta yo mukti-pade sa dāya-bhāk

"My dear Lord, one who earnestly waits for You to bestow Your causeless mercy upon him, all the while patiently suffering the reactions of his past misdeeds and offering You respectful obeisances with his heart, words, and body, is surely eligible for liberation, for it has become his rightful claim." (*Bhāg.* 10.14.8)

Such a devotee is *mukti-pade,* already liberated. More of his characteristics are mentioned next.

20 A person who neither rejoices upon achieving something pleasant nor laments upon obtaining something unpleasant, who is self-intelligent, who is unbewildered, and who knows the science of God, is already situated in transcendence.

A practicing devotee (*sādhaka*) should attempt to act in this way. However, as Śrīla Prabhupāda explains in his purport, such behavior is a symptom of a perfect devotee (*siddha*). Such a person does not identify with the transformations of the subtle body. His happiness and distress do not, therefore, bring him happiness and distress. Because he is not bewildered by what happens to him, but instead sees everything as Kṛṣṇa's mercy, he does not become entangled in matter. Text 21 continues to describe the symptoms of a person focused on the Supersoul.

21 Such a liberated person is not attracted to material sense pleasure but is always in trance, enjoying the pleasure within. In this way the self-realized person enjoys unlimited happiness, for he concentrates on the Supreme.

The practitioner uses his intelligence to reject sense gratification, and instead he seeks pleasure in the Supreme. The degree to which he replaces sensuality with spirituality is the measure of his success. Śrīla Prabhupāda explains: "The highest pleasure in terms of matter is sex pleasure. The whole world is moving under its spell, and a materialist cannot work at all without this motivation. But a person engaged in Kṛṣṇa consciousness can work with greater vigor without sex pleasure, which he avoids. That is the test in spiritual realization. Spiritual realization and sex pleasure go ill together."

When the devotee becomes connected (*yukta*) with the Supreme, he experiences unlimited happiness and loses all attraction to matter. Śrīla Viśvanātha Cakravartī Ṭhākura comments that just as a person eating sweetmeats has no inclination to eat mud, so a liberated person is not attracted to material sense pleasure.

In the next two *ślokas* Kṛṣṇa tells Arjuna why sensual desires are foolish.

22 An intelligent person does not take part in the sources of misery, which are due to contact with the material senses. O son of Kuntī, such pleasures have a beginning and an end, and so the wise man does not delight in them.

The *sādhaka* needs to fix this principle strongly in his intelligence: "Sense gratification equals misery." A *sādhaka* becomes free from the material modes by a combination of intellectual conviction and a higher taste.

The result of tolerating sense desires and not succumbing to their pushings is explained below.

23 Before giving up this present body, if one is able to tolerate the urges of the material senses and check the force of desire and anger, he is well situated and is happy in this world.

How long will we have to tolerate the pushings of the mind and senses? Does *māyā* give up? One day, do we wake up liberated, freed from the impediments caused by the mind and senses? This verse answers that sense attraction must be tolerated until death.

We can remain tolerant by fixing our consciousness on Kṛṣṇa. The pleasure of Kṛṣṇa consciousness, combined with the conviction that nothing in this world can bring lasting happiness, will help us tolerate the pushings of the body and mind.

The pleasure of spiritual realization is the topic of the next verse.

24 One whose happiness is within, who is active and rejoices within, and whose aim is inward is actually the perfect mystic. He is liberated in the Supreme, and ultimately he attains the Supreme.

Śrīla Prabhupāda writes: "Unless one is able to relish happiness from within, how can one retire from the external engagements meant for deriving superficial happiness? A liberated person enjoys happiness by factual experience. He can, therefore, sit silently at any place and enjoy the activities of life from within. Such a liberated person no longer desires external material happiness. This state is called *brahma-bhūta,* attaining which one is assured of going back to Godhead, back to home."

We must get a higher taste. It is urgent. We have to hear, chant and have good association; otherwise, over time, we will be unable to tolerate the urges of the senses.

Kṛṣṇa gives more symptoms of one seeking satisfaction in spirit, not matter.

25 Those who are beyond the dualities that arise from doubts, whose minds are engaged within, who are always busy working for the welfare of all living beings, and who are free from all sins achieve liberation in the Supreme.

After reading verses 24 and 25, we may think that achieving liberation is too difficult, and we may become discouraged. In text 24, Śrīla Prabhupāda's translation uses the word "ultimately," as if to caution us that the result won't be quickly achieved. Similarly, the qualities mentioned in these two verses are rarely found.

In the next verse, however, Kṛṣṇa speaks reassuringly.

26 Those who are free from anger and all material desires, who are self-realized, self-disciplined, and constantly endeavoring for perfection, are assured of liberation in the Supreme in the very near future.

How is it possible that something so difficult to obtain will be achieved "in the very near future"? Śrīla Prabhupāda answers this question by citing an analogous example: "By vision, by meditation, and by touch only do the fish, the tortoise, and the birds maintain their offspring. Similarly do I also, O Padmaja!" (The Supreme Lord speaking to Brahmā)

Śrīla Prabhupāda comments: "The fish brings up its offspring simply by looking at them. The tortoise brings up its offspring simply by meditation. The eggs of the tortoise are laid on land, and the tortoise meditates on the eggs while in the water. Similarly, the devotee in Kṛṣṇa consciousness, although far away from the Lord's abode, can elevate himself to that abode simply by thinking of Him constantly – by engagement in Kṛṣṇa consciousness. He does not feel the pangs of material miseries; this state of life is called *brahma-nirvāṇa,* or the absence of material miseries due to being constantly immersed in the Supreme."

Śrīla Baladeva Vidyābhūṣaṇa quotes the above analogy to indicate that for those who endeavor seriously (as described in this *Gītā* verse), perfection is readily available because the Supersoul is concerned about those who act in this fashion. By sincerely fixing their minds on the Lord, they evoke His mercy.

Kṛṣṇa has now finished His discussion of how to gain liberation by working in complete knowledge of the Supersoul. In the next two verses He explains how to achieve that same liberated condition through *aṣṭaṅga-yoga.* These two texts introduce chapter six, which covers *aṣṭāṅga-yoga* in detail.

27–28 Shutting out all external sense objects, keeping the eyes and vision concentrated between the two eyebrows, suspending the inward and outward breaths within the nostrils, and thus controlling the mind, senses, and intelligence, the transcendentalist aiming at liberation becomes free from desire, fear, and anger. One who is always in this state is certainly liberated.

Śrīla Prabhupāda explains how these verses fit into this section of the *Gītā:* "After explaining the above principles of liberation in the Supreme, the Lord gives instruction to Arjuna as to how one can come to that position by the practice of the mysticism or *yoga* known as *aṣṭāṅga-yoga,* which is divided into an eightfold procedure called *yama, niyama, āsana, prāṇāyāma, pratyāhāra, dhāraṇā, dhyāna,* and *samādhi.* In the sixth chapter the subject of *yoga* is explicitly detailed, and at the end of the fifth it is only preliminarily explained."

After giving this brief preview to chapter six, Kṛṣṇa ends this chapter by telling Arjuna how he can remain peaceful on, of all places, a battlefield.

29 A person in full consciousness of Me, knowing Me to be the ultimate beneficiary of all sacrifices and austerities, the Supreme Lord of all planets and demigods, and the benefactor and well-wisher of all living entities, attains peace from the pangs of material miseries.

Kṛṣṇa here summarizes many of the topics discussed thus far in *Bhagavad-gītā* and puts them in the context of achieving liberation. *Bhoktāraṁ yajña* and *sarva-loka maheśvaram* refer to Kṛṣṇa, not the demigods, as the final enjoyer of all sacrifices performed by one practicing *karma-kāṇḍa* or *karma-yoga. Bhoktaraṁ tapasām* refers to Kṛṣṇa as the goal and the beneficiary of the *jñānī's* attempts at austerities. *Surhṛdaṁ sarva-bhūtānām* is directed to the *yogīs* who meditate on the Supersoul, because it is the Supersoul who, as a well-wishing friend, accompanies the *jīva* from body to body.

Śrīla Viśvanātha Cakravartī Ṭhākura adds, "Kṛṣṇa is the well-wishing friend of all living beings. He is mercifully bestowing benefit through His devotees in the form of their instructions on devotional service."

Knowing Kṛṣṇa's position in relation to activities of *karma-kāṇḍa* or *karma-yoga,* understanding knowledge of Him as the goal of all *tapasya,* and finally recognizing Him as the well-wishing friend in everyone's heart brings us to the only true platform of peace: liberation from the material world.

Śrīla Prabhupāda expanded on *suhṛdaṁ sarva-bhūtānām* in a 1968 *Bhagavad-gītā* lecture:

> Kṛṣṇa is always our natural friend. That is stated in *Bhagavad-gītā: suhṛdaṁ sarva-bhūtānām. Suhṛdam* means *suhṛt.* There are different names in Sanskrit for different kinds of friends. One friend is called *bandhu,* one is called *mitra,* and one is called *suhṛt.* So Kṛṣṇa says, "I am *suhṛt,* which means "such a friend." A friend sincerely wants your happiness. A s*uhṛt* is a real friend. And *mitra* is social friendship. *Bandhu* is official friendship. But *suhṛt* means one actually desires good for his friend – "sincere friend." Kṛṣṇa is *suhṛt.* He's always wishing my good, and He is therefore canvassing me, "Please, you surrender unto Me."
>
> Just like a father says, "My dear boy, why you are acting independently? Foolishly you are suffering. Just surrender unto me. I shall give you protection." Similarly, Kṛṣṇa is a friend like a father. He's always asking, and He is going with me in every type of body. Even if I get the body of a dog, Kṛṣṇa is always there with me. Even with cats, dogs, hogs, or any lower type of animal, He has no hesitation, and He is so friendly that wherever His friend is going, He's also going there.

> As Paramātmā, He is doing friendly activities. He's sending His bona fide servant as spiritual master, He's coming as incarnations, and He's coming as a devotee, Lord Caitanya. He's helping us in so many ways. But we are so foolish that we are not accepting Him. Nobody can be a better friend than Kṛṣṇa. But we are so much unfortunate, so much captivated by the external energy, that we don't accept Kṛṣṇa as our friend. (Lecture, Seattle, October 14, 1968)

Jñāna (knowledge that we are eternal souls), renunciation, and sense control cannot actually give us liberation. We must take shelter of our dearmost friend Kṛṣṇa.

Śrīla Prabhupāda discusses this chapter in his purport: "This fifth chapter is a practical explanation of Kṛṣṇa consciousness, generally known as *karma-yoga.* The question of mental speculation as to how *karma-yoga* can give liberation is answered herewith. To work in Kṛṣṇa consciousness is to work with the complete knowledge of the Lord as the predominator. Such work is not different from transcendental knowledge." That transcendental knowledge is knowledge of the Supersoul, and that knowledge awards liberation.

Chapter Six

Dhyāna-yoga

In chapter five Kṛṣṇa explained how to achieve liberation through *niṣkāma karma-yoga,* and at the end of the chapter He explained how to achieve that same liberation through *aṣṭāṅga-yoga*. Now, in chapter six, Kṛṣṇa will describe the process of *aṣṭāṅga-yoga* in greater detail.

1 The Supreme Personality of Godhead said: One who is unattached to the fruits of his work and who works as he is obligated is in the renounced order of life, and he is the true mystic, not he who lights no fire and performs no duty.

Although one who takes *sannyāsa* ordinarily gives up performing fire sacrifices, here, for the third time, Kṛṣṇa asserts the importance of not giving up work. The true renunciant, the true mystic, performs his duty but renounces the fruit. That is Kṛṣṇa's request of Arjuna.

The phrase "lights no fire" refers to *brāhmaṇas.* One of the prescribed duties of the *brāhmaṇa-varṇa* is to perform a daily *agni-hotra* (fire sacrifice). Kṛṣṇa is again explaining that one who is unadvanced thinks, "I have knowledge; I don't have to perform my duty." Rather, an advanced soul performs his duties with detachment.

Kṛṣṇa repeats this point just before describing the *aṣṭāṅga-yoga* system so that we will not become confused. Although *aṣṭāṅga-yogīs* eventually go to the forest after renouncing their prescribed duties, Kṛṣṇa wants to make it clear that *aṣṭāṅga-yogīs,* like *niṣkāma karma-yogīs,* must first perform detached work before they are advanced enough to renounce the world.

Kṛṣṇa will now explain the relationship between *sannyāsa* and *yoga.*

2 What is called renunciation you should know to be the same as yoga, or linking oneself with the Supreme, O son of Pāṇḍu, for one can never become a yogī unless he renounces the desire for sense gratification.

Restraining the senses is not the only constituent in true renunciation of sense gratification. Even the desire for sense gratification must be renounced.

We have already learned that *karma-yoga* and *sāṅkhya-yoga* (*jñāna*) are the same in that they lead to the same goal.

Now we will learn that *sannyāsa* (renunciation) is the same as *yoga* (linking oneself with the Supreme), in that every *yogī* must be renounced, just as all *sannyāsīs* are renounced. Both *sannyāsīs* and *yogīs* reject the desire for enjoyment. In other words, a *yogī* cannot be perfect without renouncing the desire for sense gratification. As Śrīla Viśvanātha Cakravartī Ṭhākura says, "One who has not renounced his intention to enjoy sense gratification, that is to say, his hankering for material fruits, cannot be a *yogī*."

Śrīla Prabhupāda writes, "A Kṛṣṇa conscious person is simultaneously a *sannyāsī* and a *yogī*."

Kṛṣṇa now explains that the *yoga* process is divided into two levels.

3 For one who is a neophyte in the eightfold yoga system, work is said to be the means; and for one who is already elevated in yoga, cessation of all material activities is said to be the means.

The two stages of *aṣṭāṅga-yoga* are *yogārurukṣu* (the beginning stage) and *yogārūḍha* (the advanced stage). These are further divided into eight steps (*aṣṭa* means "eight," and *aṅga* means "parts"). One at the beginning stage (*yogārurukṣu*) must work; he is neither detached enough nor pure enough to renounce work. One can renounce work only at the advanced stage (*yogārūḍha*). Śrīla Baladeva Vidyābhūṣaṇa comments: "When the *yogī* has ascended to the achievement of *yoga,* of *dhyāna-yoga* in particular, when, in other words, he has become fixed in meditation, at that time *śama,* the cessation of all activities that disturb the mind, becomes the cause of his further advancement."

Of the eight steps in *aṣṭāṅga-yoga,* the first two are *yama* and *niyama,* following the prescriptions and prohibitions. After one learns to strictly follow the rules and regulations, he begins to practice *āsanas,* sitting postures (what people commonly call *haṭha-yoga*). When the *āsanas* are mastered, one begins *prāṇāyāma,* breathing exercises. The breath is intimately connected with the mind. Therefore *prāṇāyāma* helps to control the mind. When his mind is controlled, the aspiring *yogī* advances to the practice of *pratyāhāra,* withdrawing his senses from their objects. When he becomes detached, he practices first *dhāraṇā,* then *dhyāna,* different intensities of meditation. Such meditation leads to the final stage, *samādhi.*

Different transcendentalists attain distinct kinds of *samādhi.* In *samādhi,* the mind and the consciousness are fully focused on the Absolute. The *jñānī* focuses on Brahman, the Patañjali *yogī* on Paramātmā, and the *bhakti-yogī* on Kṛṣṇa.

Śrīla Viśvanātha Cakravartī Ṭhākura answers the question "Should the *aṣṭāṅga-yogī* perform his prescribed duties as long as he lives?" He says that this third text describes how in the *yogārurukṣu* (beginning) stage, one works in *niṣkāma karma-yoga* while simultaneously practicing *aṣṭāṅga-yoga.* That purifies his heart. When the aspiring *yogī* becomes elevated in his practice to the point of *yogārūḍha,* he gives up *niṣkāma karma-yoga* and practices *aṣṭāṅga-yoga* exclusively. Śrīla Baladeva Vidyābhūṣaṇa adds, "The *yogārūḍha* stage begins at *dhyāna,* which is described in the next verse."

4 A person is said to be elevated in yoga when, having renounced all material desires, he neither acts for sense gratification nor engages in fruitive activities.

Owing to his higher spiritual taste, the *yogī* renounces both material desires and the desire for fruitive pursuits. He thus attains the *yogārūḍha* platform. Such a *yogī* may choose to continue his work, which mostly consists of his prescribed duties, not out of attachment, but to set a proper example.

Nonattraction to sense objects is required for one in the *yogārūḍha* stage for the following reason.

5 One must deliver himself with the help of his mind, and not degrade himself. The mind is the friend of the conditioned soul, and his enemy as well.

6 For him who has conquered the mind, the mind is the best of friends; but for one who has failed to do so, his mind will remain the greatest enemy.

One must renounce the desire for sense gratification, or else his mind will degrade, not elevate him. Śrīla Prabhupāda emphasizes controlling the mind in his purport to text 5:

> It is stressed herein that the mind must be so trained that it can deliver the conditioned soul from the mire of nescience. In material existence one is subjected to the influence of the mind and the senses. In fact, the pure soul is entangled in the material world because the mind is involved with the false ego, which desires to lord it over material nature. Therefore, the mind should be trained so that it will not be attracted by the glitter of material nature, and in this way the conditioned soul may be saved. One should not degrade oneself by attraction to sense objects. The more one is attracted by sense objects, the more one becomes entangled in material existence. The best way to disentangle oneself is to always engage the mind in Kṛṣṇa consciousness. The word *hi* is used for emphasizing this point, i.e., that one *must* do this.

In the next three verses, Kṛṣṇa describes the symptoms of a person with a controlled mind on the *yogārūḍha* (advanced) platform.

7 For one who has conquered the mind, the Supersoul is already reached, for he has attained tranquility. To such a man happiness and distress, heat and cold, honor and dishonor are all the same.

8 A person is said to be established in self-realization and is called a yogī [or mystic] when he is fully satisfied by virtue of acquired knowledge and realization. Such a person is situated

in transcendence and is self-controlled. He sees everything – whether it be pebbles, stones, or gold – as the same.

His mind is *tṛpta,* satisfied. By what is he satisfied? By his *jñāna* (knowledge) and *vijñāna* (realization). Maintaining a satisfied mood is not easy because the mind tends to be whimsical. *Kūṭa-sthaḥ* means one is fixed or spiritually elevated. Before the mind gives up sense gratification and is able to be satisfied by *jñāna* and *vijñāna,* it may have to be beaten, just as a blacksmith beats metal on an anvil. One who has thus brought his mind under full control is eligible to give up *niṣkāma karma-yoga,* sit down, and meditate.

9 A person is considered still further advanced when he regards honest well-wishers, affectionate benefactors, the neutral, mediators, the envious, friends and enemies, the pious and the sinners all with an equal mind.

This verse describes the most advanced stages of the *yogārūḍha* platform. It is difficult for even a great sage to give up family attachment, yet Kṛṣṇa recommends *sama-buddhi:* the *yogī* must be equal to family members, friends, and enemies.

We tend to consider someone who appreciates us as a man of good discrimination, but view one who doesn't as envious. *Suhṛt* means a well-wisher. *Mitra* is a benefactor; *ari* a killer. *Udāsīna* refers to one who is neutral. A *madhya-stha* is an impartial judge – concerned, but neutrally mediating between belligerents. The *dveṣya* is envious. *Bandhu* means a well-wisher. How can we see all such persons equally? It is more difficult to see these equally than to view "pebbles, stones, or gold" equally. If one is able to achieve this platform, however, his meditation becomes uninterrupted.

In texts 10–32, Kṛṣṇa describes the practices of *aṣṭāṅga-yoga,* first in the perfected stage and then in the beginning stage.

10 A transcendentalist should always engage his body, mind, and self in relationship with the Supreme; he should live alone in a secluded place and should always carefully control his mind. He should be free from desires and feelings of possessiveness.

Having described the *yogārūḍha* stage, Kṛṣṇa now explains how to practice *yoga* in that stage. One must be *nirāśī,* completely free of material desires and possessiveness. He must also be *ekākī,* alone, in a secluded place, *rahasi.* He should not even be accompanied by disciples.

In his purport, Śrīla Prabhupāda brings Kṛṣṇa's discussion to its highest point by describing and then emphasizing *bhakti,* the topmost *yoga* practice, which Kṛṣṇa Himself will describe in the final verse of this chapter. Śrīla Prabhupāda's purport additionally describes how the direct practice of *bhakti* automatically fulfills the rigorous requirements of *aṣṭāṅga-yoga:*

> Kṛṣṇa is realized in different degrees as Brahman, Paramātmā, and the Supreme Personality of Godhead. Kṛṣṇa consciousness means, concisely, to be always engaged in the transcendental loving service of the Lord. But those who are attached to the impersonal Brahman or the localized Supersoul are also partially Kṛṣṇa conscious, because impersonal Brahman is the spiritual ray of Kṛṣṇa and the Supersoul is the all-pervading partial expansion of Kṛṣṇa. Thus the impersonalist and the meditator are also indirectly Kṛṣṇa conscious. A directly Kṛṣṇa conscious person is the topmost transcendentalist because such a devotee knows what is meant by Brahman and Paramātmā. His knowledge of the Absolute Truth is perfect, whereas the impersonalist and the meditative *yogī* are imperfectly Kṛṣṇa conscious.
>
> Nevertheless, all of these are instructed herewith to be constantly engaged in their particular pursuits so that they may come to the highest perfection sooner or later....
>
> All these perfections and precautions are perfectly executed when one is directly in Kṛṣṇa consciousness, because direct Kṛṣṇa consciousness means self-abnegation, wherein there is very little chance for material possessiveness....
>
> A Kṛṣṇa conscious person well knows that everything belongs to Kṛṣṇa, and thus he is always free from feelings of personal possession. As such, he has no hankering for anything on his own personal account. He knows how to accept things in favor of Kṛṣṇa consciousness and how to reject things unfavorable to Kṛṣṇa consciousness. He is always aloof from material things because he is always transcendental, and he is always alone,

having nothing to do with persons not in Kṛṣṇa consciousness. Therefore a person in Kṛṣṇa consciousness is the perfect *yogī*.

Kṛṣṇa next describes the basic practices of *aṣṭāṅga-yoga*.

11–12 To practice yoga, one should go to a secluded place and should lay kuśa grass on the ground and then cover it with a deerskin and a soft cloth. The seat should be neither too high nor too low and should be situated in a sacred place. The yogī should then sit on it very firmly and practice yoga to purify the heart by controlling his mind, senses, and activities and fixing the mind on one point.

The aspiring *yogī* must live alone, free from fear and attachment. He has to sit still (not stand or sleep) and focus his mind. He must sit on his own *āsana* (seat), not another's *āsana,* because *āsanas, kamaṇḍalus* (pots), and cloth should not be shared. Śrīla Prabhupāda describes aspects of the sitting place:

> *Śucau deśe pratiṣṭhāpya:* he must be situated in a very sanctified place. *Sthiram āsanam ātmanaḥ:* the *āsanam,* the sitting place, should not be changed. And how should the sitting place be selected? *Na ati ucchritam:* not too much raised nor too low. And *cailājina-kuśottaram:* "*caila*" means a cotton sitting place. Then deerskin: *yogīs* sit on either the skin of a tiger or the skin of a deer. Why? Because they are in a secluded place and these skins have some chemical effect. If you sit on a deerskin, then the reptiles and snakes won't disturb you. (Lecture, New York, September 4, 1966)

13–14 One should hold one's body, neck, and head erect in a straight line and stare steadily at the tip of the nose. Thus, with an unagitated, subdued mind, devoid of fear, completely free from sex life, one should meditate upon Me within the heart and make Me the ultimate goal of life.

After teaching proper sitting, Kṛṣṇa now teaches Arjuna how to meditate. *Acalam* means "unmoving," "fixed," and "unshaken." The *yogī* must not rock back and forth or look here and there.

He must also be a pure *brahmacārī*. The result attained after long practice is next described.

15 Thus practicing constant control of the body, mind, and activities, the mystic transcendentalist, his mind regulated, attains to the kingdom of God [or the abode of Kṛṣṇa] by cessation of material existence.

A *yogī* must know the Supersoul if he wants *śāntiṁ nirvāṇa-paramām,* the cessation of material existence. He must carefully avoid the desire for mystic *siddhis;* otherwise, he will not progress. Śrīla Prabhupāda writes in his purport: "The ultimate goal in practicing *yoga* is now clearly explained. *Yoga* practice is not meant for attaining any kind of material facility; it is to enable the cessation of all material existence. One who seeks an improvement in health or aspires after material perfection is no *yogī* according to *Bhagavad-gītā*."

Three great flaws in the processes of *karma, jñāna,* and *yoga* – dangers within each of the processes – make them hazardous for the aspiring transcendentalist. That is, they each offer powerful temptations. In *karma,* whether it be *karma-kāṇḍa* or *sakāma karma-yoga,* one tends to become attached to the fruits of one's work. With *jñāna-yoga,* the desire to merge into Brahman, thinking of the glories of freedom from both anxiety and service, tempts one. In *aṣṭāṅga-yoga,* one tends to desire mystic *siddhis* so that one becomes powerful and can even override the laws of nature. A *bhakta,* however, forever remains Kṛṣṇa's servant and thus avoids those hindrances by keeping his mind absorbed in Kṛṣṇa consciousness.

Kṛṣṇa next warns of some obstacles to the aspiring *yogī's* progress.

16 There is no possibility of one's becoming a yogī, O Arjuna, if one eats too much or eats too little, sleeps too much or does not sleep enough.

The proper balance in the stomach is one-half food, one-quarter water, and one-quarter air. If the *yogī* eats too little, the amount of air is increased and the body becomes disturbed. Sleeping must also be balanced. That is further described below.

17 He who is regulated in his habits of eating, sleeping, recreation, and work can mitigate all material pains by practicing the yoga system.

Śrīla Viśvanātha Cakravartī Ṭhākura explains that a *yogī's* recreation is walking, and Śrīla Baladeva Vidyābhūṣaṇa mentions that the *yogī* should restrict his speaking. By controlling all these activities, the *yogī* remains free from desires and strong in meditation.

In texts 10–17, Kṛṣṇa has described how to meditate. Now Kṛṣṇa will describe the perfectional stage of *aṣṭāṅga-yoga.*

18 When the yogī, by practice of yoga, disciplines his mental activities and becomes situated in transcendence – devoid of all material desires – he is said to be well established in yoga.

When the *yogī's* mind is undisturbed and remains situated in the Self, he is called *yukta:* connected, or, as in Śrīla Prabhupāda's translation, "well situated in *yoga.*"

19 As a lamp in a windless place does not waver, so the transcendentalist, whose mind is controlled, remains always steady in his meditation on the transcendent self.

This example illustrates the perfect stage of *yoga.* As a flame in a windless place does not waver, so the mind of a *yogī* in *samādhi* is perfectly steady.

20–23 In the stage of perfection called trance, or samādhi, one's mind is completely restrained from material mental activities by practice of yoga. This perfection is characterized by one's ability to see the self by the pure mind and to relish and rejoice in the self. In that joyous state, one is situated in boundless transcendental happiness, realized through transcendental senses. Established thus, one never departs from the truth, and upon gaining this he thinks there is no greater gain. Being situated in such a position, one is never shaken, even in the midst of greatest difficulty. This indeed is actual freedom from all miseries arising from material contact.

These verses describe the experience of the perfect *yogī* who has attained the Brahman platform. His fixedness is similar to that of the *sthita-prajña* described earlier (starting with Bg. 2.54). A devotee also experiences such steadiness, but his means to achieve *samādhi* is easier. Śrīla Prabhupāda confirms this at the end of his purport: "The best practice of *yoga* in this age is Kṛṣṇa consciousness, which is not baffling. A Kṛṣṇa conscious person is so happy in his occupation that he does not aspire after any other happiness. There are many impediments, especially in this age of hypocrisy, to practicing *haṭha-yoga, dhyāna-yoga,* and *jñāna-yoga,* but there is no such problem in executing *karma-yoga* or *bhakti-yoga*."

In texts 24 and 25, Kṛṣṇa prescribes the methods to attain the *yogārūḍha* (advanced) stage.

24 One should engage oneself in the practice of yoga with determination and faith and not be deviated from the path. One should abandon, without exception, all material desires born of mental speculation and thus control all the senses on all sides by the mind.

Without strong faith, one cannot possess determination. If we believe neither in the goal (*sādhya*) nor the method (*sādhana*) to achieve the goal, how will we remain determined? That applies to all spiritual practices. We require faith that following the process will award success. Perfection does not manifest quickly, especially for the *aṣṭāṅga-yogī*. Therefore the *yogī* must have fixed determination and enthusiasm that go beyond even the bounds of one life. Such a *yogī* thinks, "Even if I do not achieve perfection in this life, I must continue." He cannot become discouraged and say, "This is taking so long. Is it worth it?" In his purport, Śrīla Prabhupāda tells the wonderful story of the determined sparrow trying to recover her eggs from the ocean. He then concludes: "[T]he practice of *yoga,* especially *bhakti-yoga* in Kṛṣṇa consciousness, may appear to be a very difficult job. But if anyone follows the principles with great determination, the Lord will surely help, for God helps those who help themselves." We cannot succeed without blessings. Still, we have to show our sincerity by making a determined effort, as mentioned in the next verse.

25 Gradually, step by step, one should become situated in trance by means of intelligence sustained by full conviction, and thus the mind should be fixed on the self alone and should think of nothing else.

Śanaiḥ śanaiḥ means "gradually, step by step." Progress in *yoga* occurs slowly and steadily. Because a *yogī* cannot expect instant success, he is required to fix his intelligence and determination through hearing *śāstra*.

The means of success is next described.

26 From wherever the mind wanders due to its flickering and unsteady nature, one must certainly withdraw it and bring it back under the control of the self.

Here Kṛṣṇa uses three adjectives to describe the mind. *Niścalati* (wandering), *cañcalam* (flickering), and *asthiram* (unsteady). By steady intelligence the *yogī* must overcome all those mental tendencies. He cannot indulge his mind and gratify his senses. He must know for certain that yielding to the mind will destroy his tranquility. Rather, he should be fixed in the Self, not in his thoughts, which may be influenced by his previous passionate conditioning.

27 The yogī whose mind is fixed on Me verily attains the highest perfection of transcendental happiness. He is beyond the mode of passion, he realizes his qualitative identity with the Supreme, and thus he is freed from all reactions to past deeds.

Happiness comes to a *yogī* even before he attains perfection. Freedom from passion and ignorance situates the *yogī* in the pleasurable mode of goodness. Gradually, he realizes his qualitative identity with Brahman and becomes satisfied. A devotee's realization, however, goes beyond the *yogī's*. The devotee remains unsatisfied even after achieving his own happiness. His interest is pleasing Kṛṣṇa, which awards him far greater bliss.

In texts 28–32, Kṛṣṇa explains that the perfection of *yoga* is realizing the Supersoul.

28 Thus the self-controlled yogī, constantly engaged in yoga practice, becomes free from all material contamination and achieves the highest stage of perfect happiness in transcendental loving service to the Lord.

The previous verse described the *yogī* who attained self-realization, who realized that he is not his body but a soul qualitatively one with Brahman. This verse describes going beyond that realization to realization of the Supersoul. Thus the *yogī,* "one who is in touch with the Supreme Self," experiences *sukhena,* "transcendental happiness," because of *brahma-saṁsparśam,* "being in constant touch with the Supreme." This liberation is achieved by practicing *yoga* with a controlled mind and thereby contacting the Supersoul. Thus a *yogī* can gradually progress from an impersonal realization to a personal relationship. That means, however, that the Supersoul he is realizing will also gradually "turn into" Bhagavān.

Kṛṣṇa clarifies this point further in the next verse.

29 A true yogī observes Me in all beings and also sees every being in Me. Indeed, the self-realized person sees Me, the same Supreme Lord, everywhere.

Here it is described what a true *yogī* sees: the Supersoul within the body of all living beings. He also sees all living beings within the Supersoul. This is his vision, not simply an intellectual adjustment. The benefits of such a vision are delineated next.

30 For one who sees Me everywhere and sees everything in Me, I am never lost, nor is he ever lost to Me.

Śrīla Viśvanātha Cakravartī Ṭhākura further explains Kṛṣṇa's words: "When a *yogī* is constantly realizing Me directly with his senses, he is My worshiper and never falls down."

In his purport Śrīla Prabhupāda discusses the direct relationship between the *yogī* and the Supersoul in the context of full realization of Kṛṣṇa:

> A person in Kṛṣṇa consciousness certainly sees Lord Kṛṣṇa everywhere, and he sees everything in Kṛṣṇa. Such a person

> may appear to see all separate manifestations of the material nature, but in each and every instance he is conscious of Kṛṣṇa, knowing that everything is a manifestation of Kṛṣṇa's energy. Nothing can exist without Kṛṣṇa, and Kṛṣṇa is the Lord of everything – this is the basic principle of Kṛṣṇa consciousness. Kṛṣṇa consciousness is the development of love of Kṛṣṇa – a position transcendental even to material liberation. At this stage of Kṛṣṇa consciousness, beyond self-realization, the devotee becomes one with Kṛṣṇa in the sense that Kṛṣṇa becomes everything for the devotee and the devotee becomes full in loving Kṛṣṇa. An intimate relationship between the Lord and the devotee then exists...."I worship the primeval Lord, Govinda, who is always seen by the devotee whose eyes are anointed with the pulp of love. He is seen in His eternal form of Śyāmasundara, situated within the heart of the devotee."
>
> At this stage, Lord Kṛṣṇa never disappears from the sight of the devotee, nor does the devotee ever lose sight of the Lord. In the case of a *yogī* who sees the Lord as Paramātmā within the heart, the same applies. Such a *yogī* turns into a pure devotee and cannot bear to live for a moment without seeing the Lord within himself."

In the following verse Kṛṣṇa directly describes Supersoul realization as worshipful service to Him, if the *yogī* has proper knowledge.

31 Such a yogī, who engages in the worshipful service of the Supersoul, knowing that I and the Supersoul are one, remains always in Me in all circumstances.

In his purport, Śrīla Prabhupāda describes many of the characteristics of a *yogī* who sees the Supersoul and Kṛṣṇa "in oneness" (*ekatvam*):

> A *yogī* who is practicing meditation on the Supersoul sees within himself the plenary portion of Kṛṣṇa as Viṣṇu – with four hands, holding a conchshell, wheel, club, and lotus flower. The *yogī* should know that Viṣṇu is not different from Kṛṣṇa. Kṛṣṇa in this form of the Supersoul is situated in everyone's heart. Furthermore, there is no difference between the innumerable

> Supersouls present in the innumerable hearts of living entities. Nor is there a difference between a Kṛṣṇa conscious person always engaged in the transcendental loving service of Kṛṣṇa and a perfect *yogī* engaged in meditation on the Supersoul. The *yogī* in Kṛṣṇa consciousness – even though he may be engaged in various activities while in material existence – remains always situated in Kṛṣṇa.

By his proper worship, the *yogī* understands the actual situation of the soul in the material world. Kṛṣṇa will describe that next.

32 He is a perfect yogī who, by comparison to his own self, sees the true equality of all beings, in both their happiness and their distress, O Arjuna!

In Bg. 5.18 Kṛṣṇa spoke of the *paṇḍita's* equal vision toward all living entities. That vision, Kṛṣṇa explained, could be realized through the practice of *niṣkāma karma-yoga* at the stage of Supersoul realization. That same vision is available to the *aṣṭāṅga-yogī.*

Such a *yogī* also sees how the living entities suffer and are bewildered under the laws of *karma*. Therefore, his activities match his vision. Knowing from his own experience the distress resulting from material activities, he never acts in a way that brings distress to others.

Śrīla Prabhupāda contrasts a *yogī* and a devotee-preacher who is working for the welfare of others: "The cause of the distress of a living entity is forgetfulness of his relationship with God. And the cause of happiness is knowing Kṛṣṇa to be the supreme enjoyer of all the activities of the human being, the proprietor of all lands and planets, and the sincerest friend of all living entities....Here is a contrast between a pure devotee of the Lord and a *yogī* interested only in his personal elevation. The *yogī* who has withdrawn to a secluded place in order to meditate perfectly may not be as perfect as a devotee who is trying his best to turn every man toward Kṛṣṇa consciousness."

After hearing descriptions of *aṣṭāṅga-yoga* Arjuna analyzes his inability to follow the process.

33 Arjuna said: O Madhusūdana, the system of yoga which You have summarized appears impractical and unendurable to me, for the mind is restless and unsteady.

Can Arjuna maintain equal vision on the Battlefield of Kurukṣetra? One with such equal vision "observes Me in all beings and also sees every being in Me" (text 29) and "sees Me everywhere and sees everything in Me" (text 30). Can Arjuna really see Mahārāja Yudhiṣṭhira and Duryodhana equally? Arjuna presents his doubts to Kṛṣṇa, frankly telling Him that for him such vision is impossible. Could Arjuna, by the strength of his intelligence, see both his friends and enemies equally and simultaneously carry out his duty of fighting?

Arjuna thus points out why maintaining this outlook is so problematic.

34 For the mind is restless, turbulent, obstinate, and very strong, O Kṛṣṇa, and to subdue it, I think, is more difficult than controlling the wind.

Śrīla Viśvanātha Cakravartī Ṭhākura comments that the intelligence is sometimes compared to a sharp needle: "Even the very sharp needle of the intelligence cannot pierce the strong mind, any more than a needle can forcibly pierce iron."

Arjuna, however, compares his mind to the wind, an unstoppable enemy. The mind's unrest is also sometimes compared to a chronic disease that won't respond to medicine. The mind is *pramāthi* (always churning), *balavat* (unbreakable), and *dṛḍham* (obstinate). Its business is to accept a thing and then reject the same thing a moment later. It may then quickly accept that same thing again.

Texts 33 and 34 are Arjuna's response to Kṛṣṇa's question: "Why don't you just control your mind with your intelligence?" The next verse answers this question: "If controlling the mind is possible, by what means can I do it?"

35 Lord Śrī Kṛṣṇa said: O mighty-armed son of Kuntī, it is undoubtedly very difficult to curb the restless mind, but it is possible by suitable practice and by detachment.

Kṛṣṇa agrees with Arjuna's analysis. Śrīla Prabhupāda writes:

> The difficulty of controlling the obstinate mind, as expressed by Arjuna, is accepted by the Personality of Godhead. But at the same time He suggests that by practice and detachment it is possible. What is that practice? In the present age no one can observe the strict rules and regulations of placing oneself in a sacred place, focusing the mind on the Supersoul, restraining the senses and mind, observing celibacy, remaining alone, etc. By the practice of Kṛṣṇa consciousness, however, one engages in nine types of devotional service to the Lord. The first and foremost of such devotional engagements is hearing about Kṛṣṇa. This is a very powerful transcendental method for purging the mind of all misgivings. The more one hears about Kṛṣṇa, the more one becomes enlightened and detached from everything that draws the mind away from Kṛṣṇa. By detaching the mind from activities not devoted to the Lord, one can very easily learn *vairāgya*. *Vairāgya* means detachment from matter and engagement of the mind in spirit.

Śrīla Viśvanātha Cakravartī Ṭhākura comments: "Even when a disease is advanced, if the patient places himself under the care of an expert physician (the spiritual master), then the regular treatment (*abhyāsa,* practice, and *vairāgya,* detachment) will be effective. Kṛṣṇa calls Arjuna *mahā-bāho,* 'mighty-armed.' Arjuna's arms were so strong that he defeated even Lord Śiva. Lord Śiva, however, is not nearly as strong as the crest-jewel of all warriors, the mind. If Arjuna can control his mind by *yoga,* then he can rightly claim the title *mahā-bāho*. In this verse, Kṛṣṇa also calls Arjuna 'Kaunteya,' son of Kuntī, thereby telling Arjuna: 'Do not worry. You are the son of My aunt Kuntī. I will help you control the mind.' "

Kṛṣṇa continues instructing Arjuna on how to control the mind in the next verse.

36 For one whose mind is unbridled, self-realization is difficult work. But he whose mind is controlled and who strives by appropriate means is assured of success. That is My opinion.

Śrīla Prabhupāda writes:

> The Supreme Personality of Godhead declares that one who does not accept the proper treatment to detach the mind from material engagement can hardly achieve success in self-realization. Trying to practice *yoga* while engaging the mind in material enjoyment is like trying to ignite a fire while pouring water on it....Therefore, one must control the mind by engaging it constantly in the transcendental loving service of the Lord. Unless one is engaged in Kṛṣṇa consciousness, he cannot steadily control the mind. A Kṛṣṇa conscious person easily achieves the result of *yoga* practice without separate endeavor, but a *yoga* practitioner cannot achieve success without becoming Kṛṣṇa conscious.

Whether we practice *niṣkāma karma-yoga, jñāna-yoga, aṣṭāṅga-yoga,* or *bhakti-yoga,* we need to control the mind by *abhyāsa* and *vairāgya. Abhyāsa* means to practice the process or principles of *yoga.* We can succeed in *yoga* practice by following the procedures given by *guru* and *śāstra* and by renunciation (*vairāgya*) of unfavorable desires.

After understanding the formidability of the obstacles to progress in *yoga,* and after hearing of the processes to remove them, Arjuna speaks the next verse.

37 Arjuna said: O Kṛṣṇa, what is the destination of the unsuccessful transcendentalist, who in the beginning takes to the process of self-realization with faith but who later desists due to worldly-mindedness and thus does not attain perfection in mysticism?

Arjuna now wants to know what happens to a person who does not succeed in this practice. Such a person may have faith in the authority of the *yoga* scriptures and with such faith engage in *yoga* practice. He is not trying to cheat, but somehow his mind deviates him before he attains success. Thus, he has made progress, but he dies before he reaches perfection. Arjuna clarifies his question in the next verse.

38 O mighty-armed Kṛṣṇa, does not such a man, who is bewildered from the path of transcendence, fall away from both spiritual and material success and perish like a riven cloud, with no position in any sphere?

What happens to such a person, who is neither a materialist nor a spiritualist? As he has taken up spiritual practices, he has not been able to enjoy his senses. Thus he has reaped the benefits of neither spiritual nor material life. Does such a person have any position? Or, like a small cloud that has broken away from a big cloud, does he disintegrate?

39 This is my doubt, O Kṛṣṇa, and I ask You to dispel it completely. But for You, no one is to be found who can destroy this doubt.

Kṛṣṇa is the only one who can dispel Arjuna's doubt because He perfectly knows past, present, and future.

40 The Supreme Personality of Godhead said: Son of Pṛthā, a transcendentalist engaged in auspicious activities does not meet with destruction either in this world or in the spiritual world; one who does good, My friend, is never overcome by evil.

Kalyāṇa-kṛt, "one engaged in auspicious activities," does not refer only to the *aṣṭāṅga-yogī* but also to anyone engaged in legitimate and thus auspicious activities on the spiritual path. So Arjuna should not worry. Śrīla Baladeva Vidyābhūṣaṇa explains that by using the word *tāta,* "My friend," Kṛṣṇa is showing Arjuna special affection, addressing him as a loving father would address his son, or a spiritual master his intimate disciple.

After allaying Arjuna's fears that a fallen *yogī* loses everything, Kṛṣṇa next describes the destiny of such a transcendentalist.

41 The unsuccessful yogī, after many, many years of enjoyment on the planets of the pious living entities, is born into a family of righteous people, or into a family of rich aristocracy.

Unsuccessful *yogīs* are divided into two classes: those who fall after short practice and those who fall after long practice. The *yogī* who falls after a short period is described first. He goes to the higher planets inhabited by pious living entities. Śrīla Baladeva Vidyābhūṣaṇa says that after a prolonged life in which he has the opportunity to enjoy his senses, he again develops a distaste for sense gratification and returns to earth to take birth in a learned family of *brāhmaṇas* (*śucīnām*) or of wealthy and pious merchants (*śrīmatām*).

Śrīla Prabhupāda writes: "The real purpose of *yoga* practice is to achieve the highest perfection of Kṛṣṇa consciousness, as explained in the last verse of this chapter. But those who do not persevere to such an extent and who fail because of material allurements are allowed, by the grace of the Lord, to make full utilization of their material propensities. And after that, they are given opportunities to live prosperous lives in righteous or aristocratic families. Those who are born in such families may take advantage of the facilities and try to elevate themselves to full Kṛṣṇa consciousness."

The destination of the more advanced *yogīs* is explained as follows.

42 Or [if unsuccessful after long practice of yoga] he takes his birth in a family of transcendentalists who are surely great in wisdom. Certainly, such a birth is rare in this world.

This is a far better and rarer birth. It occurs because of the deep mental impressions (*saṁskāras*) developed by serious *yoga* practice. Śrīla Prabhupāda humbly and sweetly reveals his own situation in the purport: "By the grace of the Lord, there are still families that foster transcendentalists generation after generation. It is certainly very fortunate to take birth in such families. Fortunately, both our spiritual master, Oṁ Viṣṇupāda Śrī Śrīmad Bhaktisiddhānta Sarasvatī Gosvāmī Mahārāja, and our humble self had the opportunity to take birth in such families, by the grace of the Lord, and both of us were trained in the devotional service of the Lord from the very beginning of our lives. Later on we met by the order of the transcendental system."

43 On taking such a birth, he revives the divine consciousness of his previous life, and he again tries to make further progress in order to achieve complete success, O son of Kuru.

Spiritual advancement is never lost. Kṛṣṇa previously assured Arjuna, "In this endeavor there is no loss or diminution"

(Bg. 2.40). The *yogī* begins where he left off in his previous life. Jaḍa Bharata is an excellent example of this principle. Śrīla Prabhupāda explains, "From his life it is understood that transcendental endeavors, or the practice of *yoga,* never go in vain. By the grace of the Lord the transcendentalist gets repeated opportunities for complete perfection in Kṛṣṇa consciousness."

Kṛṣṇa explains this further in the next verse.

44 By virtue of the divine consciousness of his previous life, he automatically becomes attracted to the yogic principles – even without seeking them. Such an inquisitive transcendentalist stands always above the ritualistic principles of the scriptures.

His previous practice (*pūrvābhyāsa*) automatically attracts him (*hriyate hy avaśaḥ*), and he remains attracted despite the previous obstacles he faced. His being transcendental to *śabda-brahma,* or "above the ritualistic principles of the scriptures," refers to his being above the *karma-kāṇḍa* rituals leading to material enjoyment. He is attracted to spiritual, not material, life.

Finally, the next verse explains how and when the *yogī* will achieve his ultimate goal.

45 And when the yogī engages himself with sincere endeavor in making further progress, being washed of all contaminations, then ultimately, achieving perfection after many, many births of practice, he attains the supreme goal.

To become successful, a *yoga-bhraṣṭaḥ* (a *yogī* who has fallen from his practice) must work harder than *yogīs* who have practiced longer. Why? Because rigid practice (*prayatnāt*) is more difficult to achieve from a *śucīnām* birth (birth in a pious, religious family) or a *śrīmatām* birth (birth in a rich mercantile or royal family) than from a birth in a *yogīnāṁ dhīmatām* family (a family of transcendentalists possessing great wisdom). Children born in families of transcendentalists receive especially deep Kṛṣṇa conscious impressions and training early in their spiritual lives.

46 A yogī is greater than the ascetic, greater than the empiricist and greater than the fruitive worker. Therefore, O Arjuna, in all circumstances, be a yogī.

The *tapasvī* was mentioned in Bg. 4.28. Although he performs austerities, he has not yet acquired knowledge. The *jñānī* has knowledge and he knows *śāstra,* but his realization ends at Brahman. *Karmīs* and even *karma-yogīs* tend toward fruitive activities. Therefore they act piously by digging wells, constructing roads, and offering charity. The *yogī,* however, knows the Supersoul. He is most advanced. Thus this verse reveals the progressive rungs on the *yoga* ladder by clearly glorifying *yogīs* above *karmīs, jñānīs*, and *tapasvīs*. Kṛṣṇa now gives his final statement about the *yogī* of the highest caliber.

47 And of all yogīs, the one with great faith who always abides in Me, thinks of Me within himself, and renders transcendental loving service to Me – he is the most intimately united with Me in yoga and is the highest of all. That is My opinion.

Śrīla Baladeva Vidyābhūṣaṇa explains Kṛṣṇa's words: "Although there is a relative grading of superiority and inferiority among the *tapasvīs* and so on, still they are all inferior to My devotee, in the same way as all ordinary mountains, both tall ones and short ones, are inferior to a mountain made of gold."

He continues, "But is there anyone greater than the *yogī*? This question is answered in the words beginning *yoginām*. In the ascending hierarchy of *yoga* there are many *karma-yogīs.* Better than all of them is the one who has risen to the level of *dhyāna;* he is properly engaged (*yukta*). But one who has ascended to *samādhi* is even better engaged (*yukta-tara*). And one who has achieved *bhakti-yoga* in the form of hearing, chanting, and so on is the best (*yukta-tama*)."

Śrīla Prabhupāda explains:

> The culmination of all kinds of *yoga* practices lies in *bhakti-yoga.* All other *yogas* are but means to come to the point of *bhakti* in *bhakti-yoga. Yoga* actually means *bhakti-yoga;* all other *yogas* are progressions toward the destination of *bhakti-yoga.* From the beginning of *karma-yoga* to the end of *bhakti-yoga* is a long

> way to self-realization. *Karma-yoga,* without fruitive results, is the beginning of this path. When *karma-yoga* increases in knowledge and renunciation, the stage is called *jñāna-yoga.* When *jñāna-yoga* increases in meditation on the Supersoul by different physical processes, and the mind is on Him, it is called *aṣṭāṅga-yoga.* And when one surpasses *aṣṭāṅga-yoga* and comes to the point of the Supreme Personality of Godhead Kṛṣṇa, it is called *bhakti-yoga,* the culmination. Factually, *bhakti-yoga* is the ultimate goal, but to analyze *bhakti-yoga* minutely one has to understand these other *yogas.*

One can attain to *bhakti* through a gradual Vedic process – through *karma, jñāna,* and *yoga.* If one is fortunate, however, he can come in contact with Kṛṣṇa's pure devotee and directly take to Kṛṣṇa consciousness. By hearing the *śāstra* he learns to act in full faith, *śraddhāvān.* Gradually he progresses to the point where Kṛṣṇa has entered his very existence (*antar-ātmanā*), and the devotee becomes *mad-gata,* always absorbed in thoughts of Kṛṣṇa.

Śrīla Prabhupāda beautifully describes the result of becoming *mad-gatenāntar-ātmanā:*

> It is by great fortune that one comes to Kṛṣṇa consciousness on the path of *bhakti-yoga* to become well situated according to the Vedic direction. The ideal *yogī* concentrates his attention on Kṛṣṇa, who is called Śyāmasundara, who is as beautifully colored as a cloud, whose lotuslike face is as effulgent as the sun, whose dress is brilliant with jewels, and whose body is flower-garlanded. Illuminating all sides is His gorgeous luster, which is called the *brahmajyoti.* He incarnates in different forms such as Rāma, Nṛsiṁha, Varāha, and Kṛṣṇa, the Supreme Personality of Godhead, and He descends like a human being, as the son of Mother Yaśodā, and He is known as Kṛṣṇa, Govinda, and Vāsudeva. He is the perfect child, husband, friend, and master, and He is full with all opulences and transcendental qualities. If one remains fully conscious of these features of the Lord, he is called the highest *yogī.*

CHAPTER SEVEN

Knowledge of the Absolute

In earlier chapters Arjuna often encouraged Kṛṣṇa to speak by asking a question. At the beginning of chapter seven, however, Kṛṣṇa spontaneously explains how to attain the constant remembrance of Him that he described in the final verse of chapter six. According to that verse, remembrance of Kṛṣṇa characterizes one as the topmost *yogī.* Because this point is so important, Kṛṣṇa speaks about it without being prompted by Arjuna.

1 The Supreme Personality of Godhead said: Now hear, O son of Pṛthā, how by practicing yoga in full consciousness of Me, with mind attached to Me, you can know Me in full, free from doubt.

Kṛṣṇa begins by saying *mayy āsakta-manāḥ:* with mind attached to Me. Then Kṛṣṇa says, *yogaṁ yuñjan mad-āśrayaḥ:* by practicing *yoga* in full consciousness of Me... *asaṁśayaṁ samagraṁ māṁ yathā jñāsyasi,* you can know Me completely, without a doubt. How do we attain this? *Tac chṛṇu:* simply by hearing from Kṛṣṇa.

Hearing from Kṛṣṇa or hearing about Him develops the full faith described in Bg. 6.47. Hearing about Kṛṣṇa is essential to fix one's full consciousness on Him. Kṛṣṇa tells Arjuna to "just hear" because knowledge of Him is beyond the three modes of nature and is inaccessible through ordinary means. In his purport to Bg. 7.1, Śrīla Prabhupāda quotes the famous verses from *Śrīmad-Bhāgavatam* (1.2.17–21) starting *śṛṇvatāṁ sva-kathāḥ kṛṣṇaḥ*. These verses explain that *bhakti* begins when we hear about Kṛṣṇa.

In text 2, Kṛṣṇa further describes the knowledge He will now give Arjuna.

2 I shall now declare unto you in full this knowledge, both phenomenal and numinous. This being known, nothing further shall remain for you to know.

Kṛṣṇa glorifies knowledge about Himself. As Kṛṣṇa is everything phenomenal (material) and numinous (spiritual), grasping this knowledge leaves nothing unknown. Śrīla Prabhupāda explains: "Complete knowledge includes knowledge of the phenomenal world, the spirit behind it, and the source of both of them. This is transcendental knowledge."

Jñāna generally refers to knowing that the body and soul are different. Here, however, knowledge refers to knowledge of Kṛṣṇa and His energies. Śrīla Rāmānujācārya comments that *vijñāna* refers to knowledge of Kṛṣṇa's form.

Kṛṣṇa next says who is qualified to receive this knowledge.

3 Out of many thousands among men, one may endeavor for perfection, and of those who have achieved perfection, hardly one knows Me in truth.

Śrīla Prabhupāda writes about the potency of *bhakti:* "It is not possible for the Brahman-realized impersonalist or the Paramātmā-realized *yogī* to understand Kṛṣṇa the Supreme Personality of Godhead as the son of Mother Yaśodā or the charioteer of Arjuna. Even the great demigods are sometimes confused about Kṛṣṇa (*muhyanti yat sūrayaḥ*)."

Only a rare soul knows Kṛṣṇa in truth. Kṛṣṇa will emphasize the rarity of knowing about Him by repeating this point twice more in this chapter (texts 19 and 26). Still, in spite of such knowledge being so rarely attained, Kṛṣṇa now begins to explain it.

In the next nine verses (4–12) Kṛṣṇa explains that He is the source of both the material and spiritual energies. Because everything within our experience is a combination of these two energies, this information will enable Arjuna to see Kṛṣṇa everywhere, even as he stands on the Battlefield of Kurukṣetra.

After fixing Arjuna's attention by glorifying the knowledge He will speak, Kṛṣṇa next summarizes the entirety of matter in one verse.

4 Earth, water, fire, air, ether, mind, intelligence, and false ego – all together these eight constitute My separated material energies.

Kṛṣṇa has summed up the material world by describing its basic elements. His description ranges from gross to subtle. From these eight elements come the twenty-four elements that will be explained in chapter thirteen. The first five gross elements plus their sense objects (earth/fragrance, water/taste, fire/form, air/touch, and ether/sound) add up to ten elements. Mind, intelligence, and false ego bring the total to thirteen. The false ego is the cause of the five knowledge-acquiring senses and the five working senses. That equals twenty-three elements. Finally, we add the *mahat-tattva,* the twenty-fourth element, which is the cause of false ego. All these material elements are called *aparā,* inferior, because they lack consciousness. Kṛṣṇa has empowered this material energy to move separately and independently of His direct control. Thus it is called "separated," or *bhinnā.*

Kṛṣṇa has already explained in chapter two that the living entities are spiritual by nature. In the next two verses, Kṛṣṇa will explain that the material world consists of two parts: the material energy and the living entities (*taṭa-stha-śakti*).

5 Besides these, O mighty-armed Arjuna, there is another, superior energy of Mine, which comprises the living entities who are exploiting the resources of this material, inferior nature.

6 All created beings have their source in these two natures. Of all that is material and all that is spiritual in this world, know for certain that I am both the origin and the dissolution.

The combination of Kṛṣṇa's two energies makes up everything – both living and nonliving – in the material world. The two energies are called *kṣetra* and *kṣetra-jña,* and they will be discussed in detail in chapter thirteen. The point we are to understand here, however, is that everything ultimately consists of Kṛṣṇa, because everything is His energy.

In the next verse, Kṛṣṇa presents a simile to help Arjuna understand this point.

7 O conqueror of wealth, there is no truth superior to Me. Everything rests upon Me, as pearls are strung on a thread.

In the previous verse Kṛṣṇa told Arjuna that He is the creator and the destroyer. Now Kṛṣṇa explains that He is also the maintainer. Kṛṣṇa maintains everything, but no one can see Him, just as no one can see the thread that holds together a pearl necklace. Again, we can know Kṛṣṇa only by hearing from Him or about Him (*tac chṛṇu*) from an authorized source. If we accept Kṛṣṇa's assertion that everything material and spiritual comes from Him, we become able to see Him everywhere.

Śrīla Prabhupāda stresses that this verse presents a strong challenge to the impersonalists. Kṛṣṇa, the person, clearly states, *mattaḥ parataraṁ nānyat:* nothing is superior to Me. Kṛṣṇa explains this further in the following four verses by describing that it is He who is the essential or maintaining principle of various manifestations.

8 O son of Kuntī, I am the taste of water, the light of the sun and the moon, the syllable oṁ in the Vedic mantras; I am the sound in ether and ability in man.

We should appreciate Kṛṣṇa not only as the cause of everything but also as the essence of everything. Kṛṣṇa has already explained that the element water comes from Him, but what we most appreciate about water is its taste. That taste that quenches our thirst is Kṛṣṇa. He is its active ingredient, the essence of water.

Similarly, the essential principle of the sun and moon is light. Although sunlight heats and moonlight cools, that essential principle is Kṛṣṇa. *Oṁ* is the essence of the Vedic *mantras*. Sound is the essential element in ether. A man's ability is the essential quality he possesses by which he can become great. All these essential ingredients are Kṛṣṇa.

9 I am the original fragrance of the earth, and I am the heat in fire. I am the life of all that lives, and I am the penances of all ascetics.

We have heard that earth is one of Kṛṣṇa's energies. Here Kṛṣṇa explains that he has imbued the earth with a variety of fragrances. If we plant a rose seed (which has no fragrance) and add water (which has no fragrance), a fragrant rose will bud from the bush. Similarly, jasmine or gardenia seeds will each yield blooms with unique and wonderful fragrances that are all released from the earth.

The essence of fire is heat. Heat is necessary to cook our food. It is not only the food, however, that is maintaining us. We must also be able to digest the food. That fire of digestion is Kṛṣṇa's energy.

The soul, which is the essence of life, is an energy of Kṛṣṇa. The essence of an ascetic's life is penance, or his ability to tolerate austerities. That ability is also Kṛṣṇa's gift.

10 O son of Pṛthā, know that I am the original seed of all existences, the intelligence of the intelligent, and the prowess of all powerful men.

Śrīla Prabhupāda writes that *bījam* means "seed." The seed of material existence is *pradhāna,* the undifferentiated sum total of the material elements.

11 I am the strength of the strong, devoid of passion and desire. I am sex life which is not contrary to religious principles, O lord of the Bhāratas [Arjuna].

Thus Kṛṣṇa ends his description of how He is the essential or maintaining principle of various manifestations. The next verse provides a summary.

12 Know that all states of being – be they of goodness, passion, or ignorance – are manifested by My energy. I am, in one sense, everything, but I am independent. I am not under the modes of material nature, for they, on the contrary, are within Me.

We have now understood that Kṛṣṇa is both the cause and the essence of everything. Here Kṛṣṇa summarizes, adding that everything is under His control, including the three modes of material nature, which in turn control this world.

This verse ends Kṛṣṇa's discussion of His *para* (spiritual) and *aparā* (material) energies. At this point, one may wonder why we are prevented from seeing, knowing, and surrendering to Kṛṣṇa if He is, in one way or another, everywhere. Kṛṣṇa answers this question in the next two verses.

13 Deluded by the three modes [goodness, passion, and ignorance], the whole world does not know Me, who am above the modes and inexhaustible.

Rather than thinking of Kṛṣṇa as the source of everything, deluded people think, "As I am subject to the modes of nature, so is Kṛṣṇa." How they can understand Kṛṣṇa properly is described next.

14 This divine energy of Mine, consisting of the three modes of material nature, is difficult to overcome. But those who have surrendered unto Me can easily cross beyond it.

The three modes (*guṇas*) bind us tightly to the material world. *Guṇa* also means "rope." A rope is made strong by weaving together several strands. Similarly, these three modes woven together strongly bind the conditioned soul to illusion.

Despite their strength, the modes can be overcome by surrender. But to whom should the living entity surrender? Śrīla Viśvanātha Cakravartī Ṭhākura states that Kṛṣṇa is touching His chest and saying, *mām eva:* surrender unto Me, Śyāmasundara. Later in this chapter, Kṛṣṇa will criticize those who lack knowledge and therefore surrender to the demigods or the impersonal Brahman.

If surrender to Kṛṣṇa frees one from material nature – from birth and death – why doesn't everyone surrender, especially the learned?

15 Those miscreants who are grossly foolish, who are lowest among mankind, whose knowledge is stolen by illusion, and who partake of the atheistic nature of demons do not surrender unto Me.

Four types of people are devoid of piety, and thus they never surrender to Kṛṣṇa. Śrīla Prabhupāda writes that such people are not truly learned and therefore can be considered neither *mahājanas* nor *ācāryas*. Śrīla Prabhupāda describes each of these four types of *duṣkṛtinas* in his purport. Śrīla Viśvanātha Cakravartī Ṭhākura and Śrīla Baladeva Vidyābhūṣaṇa offer slightly different descriptions.

Mūḍhas

Śrīla Prabhupāda writes: "Most often, those who work very hard day and night to clear the burden of self-created duties say that they have no time to hear of the immortality of the living being. To such *mūḍhas,* material gains, which are destructible, are life's all in all – despite the fact that the *mūḍhas* enjoy only a very small fraction of the fruit of labor."

Śrīla Viśvanātha Cakravartī Ṭhākura writes: "*Duṣkṛtīs* are of four kinds. Some are *mūḍhas, karmīs* who are just like animals. As is stated: 'Those who are condemned by fate avoid the nectarean topics of Lord Acyuta and listen instead to impious narrations. They are just like dogs eating stool.' And: 'Who will not serve Lord Mukunda, other than one who is less than human?' "

According to Śrīla Baladeva Vidyābhūṣaṇa, Kṛṣṇa says, "Some are bewildered (*mūḍha*) by *māyā,* their intelligence dulled by fruitive work. They think that I, Lord Viṣṇu, am like Lord Indra, an agent of the law of *karma,* and that, like *jīvas,* I am subject to *karma*."

Narādhamas

Śrīla Prabhupāda writes: "In the *Gītā* the Personality of Godhead clearly states that there is no authority above Him and that He is the Supreme Truth. The civilized form of human life is meant for man's *reviving the lost consciousness* of his eternal relation with the Supreme Truth, the Personality of Godhead Śrī Kṛṣṇa, who is all-powerful. Whoever loses this chance is classified as a *narādhama.*"

"*Narādhamas,*" according to Śrīla Viśvanātha Cakravartī Ṭhākura, "having become civilized human beings by practicing devotional service for some time, later decide that devotional practices are impractical for achieving their aims in life and thus whimsically discard devotional service. The symptom of their being *adhama,* or the most fallen, is their intentional rejection of devotional service."

Śrīla Baladeva Vidyābhūṣaṇa adds: "Some people are made into the worst of men by the influence of *māyā*. Even having received a most excellent status by birth in a brahminical or high-class family, they become degraded to a low-class status by attachment to poetry or wealth. As is stated: 'Such people have been cheated by fate. Abandoning the nectar of topics about Lord Acyuta, they listen to impure narrations, just as dogs eat excrement.'"

Māyayāpahṛta-jñānīs

Śrīla Prabhupāda explains:

> In the *Gītā,* in plain and simple language, it is stated that Śrī Kṛṣṇa is the Supreme Personality of Godhead. There is none equal to or greater than Him. He is mentioned as the father of Brahmā, the original father of all human beings. In fact, Śrī Kṛṣṇa is said to be not only the father of Brahmā but also the father of all species of life. He is the root of the impersonal Brahman and Paramātmā; the Supersoul in every entity is His plenary portion. He is the fountainhead of everything, and everyone is advised to surrender unto His lotus feet. Despite all these clear statements, the *māyayāpahṛta-jñānāḥ* deride the personality of the Supreme Lord and consider Him merely another human being. They do not know that the blessed form of human life is designed after the eternal and transcendental feature of the Supreme Lord.

Māyayāpahṛta-jñānīs often follow atheistic Sāṅkhya philosophy and think that creation is enacted by material nature. Thus Śrīla Prabhupāda says that the *māyayāpahṛta-jñānīs* are "mostly very learned fellows – great philosophers, poets, literati, scientists, etc."

Śrīla Viśvanātha Cakravartī Ṭhākura states: "Some people have the qualification of having studied scripture, but their knowledge has been stolen by illusion. That is to say, they think that only the Nārāyaṇa form of God residing in Vaikuṇṭha is the eternal object of attainment by devotional service, and the mere human forms of Kṛṣṇa, Rāma, and so on are not. This is described in the words, 'Fools deride Me when I appear in My human form.' Even when those persons are apparently surrendering unto Kṛṣṇa, they actually are not surrendering to Him."

Śrīla Baladeva Vidyābhūṣaṇa explains Kṛṣṇa's words: "Others such as the proponents of Sāṅkhya philosophy, have had their knowledge stolen by *māyā*. The Sāṅkhyas belittle Me, even though My qualities of omniscience, omnipotence, and being the creator of all and the bestower of liberation are proclaimed by thousands of revealed scriptures. Instead they whimsically propose that material nature is the creator of all and the bestower of liberation. The reason that they raise hundreds of such faulty and deceptive arguments is simply the influence of *māyā*."

Asuras

Asuras take shelter of the demonic nature (*āsuraṁ bhāvam āśritāḥ*). Śrīla Prabhupāda writes that they are openly atheistic: "Such persons, whose very principle of life is to decry the Personality of Godhead, cannot surrender unto the lotus feet of Śrī Kṛṣṇa." Jarāsandha is an example of an *asura*. Although he had knowledge (*jñāna*), he hated Kṛṣṇa and even wanted to kill Him.

Śrīla Viśvanātha Cakravartī Ṭhākura says that Kṛṣṇa is stating: "Some people have taken shelter of the demoniac nature. Demons such as Jarāsandha aim and shoot arrows at My personal form, while these persons try to obliterate My personal form. They attack My form with bad logical arguments based on such evidence as the fact that My form is visible. Such persons certainly do not surrender unto Me."

Śrīla Baladeva Vidyābhūṣaṇa writes, "Some people have taken shelter of the demoniac nature by the influence of *māyā*. These are the proponents of the philosophy that the Absolute is pure spirit, without any qualities. In the same manner as *asuras* try to shoot arrows at My personal form, the source of all bliss, the Māyāvādīs attack My personal form, which is proven in *śruti* to be the eternal embodiment of living spirit.

The Māyāvādīs thus try to destroy My personal form with their arguments. The reason for such a mentality arising in them is, again, simply the influence of *māyā*."

16 O best among the Bhāratas, four kinds of pious men begin to render devotional service unto Me – the distressed, the desirer of wealth, the inquisitive, and he who is searching for knowledge of the Absolute.

Śrīla Prabhupāda clearly explains that although these souls are not pure devotees, they are pious. They can be elevated to pure devotional service by the association of a pure devotee.

When a pious soul turns to Kṛṣṇa out of distress, he is known as *ārta*. Such a person desires relief from sickness, calamity, or other material miseries, and this serves as his impetus to approach Kṛṣṇa. Gajendra is an example of an *ārta*.

A *jijñāsu* is curious. He inquisitively approaches Kṛṣṇa to understand the soul or to become self-realized. Śaunaka Ṛṣi is an example.

An *artha-arthī* may want to enjoy land, money, sons, or a wife in this life or the next. Fortunately, he asks Kṛṣṇa, not the demigods, to supply his needs. Dhruva Mahārāja is an example of an *artha-arthi*.

All of the above categories contain *sakāma* devotees. More specifically, they are *karma-miśra bhaktas*, because they ask Kṛṣṇa to fulfill their fruitive desires. The fourth category, a *jñānī*, is technically referred to as a *jñāna-miśra-bhakta* (or *yoga-miśra*). He approaches Kṛṣṇa not to have his material desires fulfilled but to gain knowledge and thus approach liberation. Therefore he is on the *niṣkāma* platform. Both Śukadeva Gosvāmī and the four Kumāras are examples of this type of pious soul.

Śrīla Baladeva Vidyābhūṣaṇa comments that a *jijñāsu* is mentioned in the Sanskrit verse between an *ārta* and an *artha-arthī* because both will naturally progress to the *jijñāsu* category as they advance in Kṛṣṇa consciousness. If they are not curious about Kṛṣṇa consciousness, then they are likely to later give up their interest in Kṛṣṇa's service.

Kṛṣṇa next tells us which of these four kinds of pious men is best.

17 Of these, the one who is in full knowledge and who is always engaged in pure devotional service is the best. For I am very dear to him, and he is dear to Me.

Kṛṣṇa here tells us that the *jñānī* is the best because the *jñānī* is free from material desires. The other three types of pious souls are also great because they turn to Kṛṣṇa, but often they leave Kṛṣṇa's service once their distress is alleviated or their material desires are fulfilled. A *jñānī's* devotional service, however, is steady. He is called *eka-bhaktiḥ,* interested only in devotional service. It is clear that Kṛṣṇa has used the term "*jñānī*" to refer to one who has abandoned his pursuit of *jñāna* and turned to *bhakti*. Such a *jñānī* loves Kṛṣṇa, and Kṛṣṇa loves him. In other words, Kṛṣṇa is not referring to one who practices *bhakti* to obtain knowledge.

Śrīla Baladeva Vidyābhūṣaṇa comments that this type of *jñānī* (the devotee in knowledge who desires only Kṛṣṇa's service) is so dear to Kṛṣṇa that the Lord is not satisfied just to characterize him as the best. He thus adds "he is dear to Me."

After hearing this verse, one may conclude that the three *karma-miśra-bhaktas* are insignificant and only a *jñānī* is important. Anticipating this, Kṛṣṇa speaks text 18.

18 All these devotees are undoubtedly magnanimous souls, but he who is situated in knowledge of Me I consider to be just like My own self. Being engaged in My transcendental service, he is sure to attain Me, the highest and most perfect goal.

Although the *jñānī* is special, the other three are also objects of Kṛṣṇa's affection because they have come to Him, even if it is to have their desires satisfied. Śrīla Viśvanātha Cakravartī Ṭhākura explains:

> Then, are the three kinds of worshipers beginning with the distressed not dear to You?
>
> "That's not the case at all," says the Lord in the verse beginning *udārāḥ* [text 18]. "Those who worship Me, taking something they want from Me, which I was prepared to give them anyway, are very dear to Me. They are giving so much to

satisfy Me, and I am very affectionate to My devotees. The *jñānī,* however, is like My own self. While worshiping Me, he does not hanker for any benefit – neither attainment of heaven, nor liberation, nor anything else. Therefore, in My opinion, such a *jñānī* is My very self, and I become subordinate to him."

The implied idea is: "I accept him as My very self because he has concluded that I, in the form of Śyāmasundara, am the supreme goal, not dissolution in the formless identity of Brahman."

In this way the *jñānī,* by possessing *bhakti* that predominates over other tendencies and is devoid of ulterior motives, comes to be considered by the *bhakta-vatsala* Personality of Godhead as His own self. But the devotee whose devotion is completely pure, who has no other desires at all, the Lord considers even greater than His own self: "My dear Uddhava, neither Lord Brahmā, Lord Śiva, Lord Saṅkarṣaṇa, the goddess of fortune nor indeed My own self are as dear to Me as you are." (*Bhāg.* 11.14.15)

Lord Kṛṣṇa is *ātmārāma,* self-satisfied. Still, He is inclined to enjoy with the *gopīs,* which indicates that He considers the *gopīs* even more dear than His own self. "Śukadeva Gosvāmī said: Smiling upon hearing despondent words from the *gopīs,* Lord Kṛṣṇa, the supreme master of all masters of mystic *yoga,* mercifully enjoyed with them, although He is self-satisfied." (*Bhāg*. 10.29.42)

How long has it taken the *jñānī* to attain to that level of devotion?

19 After many births and deaths, he who is actually in knowledge surrenders unto Me, knowing Me to be the cause of all causes and all that is. Such a great soul is very rare.

This verse stresses the rarity of pure devotion. The *ārta, jijñāsu,* and *artha-arthī* must come to the *jñānī's* level before they are eligible to go back to Godhead. This is also the clear message of the third and fifth chapters: material desires must be given up to make spiritual advancement. One has to rise to the platform of *niṣkāma* and then, from that level, fully surrender.

Bhakti is rare even among the *jñānīs* (*sa mahātmā sudurlabhaḥ*), and its development usually takes a long time (*bahūnāṁ janmanām ante*). Association with pure devotees quickens the process, because by association one hears and chants about Kṛṣṇa (the subject of the first part of this chapter), whose glories are the essence of transcendental knowledge. One thus understands that Vāsudeva, Kṛṣṇa, is everything (*vāsudevaḥ sarvam iti*).

One may then ask about the position of those who surrender, but not to Kṛṣṇa. These persons are neither among the four types of impious, unsurrendered men nor in the group of four types of pious, surrendered souls. Kṛṣṇa answers this question in the next three verses.

20 Those whose intelligence has been stolen by material desires surrender unto demigods and follow the particular rules and regulations of worship according to their own natures.

Śrīla Prabhupāda explains, "Less intelligent people who have lost their spiritual sense take shelter of demigods for immediate fulfillment of material desires. Generally, such people do not go to the Supreme Personality of Godhead, because they are in the lower modes of nature (ignorance and passion) and therefore worship various demigods."

Under the influence of the lower modes, the less intelligent foolishly think the demigods can fulfill their desires more quickly and effectively than Kṛṣṇa. In fact, Kṛṣṇa does fulfill His devotees' desires, but it takes longer, for He simultaneously purifies the hearts of all who approach Him.

21 I am in everyone's heart as the Supersoul. As soon as one desires to worship some demigod, I make his faith steady so that he can devote himself to that particular deity.

22 Endowed with such a faith, he endeavors to worship a particular demigod and thus obtains his desires. But in actuality these benefits are bestowed by Me alone.

The fruits that demigods offer their worshipers are ultimately awarded by Kṛṣṇa. Even the faith that demigod worshipers possess is given by Kṛṣṇa and not by the demigods. Although all is ultimately given by Kṛṣṇa, still, because demigod worshipers have not directly approached Kṛṣṇa, they cannot be liberated.

Kṛṣṇa will now compare the destination of demigod worshipers with that of His *bhaktas*.

23 Men of small intelligence worship the demigods, and their fruits are limited and temporary. Those who worship the demigods go to the planets of the demigods, but My devotees ultimately reach My supreme planet.

As the demigods eventually perish, so do the fruits that they offer. Both Kṛṣṇa and the demigods give fruits to their worshipers; but the demigods' followers are called *alpa-medhas,* less intelligent, because what they obtain will not long endure. Kṛṣṇa's devotees, even those who have material desires, will ultimately return to the eternal, spiritual world.

Despite Kṛṣṇa's words, some say that one achieves the Absolute Truth regardless of whom one worships. Śrīla Prabhupāda confronts this challenge in his purport:

> Here the point may be raised that if the demigods are different parts of the body of the Supreme Lord, then the same end should be achieved by worshiping them. However, worshipers of the demigods are less intelligent because they don't know to what part of the body food must be supplied. Some of them are so foolish that they claim that there are many parts and many ways to supply food.…Can anyone supply food to the body through the ears or eyes? They do not know that these demigods are different parts of the universal body of the Supreme Lord, and in their ignorance they believe that each and every demigod is a separate God and a competitor of the Supreme Lord. Not only are demigods parts of the Supreme Lord, but ordinary living entities are also.

One may complain that demigod worshipers put the same amount of effort into their pursuits as do the *bhaktas*. Why, then, do their results differ so vastly? Śrīla Viśvanātha Cakravartī Ṭhākura answers: "We go to whomever we worship.

The demigods, along with their fruits, will all be destroyed, whereas Kṛṣṇa, His service, His devotees, and His abode are all eternal."

Śrīla Prabhupāda mentions, however, that if the demigods are worshiped with an understanding of their position as the Lord's expansions, then the result of worshiping them is permanent. Bharata Mahārāja is an example of one who worshiped the demigods as Lord Viṣṇu's agents and not for material rewards.

In addition to the demigod worshipers, another class of men who surrender, but improperly, are the impersonalists. They are described next.

24 Unintelligent men, who do not know Me perfectly, think that I, the Supreme Personality of Godhead, Kṛṣṇa, was impersonal before and have now assumed this personality. Due to their small knowledge, they do not know My higher nature, which is imperishable and supreme.

Kṛṣṇa just described demigod worshipers as possessing small intelligence. Here He labels the impersonalists *abuddhayaḥ*, even less intelligent. *Abuddhayaḥ* can also be translated as "possessing no intelligence." Śrīla Prabhupāda systematically reveals their misconceptions in his lengthy purport.

If Kṛṣṇa and His form, characteristics, abode, and worshipers are all eternal, why can't He be seen? Why can't impersonalists, who are detached from matter and are therefore also transcendentalists, see Him?

25 I am never manifest to the foolish and unintelligent. For them I am covered by My internal potency, and therefore they do not know that I am unborn and infallible.

Because of the impersonalists' foolishness, Kṛṣṇa covers them with His *māyā* potency. They can neither see nor understand Him. Does that covering work both ways? Does *māyā* also prevent Kṛṣṇa from knowing them, as a closed stage curtain simultaneously blocks the audience's vision of the actors and the actors' vision of the audience?

26 O Arjuna, as the Supreme Personality of Godhead, I know everything that has happened in the past, all that is happening in the present, and all things that are yet to come. I also know all living entities; but Me no one knows.

Śrīla Baladeva Vidyābhūṣaṇa poses a question: "If a living entity can be covered by *māyā* and fall into ignorance, can this also happen to Kṛṣṇa?" "No!" he answers. *Māyā* is inferior to Kṛṣṇa and is controlled by Kṛṣṇa's prowess. She carries out His orders from afar and cannot affect Him.

Viśvanātha Cakravartī Ṭhākura explains Kṛṣṇa's words: "*Māyā* has no power to bewilder her own shelter. Therefore neither the external *māyā* nor the internal Yogamāyā can ever cover My awareness. And no one knows Me completely – no materialistic or transcendental person, such as Mahārudra, or anyone else – even the most omniscient person. That is because either *māyā* or Yogamāyā, as is appropriate in each individual case, is always covering everyone's awareness."

"*Māṁ tu veda na kaścana*" signifies that one who truly knows Kṛṣṇa is very rare.

In the next four verses, Kṛṣṇa describes how and when the living entities become covered by *māyā*. He also explains how they can become free from *māyā*.

27 O scion of Bharata, O conqueror of the foe, all living entities are born into delusion, bewildered by dualities arisen from desire and hate.

From the beginning of creation, the conditioned living entities are born into the illusory world of duality – desire and hate. They thus desire (*icchā*) one set of sense objects and are repulsed (*dveśa*) by another set, and they are capable of being repulsed by objects to which they were attracted only moments before. At times they are repulsed by thoughts of a Supreme who is beyond themselves.

Śrīla Prabhupāda says: "Such deluded persons, symptomatically, dwell in dualities of dishonor and honor, misery and happiness, woman and man, good and bad, pleasure and pain, etc., thinking, 'This is my wife; this is my house; I am the master of this house; I am the husband of this wife.' These are the dualities of delusion. Those who are so deluded by dualities are completely foolish and therefore cannot understand the Supreme Personality of Godhead."

This point further reveals the rarity of the *jñānī,* because, as described in texts 16–19, *jñānīs* are beyond being fooled by dualities of happiness and distress, male and female, and so on.

One may ask, after hearing text 27, whether anyone is, in fact, capable of overcoming illusion and becoming a devotee.

28 Persons who have acted piously in previous lives and in this life and whose sinful actions are completely eradicated are freed from the dualities of delusion, and they engage themselves in My service with determination.

Pious persons are qualified to take to devotional service, not exactly because of their piety, but because their piety attracts a pure devotee's mercy. It is the mercy of the Lord's devotee, and nothing else, that destroys sins and establishes faith in *bhakti.* Thus it is the *bhakta's* business to distribute Kṛṣṇa consciousness to others. Śrīla Prabhupāda writes, "All the devotees of the Lord traverse this earth just to recover the conditioned souls from their delusion."

Śrīla Baladeva Vidyābhūṣaṇa's comment points directly to the unique, magnanimous contribution of Śrīla Prabhupāda:

> But do we ever find devotion for You in anyone? It seems that this would not be the case, judging by Your statement that all beings in creation are born into delusion.
>
> [This is answered:] Those living beings who have received the merciful glance of the topmost pure souls will have all their sinful reactions destroyed. As stated in *śruti:* "The personal servants of Lord Viṣṇu wander this world to purify the conditioned souls."
>
> What characteristics are found in those who receive such mercy? This is answered by the phrase *puṇya-karmaṇām:* their activity of taking the *darśana* of great souls is *puṇya,* "attractive or charming."
>
> "Becoming firm in their vows and gaining determination by virtue of the association of great souls, they are freed from the

delusion of duality. Coming to understand the truth about Me, they engage in worshiping Me."

How munificent, then, was Śrīla Prabhupāda! He so widely cast his purifying glance that it fell on even the impious and those engaged in most unfortunate works, and thus he created their *puṇya-karmaṇām.*

Another kind of devotee – one with mixed intentions – is described next.

29 Intelligent persons who are endeavoring for liberation from old age and death take refuge in Me in devotional service. They are actually Brahman because they entirely know everything about transcendental activities.

Here Kṛṣṇa describes a fourth kind of *sakāma* devotee, one whose devotion is mixed with the desire for liberation from the cycle of birth and death. His position will be further discussed in chapter eight. Such a devotee is Brahman and knows everything about *adhyātma* (the self, or *jīva*) and *karma* (activities). Those three terms will also be explained in chapter eight, along with three more terms mentioned in the next verse.

30 Those in full consciousness of Me, who know Me, the Supreme Lord, to be the governing principle of the material manifestation, of the demigods, and of all methods of sacrifice, can understand and know Me, the Supreme Personality of Godhead, even at the time of death.

Three additional concepts are mentioned: *adhibhūta, adhidaiva,* and *adhiyajña.* Arjuna will ask about their meanings in the beginning of the next chapter.

By naming Himself as the governing principle behind the material manifestation, the demigods and acts of sacrifice, Kṛṣṇa directs the knowledge, desires, and service of many classes of individuals toward His lotus feet. The benefit of that – and this has special significance to Arjuna because he is standing on a battlefield about to fight – is that one with this consciousness can know Kṛṣṇa at the time of death.

Chapter Eight

Attaining the Supreme

Arjuna will now inquire about the six terms Kṛṣṇa used at the end of chapter seven: Brahman, *adhyātma, karma, adhibhūta, adhidaiva,* and *adhiyajña.*

Kṛṣṇa describes these terms one by one in the order that Arjuna asks about them. Later in the chapter, Kṛṣṇa also discusses *yoga-miśra-bhakti* (devotional service mixed with *yoga*), *śuddha-bhakti* (unmixed, pure devotional service) and the factors that determine a soul's destination when it leaves the body.

1 Arjuna inquired: O my Lord, O Supreme Person, what is Brahman? What is the self? What are fruitive activities? What is this material manifestation? And what are the demigods? Please explain this to me.

Arjuna first asks, "What is Brahman?" He wants to know if Brahman refers to the *jīva* or the Paramātmā. Śrīla Prabhupāda writes: "*Ahaṁ brahmāsmi:* I am spirit. It is said that one should understand that he is Brahman, spirit soul. This Brahman conception of life is also in devotional service,... The pure devotees are transcendentally situated on the Brahman platform, and they know everything about transcendental activities....Only persons who perform activities in Kṛṣṇa consciousness (*mām āśritya*) are actually entitled to be called Brahman, because they are actually endeavoring to reach the Kṛṣṇa planet. Such persons have no misgivings about Kṛṣṇa, and thus they are factually Brahman." (Bg. 7.29, purport)

Śrīla Baladeva Vidyābhūṣaṇa analyzes Arjuna's remaining questions as follows: "What is the *adhyātma*?" asks if the *adhyātma,* the self, pertains to the gross or subtle body.

"What is *karma*?" asks if *karma* (activity) refers to fruitive or spiritual activity and why, if they are equivalent, he should fight.

In "What is the *adhibhūta*?" Arjuna is asking, "What gross, physical things are you referring to – items such as pots or the bodies of living beings?"

"Who is the *adhidaiva*?" asks if the *adhidaiva,* the governor of the demigods, is a demigod or the *virāṭ-puruṣa* (the universal form of the Lord).

The prefix *adhi* is significant. One definition of it is "above, over and above." In another respect, then, Arjuna is asking about the identity of the *adhi,* the one above or ruling over the body, the physical manifestation, and the demigods.

In the next verse, he will ask about the identity of the one above all sacrifices, and further, where that Lord resides.

2 Who is the Lord of sacrifice, and how does He live in the body, O Madhusūdana? And how can those engaged in devotional service know You at the time of death?

Arjuna now inquires about the sixth term, *adhiyajña*. By inquiring about *adhiyajña* Arjuna wants to understand the identity of the one who is ultimately worshiped by the performance of sacrifice. Is it Viṣṇu? A demigod? And whoever He is, where in the body does He live?

In this verse, Arjuna asks an additional question, the answer to which becomes a major topic in this chapter: "How can those engaged in devotional service, the self-controlled, know You at the time of death?"

In the next two verses, Kṛṣṇa quickly answers Arjuna's first six questions.

3 The Supreme Personality of Godhead said: The indestructible, transcendental living entity is called Brahman, and his eternal nature is called adhyātma, the self. Action pertaining to the development of the material bodies of the living entities is called karma, or fruitive activities.

Arjuna's questions and Kṛṣṇa's answers are as follows:

1) What is Brahman? Kṛṣṇa tells Arjuna that the *jīva* is Brahman. Śrīla Prabhupāda writes: "Brahman is indestructible and eternally existing, and its constitution is not changed at any

time. But beyond Brahman there is Parabrahman. Brahman refers to the living entity, and Parabrahman refers to the Supreme Personality of Godhead."

2) What is the self? The nature of the *jiva*, the *adhyātma*, or self, is to eternally serve. Śrīla Prabhupāda writes: "The constitutional position of the living entity is different from the position he takes in the material world. In material consciousness his nature is to try to be the lord of matter, but in spiritual consciousness, Kṛṣṇa consciousness, his position is to serve the Supreme."

3) What is *karma*? *Karma* is not simply activity but specifically activity that develops a material body. Śrīla Prabhupāda writes: "When the living entity is in material consciousness, he has to take on various bodies in the material world. That is called *karma*, or varied creation by the force of material consciousness." Śrīla Prabhupāda's purport also gives a technical description of *karma* from the *Chāndogya Upaniṣad*. *Karma*, in this technical sense, specifically refers to the journey of a *jīva* to the heavenly planets, his return to earth, and his acquiring a human body after falling from the heavens in the form of rain.

In answering Arjuna's first three questions, Kṛṣṇa has clarified the difference between the body and the soul. He has also explained the difference between the activity of the body, which causes the soul's bondage, and the spiritual activity of the soul executed in the material world, which causes neither *karma* nor bondage. In other words, the soul is spiritual, its nature is devotional service to Kṛṣṇa, and its *karma* is the material body, or its conditioned nature.

4 O best of the embodied beings, the physical nature, which is constantly changing, is called adhibhūta [the material manifestation]. The universal form of the Lord, which includes all the demigods, like those of the sun and moon, is called adhidaiva. And I, the Supreme Lord, represented as the Supersoul in the heart of every embodied being, am called adhiyajña [the Lord of sacrifice].

4) What is the *adhibhūta*? Śrīla Prabhupāda writes: "The physical nature is constantly changing. Material bodies generally pass

through six stages: they are born, they grow, they remain for some duration, they produce some by-products, they dwindle, and then they vanish. This physical nature is called *adhibhūta*. It is created at a certain point and will be annihilated at a certain point." Kṛṣṇa is the ultimate governor of the ever-changing material nature.

5) Who is the *adhidaiva*? Śrīla Prabhupāda says, "The conception of the universal form of the Supreme Lord, which includes all the demigods and their different planets, is called *adhidaivata*." Śrīla Prabhupāda further describes the universal form, the *adhidaivata-virāṭ-rūpa,* in his purport to *Bhāg.* 2.1.29:

> The conception of the *virāṭ-puruṣa,* or the gigantic form of the Supreme Lord, is said to include all the dominating demigods as well as the dominated living beings. Even the minutest part of a living being is controlled by the empowered agency of the Lord. Since the demigods are included in the gigantic form of the Lord, worship of the Lord, whether in His gigantic material conception or in His eternal transcendental form as Lord Śrī Kṛṣṇa, also appeases the demigods and all the other parts and parcels, as much as watering the root of a tree distributes energy to all of the tree's other parts. Consequently, for a materialist also, worship of the universal gigantic form of the Lord leads one to the right path. One need not risk being misled by approaching many demigods for fulfillment of different desires. The real entity is the Lord Himself, and all others are imaginary, for everything is included in Him only.

6) Who is the *adhiyajña*? Where in the body does He live? Kṛṣṇa, as the Supreme Lord and Supersoul, is the enjoyer of all sacrifice (*adhiyajña*). Śrīla Prabhupāda writes: "Present in the body along with the individual soul is the Supersoul, a plenary representation of Lord Kṛṣṇa. The Supersoul is called the Paramātmā or *adhiyajña* and is situated in the heart."

In conclusion, when we perform sacrifices or we worship the demigods or the continuously changing material manifestation, we indirectly worship Kṛṣṇa Himself. If, however, we worship

Kṛṣṇa as the governing principle behind all three, then we can know Him "even at the time of death." And that is the answer in brief to Arjuna's final question: "How can those engaged in devotional service know You at the time of death?"

At the end of the seventh chapter, Kṛṣṇa said, "Those in full consciousness of Me, who know Me, the Supreme Lord, to be the governing principle of the material manifestation, of the demigods, and of all methods of sacrifice, can understand and know Me, the Supreme Personality of Godhead, even at the time of death." Kṛṣṇa explained in this verse the potency of knowing and remembering Him at the time of death through understanding Him as *adhibhūta,* the Lord controlling all material transformations; *adhidaiva,* the source of the *virāṭ-rūpa* and the demigods; and *adhiyajña,* the one whom the process of Vedic sacrifice is meant to please. Knowing Kṛṣṇa as the Supreme Lord in these ways allows Arjuna to work as His servant even on the battlefield and to fight on the spiritual (Brahman) platform in his actual identity. Such activities produce no *karma* and therefore do not develop another material body. Arjuna can now focus His mind on Kṛṣṇa and fight.

What is the result if one thinks of Kṛṣṇa at the time of death? Kṛṣṇa answers this question in texts 5–8.

5 And whoever, at the end of his life, quits his body, remembering Me alone, at once attains My nature. Of this there is no doubt.

6 Whatever state of being one remembers when he quits his body, O son of Kuntī, that state he will attain without fail.

Kṛṣṇa has just explained what happens when His devotees remember Him at the moment of death. The general law has also been stated: We attain in our next life whatever we remember at the time of death. Śrīla Prabhupāda's description of Bharata Mahārāja becoming a deer illustrates the point:

> Mahārāja Bharata, although a great personality, thought of a deer at the end of his life, and so in his next life he was transferred into the body of a deer. Although as a deer he remembered his past activities, he had to accept that animal body. Of

course, one's thoughts during the course of one's life accumulate to influence one's thoughts at the moment of death, so this life creates one's next life. If in one's present life one lives in the mode of goodness and always thinks of Kṛṣṇa, it is possible for one to remember Kṛṣṇa at the end of one's life. That will help one be transferred to the transcendental nature of Kṛṣṇa. If one is transcendentally absorbed in Kṛṣṇa's service, then his next body will be transcendental (spiritual), not material.

Whatever one's nature is saturated with (*sadā tad-bhāva-bhāvitaḥ*), one attains that – always – without fail.

Arjuna, perhaps relieved upon hearing this, may have thought, "Kṛṣṇa is telling me to remember Him. That is much better advice than telling me to fight." Kṛṣṇa, however, clears away this possible misconception in the next verse.

7 Therefore, Arjuna, you should always think of Me in the form of Kṛṣṇa and at the same time carry out your prescribed duty of fighting. With your activities dedicated to Me and your mind and intelligence fixed on Me, you will attain Me without doubt.

Often devotees wonder if it is necessary to remember Kṛṣṇa while they do their duty or whether doing their duty for Kṛṣṇa is sufficient. Here is Kṛṣṇa's answer. We should remember Kṛṣṇa *and* do our prescribed duties. Even though it may be difficult to remember Kṛṣṇa while we work, it will be far more difficult to remember Him at the time of death when our consciousness is disturbed and overwhelmed with pain. Therefore Kṛṣṇa wants us to practice now. Kṛṣṇa will repeat His desire for us to constantly remember Him in Bg. 18.57 and in other verses.

It is interesting that Kṛṣṇa says *mām anusmara* ("go on remembering Me") even before *yudhya ca* ("and fight"). We should remember Kṛṣṇa in devotion and work for His pleasure.

To remember Kṛṣṇa is so important that Kṛṣṇa repeats the point in the next verse.

8 He who meditates on Me as the Supreme Personality of Godhead, his mind constantly engaged in remembering Me, undeviated from the path, he, O Pārtha, is sure to reach Me.

Remembering Kṛṣṇa is such a powerful practice that it can even empower us to conquer our conditioned natures. We have different strengths, weaknesses, attachments, and misgivings according to our association with the modes of material nature. We can conquer our limitations, by Kṛṣṇa's mercy, through always remembering Him. However, as Kṛṣṇa states in Bg. 6.35, remembering Him takes constant practice and determination.

Kṛṣṇa next tells us how He can be remembered.

9 One should meditate on the Supreme Person as the one who knows everything, as He who is the oldest, who is the controller, who is smaller than the smallest, who is the maintainer of everything, who is beyond all material conception, who is inconceivable, and who is always a person. He is luminous like the sun, and He is transcendental, beyond this material nature.

Kṛṣṇa gives us ten ways to meditate on Him. Meditating on the Lord as the possessor of these specific qualities enables one to realize Him as the Supersoul, whom the *yogīs* meditate on as the goal of their *yoga* practice.

Thus Kṛṣṇa is discussing *bhakti,* but *bhakti* mixed with the aspirations of a *yogī* seeking liberation from the cycle of birth and death (*yoga-miśra bhakti*). In texts 10–13, Kṛṣṇa will explain the practices of these *yogīs,* who were also described in Bg. 7.29. Śrīla Prabhupāda says in his purport to that verse: "Those who are engaged in worshiping the form or *arcā* of the Lord, or who are engaged in meditation on the Lord simply for liberation from material bondage, also know, by the grace of the Lord, the purports of Brahman, *adhibhūta,* etc..."

10 One who, at the time of death, fixes his life air between the eyebrows and, by the strength of yoga, with an undeviating mind, engages himself in remembering the Supreme Lord in full devotion, will certainly attain to the Supreme Personality of Godhead.

The ultimate message of these verses is to remember Kṛṣṇa. That is *yoga's* goal. Fixing the life air between the eyebrows is useful only to assist a *yogī* in remembering Kṛṣṇa. Additional aids are mentioned in the next three verses.

11 Persons who are learned in the Vedas, who utter oṁkāra, and who are great sages in the renounced order enter into Brahman. Desiring such perfection, one practices celibacy. I shall now briefly explain to you this process by which one may attain salvation.

12 The yogic situation is that of detachment from all sensual engagements. Closing all the doors of the senses and fixing the mind on the heart and the life air at the top of the head, one establishes himself in yoga.

13 After being situated in this yoga practice and vibrating the sacred syllable oṁ, the supreme combination of letters, if one thinks of the Supreme Personality of Godhead and quits his body, he will certainly reach the spiritual planets.

Again, the important principle is *mām anusmara:* practice *yoga,* practice celibacy, chant *oṁ* – and remember Kṛṣṇa.

Having explained the practices of *yoga-miśra bhakti,* or how one attached to *yoga* and liberation can remember Him, Kṛṣṇa next discusses pure devotional service.

14 For one who always remembers Me without deviation, I am easy to obtain, O son of Pṛthā, because of his constant engagement in devotional service.

Śrīla Prabhupāda mentions in his purport that pure *bhakti* is indicated in this verse by the words *ananya-cetāḥ,* "without deviation of the mind."

> This verse especially describes the final destination attained by the unalloyed devotees who serve the Supreme Personality of Godhead in *bhakti-yoga*. Previous verses have mentioned four different kinds of devotees, the distressed, the inquisitive, those who seek material gain, and the speculative philosophers. Different processes of liberation have also been described: *karma-yoga, jñāna-yoga,* and *haṭha-yoga.* The principles of

these *yoga* systems have some *bhakti* added, but this verse particularly mentions pure *bhakti-yoga,* without any mixture of *jñāna, karma,* or *haṭha.* As indicated by the word *ananya-cetāḥ,* in pure *bhakti-yoga* the devotee desires nothing but Kṛṣṇa. A pure devotee does not desire promotion to heavenly planets, nor does he seek oneness with the *brahmajyoti* or salvation or liberation from material entanglement. A pure devotee does not desire anything. In the *Caitanya-caritāmṛta* the pure devotee is called *niṣkāma,* which means he has no desire for self-interest. Perfect peace belongs to him alone, not to them who strive for personal gain. Whereas a *jñāna-yogī, karma-yogī,* or *haṭha-yogī* has his own selfish interests, a perfect devotee has no desire other than to please the Supreme Personality of Godhead. Therefore the Lord says that for anyone who is unflinchingly devoted to Him, He is easy to attain.

Ananya-cetāḥ means undeviating, with no desire for heavenly pleasure or liberation. *Satatam* and *nityaśaḥ* mean always serving, with no break – for one's entire life – without consideration of time and place. Kṛṣṇa is so pleased by such an attitude that He becomes *su-labhaḥ,* easy to obtain, even if one is not yet on that platform but only desiring to reach it. Kṛṣṇa removes all obstacles from such a devotee's path. A vivid example illustrating the importance of *ananya-cetā bhakti* is found in Lord Caitanya's *līlā*.

Once Lord Caitanya went to evacuate. When He returned, He was holding His tongue. When the devotees saw this peculiar sight, they asked Him why He was doing that. Mahāprabhu replied that His tongue was acting so improperly that it wouldn't stop chanting Hare Kṛṣṇa even when He was engaged in such a filthy activity. Therefore He was forced to hold His tongue to restrain it. At that time, a small boy named Gopāla bravely spoke up.

Gopāla said, "No, no, this isn't the correct philosophy. Kṛṣṇa's names are pure and should be chanted at all times. For instance, if one were about to die, would he think, 'Oh, this is an inauspicious, dirty time and therefore I shouldn't chant?' No, at all times, regardless of the external purity of the situation, one should remember Kṛṣṇa and chant His names."

Śrī Caitanya Mahāprabhu replied, "You have properly understood the philosophy. You are my *guru*. You are Gopāla Guru."

Texts 15 and 16 describe the result one achieves by practicing pure *bhakti*.

15 After attaining Me, the great souls, who are yogīs in devotion, never return to this temporary world, which is full of miseries, because they have attained the highest perfection.

Śrīla Viśvanātha Cakravartī Ṭhākura explains, "Such devotees enter Kṛṣṇa's pastimes and happily take birth when Kṛṣṇa appears in the house of Vasudeva as his son."

16 From the highest planet in the material world down to the lowest, all are places of misery wherein repeated birth and death take place. But one who attains to My abode, O son of Kuntī, never takes birth again.

Kṛṣṇa makes it clear that His planet is supreme. The term *mām upetya* used in both texts 15 and 16 means "achieving Me." Kṛṣṇa, through repetition, emphasizes this, because He does not want us bewildered by a desire to go to the heavenly planets. He therefore clearly states that every situation in the material world is miserable. We should desire only *mām upetya,* to achieve Him.

To further establish the point, Kṛṣṇa compares the material world with the spiritual nature in texts 17–22.

17 By human calculation, a thousand ages taken together form the duration of Brahmā's one day. And such also is the duration of his night.

18 At the beginning of Brahmā's day, all living entities become manifest from the unmanifest state, and thereafter, when the night falls, they are merged into the unmanifest again.

19 Again and again, when Brahmā's day arrives, all living entities come into being, and with the arrival of Brahmā's night they are helplessly annihilated.

Kṛṣṇa is preparing a contrast to describe the benefit of leaving the material world for the spiritual world. Here Kṛṣṇa explains that even Brahmaloka, the most wonderful planet, is influenced by time. How does time affect us? Time forces the annihilation of every material body. Death, the annihilation of our body, rips us away from all the attachments we have developed over a lifetime. *Bhūtvā bhūtvā pralīyate:* this happens again and again. In addition, we are intermittently forced into an unmanifest state for a thousand *yuga* cycles – something not at all pleasant for the active soul.

Kṛṣṇa kindly describes this to awaken our detachment and renunciation, based on the realization that no happiness exists within matter for the eternal soul.

Next, Kṛṣṇa contrasts this disastrous situation with what those who become Kṛṣṇa conscious attain.

20 Yet there is another unmanifest nature, which is eternal and is transcendental to this manifested and unmanifested matter. It is supreme and is never annihilated. When all in this world is annihilated, that part remains as it is.

21 That which the Vedāntists describe as unmanifest and infallible, that which is known as the supreme destination, that place from which, having attained it, one never returns – that is My supreme abode.

These verses explain the *paramāṁ gatim,* the supreme abode mentioned in Bg. 8.15. That place is eternal and transcendental, and it is that supreme abode for which we hanker. Unfortunately, we search for it within the realm of time and matter. When we attain Kṛṣṇa's supreme abode, we, along with Kṛṣṇa's other devotees, will continuously exult in our loving relationship with Him. What a striking contrast to the material world! In the material sphere we are "again and again...helplessly annihilated." Spiritual life, however, carries us to the supreme destination, which is never annihilated.

The term *avyakta* does not mean "formless" in this context, but "materially unmanifest." That which is *avyakta* is composed of Kṛṣṇa's internal energy.

Kṛṣṇa next tells us how to attain that abode.

22 The Supreme Personality of Godhead, who is greater than all, is attainable by unalloyed devotion. Although He is present in His abode, He is all-pervading, and everything is situated within Him.

Here the words *tv ananyayā* reiterate the statement made in Bg. 8.14. *Ananya-cetāḥ satataṁ yo māṁ smarati nityaśaḥ:* our desires must be undeviatedly focused on Kṛṣṇa. Maintaining desires for *jñāna, karma, yoga,* and so on, prevents us from attaining Kṛṣṇa.

Kṛṣṇa has now concluded describing the spiritual world and the process of reaching it. In the final six verses of this chapter Kṛṣṇa discusses the process by which a soul should leave his body to attain the Supreme.

23 O best of the Bhāratas, I shall now explain to you the different times at which, passing away from this world, the yogī does or does not come back.

These four verses (23–26) pertain to the *jñāna-yogīs, karma-yogīs,* and *aṣṭāṅga-yogīs,* and they explain how *yogīs* must carefully plan their deaths so they will not return to the material world. The last two verses of this chapter (27–28) are for the devotees.

24 Those who know the Supreme Brahman attain that Supreme by passing away from the world during the influence of the fiery god, in the light, at an auspicious moment of the day, during the fortnight of the waxing moon, or during the six months when the sun travels in the north.

This verse is for the *jñāna-yogī*. Śrīla Prabhupāda writes: "When fire, light, day, and the fortnight of the moon are mentioned, it is to be understood that over all of them there are various presiding deities who make arrangements for the passage of the soul. At the time of death, the mind carries one on the path to a new life. If one leaves the body at the time designated above, either accidentally or by arrangement, it is possible for him to attain the impersonal *brahmajyoti*."

When one leaves by this method, the fire god takes him up to a certain point and hands him over to the next demigod, who turns him over to another. He passes through segment after segment of the universe until he reaches Brahman.

The next verse discusses the destination of the *karma-kāṇḍī,* or fruitive worker. Unfortunately, after completing his allotted period of heavenly enjoyment, he must return again to earth.

25 The mystic who passes away from this world during the smoke, the night, the fortnight of the waning moon, or the six months when the sun passes to the south reaches the moon planet but again comes back.

This verse repeats what Śrīla Prabhupāda discussed in the purport to Bg. 8.3: The *karma-kāṇḍī,* devoid of true spiritual desire, returns again to earth when his pious credits are nearly exhausted.

26 According to Vedic opinion, there are two ways of passing from this world – one in light and one in darkness. When one passes in light, he does not come back; but when one passes in darkness, he returns.

This verse summarizes the two paths discussed in verses 24 and 25. These two paths always exist because the material world is beginningless.

How does knowledge of these paths affect devotees?

27 Although the devotees know these two paths, O Arjuna, they are never bewildered. Therefore be always fixed in devotion.

Devotees remain unconcerned about these two paths because their attention is focused only on devotional service. Simultaneously, their understanding of the adverse consequences of engaging in fruitive activities, as outlined in text 25, serves to intensify their commitment. The final verse in this chapter underscores the knowledge that fixes a devotee on the path of devotion.

28 A person who accepts the path of devotional service is not bereft of the results derived from studying the Vedas, performing austere sacrifices, giving charity or pursuing philosophical and fruitive activities. Simply by performing devotional service, he attains all these, and at the end he reaches the supreme eternal abode.

This verse summarizes chapters seven and eight by describing the supreme position of the *bhakti* path. At the end of chapter six (46–47), we heard that devotees are greater than ascetics (*tapasvīs*), empiricists (*jñānīs*), and fruitive workers (*karmīs*). This verse clarifies that point by explaining *how* a devotee is best. By his devotion, a devotee automatically gains the results of all other paths without even desiring them. More importantly, however, devotees enter the spiritual world.

Śrīla Prabhupāda places these two chapters in the context of the entire *Bhagavad-gītā:* "The words *idaṁ viditvā* indicate that one should understand the instructions given by Śrī Kṛṣṇa in this chapter and the seventh chapter of *Bhagavad-gītā*. One should try to understand these chapters not by scholarship or mental speculation but by hearing them in association with devotees. Chapters seven through twelve are the essence of *Bhagavad-gītā*. The first six and the last six chapters are like coverings for the middle six chapters, which are especially protected by the Lord. If one is fortunate enough to understand *Bhagavad-gītā* – especially these middle six chapters – in the association of devotees, then his life at once becomes glorified beyond all penances, sacrifices, charities, speculations, etc., for one can achieve all the results of these activities simply by Kṛṣṇa consciousness."

Chapter Nine

The Most Confidential Knowledge

Chapter seven and chapter nine share various themes: hearing from Kṛṣṇa (7.1–2 / 9.1–2); the relationship between Kṛṣṇa and material nature (7.4–7, 7.12 / 9.4–10); Kṛṣṇa's potency manifested within matter (7.8–11 / 9.16–19); worship of demigods contrasted with worship of Kṛṣṇa (7.20–23 / 9.20–28); and the impersonalists' knowledge of Kṛṣṇa contrasted with that of devotees (7.24–26 / 9.11–15).

Despite those thematic similarities, chapter nine, not seven, is entitled "The Most Confidential Knowledge." Śrīla Prabhupāda writes in his first purport to this chapter: "The matters which are described in the ninth chapter deal with unalloyed pure devotion. Therefore this is called the most confidential."

Śrīla Viśvanātha Cakravartī Ṭhākura describes Kṛṣṇa's explanation of the progression within the *Gītā* chapters as follows: "The knowledge useful for liberation taught in the second, third, and subsequent chapters is confidential. The knowledge useful for attaining Me taught in the seventh and eighth chapters is more confidential, because by that knowledge the truth about the Personality of Godhead is known. That knowledge is the science of devotional service. In this chapter, however, the word 'knowledge' needs to be interpreted as meaning *bhakti*. It is not the same knowledge described in the first six chapters."

In the eighth chapter, Kṛṣṇa explained that His devotee, fixed solely on Him (*ananya*), surpasses both the path of light and the path of darkness. In this chapter, Kṛṣṇa will explain, again without being prompted by Arjuna, how to become an *ananya-bhakta*. It starts with hearing.

1 The Supreme Personality of Godhead said: My dear Arjuna, because you are never envious of Me, I shall impart to you this most confidential knowledge and realization, knowing which you shall be relieved of the miseries of material existence.

The first three verses of this chapter glorify its contents. Later, Kṛṣṇa will describe His inconceivable opulence, which will help fix a nonenvious soul in unswerving devotional service by increasing his knowledge, appreciation, and awe.

This verse makes three points: 1) one becomes advanced by hearing about Kṛṣṇa, 2) one must be nonenvious to hear properly, and 3) one becomes free from material miseries when he hears properly and cultivates devotional practices.

2 This knowledge is the king of education, the most secret of all secrets. It is the purest knowledge, and because it gives direct perception of the self by realization, it is the perfection of religion. It is everlasting, and it is joyfully performed.

Su-sukham indicates that this knowledge will bring us great happiness and that its application, devotional service, is joyfully performed. *Bhakti-yoga* is joyfully performed because it entails using our senses in Kṛṣṇa's service. *Bhakti-yoga* does not require, as *jñāna-yoga* does, that we renounce all activities. Renouncing sense activities does not bring joy, but, rather, dryness and misery.

Bhakti-yoga is also easy to perform. As we will find out in text 26, a devotee need offer Kṛṣṇa only a leaf, flower, fruit, and water to satisfy Him.

Pure devotional service is beyond the modes of nature and transcends liberation. Therefore it is eternal. *Avyayam* implies that a devotee's advancement can never be destroyed.

Śrīla Baladeva Vidyābhūṣaṇa asserts that *rāja-vidyā rāja-guhyam* indicates "the knowledge of kings, the secret of kings." It is "the knowledge, or more exactly, the meditational worship, of those who, like kings, have magnanimous, compassionate hearts. They are unlike the cripple-hearted *karmīs*, who worship demigods with the desire to attain sons and other material benefits. Kings, even when they fail to hide their treasures of gems and other valuables, keep their private counsel very hidden. In the same way, even when My devotees do not conceal other kinds of knowledge, they keep this knowledge concealed."

The word *pavitram* means that this knowledge purifies all four stages of sinful reactions. In his purport Śrīla Prabhupāda quotes a verse from the *Padma Purāṇa* to substantiate this point. Different stages of reactions to sinful activities can be observed. Some reactions are already fructified and are giving us distress and pain (*prārabdha*). Sinful reactions may be just waiting to take effect (*phalonmukha*), reactions may be still further dormant (*kūṭa*), or the reactions may be in a seedlike state (*bīja*). In any case, all types of sinful reactions are vanquished one after another if a person engages in the devotional service of Lord Viṣṇu.

Śrīla Baladeva Vidyābhūṣaṇa says, "Because this *dharma* (*bhakti-yoga*) is so joyfully performed, one may wonder who would remain in *saṁsāra*." Kṛṣṇa addresses this point in the next verse.

3 Those who are not faithful in this devotional service cannot attain Me, O conqueror of enemies. Therefore they return to the path of birth and death in this material world.

The faithless cannot attain Kṛṣṇa. Despite Kṛṣṇa's repeated words, they cannot accept the supreme position of *bhakti*. Thus they take birth again and again in this world.

Kṛṣṇa has completed His glorification of the knowledge He will speak. In the next group of verses (4–10), He begins describing His own *acintya-bhedābheda* relationship with the material world.

4 By Me, in My unmanifested form, this entire universe is pervaded. All beings are in Me, but I am not in them.

By the term "unmanifested form" (*avyakta-mūrtinā*), Kṛṣṇa explains that although His form is ever present, we cannot see it with our gross senses. To confirm this point, Śrīla Prabhupāda quotes the verse beginning *ataḥ śrī-kṛṣṇa-nāmādi* from *Bhakti-rasāmṛta-sindhu* (which is originally from the *Padma Purāṇa*). It says that because Kṛṣṇa's form, qualities, pastimes, etc., are all on the absolute platform, material senses cannot apprehend them; but when a conditioned soul is awakened to Kṛṣṇa consciousness and renders service by using his tongue to chant the Lord's holy name and taste the remnants of the Lord's food, the tongue is purified, and one's understanding of Kṛṣṇa gradually blossoms.

Here, Kṛṣṇa begins to describe His simultaneous connectedness and nonconnectedness with matter. The material world rests on His energy, but He is aloof. He is the source of the material world, and He maintains it, but He does not directly associate with it. He is free from material nature, but material nature is not free from Him.

Gaining *aiśvarya-jñāna,* knowledge of Kṛṣṇa's inconceivably opulent potency – all matter rests on Him yet He remains aloof – should stimulate our reverence and devotion.

5 And yet everything that is created does not rest in Me. Behold My mystic opulence! Although I am the maintainer of all living entities and although I am everywhere, I am not a part of this cosmic manifestation, for My Self is the very source of creation.

Śrīla Baladeva Vidyābhūṣaṇa explains that Kṛṣṇa has presented an apparent contradiction. He first said, "All beings are in Me," yet now He says the opposite: "And yet everything that is created does not rest in Me." Within the realm of Kṛṣṇa's inconceivable potency, or His *yogam aiśvaram* (mystic opulence), everything rests in Kṛṣṇa, but that does not present even the smallest of burdens to Him. He maintains all that exists while remaining completely separate and detached in the spiritual world.

To help us understand His inconceivable and mystical relationship with the material energy, Kṛṣṇa offers an analogous example.

6 Understand that as the mighty wind, blowing everywhere, rests always in the sky, all created beings rest in Me.

Although all living entities are within Kṛṣṇa, are dependent on Kṛṣṇa and are supported by Kṛṣṇa, they nevertheless act independently. How can one who is completely dependent act independently? This is an inconceivable feature of the relationship between the living entities and Kṛṣṇa.

Kṛṣṇa provides an analogy to help us understand. The sky,

like an upside-down bowl, contains the wind. In the same way, "all created beings rest in Me." Just as the sky is detached from the wind, the wind, though in the sky, blows freely and independently. The sky restricts only the area of movement, not the movement itself.

Kṛṣṇa thus limits the activities of the conditioned living entities, regardless of the extent of their power, to the circumference of the material world. Within the material sphere they are free, and Kṛṣṇa is detached from their independently enacted activities and from the reactions their activities generate. The living entities are thus simultaneously fully dependent on Kṛṣṇa and independent of Him.

Śrīla Viśvanātha Cakravartī Ṭhākura raises a question: Because Kṛṣṇa has described, by an analogous example, His *acintya-śakti,* or inconceivable mystic power, hasn't His explanation made the inconceivable conceivable? He writes: "But then how is the Lord's mystic power inconceivable, which He claimed it to be in His statement, 'Just see My mystic power'? After all, we now have a conceivable example explaining His mystic power."

He then answers: "The sky is nonattached to the wind, which is contained within it, because the sky and wind are unconscious matter [and matter does not form attachments]. However, only in one case does living spirit remain nonattached while living in this world and controlling it, and that is in the case of the supreme controller. In this way the inconceivability [of the supreme controller's being nonattached] is established. The example of the nonattached sky is nonetheless offered in order to give ordinary people an opportunity to begin to understand this subject."

Kṛṣṇa began His explanation of His inconceivable relationship with the material world in chapter five (texts 14–15) by saying, "I do nothing. The material nature is the doer." As Śrīla Prabhupāda confirms in his purport to this verse, however, Kṛṣṇa is nevertheless the cause of the material nature and "not a blade of grass moves without the will of the Supreme Personality of Godhead." Śrīla Viśvanātha Cakravartī Ṭhākura concludes by saying, "This is Kṛṣṇa's inconceivable potency, and we can only fold our hands and offer respects to His greatness."

In texts 4–6, Kṛṣṇa discussed His relationship to the maintenance of the material world. Now He will explain destruction and creation.

7 O son of Kuntī, at the end of the millennium all material manifestations enter into My nature, and at the beginning of another millennium, by My potency, I create them again.

8 The whole cosmic order is under Me. Under My will it is automatically manifested again and again, and under My will it is annihilated at the end.

These verses are similar to Bg. 8.18–19. If Kṛṣṇa, the *parameśvara,* is aloof, as He claims, how does everything in the material world continue? Here Kṛṣṇa explains that everything goes on by "My will." He does not Himself create or destroy, but the material nature acts by His desire.

That the cosmic order is "automatically manifested" also points to Kṛṣṇa's detachment. Everything moves by His will and automatically manifests because He empowers the material nature to act.

Kṛṣṇa's relationship with the material world is amazing, yet still more amazing is that He, the ultimate controller of all, ran in fear from Mother Yaśodā! He stole butter and then became afraid that His mother would punish Him. He is all-knowing and all-powerful, yet tears flowed from His eyes, and He trembled. When Queen Kuntī – who knew Kṛṣṇa's actual position – heard this, she was astonished. Kṛṣṇa's pastimes – within both the material energy and the spiritual energy – are inconceivable. If Kṛṣṇa's potency could fit into our understanding, He, like our intelligence, would be finite.

One may note that cosmic creation, maintenance, and destruction are enacted by Kṛṣṇa's arrangement, yet He generates no karmic reactions for His work, as do the living entities. Why?

9 O Dhanañjaya, all this work cannot bind Me. I am ever detached from all these material activities, seated as though neutral.

As a person who works dutifully in a detached spirit remains aloof from the reactions of his work, so Kṛṣṇa becomes neither transformed nor entangled in material events and their reactions because He always remains aloof and detached. The point in this verse is similar to the points made in Bg. 3.21–24.

Kṛṣṇa now explains how He is neutral.

10 This material nature, which is one of My energies, is working under My direction, O son of Kuntī, producing all moving and nonmoving beings. Under its rule this manifestation is created and annihilated again and again.

Mayā means "by My," *adhi* means "from above," and *akṣa* means "eyes." Thus *mayādhyakṣeṇa* means "under My eyes." Everything is done under Kṛṣṇa's supervision.

Śrīla Viśvanātha Cakravartī Ṭhākura gives an analogous example to explain Kṛṣṇa's words: "The governmental business of a king, like Ambarīṣa Mahārāja, is carried out by his ministers (*prakṛtis*), while the uninvolved king merely remains present. All the same, unless the king is present on his throne, the ministers are incapable of doing anything. In the same way, unless I give My support as the supervisor, material nature (*prakṛti*) cannot do anything."

Śrīla Prabhupāda's purport summarizes Kṛṣṇa's relationship with the material world:

> Because He glances over material nature, there is undoubtedly activity on the part of the Supreme Lord, but He has nothing to do with the manifestation of the material world directly. This example is given in the *smṛti:* when there is a fragrant flower before someone, the fragrance is touched by the smelling power of the person, yet the smelling and the flower are detached from one another. There is a similar connection between the material world and the Supreme Personality of Godhead; actually He has nothing to do with this material world, but He creates by His glance and ordains. In summary, material nature, without the superintendence of the Supreme Personality of Godhead, cannot do anything. Yet the Supreme Personality is detached from all material activities.

The question may then be asked, "Why don't people respect Kṛṣṇa, who is the most glorious personality?"

11 Fools deride Me when I descend in the human form. They do not know My transcendental nature as the Supreme Lord of all that be.

That Kṛṣṇa, who appears in a humanlike form, is the Supreme Personality of Godhead and is even higher than the four-armed Viṣṇu form is not easy to accept. Even Lord Brahmā became bewildered about Kṛṣṇa's identity. After Kṛṣṇa killed Aghāsura, Brahmā saw Him as a cowherd boy surrounded by His friends, with a lump of food held in His left hand. Brahmā could not accept this boy as his master, the Supreme Lord, the source of innumerable universes.

Rather than accepting Him as He is, some consider Him simply a powerful man. Others think He has acquired His wonderful form and qualities by *karma* and *tapasya.* Still others consider the Supreme to be impersonal and devoid of attributes. They think that since absolute oneness cannot be understood, it assumes a form and descends as Kṛṣṇa, Rāma, and other *avatāras* through contact with the material mode of goodness.

Kṛṣṇa's opinion about such speculations is expressed in this verse. *Avajānanti māṁ mūḍhā mānuṣīṁ tanum āśritam:* "Fools deride My descent, thinking that I have assumed this human form."

In contrast, Śrīla Prabhupāda discusses how devotees accept Kṛṣṇa's form: "Although the foolish cannot imagine how Kṛṣṇa, who appears just like a human being, can control the infinite and the finite, those who are pure devotees accept this, for they know that Kṛṣṇa is the Supreme Personality of Godhead. Therefore they completely surrender unto Him and engage in Kṛṣṇa consciousness, devotional service of the Lord."

What happens to those who, in bewilderment, disrespect Kṛṣṇa's form?

12 Those who are thus bewildered are attracted by demonic and atheistic views. In that deluded condition, their hopes for

liberation, their fruitive activities, and their culture of knowledge are all defeated.

Śrīla Viśvanātha Cakravartī Ṭhākura explains that if one is practicing *aṣṭāṅga-yoga* for liberation, or if one is practicing *karma-kāṇḍa* rituals for material well-being, or if one is practicing *jñāna-yoga* for knowledge and Brahman realization, all his aspirations will be crushed if he misunderstands Kṛṣṇa's form to be material. No success is awarded to those refusing to accept Kṛṣṇa's transcendental form.

One modern politician wrote a commentary on the *Rāmāyaṇa* and said that Lord Rāma, by acting as a *kṣatriya* and fighting to protect Sītādevī, proved the omnipotence of the modes of material nature. How? Because by acting in that way, claimed the author, the Lord revealed that even when God descends into the material world, He becomes controlled by the modes of nature. How foolish! How can God be controlled by His own energies?

The hopes, knowledge, and fruitive desires of one who thinks in that way are destroyed by such inappropriate, illogical and demoniac conclusions. Māyāvādīs, who say that Brahman affected by the mode of goodness becomes *īśvara,* an incarnation, are particularly ruined.

What about those who do accept Kṛṣṇa as He has revealed Himself?

13 O son of Pṛthā, those who are not deluded, the great souls, are under the protection of the divine nature. They are fully engaged in devotional service because they know Me as the Supreme Personality of Godhead, original and inexhaustible.

Śrīla Prabhupāda describes the undeluded *mahātmā* who is situated within the divine nature: "The *mahātmā* does not divert his attention to anything outside Kṛṣṇa, because he knows perfectly well that Kṛṣṇa is the original Supreme Person, the cause of all causes. There is no doubt about it. Such a *mahātmā,* or great soul, develops through association with other *mahātmās,* pure devotees. Pure devotees are not even attracted by Kṛṣṇa's other features, such as the four-armed Mahā-viṣṇu. They are simply attracted by the two-armed form of Kṛṣṇa."

What are the activities of such great souls, and how do they serve the Lord?

14 Always chanting My glories, endeavoring with great determination, bowing down before Me, these great souls perpetually worship Me with devotion.

Śrīla Viśvanātha Cakravartī Ṭhākura explains: "A *mahātmā* always serves and glorifies Kṛṣṇa, regardless of time and place. He offers his obeisances and chants a fixed number of rounds with great determination. The word *mām* is used twice in this verse. The repetition emphasizes that these activities are offered to Kṛṣṇa and to no one else."

In this section we have heard about those who worship Kṛṣṇa and those who do not. Now in text 15, Kṛṣṇa mentions three types of worshipers who worship Him indirectly. Such persons do not realize that it is Kṛṣṇa they are worshiping.

15 Others, who engage in sacrifice by the cultivation of knowledge, worship the Supreme Lord as the one without a second, as diverse in many, and in the universal form.

In his purport, Śrīla Prabhupāda mentions three levels of Kṛṣṇa worshipers: 1) the *mahātmās,* 2) the *sukṛtinas* (mentioned in Bg. 7.16), and 3) three kinds of *jñānīs* who worship the Absolute Truth. It is these *jñānīs* who are being discussed in this verse. Śrīla Prabhupāda says about them:

> [T]hese are divided into three: 1) he who worships himself as one with the Supreme Lord, 2) he who concocts some form of the Supreme Lord and worships that, and 3) he who accepts the universal form, the *viśva-rūpa* of the Supreme Personality of Godhead, and worships that. Out of the above three, the lowest, those who worship themselves as the Supreme Lord, thinking themselves to be monists, are most predominant....The second class includes the worshipers of the demigods, those who by imagination consider any form to be the form of the Supreme Lord. And the third class includes those who cannot conceive of anything beyond the manifestation of this material

universe. They consider the universe to be the supreme organism or entity and worship that. The universe is also a form of the Lord.

The first type of *jñānī* mentioned is the one who worships himself as one (*ekatvena*) with the Supreme. This person is the lowest of the three. Although he is a monist, he is still considered to be worshiping God because he understands that he is eternal and is not his material body. Those in this category are the most predominant.

Above them are the demigod worshipers who imagine a favorite demigod as the Supreme Lord (*pṛthaktvena bahudhā*).

The best of the three is one who, considering the universe as the supreme entity, conceives of the Lord's universal form within the manifest universe (*viśvataḥ-mukham*) and worships that.

Kṛṣṇa has already discussed the results gained by the *ekatvena* worshiper in verses 11 and 12. In the next four verses He will explain how to recognize and worship Him in His universal form. Further on in this chapter, Kṛṣṇa will also discuss the results of demigod worship.

16 But it is I who am the ritual, I the sacrifice, the offering to the ancestors, the healing herb, the transcendental chant. I am the butter and the fire and the offering.

17 I am the father of this universe, the mother, the support, and the grandsire. I am the object of knowledge, the purifier, and the syllable oṁ. I am also the Ṛg, the Sāma, and the Yajur Vedas.

18 I am the goal, the sustainer, the master, the witness, the abode, the refuge, and the most dear friend. I am the creation and the annihilation, the basis of everything, the resting place and the eternal seed.

19 O Arjuna, I give heat, and I withhold and send forth the rain. I am immortality, and I am also death personified. Both spirit and matter are in Me.

Kṛṣṇa is explaining in these verses how to see Him within the objects of this world. Śrīla Prabhupāda summarizes this point in his purport: "Since Kṛṣṇa is both matter and spirit, the gigantic universal form comprising all material manifestations is also Kṛṣṇa, and His pastimes in Vṛndāvana as two-handed Śyāmasundara, playing on a flute, are those of the Supreme Personality of Godhead."

Next, Kṛṣṇa describes the one who worships the demigods as if they were the Supreme and does not directly worship their source and empowering agent, the Supreme Lord.

20 Those who study the Vedas and drink the soma juice, seeking the heavenly planets, worship Me indirectly. Purified of sinful reactions, they take birth on the pious, heavenly planet of Indra, where they enjoy godly delights.

Students of the *Vedas* generally worship the demigods. As mentioned before, if such persons worship Kṛṣṇa through their worship of the demigods, they are properly situated. If they worship the demigods as independent deities, however, they are purified and attain the heavenly kingdom. What ultimately happens to such improper worshipers of the demigods?

21 When they have thus enjoyed vast heavenly sense pleasure and the results of their pious activities are exhausted, they return to this mortal planet again. Thus those who seek sense enjoyment by adhering to the principles of the three Vedas achieve only repeated birth and death.

This verse and text 20 describe the result of demigod worship, and how such worshipers obtain the necessities of life and satisfy their desires. Now Kṛṣṇa will explain the process by which the unalloyed devotees, whose only desire is to perpetually worship Him, are maintained and receive their necessities.

22 But those who always worship Me with exclusive devotion, meditating on My transcendental form – to them I carry what they lack, and I preserve what they have.

Paryupāsate (properly worship) and *nityābhiyuktānām* (always fixed in devotion) indicate a devotee's absorption in pure Kṛṣṇa consciousness. Śrīla Prabhupāda writes: "One who is unable to live for a moment without Kṛṣṇa consciousness cannot but think of Kṛṣṇa twenty-four hours a day, being engaged in devotional service by hearing, chanting, remembering, offering prayers, worshiping, serving the lotus feet of the Lord, rendering other services, cultivating friendship, and surrendering fully to the Lord."

With such determination in their practice of *sādhana,* the devotees neglect even their own maintenance and do not care for liberation. They leave both responsibilities to Kṛṣṇa, and thus Kṛṣṇa personally delivers them. (This contrasts with the description given of the *yogī* in Bg. 8.24, where it is said that the demigods, in shifts, arrange for the soul's passage higher and higher through the material realm to the ultimate destination of the *brahmajyoti.*)

One may ask, "What kind of devotee would give his worshipful Deity, Kṛṣṇa, such a burden?" However, Kṛṣṇa does not consider maintaining His devotee a burden. He wants to serve His devotee. Kṛṣṇa is so powerful that simply by exerting His will, He can create unlimited universes; maintaining His devotees is not a burden. Rather, it is His pleasure.

When the *brāhmaṇa,* Arjunācārya, was writing his commentary on the *Gītā,* he saw this verse and thought it a mistake to believe that the Lord would personally carry whatever was needed to each devotee. Arjunācārya therefore scratched out *vahāmi* ("I carry") and inserted *karomi* ("I have it done"). Arjunācārya was extremely poor. After making the change in the text, as he did every day, he went out begging.

While he was gone, his wife heard a knock at the door. Two beautiful boys fearfully insisted that she quickly accept the food that her husband had forced them to bring. These beautiful boys were anxious to get away from her house because, They told her, the great *brāhmaṇa* scholar, Arjunācārya, would probably beat Them again. When Arjunācārya's wife expressed disbelief that her husband had beat such boys, one said, "See?" And the dark boy turned to show her the marks on His back where He had been struck. Then They both dashed away.

Arjunācārya's wife was bewildered, and she began to cook and eat the food the boys had brought. Upon Arjunācārya's return, he saw his wife eating. He was shocked. According to the Vedic system, a wife never eats before she has fed her husband.

When he challenged her, she replied, "Ācārya, why have you acted so inappropriately and become so cruel?" She then told him that two beautiful boys had come, left a bountiful supply of food, and after the dark boy had showed her the marks on His back, They had rushed away. The *ācārya* thought for a few moments and then asked what the boys looked like. Upon hearing that one had a beautiful darkish complexion and the other was white, he could understand that his fortunate wife had been blessed with the *darśana* of Kṛṣṇa and Balarāma. The "beating" marks on the beautiful dark boy's back were the result of the *ācārya's* having scratched out the word *vahāmi*. Kṛṣṇa had been forced to come personally to prove the truth of His words, "I carry what they lack."

Text 15 informed us that demigod worshipers worship Kṛṣṇa indirectly. The next text answers the question, "Do demigod worshipers, as they too are ultimately worshipers of Kṛṣṇa, receive the same result as Kṛṣṇa's unalloyed devotees?"

23 Those who are devotees of other gods and who worship them with faith actually worship only Me, O son of Kuntī, but they do so in a wrong way.

Such persons are worshiping, but with improper knowledge and with an improper process. *Vidhi-pūrvakam* means to follow the actual rules and regulations; *avidhi-pūrvakam* means not to follow them, or to follow in a wrong way, against the actual injunctions of the *śāstra* and without the conscious worship of Kṛṣṇa as the Supreme Lord.

Śrīla Prabhupāda compares such *avidhi-pūrvakam* worship to watering the leaves and branches of a tree while neglecting to water the root. What happens to such worshipers?

24 I am the only enjoyer and master of all sacrifices. Therefore, those who do not recognize My true transcendental nature fall down.

Demigod worshipers, after great endeavor to follow the *Vedas,* simply "fall down to material existence and do not achieve the desired goal of life," Śrīla Prabhupāda writes.

To contrast the destinations of demigod worshipers and *kṛṣṇa-bhaktas,* Kṛṣṇa speaks verse 25.

25 Those who worship the demigods will take birth among the demigods; those who worship the ancestors go to the ancestors; those who worship ghosts and spirits will take birth among such beings; and those who worship Me will live with Me.

Worshipers go where their faith is reposed, as their consciousness naturally carries them to that to which they are attracted. Kṛṣṇa has clearly outlined our choices: we have to accept one object of worship or another as our goal. To encourage us to choose correctly, He speaks the final nine verses of this chapter. These verses plead with us, for our own benefit, to become His exclusive devotees.

26 If one offers Me with love and devotion a leaf, a flower, a fruit, or water, I will accept it.

To worship the demigods properly, one is required to perform elaborate sacrifices governed by intricate rules. Numerous pure and trained priests, and huge amounts of ghee and other difficult-to-obtain ingredients are needed before one can perform such *yajñas*.

Worshiping Kṛṣṇa is simple. *Patram, puṣpam, phalam,* and *toyam* are all in the singular. Kṛṣṇa asks only for a leaf, a flower, water, or a piece of fruit. His request is not even for all of them! His actual desire is to taste the *bhakti* of His devotee's offering. Therefore He mentions *bhakti* twice in this verse for emphasis. The demigods are pleased by the offering; Kṛṣṇa is pleased by devotion.

A devotee not only offers these items to Kṛṣṇa with devotion but bases his entire life on rendering pleasing service to Kṛṣṇa. Therefore, the essential ingredients of an offering (the sentiments of *bhakti*) are not only evoked at the time of the offering but are cultivated throughout a devotee's life. The garden in which the grains, vegetables, fruits, and flowers are sown and grown is watered with devotion to Kṛṣṇa. The flowers are picked and the food cooked with devotion. Finally, the items are served and offered to Kṛṣṇa. Kṛṣṇa says that He accepts (*aśnāmi*) such offerings because His devotee's *bhakti* has given Him an appetite.

This verse and texts 14 and 22 describe advanced stages of devotion. In the next verse, according to Viśvanātha Cakravartī Ṭhākura, Kṛṣṇa describes a step below this – *niṣkāma karma-yoga* – for those who are not yet able to practice pure devotional service.

27 Whatever you do, whatever you eat, whatever you offer or give away, and whatever austerities you perform – do that, O son of Kuntī, as an offering to Me.

Niṣkāma karmīs are attached to the specific work they perform. To them Kṛṣṇa therefore says that whatever you are *already* doing, "do that as an offering to Me." First perform the activity and then surrender its fruit to Kṛṣṇa.

Bhakti is different. In *bhakti,* we first surrender to the order of *guru* and Kṛṣṇa and then act. We make no distinction between the activity and its fruit. Everything is offered in surrender to Kṛṣṇa's lotus feet.

Śrīla Prabhupāda confirmed that this verse refers to *karma-yoga,* technically different from *bhakti-yoga,* in a lecture on the prayers of Queen Kuntī, given in Māyāpur in 1974:

> Kṛṣṇa is meant for the *paramahaṁsa* and *muni,* very, very exalted persons. *Yoga* means "contact" or "having connection." *Bhakti-yoga* means directly connecting with Kṛṣṇa, or God. Other *yogas* are not directly connected. When there is *karma-yoga,* it is adulterated. It is not pure. *Karma-yoga* means *yat karoṣi yad aśnāsi yaj juhoṣi dadāsi yat.* In the beginning one cannot take to pure *bhakti-yoga.* Therefore *karma-yoga* is recommended. People are interested in different types of work. Therefore Kṛṣṇa says, *yat karoṣi:* "Never mind, whatever you are doing." So how does it become *karma-yoga*? Now, *kuruṣva tad mad-arpaṇam:* "You give it to Me." Kṛṣṇa says, "All right, go on. You are attached to business. You go on doing that. But

the money earned out of your business, you give to Me." This is *karma-yoga*. "It doesn't matter, whatever you are doing, but the ultimate result, you give to Me."

The next verse describes the results of *niṣkāma karma-yoga*.

28 In this way you will be freed from bondage to work and its auspicious and inauspicious results. With your mind fixed on Me in this principle of renunciation, you will be liberated and come to Me.

Śrīla Viśvanātha Cakravartī Ṭhākura explains: "He [the person described in the previous verse] not only becomes liberated but also achieves *vimukti.* He becomes exceptional (*viśiṣṭa*) among those who are liberated and comes into My proximity in order to serve Me directly."

Śrīla Baladeva Vidyābhuṣaṇa explains: "The consequence of such devotion is described in the verse beginning *śubhā* [text 28]. When you engage in the kind of devotional service characterized by offering all works to Me under My order, then you become freed from the bondage of material activities. You not only become *mukta,* liberated from material activities, but *vimukta,* and come to Me. You become exceptional among those who are liberated and come near Me in order to serve Me directly."

Devotees of the Lord are so special. *Nārāyaṇa-parāḥ sarve na kutaścana bibhyati/ svargāpavarga-narakeṣv api tulyārtha-darśinaḥ:* "Devotees solely engaged in the devotional service of the Supreme Personality of Godhead, Nārāyaṇa, never fear any condition of life. For them the heavenly planets, liberation, and the hellish planets are all the same, for such devotees are interested only in the service of the Lord." (*Bhāg.* 6.17.28)

Kṛṣṇa stated earlier that He delivers His devotees and annihilates the miscreants, but shouldn't the Supreme Lord, who is the father of all living entities, treat all – both the good and bad – equally? Is Kṛṣṇa partial?

29 I envy no one, nor am I partial to anyone. I am equal to all. But whoever renders service unto Me in devotion is a friend, is in Me, and I am also a friend to him.

Kṛṣṇa is compared to rain. Trees absorb rainwater and then grow and produce fruits. Some trees produce bitter fruits and others produce sweet ones. Does this mean the rain is partial? No. Similarly, regardless of a living entity's situation, Kṛṣṇa nourishes everyone equally. Śrīla Baladeva Vidyābhūṣaṇa explains the Lord's mood, described in the first half of this verse, as the mood of the Supersoul, the Paramātmā: "Sending forth and maintaining all kinds of beings among the demigods, humans, animals, nonmoving creatures, and so on, I, the Lord of all, am equal. I am just like a cloud pouring rain on all kinds of seeds. Among all these creatures, none are My enemies and none are especially dear to Me."

The second half of this verse, however, confirms Kṛṣṇa's partiality to His devotee in His feature as Bhagavān. Earlier in this chapter, Kṛṣṇa described that although the material world rests on Him, He remains aloof from it. Here, on the contrary, we find that Kṛṣṇa does not remain aloof from His devotees. Śrīla Prabhupāda writes:

> One may question here that if Kṛṣṇa is equal to everyone and no one is His special friend, then why does He take a special interest in the devotees who are always engaged in His transcendental service? But this is not discrimination; it is natural. Any man in this material world may be very charitably disposed, yet he has a special interest in his own children. The Lord claims that every living entity – in whatever form – is His son, and so He provides everyone with a generous supply of the necessities of life. He is just like a cloud which pours rain all over, regardless of whether it falls on rock or land or water. But for His devotees, He gives specific attention….The very phrase "Kṛṣṇa consciousness" suggests that those who are in such consciousness are living transcendentalists, situated in Him. The Lord says here distinctly, *mayi te:* "They are in Me." Naturally, as a result, the Lord is also in them….If a reciprocal relationship is not present between the devotee and the Lord, then there is no personalist philosophy.

Kṛṣṇa vowed, *ye yathā māṁ prapadyante tāṁs tathaiva bhajāmy aham:* "As all surrender to Me, I reward them accordingly."

Here He confirms that He reciprocates even more personally with His devotees who love Him. He is not like a *kalpa-vṛkṣa* tree, who responds equally to all requests. Rather, He is willing to become the enemy of His devotee's enemy. As Kṛṣṇa told Duryodhana, "Anyone who is envious of the Pāṇḍavas is envious of Me and is My enemy."

Śrīla Prabhupāda beautifully describes this relationship between Kṛṣṇa and His devotees in his purport: "When a diamond is set in a golden ring, it looks very nice. The gold is glorified, and at the same time the diamond is glorified. The Lord and the living entity eternally glitter, and when a living entity becomes inclined to the service of the Supreme Lord he looks like gold. The Lord is a diamond, and so this combination is very nice."

Kṛṣṇa personally maintains and cares for His devotees. Even if His devotee were to perform a heinous act, Kṛṣṇa would nevertheless protect and purify him.

30 Even if one commits the most abominable action, if he is engaged in devotional service he is to be considered saintly because he is properly situated in his determination.

The power of the devotee's determination to perform *bhakti* exclusively causes Kṛṣṇa to uplift and protect him even if he has acted improperly. Śrīla Prabhupāda's purport confirms this:

> The words *sādhur eva,* "he is saintly," are very emphatic. They are a warning to the nondevotees that because of an accidental falldown a devotee should not be derided; he should still be considered saintly even if he has accidentally fallen down. And the word *mantavyaḥ* is still more emphatic. If one does not follow this rule, and derides a devotee for his accidental falldown, then one is disobeying the order of the Supreme Lord. The only qualification of a devotee is to be unflinchingly and exclusively engaged in devotional service....On the other hand, one should not misunderstand that a devotee in transcendental devotional service can act in all kinds of abominable ways; this verse only refers to an accident due to the strong power of material connections.

Thus a devotee should not commit sins, thinking, "I'm a devotee, and therefore I can act according to my whim." Such a mentality is the seventh offense against chanting the holy name of the Lord. *Na vidyate tasya yamair hi śuddhiḥ:* those who adopt that mentality will never be purified, even if carried to the court of Yamarāja, the superindendent of death.

Thus Kṛṣṇa's words glorify the strength of *bhakti* and reveal His partiality toward His unalloyed devotees.

Still, the question may be raised: "How can a person who is *su-durācāra* (committing highly improper activities) be regarded as saintly?"

31 He quickly becomes righteous and attains lasting peace. O son of Kuntī, declare it boldly that My devotee never perishes.

Such a fixed devotee is quickly purified by his desire to remember the Lord. As Śrīla Prabhupāda points out, there is no need for him to perform ceremonial atonement (*prāyaścitta*). Devotion alone is sufficient.

Śrīla Viśvanātha Cakravartī Ṭhākura comments on verses 30–31 as follows:

> One might ask, "But if someone is corrupted by such bad behavior, how can he be a *sādhu*?"
>
> This is answered: "He should be considered as such and thought of as a *sādhu*." "He should be considered" is an injunctive statement. If this injunction is disobeyed, there will be unfavorable consequences. In other words, "The evidence for the truth of this is that it is simply My command."
>
> "Well," someone might say, "one may be considered a *sādhu* partially, to the extent that he is worshiping You. But to the extent that he is usurping other men's wives and property, he is not to be considered a *sādhu*."
>
> This is answered by the word *eva,* only: "He should only be considered a *sādhu,* in all ways, completely."
>
> We should never view him as not a *sādhu*. His determination is completely fixed: "I may go to hell or obtain an animal birth because of my unavoidable sinful reactions, but I will never give up my exclusive worship of Śrī Kṛṣṇa." Such determination is praiseworthy.

"But," one might ask, "why do You accept the worship of such an irreligious person? Why do you consume the food and drink offered by one whose heart is contaminated by lust, anger, and other faults?"

In response, the Lord says, "He quickly becomes religious." This is not expressed as "He is going to quickly become" or "He will soon achieve peace." Rather, the present tense is used: "he becomes" and "he attains."

The Lord continues, "This means that immediately after he commits impiety, he remembers Me and feels remorse. He thus quickly becomes religious. He thinks, 'Alas! Alas! There is no person more fallen than me. I defile the reputation of the community of devotees. Damn me!' Again and again feeling remorse like this, he achieves complete peace and detachment."

"Well," one may say, "if he actually becomes religious, there can be no argument about such a person. But what about a devotee whose behavior is wicked and who fails to give up his bad behavior throughout his whole life? What can be said about him?"

Always affectionate to His devotees, the Lord responds to this doubt with complete confidence and with some anger, in the words beginning *kaunteya:* "My devotee never perishes. Even when he dies, he never falls down."

To encourage Arjuna, who is disturbed with sorrow and apprehension over the thought that hard-hearted quibblers who indulge in false logic will not accept this, the Lord says, "O Kaunteya, go to the assembly of these disputants, and making a loud sound with drums and cymbals, raise your arms fearlessly and declare My promise: 'I, Kṛṣṇa, am the Supreme Lord, and even if My devotee is wicked in his behavior, he will never perish. On the contrary, such a devotee is sure to become successful.' Their bad logic will be shattered by this confident declaration. They will certainly take shelter of you as their *guru*." Such is the interpretation given by Śrīdhara Svāmī in his commentary.

Someone may ask, "But why doesn't the Personality of Godhead Himself make this promise? Why does he instead deputize Arjuna to promise? In the same way as the Lord will later say, 'Without a doubt you will come to Me. I promise you this because you are very dear to Me,' why doesn't He now say,

'Kaunteya, I promise that My devotee will never perish'?"

Here is the answer. At that moment, the Lord was thinking, "I am very affectionate to My devotees and cannot tolerate their being discredited at all. I will often even break My own promise and let Myself be discredited to protect My devotee's promise. For example, I will soon fight with Bhīṣma and discard My own promise in order to protect Bhīṣma's promise. Thus atheistic, logical quibblers will only laugh if I now offer My own promise, but they will have to acknowledge Arjuna's promise as if it were written in stone. Therefore I will have Arjuna make this promise."

Kṛṣṇa continues glorifying the path of *bhakti.*

32 O son of Pṛthā, those who take shelter in Me, though they be of lower birth – women, vaiśyas [merchants], and śūdras [workers] – can attain the supreme destination.

This verse is a continuation of Kṛṣṇa's declaration, and so it also glorifies the potency of *bhakti:* even the most sinful can become purified by devotional service. Here Kṛṣṇa speaks about those who have taken a lower birth.

The next verse describes those who have taken higher births.

33 How much more this is so of the righteous brāhmaṇas, the devotees, and the saintly kings. Therefore, having come to this temporary, miserable world, engage in loving service unto Me.

Kṛṣṇa is saying, "Those of lower birth get purified by devotional service, what to speak of those who have taken a higher birth."

The term *anityam,* as Śrīla Prabhupāda explains in his purport, means "not eternal." To describe the material world, Kṛṣṇa has used this word, not the word *mithyā,* false. Māyāvādīs say that this world is false, but Śrīla Prabhupāda says, "We can understand from *Bhagavad-gītā* that the world is not false; it is temporary." To seek happiness where everything is temporary is called delusion.

Kṛṣṇa concludes text 33 with the words *bhajasva mām,* "engage in loving service unto Me." In the next text, Kṛṣṇa will clearly tell us how to do so.

34 Engage your mind always in thinking of Me, become My devotee, offer obeisances to Me, and worship Me. Being completely absorbed in Me, surely you will come to Me.

Kṛṣṇa here gives four confidential instructions: 1) *man-manāḥ:* always think of me; 2) *bhava mad-bhaktaḥ:* become My devotee; 3) *mad-yājī:* worship Me; and 4) *māṁ namaskuru:* offer obeisances to Me.

First, Kṛṣṇa tells us to always think of Him. It is not sufficient to work hard for Kṛṣṇa while our minds wander. Śrīla Baladeva Vidyābhūṣaṇa comments that here Kṛṣṇa says to Arjuna: "A so-called 'devotee' of a king, the king's servant, is actually thinking about his own wife and so on. His thoughts are not fixed on the king. Thus he is not actually the king's devotee. You, however, in contrast with such a person, should be absorbed in thinking of Me and should be My devotee. Your mind should always be fixed, like an uninterrupted flow of honey, on Me, the son of Vasudeva. You should think of Me as your own master and as the very goal of your life."

The *Bhagavad-gītā* is the essence of all Vedic literature. The middle six chapters are the essence of the *Gītā,* and the ninth and tenth chapters are the essence of the middle six chapters. Finally, the last verse of this chapter, which is exactly in the middle of the *Gītā,* and which will be repeated practically verbatim at the end of the *Gītā,* is the most confidential and essential *śloka.* It is the essence of the essence of the essence and the most confidential of all knowledge: Become a pure devotee of Lord Kṛṣṇa.

One may question whether this verse beginning *man-manā bhava mad-bhakto* is actually the essence of the *Gītā.* Noting that almost the same verse appears again as Bg. 18.65, one may think that Bg. 18.66, *sarva-dharmān parityajya*...is actually the essence, not 18.65. Actually, both verses are the same in that, in both, Kṛṣṇa offers the same instruction. Text 18.66 expresses Kṛṣṇa's desire that Arjuna surrender, and text 18.65 explains the components of that surrender.

In Bg. 18.64, just before these essential verses, Kṛṣṇa states, *sarva-guhya-tamaṁ bhūyaḥ śṛṇu me paramaṁ vacaḥ:* "I am speaking My supreme instruction, the most confidential knowledge of all." *Sarva-guhya-tamam* means "the most confidential of all." *Bhūyaḥ* means "again." Kṛṣṇa speaks the verse here in chapter nine and again as text 18.65. Kṛṣṇa also clearly says that these verses, 18.65 and 18.66, are the most confidential knowledge of all and are His supreme instruction. Śrīla Prabhupāda has many times explained this same point. In his purport to Bg. 18.65, he writes: "The most confidential part of knowledge is that one should become a pure devotee of Kṛṣṇa and always think of Him and act for Him. . . .Concentration of the mind on the form of Kṛṣṇa constitutes the most confidential part of knowledge, and this is disclosed to Arjuna because Arjuna is the most dear friend of Kṛṣṇa's."

In his purport to *Śrīmad-Bhāgavatam* 3.24.32, Śrīla Prabhupāda writes: "In *Bhagavad-gītā* Lord Kṛṣṇa advised Arjuna many times to surrender unto Him, especially at the end of the ninth chapter – *man-manā bhava mad-bhakto:* 'If you want to be perfect, just always think of Me, become My devotee, worship Me, and offer your obeisances to Me. In this way you will understand Me, the Personality of Godhead, and ultimately you will come back to Me, back to Godhead, back home.' "

In his purport to *Śrīmad-Bhāgavatam* 5.26.37, Śrīla Prabhupāda says:

> The complete purpose of this material world will be fulfilled when we resume our spiritual identities and go back home, back to Godhead. The very simple method for doing this is prescribed by the Supreme Personality of Godhead. *Sarva-dharmān parityajya mām ekaṁ śaraṇaṁ vraja.* One should be neither pious nor impious. One should be a devotee and surrender to the lotus feet of Kṛṣṇa. This surrendering process is also very easy. Even a child can perform it. *Man-manā bhava mad-bhakto mad-yājī māṁ namaskuru.* One must always simply think of Kṛṣṇa by chanting Hare Kṛṣṇa, Hare Kṛṣṇa, Kṛṣṇa Kṛṣṇa, Hare Hare/ Hare Rāma, Hare Rāma, Rāma Rāma, Hare Hare. One should become Kṛṣṇa's devotee, worship Him and offer obeisances to Him. Thus one should engage all the activities of his life in the service of Lord Kṛṣṇa.

In a lecture on *Śrīmad-Bhāgavatam* 1.15.51, Śrīla Prabhupāda said:

> And the very simple thing is, *ya idaṁ paramaṁ guhyaṁ mad-bhakteṣv abhidhāsyati:* this confidential service, preaching of *Bhagavad-gītā* – what is that? *Bhagavad-gītā* preaching – the essence is: *sarva-dharmān parityajya mām ekaṁ śaraṇaṁ vraja.* Simply go and preach. This very thing. Kṛṣṇa says, *man-manā bhava mad-bhakto mad-yājī māṁ namaskuru.* This is Kṛṣṇa's desire. Preach to the world: "Just be Kṛṣṇa conscious." *Man-manā.* "Just become Kṛṣṇa's devotee." *Man-manā bhava mad-bhakto mad-yājī.* "Just worship Kṛṣṇa." *Namaskuru.* "Just offer your obeisances to Kṛṣṇa." Four words. Then you become a preacher. It is not very difficult to become a preacher and to become a spiritual master. How? Very simple thing. Go and speak what Kṛṣṇa says. That's all. (Lecture, Los Angeles, December 28, 1973)

Chapter Ten

The Opulence of the Absolute

At the end of the ninth chapter, Kṛṣṇa described pure devotional service and how He reciprocates with His devotees. Kṛṣṇa concluded that chapter with His *most* confidential instruction – *man-manā bhava mad-bhakto:* "Engage your mind always in thinking of Me, become My devotee." Kṛṣṇa will now continue to reveal the confidential essence of knowledge (*rāja-vidyā rāja-guhyam*). Chapter ten is entitled "The Opulence of the Absolute" (*vibhūti-yoga*), and herein Kṛṣṇa describes further His opulences, potencies and position.

1 The Supreme Personality of Godhead said: Listen again, O mighty-armed Arjuna. Because you are My dear friend, for your benefit I shall speak to you further, giving knowledge that is better than what I have already explained.

Śrīla Prabhupāda comments: "Previously, beginning with the seventh chapter, the Lord has already explained His different energies and how they are acting. Now in this chapter He explains His specific opulences to Arjuna. In the previous chapter He has clearly explained His different energies to establish devotion in firm conviction. Again in this chapter He tells Arjuna about His manifestations and various opulences."

Kṛṣṇa has just established that devotion to Him is the goal of life, and He now discusses His opulences to increase Arjuna's devotion. How does knowing Kṛṣṇa's opulences increase one's devotion? Imagine discovering that an intimate friend is really a famous billionaire. He is so powerful that when he snaps his fingers, people line up in their eagerness to serve him. We then realize, "What a wonderful friend we have!" Our understanding of his opulence and power has naturally enhanced our appreciation of him. We feel fortunate to be friends with someone so great. Similarly, when a devotee understands Kṛṣṇa's greatness in detail, he feels increased gratitude for his good fortune in being able to reciprocate intimately with such a great and powerful Lord.

Kṛṣṇa's opulence is simultaneously knowable and unknowable. Is this a contradiction? No, because we can know the unknowable to some degree, not through our own limited abilities, but when Kṛṣṇa reveals Himself to us. Even a fraction of knowledge about Kṛṣṇa's otherwise unknowable position inspires us to serve Him.

In this verse, Kṛṣṇa glorifies the knowledge He will speak by saying He is "giving knowledge that is better" than what He has already explained.

2 Neither the hosts of demigods nor the great sages know My origin or opulences, for, in every respect, I am the source of the demigods and sages.

It is impossible for anyone to fully understand his own source. Kṛṣṇa is the source of the demigods – the demigods are His creations – so even the demigods are unable to know Him. Śrīla Viśvanātha Cakravartī Ṭhākura comments that if one puts forward the argument that the reason demigods are unable to know Kṛṣṇa is because they are too attached to sense gratification, Kṛṣṇa defeats that argument in this verse. He says that even the sages – who are detached from sense gratification – cannot know Him. No one can understand Kṛṣṇa's origin and opulence without hearing from Him or His devotees.

In the next verse Kṛṣṇa explains the result of understanding Him properly.

3 He who knows Me as the unborn, as the beginningless, as the Supreme Lord of all the worlds – he only, undeluded among men, is freed from all sins.

In Bg. 4.9, Kṛṣṇa says, *janma karma ca me divyam evaṁ yo vetti tattvataḥ/ tyaktvā dehaṁ punar janma naiti mām eti so 'rjuna:* "One who knows the transcendental nature of My appearance and activities does not, upon leaving the body, take his birth again in this material world, but attains My eternal abode, O Arjuna."

Śrīla Baladeva Vidyābhūṣaṇa comments that only Kṛṣṇa possesses all three characteristics mentioned in Bg. 10.3. Śrīla Viśvanātha Cakravartī Ṭhākura comments that Brahmā is *aja* (unborn), but not *anādi* (beginningless or without an origin).

Śrī Kṛṣṇa, the inconceivably potent Lord, remains unborn though He appears to take birth as the son of Vasudeva and act as the darling son of Yaśodādevī. In the Dāmodara-līlā, Yaśodāmayī tied together length after length of rope, but no amount of rope was sufficient to circumscribe His unlimited waist, and the rope always remained two inches too short. Yet, inconceivably, the Lord's waist at that time was already encircled by a black thread and bell, which had been previously tied by Yaśodā to attract good fortune for her son.

Equally inconceivable is that Kṛṣṇa, the *loka-maheśvara,* the master of all, allowed Himself to be controlled by Arjuna as He drove Arjuna's chariot on the battlefield. Understanding Kṛṣṇa's inconceivable nature with faith frees us from sin and awards liberation. Only by associating with Kṛṣṇa's devotees will one understand Kṛṣṇa's inconceivable potency and become freed from sin and achieve liberation.

Kṛṣṇa next describes how all qualities possessed by living entities come from Him.

4–5 Intelligence, knowledge, freedom from doubt and delusion, forgiveness, truthfulness, control of the senses, control of the mind, happiness and distress, birth, death, fear, fearlessness, nonviolence, equanimity, satisfaction, austerity, charity, fame and infamy – all these various qualities of living beings are created by Me alone.

Kṛṣṇa is the source of everything. Śrīla Prabhupāda writes: "Of whatever we find, good or bad, the origin is Kṛṣṇa. Nothing can manifest itself in this material world which is not in Kṛṣṇa. That is knowledge; although we know that things are differently situated, we should realize that everything flows from Kṛṣṇa."

The qualities born of goodness are helpful in knowing Kṛṣṇa and are awarded to devotees by Kṛṣṇa Himself. Śrīla Prabhupāda writes: "All these qualities are manifest throughout the universe in human society and in the society of the demigods. . . .Now, for one who wants to advance in Kṛṣṇa consciousness, Kṛṣṇa creates all these qualities, but the person develops them himself from within. One who engages in the devotional service of the Supreme Lord develops all the good qualities, as arranged by the Supreme Lord."

Yet despite the helpfulness of these qualities, because they are born of goodness, they cannot on their own reveal Kṛṣṇa, who is beyond the mode of goodness. Nor can the great sages and demigods, who are born of Kṛṣṇa and are situated in goodness, know Kṛṣṇa through their own abilities. Śrīla Viśvanātha Cakravartī Ṭhākura explains Kṛṣṇa's words: " 'The knowers of *śāstra* cannot understand the truth about Me by their own intelligence, because intelligence is born of goodness and the other modes of *māyā.* So even though they originate from Me, the great sages and demigods are incapable of understanding Me, who am beyond the modes.' "

6 The seven great sages and before them the four other great sages and the Manus [progenitors of mankind] come from Me, born from My mind, and all the living beings populating the various planets descend from them.

Kṛṣṇa's position cannot be accurately ascertained either through the qualities born of goodness or by the sages, progenitors, and their descendants. Can Kṛṣṇa ever be known?

Śrīla Prabhupāda explains in his purport to text 2:

> As stated in the *Brahma-saṁhitā,* Lord Kṛṣṇa is the Supreme Lord. No one is greater than Him; He is the cause of all causes. Here it is also stated by the Lord personally that He is the cause of all the demigods and sages. Even the demigods and great sages cannot understand Kṛṣṇa; they can understand neither His name nor His personality, so what is the position of the so-called scholars of this tiny planet? No one can understand why this Supreme God comes to earth as an ordinary human being and executes such wonderful, uncommon activities. One should know, then, that scholarship is not the qualification necessary to understand Kṛṣṇa. . . .
>
> Here the Lord indirectly says that if anyone wants to know the Absolute Truth, "Here I am present as the Supreme

Personality of Godhead. I am the Supreme." One should know this. Although one cannot understand the inconceivable Lord who is personally present, He nonetheless exists. We can actually understand Kṛṣṇa, who is eternal, full of bliss and knowledge, simply by studying His words in *Bhagavad-gītā* and *Śrīmad-Bhāgavatam.*

Śrīla Prabhupāda mentions that the twenty-five persons spoken of in this verse (eleven sages and fourteen Manus) are the source of all progeny in the universe. Even these exalted personalities can accurately learn about Kṛṣṇa only by hearing directly from Him or His devotees.

7 One who is factually convinced of this opulence and mystic power of Mine engages in unalloyed devotional service; of this there is no doubt.

Kṛṣṇa clearly states here that knowing His opulence fixes one in devotion. This verse provides the impetus for Arjuna's request in text 16 for Kṛṣṇa to describe His opulence in detail.

The next four verses, the *catur-ślokī* of the *Bhagavad-gītā,* summarize the entire *Gītā.* In text 8, Kṛṣṇa sums up His opulences and explains the result of truly knowing those opulences: one becomes a pure devotee. In text 9, He describes how pure devotees worship Him. In texts 10 and 11, He describes His reciprocation with their loving worship.

8 I am the source of all spiritual and material worlds. Everything emanates from Me. The wise who perfectly know this engage in My devotional service and worship Me with all their hearts.

Everything emanates from Kṛṣṇa. He is *svayaṁ bhagavān,* the Supreme Personality of Godhead. It is not only Kṛṣṇa who says this about Himself, however, and Śrīla Prabhupāda provides numerous quotations from Vedic literature to support Kṛṣṇa's statement.

In his purport, Śrīla Prabhupāda explains that one who understands Kṛṣṇa perfectly from a bona fide spiritual master will worship Him with great love and attention. Thus knowing of His greatness leads to full surrender, and full surrender is followed by *bhāva,* love.

How do devotees worship Kṛṣṇa "with all their hearts"?

9 The thoughts of My pure devotees dwell in Me, their lives are fully devoted to My service, and they derive great satisfaction and bliss from always enlightening one another and conversing about Me.

Śrīla Baladeva Vidyābhūṣaṇa comments that *mad-gata-prāṇāḥ* indicates that Kṛṣṇa is the life of His devotees. They cannot live without Him any more than a fish can live when taken from water. Kṛṣṇa is their life, and *kṛṣṇa-kathā,* talking about Kṛṣṇa, is their nourishment. Thus devotees converse about Kṛṣṇa among themselves in great love. They loudly chant Kṛṣṇa's names and discuss His pastimes, form, and attributes. A pure devotee's attraction to Kṛṣṇa is as natural as the attraction between young boys and girls.

Now that Kṛṣṇa has described the worship by His devotees, He will explain His reciprocation with them.

10 To those who are constantly devoted to serving Me with love, I give the understanding by which they can come to Me.

Kṛṣṇa's devotees understand Him not only by hearing about Him but also because Kṛṣṇa enters their hearts and reveals Himself to them. Śrīla Viśvanātha Cakravartī Ṭhākura here defines *buddhi-yoga* as Kṛṣṇa's direct inspiration. Because the devotees intensely desire to know Kṛṣṇa, He gives them complete understanding of Himself. Śrīla Prabhupāda discusses this point in his purport: "A person may have a bona fide spiritual master and may be attached to a spiritual organization, but still, if he is not intelligent enough to make progress, then Kṛṣṇa from within gives him instructions so that he may ultimately come to Him without difficulty. The qualification is that a person always engage himself in Kṛṣṇa consciousness and with love and devotion render all kinds of services." Śrīla Prabhupāda stresses the wonderful inspiration Kṛṣṇa gives to reciprocate with His pure devotee's loving worship.

The living entity has been covered by ignorance since time immemorial. Therefore, is he actually capable of achieving true inspiration, knowledge and realization?

11 To show them special mercy, I, dwelling in their hearts, destroy with the shining lamp of knowledge the darkness born of ignorance.

Śrīla Viśvanātha Cakravartī Ṭhākura explains Kṛṣṇa's thinking as follows: " 'I become *ātma-bhāva-stha:* Like a bee inside the whorl of a lotus, I become situated in their *bhāva.* In My transcendental personal form, I reveal My qualities, and with the shining lamp of knowledge of these qualities, I destroy the darkness of the ignorance of *anādi-karma* (beginningless *karma*), which obstructs true knowledge, and manifests as hankering for things other than Me.' "

This grace – the gift of transcendental knowledge that removes ignorance – is how Kṛṣṇa reciprocates with His devotee's loving service. Śrīla Prabhupāda explains this sweetly in his purport:

> Man can go on speculating for several millions of years, and if he is not devoted, if he is not a lover of the Supreme Truth, he will never understand Kṛṣṇa, or the Supreme Truth. Only by devotional service is the Supreme Truth, Kṛṣṇa, pleased, and by His inconceivable energy He can reveal Himself to the heart of the pure devotee. The pure devotee always has Kṛṣṇa within his heart; and with the presence of Kṛṣṇa, who is just like the sun, the darkness of ignorance is at once dissipated. This is the special mercy rendered to the pure devotee by Kṛṣṇa....The pure devotee does not have to worry about the material necessities of life; he need not be anxious, because when he removes the darkness from his heart, everything is provided automatically by the Supreme Lord, who is pleased by the loving devotional service of the devotee. This is the essence of the teachings of *Bhagavad-gītā.* By studying *Bhagavad-gītā,* one can become a soul completely surrendered to the Supreme Lord and engage himself in pure devotional service. As the Lord takes charge, one becomes completely free from all kinds of materialistic endeavors.

According to Śrīla Baladeva Vidyābhūṣaṇa, Kṛṣṇa's reply to the question about how a living entity who has been covered by ignorance since time immemorial can attain true enlightenment is as follows:

> The devotees themselves need not endeavor. "No, not at all! To show them special mercy, I bestow upon them (but not upon any other *yogīs*) the lamplight of knowledge. In other words, they don't have to worry about how to achieve My mercy because I personally endeavor to give it to them. I am *ātma-bhāva-stha,* situated within the workings of their intelligence. Because the knowledge that I give them can be revealed only by Me, it is not something in the material mode of goodness. It is even something distinct from the normal transcendental knowledge arising from devotional service. With this lamp of knowledge I destroy their ignorance. Because I personally destroy their ignorance, why should they have to endeavor? According to My own words, 'To those who always worship Me with devotion, I carry what they lack and I preserve what they have,' I accept as My personal burden the supply of all their necessities, both material and spiritual."
>
> These four verses are the essence of *Bhagavad-gītā,* and they are thus called the *catuḥ-ślokī Gītā*. They remove the distress of all living beings and bring about all auspiciousness.

Understanding who Kṛṣṇa is and how He reciprocates with His pure devotees, we naturally desire to surrender unto Him. When we surrender unto the all-powerful, all-knowing Supreme Personality of Godhead, we attain true security and peace. Devotees see everything as Kṛṣṇa's mercy and thus know that nothing unfavorable can befall them. Their faith and knowledge grant them peace even in the most difficult circumstances.

Now, for the first time since Bg. 8.2, Arjuna will speak. In the next seven verses, Arjuna expresses his acceptance of everything Kṛṣṇa has said and asks to hear more.

12–13 Arjuna said: You are the Supreme Personality of Godhead, the ultimate abode, the purest, the Absolute Truth. You are the eternal, transcendental, original person, the unborn, the

greatest. All the great sages such as Nārada, Asita, Devala, and Vyāsa confirm this truth about You, and now You Yourself are declaring it to me.

Arjuna calls Kṛṣṇa *pavitraṁ paramam,* the supreme pure. One who knows Him as such also becomes pure.

In the next five verses Arjuna requests Kṛṣṇa to tell him more about His glories.

14 O Kṛṣṇa, I totally accept as truth all that You have told me. Neither the demigods nor the demons, O Lord, can understand Your personality.

Śrīla Prabhupāda states that Arjuna is teaching us the mood in which we should accept Kṛṣṇa's words. Śrīla Baladeva Vidyābhūṣaṇa comments that Arjuna calls Kṛṣṇa "Keśava." *Ke* refers to Lord Brahmā, *śa* to Lord Śiva, and *va* indicates that Kṛṣṇa binds Brahmā and Śiva with knowledge of Himself; He thus makes them His devotees. How then can they independently understand Kṛṣṇa, what to speak of Him being known by less powerful demigods or the demons? Therefore only Kṛṣṇa can truly know Himself, and Arjuna will point this out in the next verse.

15 Indeed, You alone know Yourself by Your own internal potency, O Supreme Person, origin of all, Lord of all beings, God of gods, Lord of the universe!

As the Lord of the universe, Kṛṣṇa protects the world through His teachings, such as the *Bhagavad-gītā.*

Arjuna will now request Kṛṣṇa to explain even more about Himself.

16 Please tell me in detail of Your divine opulences by which You pervade all these worlds.

17 O Kṛṣṇa, O supreme mystic, how shall I constantly think of You, and how shall I know You? In what various forms are You to be remembered, O Supreme Personality of Godhead?

Arjuna asks Kṛṣṇa to tell him of His opulence, though Kṛṣṇa has already explained that He is everything (*ahaṁ sarvasya prabhavaḥ*). Arjuna, however, is requesting more information. Why? Because he wants to think of Kṛṣṇa. Kṛṣṇa recommended this process to Arjuna at the end of chapter six (*mad-gatenāntar-ātmanā:* always abide in Me, think of Me within yourself) and in the last verse of chapter nine (*man-manā bhava mad-bhaktaḥ:* always think of Me and become My devotee). Kṛṣṇa also told Arjuna in Bg. 10.7 that being factually convinced of His opulence will purify him and inspire him to engage in pure devotional service. Therefore Arjuna wants to hear more about Kṛṣṇa from Kṛṣṇa Himself.

Śrīla Prabhupāda explains that Arjuna has asked about Kṛṣṇa's all-pervading opulence on behalf of the common man, who finds it easier to concentrate his mind on physical representations than on Kṛṣṇa's spiritual form. Śrīla Prabhupāda writes: "The superior devotee is concerned not only for his own understanding but for the understanding of all mankind. So Arjuna, out of his mercy, because he is a Vaiṣṇava, a devotee, is opening for the common man the understanding of the all-pervasiveness of the Supreme Lord."

18 O Janārdana, again please describe in detail the mystic power of Your opulences. I am never satiated in hearing about You, for the more I hear the more I want to taste the nectar of Your words.

Śrīla Viśvanātha Cakravartī Ṭhākura describes an objection that could be raised by Kṛṣṇa: "'But haven't I already said that all things are My opulent expansions, in My statement "I am the source of all things"? And haven't I already described devotional service in My words "Understanding this, the wise worship Me"?'

"Arjuna responds to this in the verse beginning *vistareṇa* [text 18]: 'O Janārdana, with the sweet nectar of Your instructions, You are generating in me a greed to hear, thus agitating me and impelling me to beg for more. What else then can I do, but beg?' While imbibing the nectar of Kṛṣṇa's instructions, Arjuna's ears are acquiring the ability to taste, as if they were tongues."

Kṛṣṇa now describes His opulences, which He will continue to do for the remainder of this chapter.

19 The Supreme Personality of Godhead said: Yes, I will tell you of My splendorous manifestations, but only of those which are prominent, O Arjuna, for My opulence is limitless.

Kṛṣṇa begins His description by saying *hanta*. *Hanta* is a form of address expressing tenderness. Kṛṣṇa is so pleased by Arjuna's inquiry that He reciprocates by saying, "Oh, *hanta* [yes], I will speak about My opulences."

Kṛṣṇa will now describe how we may remember Him when viewing the greatest manifestations in this world, but first He explains that He is the Supersoul in everyone's heart.

20 I am the Supersoul, O Arjuna, seated in the hearts of all living entities. I am the beginning, the middle, and the end of all beings.

In this verse and the next twenty verses, Kṛṣṇa lists various objects or groups of living entities and states that He is their essence or the chief member of each group.

21 Of the Ādityas I am Viṣṇu, of lights I am the radiant sun, of the Maruts I am Marīci, and among the stars I am the moon.

22 Of the Vedas I am the Sāma Veda; of the demigods I am Indra, the king of heaven; of the senses I am the mind; and in living beings I am the living force [consciousness].

Because the mind is the most difficult sense to control, it is considered the greatest sense and therefore is represented by Kṛṣṇa.

23 Of all the Rudras I am Lord Śiva, of the Yakṣas and Rākṣasas I am the Lord of wealth [Kuvera], of the Vasus I am fire [Agni], and of mountains I am Meru.

24 Of priests, O Arjuna, know Me to be the chief, Bṛhaspati. Of generals I am Kārtikeya, and of bodies of water I am the ocean.

The ocean is so great that it neither increases when rivers and rains pour into it nor decreases when its waters evaporate.

25 Of the great sages I am Bhṛgu; of vibrations I am the transcendental oṁ. Of sacrifices I am the chanting of the holy names [japa], and of immovable things I am the Himālayas.

Japa is the simplest form of sacrifice. *Yajñānāṁ japa-yajño 'smi:* "Of sacrifices, I am the chanting of the holy names," Kṛṣṇa says. In his purport, Śrīla Prabhupāda explains, "Of all sacrifices, the chanting of Hare Kṛṣṇa, Hare Kṛṣṇa, Kṛṣṇa Kṛṣṇa, Hare Hare/ Hare Rāma, Hare Rāma, Rāma Rāma, Hare Hare is the purest representation of Kṛṣṇa."

26 Of all trees I am the banyan tree, and of the sages among the demigods I am Nārada. Of the Gandharvas I am Citraratha, and among perfected beings I am the sage Kapila.

Nāra means "mankind" or "spiritual." *Da* means "giving or granting." Nārada, who has disciples all over the universe, gives God to everyone.

Citraratha was Arjuna's friend, and he taught Arjuna the art of singing.

27 Of horses know Me to be Uccaiḥśravā, produced during the churning of the ocean for nectar. Of lordly elephants I am Airāvata, and among men I am the monarch.

28 Of weapons I am the thunderbolt; among cows I am the surabhi. Of causes for procreation I am Kandarpa, the god of love, and of serpents I am Vāsuki.

29 Of the many-hooded Nāgas I am Ananta, and among the aquatics I am the demigod Varuṇa. Of departed ancestors I am Aryamā, and among the dispensers of law I am Yama, the lord of death.

The *sarpas* mentioned in text 28 refer to one-headed snakes; the *nāgas* referred to in this verse are many-hooded.

30 Among the Daitya demons I am the devoted Prahlāda, among subduers I am time, among beasts I am the lion, and among birds I am Garuḍa.

Time, as Kṛṣṇa mentions in Bg. 11.32, is the great destroyer of the world. By time's influence, everything within this world is created, maintained, and destroyed.

31 Of purifiers I am the wind, of the wielders of weapons I am Rāma, of fishes I am the shark, and of flowing rivers I am the Ganges.

Śrīla Baladeva Vidyābhūṣaṇa comments that the Rāma referred to here is Paraśurāma because Kṛṣṇa is explaining His *vibhūtis,* His opulences, not His incarnations. Paraśurāma is a living entity empowered (*śakty-āveśa*) to wield weapons.

32 Of all creations I am the beginning and the end and also the middle, O Arjuna. Of all sciences I am the spiritual science of the self, and among logicians I am the conclusive truth.

In text 20, Kṛṣṇa said He was the beginning, middle, and end of all beings. Śrīla Baladeva Vidyābhūṣaṇa says that in that verse He was referring to all *sentient* beings. Here, however, Kṛṣṇa says that He is also the beginning, middle, and end of every nonsentient creation.

Nyāya, logic, teaches various ways to reach a conclusion, including *vitaṇḍā, vāda,* and *jalpa*. Kṛṣṇa says, "I am *vāda,* the natural conclusion." *Vāda* is debate carried out fairly according to standard rules, without trying to force the establishment of a particular conclusion. *Vitaṇḍā* is quibbling, or merely destructive argument in which one tries to defeat the opponent by any means possible, but does nothing substantial to positively prove one's own thesis. *Jalpa,* using various deceptive means to fool the opposition, is unfair argument. *Vitaṇḍā* and *jalpa* are forms of argument in which winning, not necessarily determining the truth, is the main consideration.

33 Of letters I am the letter A, and among compound words I am the dual compound. I am also inexhaustible time, and of creators I am Brahmā.

34 I am all-devouring death, and I am the generating principle of all that is yet to be. Among women I am fame, fortune, fine speech, memory, intelligence, steadfastness, and patience.

Death is described here as *sarva-haraḥ,* all-devouring, because it takes everything away, including our memories.

Many qualities in the Sanskrit language are considered feminine, and among them, these seven represent Kṛṣṇa. Men may also possess these qualities. Śrīla Prabhupāda explains in his purport: "The seven opulences listed – fame, fortune, fine speech, memory, intelligence, steadfastness, and patience – are considered feminine. If a person possesses all of them or some of them he becomes glorious."

35 Of the hymns in the Sāma Veda I am the Bṛhat-sāma, and of poetry I am the Gāyatrī. Of months I am Mārgaśīrṣa [November-December], and of seasons I am flower-bearing spring.

36 I am also the gambling of cheats, and of the splendid I am the splendor. I am victory, I am adventure, and I am the strength of the strong.

Kṛṣṇa infuses objects with splendor, and we thus experience them as splendid.

37 Of the descendants of Vṛṣṇi I am Vāsudeva, and of the Pāṇḍavas I am Arjuna. Of the sages I am Vyāsa, and among great thinkers I am Uśanā.

38 Among all means for suppressing lawlessness I am punishment, and of those who seek victory I am morality. Of secret things I am silence, and of the wise I am the wisdom.

39 Furthermore, O Arjuna, I am the generating seed of all existences. There is no being – moving or nonmoving – that can exist without Me.

Kṛṣṇa herein explains how we can see Him everywhere. Without Kṛṣṇa, nothing can be, and no one – moving or nonmoving – can exist. Whenever we see anything, we can think, "The existence of this person, this tree, this building, this universe rests on Kṛṣṇa. Nothing exists without Him."

After speaking this verse, which by itself can award us the vision to see Him everywhere, Kṛṣṇa sums up chapter ten.

40 O mighty conqueror of enemies, there is no end to My divine manifestations. What I have spoken to you is but a mere indication of My infinite opulences.

41 Know that all opulent, beautiful, and glorious creations spring from but a spark of My splendor.

Everything opulent, beautiful, glorious, or strong should be seen as simply part of Kṛṣṇa's splendor, because all opulences, even those not specifically mentioned in this chapter, emanate from Kṛṣṇa.

Kṛṣṇa concludes this chapter by repeating His basic message, but He adds one more point.

42 But what need is there, Arjuna, for all this detailed knowledge? With a single fragment of Myself I pervade and support this entire universe.

Everything – not only those things possessing extraordinary opulence, beauty, or strength – exists, sustained by Kṛṣṇa's power. *Ekāṁśena* (*eka,* "by one"; *aṁśena,* "part") does not refer directly to Kṛṣṇa, but to His expansion, the Supersoul. Śrīla Prabhupāda explains this in his purport, as he summarizes the entire chapter: "If, however, one thoroughly studies the different descriptions of the opulences and expansions of Kṛṣṇa's energy, then one can understand without any doubt the position of Lord Śrī Kṛṣṇa and can fix his mind in the worship of Kṛṣṇa without deviation. The Lord is all-pervading by the expansion of His partial representation, the Supersoul, who enters into everything that is. Pure devotees, therefore, concentrate their minds in Kṛṣṇa consciousness in full devotional service; therefore they are always situated in the transcendental position. Devotional service and worship of Kṛṣṇa are very clearly indicated in this chapter in verses eight through eleven. That is the way of pure devotional service."

Chapter Eleven

The Universal Form

Although Kṛṣṇa is driving Arjuna's chariot, He pervades and supports the entire universe. Arjuna therefore wishes to see Kṛṣṇa's all-pervading form. Thus, after two introductory verses, Arjuna asks Kṛṣṇa to reveal His universal form.

1 Arjuna said: By my hearing the instructions You have kindly given me about these most confidential spiritual subjects, my illusion has now been dispelled.

2 O lotus-eyed one, I have heard from You in detail about the appearance and disappearance of every living entity and have realized Your inexhaustible glories.

3 O greatest of all personalities, O supreme form, though I see You here before me in Your actual position, as You have described Yourself, I wish to see how You have entered into this cosmic manifestation. I want to see that form of Yours.

In Bg. 10.16 Arjuna asked to hear in detail of Kṛṣṇa's unlimited opulence, but Kṛṣṇa gave only eighty-two examples. Arjuna, having heard but a fragment of Kṛṣṇa's glories, is now eager to see Kṛṣṇa's all-pervading form of unlimited opulence.

Śrīla Viśvanātha Cakravartī Ṭhākura, representing Arjuna, comments: "Because You have said, 'With a single fragment of Myself I support this entire universe,' I have no problem believing this as factual. Still, I want to know everything in detail." Actually, Arjuna will gain nothing for himself by seeing this form. *Yathā* ("as it is") means that Arjuna already accepts Kṛṣṇa's two-armed form as supreme. He calls Kṛṣṇa both *puruṣottama* and *parameśvara,* the best of personalities and the Supreme Lord. Why then does Arjuna ask to see – as Śrīla Prabhupāda calls it in his purport to Bg. 11.8 – Kṛṣṇa's "godless display of opulences," a form that devotees generally never wish to see? Śrīla Prabhupāda offers Arjuna's reasons in his purports to texts 1 and 3:

> Now, as far as Arjuna is concerned, he says that his illusion is over. This means that Arjuna no longer thinks of Kṛṣṇa as a mere human being, as a friend of his, but as the source of everything. Arjuna is very enlightened and is glad that he has such a great friend as Kṛṣṇa, but now he is thinking that although he may accept Kṛṣṇa as the source of everything, others may not. So in order to establish Kṛṣṇa's divinity for all, he is requesting Kṛṣṇa in this chapter to show His universal form.…Arjuna wants to see the universal form to set a criterion, for in the future there would be so many impostors who would pose themselves as incarnations of God. The people, therefore, should be careful; one who claims to be Kṛṣṇa should be prepared to show his universal form to confirm his claim to the people.

Arjuna continues making his request in text 4.

4 If You think that I am able to behold Your cosmic form, O my Lord, O master of all mystic power, then kindly show me that unlimited universal Self.

The word *yogeśvara,* master of all mystic power, is used by Arjuna to indicate that he believes Kṛṣṇa, by His mystic power, can enable him to see the universal form. The word *prabhu* as used here means "one with the capacity, power, and strength" to show the universal form. Śrīla Prabhupāda explains these points in his purport: "Arjuna could understand that for a living entity it is not possible to understand the unlimited infinite. If the infinite reveals Himself, then it is possible to understand the nature of the infinite by the grace of the infinite. The word *yogeśvara* is also very significant here because the Lord has inconceivable power. If He likes, He can reveal Himself by His grace, although He is unlimited. Therefore Arjuna pleads for the inconceivable grace of Kṛṣṇa. He does not give Kṛṣṇa orders. Kṛṣṇa is not obliged to reveal Himself unless one surrenders fully in Kṛṣṇa consciousness and engages in devotional service."

Kṛṣṇa responds by offering to show Arjuna the opulences he spoke of in chapter ten.

5 The Supreme Personality of Godhead said: My dear Arjuna, O son of Pṛthā, see now My opulences, hundreds and thousands of varied divine and multicolored forms.

6 O best of the Bhāratas, see here the different manifestations of Ādityas, Vasus, Rudras, Aśvinī-kumāras, and all the other demigods. Behold the many wonderful things which no one has ever seen or heard of before.

7 O Arjuna, whatever you wish to see, behold at once in this body of Mine! This universal form can show you whatever you now desire to see and whatever you may want to see in the future. Everything – moving and nonmoving – is here completely, in one place.

Kṛṣṇa used the word *paśya* ("see") four times in the last three verses. He is emphasizing that Arjuna should see this wonderful universal form, never before seen, though once He showed an aspect of it to Duryodhana.

In an attempt to avoid the Battle of Kurukṣetra, Mahārāja Yudhiṣṭhira sent Kṛṣṇa to Duryodhana as a messenger of peace. Duryodhana's and Karṇa's response, however, was foolish. To express disdain for the Pāṇḍavas' strength, they plotted to bind Kṛṣṇa with ropes and throw Him into prison. Only a great devotee such as Yaśodādevī, however, can evoke submission from the unlimitedly powerful Lord and bind Him. Binding Kṛṣṇa was impossible for Duryodhana because he was envious and devoid of *bhakti*. Duryodhana's and Karṇa's attempt only caused Kṛṣṇa to laugh and say, "You cannot bind Me. I exist everywhere!" At that time, Kṛṣṇa showed part of His universal form to Duryodhana, who became frightened but remained unsubmissive. Duryodhana continued minimizing Kṛṣṇa, despite His show of power, by saying, "Oh, Kṛṣṇa simply has mystic powers."

The universal form shown to Duryodhana was not the same as the universal form Kṛṣṇa will now show Arjuna.

Śrīla Prabhupāda explains the significance of the word *eka-stham* in his purport to text 7. Arjuna will be able to see the whole universe, including all space and time – past, present, and future – *eka-stham,* while sitting in one place.

8 But you cannot see Me with your present eyes. Therefore I give you divine eyes. Behold My mystic opulence!

Kṛṣṇa uses the word *divyam* to describe the "divine" eyes or vision He will award Arjuna to enable him to behold His universal form. Śrīla Prabhupāda further explains this in his purport to *Śrīmad-Bhāgavatam* 2.1.24: "A pure devotee of the Lord, being unaccustomed to looking into such a mundane gigantic form of the Lord, requires special vision for the purpose. The Lord, therefore, favored Arjuna with special vision for looking into His *virāṭ-rūpa,* which is described in the eleventh chapter of the *Bhagavad-gītā.*"

Śrīla Viśvanātha Cakravartī Ṭhākura poses and then answers the following question: "Why should Arjuna, who directly perceives with his own eyes the sweetness of the supreme person, be unable to perceive a partial expansion of the Lord and need to receive divine eyes? Some explain this by saying that those most excellent eyes which perceive the sweetness of the supreme person's human pastimes are exclusive in their scope of perception; they do not perceive the opulence of the Lord's godlike pastimes. After all, a tongue tasting crystal sugar cannot simultaneously experience the taste of unrefined *gur,* or sugarcane."

In his purport, Śrīla Prabhupāda shows that Arjuna's attainment of "divine vision" was not a sign of Arjuna's advancing.

> A pure devotee does not like to see Kṛṣṇa in any form except His form with two hands; a devotee must see His universal form by His grace, not with the mind but with spiritual eyes. To see the universal form of Kṛṣṇa, Arjuna is told not to change his mind but his vision. The universal form of Kṛṣṇa is not very important; that will be clear in subsequent verses. Yet because Arjuna wanted to see it, the Lord gives him the particular vision required to see that universal form.

> Devotees who are correctly situated in a transcendental relationship with Kṛṣṇa are attracted by loving features, not by a godless display of opulences. The playmates of Kṛṣṇa, the friends of Kṛṣṇa, and the parents of Kṛṣṇa never want Kṛṣṇa to show His opulences. They are so immersed in pure love that they do not even know that Kṛṣṇa is the Supreme Personality of Godhead. In their loving exchange they forget that Kṛṣṇa is the Supreme Lord. In the *Śrīmad-Bhāgavatam* it is stated that the boys who play with Kṛṣṇa are all highly pious souls and after many, many births they are able to play with Kṛṣṇa. Such boys do not know that Kṛṣṇa is the Supreme Personality of Godhead. They take Him as a personal friend.

Again, as in his purports to texts 2 and 3, Śrīla Prabhupāda explains the actual purpose behind Arjuna's desire:

> The fact is that the devotee is not concerned with seeing the *viśva-rūpa,* the universal form, but Arjuna wanted to see it to substantiate Kṛṣṇa's statements so that in the future people could understand that Kṛṣṇa not only theoretically or philosophically presented Himself as the Supreme but actually presented Himself as such to Arjuna. Arjuna must confirm this because Arjuna is the beginning of the *paramparā* system. Those who are actually interested in understanding the Supreme Personality of Godhead, Kṛṣṇa, and who follow in the footsteps of Arjuna should understand that Kṛṣṇa not only theoretically presented Himself as the Supreme, but actually revealed Himself as the Supreme.
>
> The Lord gave Arjuna the necessary power to see His universal form because He knew that Arjuna did not particularly want to see it, as we have already explained.

Until this point, Kṛṣṇa has only spoken about the universal form. In the next verse, Kṛṣṇa gives Arjuna *divya-cakṣuḥ,* the divine eyes that will allow Arjuna to see it.

9 Sañjaya said: O King, having spoken thus, the Supreme Lord of all mystic power, the Personality of Godhead, displayed His universal form to Arjuna.

Sañjaya, also empowered to see the universal form, next describes Arjuna's vision.

10–11 Arjuna saw in that universal form unlimited mouths, unlimited eyes, unlimited wonderful visions. The form was decorated with many celestial ornaments and bore many divine upraised weapons. He wore celestial garlands and garments, and many divine scents were smeared over His body. All was wondrous, brilliant, unlimited, all-expanding.

The word *divya* is used four times in these two verses to describe the extraordinary ornaments, weapons, garlands, and fragrances of the universal form. Śrīla Prabhupāda describes the word *aneka* ("many") in the purport, showing that Arjuna saw unlimited manifestations distributed throughout the universe.

12 If hundreds of thousands of suns were to rise at once into the sky, their radiance might resemble the effulgence of the Supreme Person in that universal form.

The universal form is wondrous, brilliant, unlimited, and all-expanding. Sañjaya uses a metaphor to compare the effulgence of the Supreme Lord to something imaginable: the simultaneous rising of hundreds of thousands of suns. He does this to aid Dhṛtarāṣṭra's understanding, as Śrīla Prabhupāda's purport to this verse explains.

13 At that time Arjuna could see in the universal form of the Lord the unlimited expansions of the universe situated in one place although divided into many, many thousands.

Śrīla Prabhupāda explains: "The word *tatra* ('there') is very significant. It indicates that both Arjuna and Kṛṣṇa were sitting on the chariot when Arjuna saw the universal form. Others on the battlefield could not see this form, because Kṛṣṇa gave the vision only to Arjuna. Arjuna could see in the body of Kṛṣṇa many thousands of planets. As we learn from Vedic scriptures, there are many universes and many planets. Some of them are made of earth, some are made of gold, some are made of jewels, some are very great, some are not so great, etc. Sitting on his chariot, Arjuna could see all these. But no one could understand what was going on between Arjuna and Kṛṣṇa."

14 Then, bewildered and astonished, his hair standing on end, Arjuna bowed his head to offer obeisances and with folded hands began to pray to the Supreme Lord.

Śrīla Baladeva Vidyābhūṣaṇa explains that Arjuna, in astonishment, now sees the universal form. Astonishment or wonder is one of the secondary *rasas*. Impelled by Kṛṣṇa's universal form, Arjuna now relishes this *rasa*.

15 Arjuna said: My dear Lord Kṛṣṇa, I see assembled in Your body all the demigods and various other living entities. I see Brahmā sitting on the lotus flower, as well as Lord Śiva and all the sages and divine serpents.

16 O Lord of the universe, O universal form, I see in Your body many, many arms, bellies, mouths, and eyes, expanded everywhere, without limit. I see in You no end, no middle, and no beginning.

17 Your form is difficult to see because of its glaring effulgence, spreading on all sides, like blazing fire or the immeasurable radiance of the sun. Yet I see this glowing form everywhere, adorned with various crowns, clubs, and discs.

18 You are the supreme primal objective. You are the ultimate resting place of all this universe. You are inexhaustible, and You are the oldest. You are the maintainer of the eternal religion, the Personality of Godhead. This is my opinion.

The universal form is dazzling and radiant. In text 17, Arjuna describes it as *aprameyam,* immeasurable, and in text 18, he attempts to describe the immeasurable.

19 You are without origin, middle, or end. Your glory is unlimited. You have numberless arms, and the sun and moon are Your eyes. I see You with blazing fire coming forth from Your mouth, burning this entire universe by Your own radiance.

The "blazing fire" coming from the mouth of the universal form is "burning this entire universe." This is the beginning of the description of Kṛṣṇa's *kāla-rūpa,* His form as time. This description continues through text 30.

20 Although You are one, You spread throughout the sky and the planets and all space between. O great one, seeing this wondrous and terrible form, all the planetary systems are perturbed.

Kṛṣṇa has allowed the demigods to see His universal form. Arjuna is also able to see those demigods.

21 All the hosts of demigods are surrendering before You and entering into You. Some of them, very much afraid, are offering prayers with folded hands. Hosts of great sages and perfected beings, crying "All peace!" are praying to You by singing the Vedic hymns.

The demigods are taking shelter of the Lord and crying, *pāhi, pāhi:* "Please protect us." The sages are begging the Lord, *svasti:* "Let there be peace, good fortune and well being for all!"

22 All the various manifestations of Lord Śiva, the Ādityas, the Vasus, the Sādhyas, the Viśvedevas, the two Aśvīs, the Maruts, the forefathers, the Gandharvas, the Yakṣas, the Asuras, and the perfected demigods are beholding You in wonder.

23 O mighty-armed one, all the planets with their demigods are disturbed at seeing Your great form, with its many faces, eyes, arms, thighs, legs, and bellies and Your many terrible teeth; and as they are disturbed, so am I.

Arjuna also becomes afraid, and his mood here changes from astonishment to fear.

24 O all-pervading Viṣṇu, seeing You with Your many radiant colors touching the sky, Your gaping mouths, and Your great glowing eyes, my mind is perturbed by fear. I can no longer maintain my steadiness or equilibrium of mind.

25 O Lord of lords, O refuge of the worlds, please be gracious to me. I cannot keep my balance seeing thus Your blazing deathlike faces and awful teeth. In all directions I am bewildered.

The *kālānala* ("the fire of death") mentioned here to describe the universal form's blazing deathlike faces is the fire of destruction at the end of the universe.

26–27 All the sons of Dhṛtarāṣṭra, along with their allied kings, and Bhīṣma, Droṇa, Karṇa – and our chief soldiers also – are rushing into Your fearful mouths. And some I see trapped with heads smashed between Your teeth.

Texts 26 through 30 describe future occurrences that Arjuna sees within the *kāla-rūpa*. In Bg. 11.7, Kṛṣṇa said that Arjuna could see "whatever [he] may want to see in the future." In these texts Arjuna sees that Bhīṣma, Droṇa, and Karṇa – the three most feared members of the opposing army – will be destroyed.

28 As the many waves of the rivers flow into the ocean, so do all these great warriors enter blazing into Your mouths.

29 I see all people rushing full speed into Your mouths, as moths dash to destruction in a blazing fire.

Śrīla Baladeva Vidyābhūṣaṇa describes the significance of these two analogies – waves of the river flowing into the ocean and moths entering fire – which depict distinct entrances by different warriors into the blazing mouths. Rivers flow into the ocean naturally, without intentional effort, and moths consciously enter fire and perish. Some of the warriors, by their demoniac behavior, are consciously destroying themselves.

30 O Viṣṇu, I see You devouring all people from all sides with Your flaming mouths. Covering all the universe with Your effulgence, You are manifest with terrible, scorching rays.

Here Arjuna describes the universal form's effulgence as covering this universe. It is inescapable and all-pervading.

Arjuna next asks two questions.

31 O Lord of lords, so fierce of form, please tell me who You are. I offer my obeisances unto You; please be gracious to me. You are the primal Lord. I want to know about You, for I do not know what Your mission is.

Arjuna asks: "Who are you?" and "What is Your mission?" Kṛṣṇa answers in the next verse.

32 The Supreme Personality of Godhead said: Time I am, the great destroyer of the worlds, and I have come here to destroy all people. With the exception of you [the Pāṇḍavas], all the soldiers here on both sides will be slain.

What is Kṛṣṇa's all-destructive form? *Kāla-rūpa,* time. What is the mission of the *kāla-rūpa*? Destruction of all the soldiers except the Pāṇḍavas. Śrīla Prabhupāda writes: "The Lord is saying that even if Arjuna did not fight, every one of them would be destroyed, for that was His plan. If Arjuna stopped fighting, they would die in another way. Death could not be checked, even if he did not fight. In fact, they were already dead." Arjuna cannot save anyone's life by not fighting, but he has the choice whether or not to participate in the battle. Kṛṣṇa, however, wants Arjuna to perform his duty. Even though the opposition is already dead, He wishes Arjuna to fight as His instrument.

33 Therefore get up. Prepare to fight and win glory. Conquer your enemies and enjoy a flourishing kingdom. They are already put to death by My arrangement, and you, O Savyasācī, can be but an instrument in the fight.

Savyasācī also means "one who can fight ambidexterously, with either hand, left or right." Kṛṣṇa therefore encourages Arjuna to now use all his skills to fight, without pride, because *pūrvam eva,* "by previous arrangement," not because of Arjuna's skills, the warriors are as good as dead.

34 Droṇa, Bhīṣma, Jayadratha, Karṇa, and the other great warriors have already been destroyed by Me. Therefore, kill them and do not be disturbed. Simply fight, and you will vanquish your enemies in battle.

In Bg. 2.6, Arjuna expressed his uncertainty as to who would win the battle. Here Kṛṣṇa says, *jetā asi,* "You will conquer," to certify that Arjuna will be victorious. Kṛṣṇa also adds Jayadratha's name to the three warriors already mentioned in text 26. Although he is not as powerful as the others, Jayadratha was given a boon by Lord Śiva to be able to stop the Pāṇḍavas once. Because Arjuna knows this, he is concerned about Jayadratha. Kṛṣṇa assures Arjuna that his concern is unwarranted.

Next, Sañjaya introduces a change of speakers.

35 Sañjaya said to Dhṛtarāṣṭra: O king, after hearing these words from the Supreme Personality of Godhead, the trembling Arjuna offered obeisances with folded hands again and again. He fearfully spoke to Lord Kṛṣṇa in a faltering voice, as follows.

Arjuna is called Kirīṭī because he often wore a brilliant celestial helmet by that name given to him by Indra after Arjuna defeated Indra's enemies. Although Arjuna possessed so much power, he stood afraid and trembled in the presence of the universal form. Yet valiant Arjuna remained able to speak.

36 Arjuna said: O master of the senses, the world becomes joyful upon hearing Your name, and thus everyone becomes attached to You. Although the perfected beings offer You their respectful homage, the demons are afraid, and they flee here and there. All this is rightly done.

In this, the first of eleven verses of prayers, Arjuna describes both the fearful and pleasing features of Kṛṣṇa's universal form.

37 O great one, greater even than Brahmā, You are the original creator. Why then should they not offer their respectful obeisances unto You? O limitless one, God of gods, refuge of the universe! You are the invincible source, the cause of all causes, transcendental to this material manifestation.

38 You are the original Personality of Godhead, the oldest, the ultimate sanctuary of this manifested cosmic world. You are the

knower of everything, and You are all that is knowable. You are the supreme refuge, above the material modes. O limitless form! This whole cosmic manifestation is pervaded by You!

39 You are air, and You are the supreme controller! You are fire, You are water, and You are the moon! You are Brahmā, the first living creature, and You are the great-grandfather. I therefore offer my respectful obeisances unto You a thousand times, and again and yet again!

40 Obeisances to You from the front, from behind, and from all sides! O unbounded power, You are the master of limitless might! You are all-pervading, and thus You are everything!

Arjuna, feeling so much reverence while seeing this wondrous and unbounded form, offers Him respectful obeisances again and again.

41–42 Thinking of You as my friend, I have rashly addressed You "O Kṛṣṇa," "O Yādava," "O my friend," not knowing Your glories. Please forgive whatever I may have done in madness or in love. I have dishonored You many times, jesting as we relaxed, lay on the same bed, or sat or ate together, sometimes alone and sometimes in front of many friends. O infallible one, please excuse me for all those offenses.

Śrīla Viśvanātha Cakravartī Ṭhākura explains that Arjuna is lamenting his previous, over-familiar relationship with Kṛṣṇa. For example, he would usually call Kṛṣṇa "Kṛṣṇa," and not the more honorific "Śrī Kṛṣṇa." Arjuna's referring to Kṛṣṇa as "Kṛṣṇa" also indicates that Kṛṣṇa is the son of Vasudeva, who was merely a minister, whereas Arjuna's father, Paṇḍu, was a great warrior. Similarly, Arjuna, a member of the royal Pāṇḍava dynasty, would refer to Kṛṣṇa as "Yādava," a member of a family unable to rule. Furthermore, Arjuna would at times say, "O my friend" as if being condescendingly kind: "Although I am superior to You, out of my affection I accept You as my friend." Now aware of Kṛṣṇa's actual position, Arjuna feels ashamed and begs forgiveness.

43 You are the father of this complete cosmic manifestation, of the moving and the nonmoving. You are its worshipable chief, the supreme spiritual master. No one is equal to You, nor can anyone be one with You. How then could there be anyone greater than You within the three worlds, O Lord of immeasurable power?

44 You are the Supreme Lord, to be worshiped by every living being. Thus I fall down to offer You my respectful obeisances and ask Your mercy. As a father tolerates the impudence of his son, or a friend tolerates the impertinence of a friend, or a wife tolerates the familiarity of her partner, please tolerate the wrongs I may have done You.

Arjuna falls to the ground.

45 After seeing this universal form, which I have never seen before, I am gladdened, but at the same time my mind is disturbed with fear. Therefore please bestow Your grace upon me and reveal again Your form as the Personality of Godhead, O Lord of lords, O abode of the universe.

Arjuna is glad that his friend Kṛṣṇa is so powerful that He is able to exhibit such an incredible form. Nevertheless, beholding that awesome form filled him with fear. His curiosity now satisfied, Arjuna asks Kṛṣṇa to conceal His universal form and again reveal Himself as Kṛṣṇa. First, however, Arjuna will request Kṛṣṇa to reveal His Nārāyaṇa form.

46 O universal form, O thousand-armed Lord, I wish to see You in Your four-armed form, with helmeted head and with club, wheel, conch, and lotus flower in Your hands. I long to see You in that form.

47 The Supreme Personality of Godhead said: My dear Arjuna, happily have I shown you, by My internal potency, this supreme universal form within the material world. No one before you has ever seen this primal form, unlimited and full of glaring effulgence.

Kṛṣṇa's display of the universal form indicates that it is not supreme. Rather, it is contained within Kṛṣṇa's two-armed form. Arjuna was unable to see it previously because Kṛṣṇa's internal energy, His *yoga-māyā,* covered Arjuna's vision. Kṛṣṇa has already declared, at the end of chapter ten, that He, not His universal form, is Supreme – *ekāṁśena sthito jagat:* "With a single fragment of Myself I pervade and support this entire universe."

Śrīla Viśvanātha Cakravartī Ṭhākura says that Kṛṣṇa now asked Arjuna a question: "My dear Arjuna, at your request I showed you this partial expansion of Mine, the *virāṭ-puruṣa.* So why has your mind now become disturbed, and why are you saying to Me, 'Please be kind to me,' and requesting Me to show you My human form?"

Śrīla Prabhupāda mentions in his purport that the universal form seen by Arjuna is different from the one shown to Duryodhana. The form Duryodhana saw displayed neither the same effulgence nor possessed the *kāla* feature.

Kṛṣṇa Himself confirms in the next verse the uniqueness of the form He showed Arjuna.

48 O best of the Kuru warriors, no one before you has ever seen this universal form of Mine, for neither by studying the Vedas, nor by performing sacrifices, nor by charity, nor by pious activities, nor by severe penances can I be seen in this form in the material world.

Neither *sādhana* nor personal endeavor can enable one to see the universal form because it can be seen only by Kṛṣṇa's devotees who have received the specific benediction to see it.

49 You have been perturbed and bewildered by seeing this horrible feature of Mine. Now let it be finished. My devotee, be free again from all disturbances. With a peaceful mind you can now see the form you desire.

Śrīla Prabhupāda writes in his purport: "In the beginning of *Bhagavad-gītā* Arjuna was worried about killing Bhīṣma and Droṇa, his worshipable grandfather and master. But Kṛṣṇa said that he need not be afraid of killing his grandfather. When the sons of Dhṛtarāṣṭra tried to disrobe Draupadī in the assembly of the Kurus, Bhīṣma and Droṇa were silent, and for such negligence of duty they should be killed. Kṛṣṇa showed His universal form to Arjuna just to show him that these people were already killed for their unlawful action. That scene was shown to Arjuna because devotees are always peaceful and they cannot perform such horrible actions. The purpose of the revelation of the universal form was shown; now Arjuna wanted to see the four-armed form, and Kṛṣṇa showed him."

50 Sañjaya said to Dhṛtarāṣṭra: The Supreme Personality of Godhead, Kṛṣṇa, having spoken thus to Arjuna, displayed His real four-armed form and at last showed His two-armed form, thus encouraging the fearful Arjuna.

Śrīla Prabhupāda explains in his purport:

> When Kṛṣṇa appeared as the son of Vasudeva and Devakī, He first of all appeared as four-armed Nārāyaṇa, but when He was requested by His parents, He transformed Himself into an ordinary child in appearance. Similarly, Kṛṣṇa knew that Arjuna was not interested in seeing a four-handed form, but since Arjuna asked to see this four-handed form, Kṛṣṇa also showed him this form again and then showed Himself in His two-handed form. The word *saumya-vapuḥ* is very significant. *Saumya-vapuḥ* is a very beautiful form; it is known as the most beautiful form. When He was present, everyone was attracted simply by Kṛṣṇa's form, and because Kṛṣṇa is the director of the universe, He just banished the fear of Arjuna, His devotee, and showed him again His beautiful form of Kṛṣṇa. In the *Brahma-saṁhitā* (5.38) it is stated, *premāñjana-cchurita-bhakti-vilocanena:* only a person whose eyes are smeared with the ointment of love can see the beautiful form of Śrī Kṛṣṇa.

51 When Arjuna thus saw Kṛṣṇa in His original form, he said: O Janārdana, seeing this humanlike form, so very beautiful, I am now composed in mind, and I am restored to my original nature.

52 The Supreme Personality of Godhead said: My dear Arjuna, this form of Mine you are now seeing is very difficult to behold. Even the demigods are ever seeking the opportunity to see this form, which is so dear.

53 The form you are seeing with your transcendental eyes cannot be understood simply by studying the Vedas, nor by undergoing serious penances, nor by charity, nor by worship. It is not by these means that one can see Me as I am.

Text 53 indirectly glorifies *bhakti* by using negatives. Kṛṣṇa here mentions that the paths He has discussed in chapters one through six will not provide us the means by which we can truly see Him in His most confidential, two-armed form. What, then, is the method by which we can see Kṛṣṇa?

54 My dear Arjuna, only by undivided devotional service can I be understood as I am, standing before you, and can thus be seen directly. Only in this way can you enter into the mysteries of My understanding.

This verse directly glorifies *bhakti*. The word *ananya* emphasizes that devotional service should be undivided, with no influence of *karma* and *jñāna*. The word *praveṣṭum,* "to enter into," is used in the sense of entering a city. When we enter a city, we don't become the city.

55 My dear Arjuna, he who engages in My pure devotional service, free from the contaminations of fruitive activities and mental speculation, he who works for Me, who makes Me the supreme goal of his life, and who is friendly to every living being – he certainly comes to Me.

Kṛṣṇa herein gives Arjuna five powerful instructions on how to render pure devotional service. By executing these five instructions, a devotee can be carried to the Lord. Śrīla Prabhupāda discusses each instruction in his purport:

1) *Bhakti* must be performed purely (*mad-bhaktaḥ*). The devotee must fully engage in the nine processes of devotional

service. The only goal is Kṛṣṇa's service, with no desire for attainments in this world.

2) *Bhakti* must be free from *karma* and *jñāna* (*saṅga-varjitaḥ*). A devotee should not associate with persons who are against Kṛṣṇa, and he should not become attracted to anything but pure devotion. A devotee, at the same time, should not be envious of those who are inimical, because the *karma* of such a person has awarded him that mentality. Devotees should remain disentangled from such a person's *karma*.

3) The work of *bhaktas* must be for Kṛṣṇa (*mat-karma-kṛt*). A devotee should use his energy fully in Kṛṣṇa's service while remaining detached from the fruits of his work.

4) Kṛṣṇa must be the goal of life (*mat-paramaḥ*). The devotee should remain unattracted to both heavenly and impersonal destinations.

5) The devotee must be friendly to all (*nirvairaḥ*). He must compassionately desire to give Kṛṣṇa consciousness to others.

In chapter seven, Kṛṣṇa described Himself as the Supreme Lord and said that we can see everything in this world as an expansion of two of His energies. In chapter nine, Kṛṣṇa again explained that everything comes from Him and should be seen in relationship to Him. Kṛṣṇa concluded chapter nine by saying that everyone, regardless of birth, should worship Him with devotion. In chapter ten, Kṛṣṇa explained His opulences and said, *ahaṁ sarvasya prabhavo mattaḥ sarvaṁ pravartate:* "I am the source of all spiritual and material worlds. Everything emanates from Me." At the end of chapter ten, Kṛṣṇa stated, *ekāṁśena sthito jagat:* "With a single fragment of Myself I pervade and support this entire universe."

After explaining this confidential knowledge to Arjuna, Kṛṣṇa proved His words by displaying His universal form before Arjuna, Sañjaya, and the demigods. Kṛṣṇa thus established the future criterion for those who claim to be God. Caitanya Mahāprabhu, who is the Supreme Lord, also showed His universal form at the home of Śrīvāsa Ṭhākura.

Śrīla Prabhupāda's purport sweetly concludes this chapter: "In summary, the universal form of Kṛṣṇa, which is a temporary manifestation, and the form of time which devours everything, and even the form of Viṣṇu, four-handed, have all been exhibited by Kṛṣṇa. Thus Kṛṣṇa is the origin of all these manifestations. It is not that Kṛṣṇa is a manifestation of the original *viśva-rūpa,* or Viṣṇu. Kṛṣṇa is the origin of all forms. There are hundreds and thousands of Viṣṇus, but for a devotee no form of Kṛṣṇa is important but the original form, two-handed Śyāmasundara. In the *Brahma-saṁhitā* it is stated that those who are attached to the Śyāmasundara form of Kṛṣṇa in love and devotion can see Him always within the heart and cannot see anything else. One should understand, therefore, that the purport of this eleventh chapter is that the form of Kṛṣṇa is essential and supreme."

Chapter Twelve

Devotional Service

By observing what is stated at a long passage's beginning and end, one is pointed toward understanding that passage's theme. The *Gītā's* middle set of six chapters – the set emphasizing *bhakti-yoga* – began with *bhakti,* prefaced by the final verse of chapter six: *yogінām api sarveṣāṁ, mad-gatenāntar-ātmanā/ śraddhāvān bhajate yo māṁ, sa me yuktatamo mataḥ,* "And of all *yogīs,* the one with great faith who always abides in Me, thinks of Me within himself, and renders transcendental loving service to Me – he is the most intimately united with Me in *yoga* and is the highest of all. That is My opinion."

Arjuna therefore wants the end of this set of chapters – chapter twelve – to conclude with Kṛṣṇa discussing *bhakti.* He especially wants this because the vivid description of the universal form in chapter eleven naturally fills us with awe, reverence, and fear, none of which are conducive to advanced Kṛṣṇa consciousness. In addition, to help us avoid mistaking the universal form – impersonalism within matter – as the supreme aspect of the Absolute Truth, and to ensure that all recognize the superiority of *bhakti* (devotional work to attain the loving service of Kṛṣṇa) over *jñāna* (the renunciation of work to attain impersonal realization), Arjuna now questions Kṛṣṇa.

1 Arjuna inquired: Which are considered to be more perfect, those who are always properly engaged in Your devotional service or those who worship the impersonal Brahman, the unmanifested?

Śrīla Prabhupāda describes two types of impersonalists in his purport to *Śrīmad-Bhāgavatam* 2.10.35: "The impersonalists think of the Absolute Personality of Godhead in two different ways. . . .On the one hand they worship the Lord in His *viśva-rūpa,* or all-pervading universal form, and on the other they think of the Lord's unmanifested, indescribable, subtle form. The theories of pantheism and monism are respectively applicable to these two conceptions of the Supreme as gross and subtle, but both of them are rejected by the learned pure devotees of the Lord."

In his purport to this *Gītā* verse, Śrīla Prabhupāda explains:

> Kṛṣṇa has now explained about the personal, the impersonal, and the universal and has described all kinds of devotees and *yogīs*. Generally, the transcendentalists can be divided into two classes. One is the impersonalist, and the other is the personalist....Now Arjuna is trying to settle the question of which process is easier and which of the classes is most perfect. In other words, he is clarifying his own position because he is attached to the personal form of Kṛṣṇa. He is not attached to the impersonal Brahman. He wants to know whether his position is secure. The impersonal manifestation, either in this material world or in the spiritual world of the Supreme Lord, is a problem for meditation. Actually, one cannot perfectly conceive of the impersonal feature of the Absolute Truth. Therefore Arjuna wants to say, "What is the use of such a waste of time?" In the eleventh chapter Arjuna experienced that to be attached to the personal form of Kṛṣṇa is best because he could thus understand all other forms at the same time and there was no disturbance to his love for Kṛṣṇa. This important question asked of Kṛṣṇa by Arjuna will clarify the distinction between the impersonal and personal conceptions of the Absolute Truth.

Next, Kṛṣṇa's reply.

2 The Supreme Personality of Godhead said: Those who fix their minds on My personal form and are always engaged in worshiping Me with great and transcendental faith are considered by Me to be most perfect.

Kṛṣṇa's answer is clear: Devotees engaged in His service are better. Śrīla Prabhupāda's purport gives practical examples of Kṛṣṇa conscious work on the transcendental platform: "Sometimes he chants, sometimes he hears or reads books about Kṛṣṇa, or sometimes he cooks *prasāda* or goes to the marketplace to purchase something for Kṛṣṇa, or sometimes he washes the temple or the dishes – whatever he does, he does not let a single moment pass without devoting his activities to Kṛṣṇa. Such action is in full *samādhi*."

Arjuna is happy to hear that devotional service is superior, but he wonders, "What is the attainment of an impersonalist, who, renouncing work, is able to 'fully worship the unmanifested'?"

3–4 But those who fully worship the unmanifested, that which lies beyond the perception of the senses, the all-pervading, inconceivable, unchanging, fixed, and immovable – the impersonal conception of the Absolute Truth – by controlling the various senses and being equally disposed to everyone, such persons, engaged in the welfare of all, at last achieve Me.

Those worshiping the impersonal certainly achieve Kṛṣṇa – *prāpnuvanti mām eva* – but only His effulgence, the *brahmajyoti,* His *nirviśeṣa,* or formless aspect, devoid of attributes and activities. Or, if by good fortune, they later meet an exalted devotee, they may accept the personal path and eventually achieve Kṛṣṇa's service.

Having replied that personal realization is superior, Kṛṣṇa now informs Arjuna of the inferiority of the impersonalist's process of realization.

5 For those whose minds are attached to the unmanifested, impersonal feature of the Supreme, advancement is very troublesome. To make progress in that discipline is always difficult for those who are embodied.

The impersonalist's path of renunciation of activities is troublesome and miserable. Why? The embodied soul's senses are always demanding engagement and want to contact sense objects. However, no spiritual activity exists for one who has renounced work. Nor is the impersonalist able to fix his mind on the goal of his meditation practices. For how can one conceive of the inconceivable?

We may argue that a devotee also experiences trouble on his path because he too must follow rules and regulations that restrict the contact of the senses with their objects. However, a devotee's misery is reduced because he experiences Kṛṣṇa's presence. Rejecting *māyā's* demands for Kṛṣṇa's service actually brings him pleasure.

Impersonalists may read this verse and respond, "Because Kṛṣṇa has certified the path of renunciation and meditation as troublesome, I will engage in devotional service to Kṛṣṇa, though I know that His form is temporary. Thus I will soon achieve Brahman." However, in Bg. 9.11–12, Kṛṣṇa has already nullified the validity of *bhakti* practiced in this fashion. *Avajānanti māṁ mūḍhā, mānuṣīṁ tanum āśritam/ paraṁ bhāvam ajānanto, mama bhūta-maheśvaram:* "Fools deride Me when I descend in the human form. They do not know My transcendental nature as the Supreme Lord of all that be." *Moghāśā mogha-karmāṇo, mogha-jñānā vicetasaḥ/ rākṣasīm āsurīṁ caiva, prakṛtiṁ mohinīṁ śritāḥ:* "Those who are thus bewildered are attracted by demonic and atheistic views. In that deluded condition, their hopes for liberation, their fruitive activities, and their culture of knowledge are all defeated."

Those who think of Kṛṣṇa's form as a temporary object which may be worshiped to facilitate impersonal realization are bewildered, and their hopes for knowledge are baffled.

The ease of attaining the desired goal by practicing true *bhakti* is next described.

6–7 But those who worship Me, giving up all their activities unto Me and being devoted to Me without deviation, engaged in devotional service and always meditating upon Me, having fixed their minds upon Me, O son of Pṛthā – for them I am the swift deliverer from the ocean of birth and death.

Although a devotee may experience difficulties, he has faith in Kṛṣṇa's promise to personally care for him and deliver him. Śrīla Prabhupāda powerfully expresses this:

> The purport of this verse is that a devotee does not need to practice *aṣṭāṅga-yoga* in order to transfer his soul to the spiritual planets. The responsibility is taken by the Supreme Lord Himself. He clearly states here that He Himself becomes the deliverer. A child is completely cared for by his parents, and thus his position is secure. Similarly, a devotee does not need to

> endeavor to transfer himself by *yoga* practice to other planets. Rather, the Supreme Lord, by His great mercy, comes at once, riding on His bird carrier Garuḍa, and at once delivers the devotee from material existence. Although a man who has fallen in the ocean may struggle very hard and may be very expert in swimming, he cannot save himself. But if someone comes and picks him up from the water, then he is easily rescued. Similarly, the Lord picks up the devotee from this material existence. One simply has to practice the easy process of Kṛṣṇa consciousness and fully engage himself in devotional service.

A devotee's responsibility is to cultivate devotion and eagerness to serve Kṛṣṇa. Kṛṣṇa then accepts full responsibility for rescuing His devotee from *māyā*. The devotee's mood is so pure that he doesn't even desire the liberation the Lord is willing to bestow upon him. Lord Caitanya prays, *janmani janmanīśvare bhavatād bhaktir ahaituki tvayi:* "All I want is Your devotional service, even if it means taking birth after birth in the material world." That intense, fully pure, and devotional desire of a devotee to serve Kṛṣṇa attracts His full mercy.

In the next five verses (8–12), Kṛṣṇa, beginning with the highest stage, describes levels of achievement in *bhakti*.

8 Just fix your mind upon Me, the Supreme Personality of Godhead, and engage all your intelligence in Me. Thus you will live in Me always, without a doubt.

A *jñānī* tries to fix his mind on the unmanifest (*avyakta*) and the reality of his spiritual existence as a soul. Kṛṣṇa's direct order to His devotee, however, is given here: "Always fix your mind on My all-attractive, beautiful form." To emphasize this instruction, Kṛṣṇa uses the word *mayi,* "on Me," three times in this verse. By always meditating on Kṛṣṇa in line with śāstric direction, one will undoubtedly always live with Kṛṣṇa. Thus Kṛṣṇa has explained the most advanced stage: to always think of Him in attachment and transcendental affection.

Because constant remembrance of Kṛṣṇa is exalted consciousness, one naturally wonders, "What practice should I follow if I am unable to always remember Kṛṣṇa?" Kṛṣṇa's reply describes the next level down.

9 My dear Arjuna, O winner of wealth, if you cannot fix your mind upon Me without deviation, then follow the regulative principles of bhakti-yoga. In this way develop a desire to attain Me.

Kṛṣṇa calls Arjuna Dhanañjaya, "the winner of wealth," because Arjuna obtained riches by fighting. Kṛṣṇa now requests Arjuna to fight his mind and obtain the wealth of meditation on Him.

Kṛṣṇa has already discussed *abhyāsa-yoga* in Bg. 6.35. *Abhyāsa-yoga* is the constant practice of thinking of Kṛṣṇa.

Śrīla Prabhupāda describes the practices of *sādhana* that elevate one to the stage of attachment to Kṛṣṇa: "To practice the regulative principles of *bhakti-yoga* one should, under the guidance of an expert spiritual master, follow certain principles: one should rise early in the morning, take bath, enter the temple and offer prayers, and chant Hare Kṛṣṇa, then collect flowers to offer to the Deity, cook foodstuffs to offer to the Deity, take *prasāda,* and so on. There are various rules and regulations which one should follow. And one should constantly hear *Bhagavad-gītā* and *Śrīmad-Bhāgavatam* from pure devotees. This practice can help anyone rise to the level of love of God."

In *Bhakti-rasāmṛta-sindhu,* Śrīla Rūpa Gosvāmī has quoted a statement from the *Padma Purāṇa* that describes constant remembrance of Kṛṣṇa as the goal of all *sādhana* practices. *Smartavyaḥ satataṁ viṣṇur, vismartavyo na jātucit/ sarve vidhi-niṣedhāḥ, syur etayor eva kiṅkarāḥ:* "Kṛṣṇa is the origin of Lord Viṣṇu. He should always be remembered and never be forgotten at any time. All the rules and prohibitions mentioned in the *śāstras* should be the servants of these two principles."

But what should one do if he finds himself unable, even by practice, to always think of Kṛṣṇa?

10 If you cannot practice the regulations of bhakti-yoga, then just try to work for Me, because by working for Me you will come to the perfect stage.

The previous two verses dealt primarily with engaging our mind, the chief of the internal senses. This verse refers to engaging our external senses in Kṛṣṇa's service as a means of further advancement. Even if we are unable to think of Kṛṣṇa, we can make progress by working for Him. This platform is called *niṣkāma karma-yoga.*

Again, Śrīla Prabhupāda gives practical instructions for one at this stage of spiritual development: "If one has sufficient money, he can help in building an office or temple for propagating Kṛṣṇa consciousness. Or he can help with publications. There are various fields of activity, and one should be interested in such activities. If one cannot sacrifice the results of his activities, the same person can still sacrifice some percentage to propagate Kṛṣṇa consciousness. This voluntary service to the cause of Kṛṣṇa consciousness will help one to rise to a higher state of love for God, whereupon one becomes perfect."

In his purport Śrīla Prabhupāda has also defined the next step down from *niṣkāma karma-yoga, sakāma karma-yoga,* by saying, "If one cannot sacrifice the results of his activities, the same person can still sacrifice some percentage to propagate Kṛṣṇa consciousness."

What can we do if we are unable to act on any of the above stages?

11 If, however, you are unable to work in this consciousness of Me, then try to act giving up all results of your work and try to be self-situated.

Śrīla Prabhupāda writes:

> It may be that one is unable even to sympathize with the activities of Kṛṣṇa consciousness because of social, familial, or religious considerations or because of some other impediments. . . . For one who has such a problem, it is advised that he sacrifice the accumulated result of his activities to some good cause. Such procedures are described in the Vedic rules. . . . Thus one may gradually become elevated to the state of knowledge. It is also found that when one who is not even interested in the activities of Kṛṣṇa consciousness gives charity to some hospital or some other social institution, he gives up the hard-earned results of his activities. That is also recommended here because by the practice of giving up the fruits of one's activities one is sure to purify his mind gradually, and in that

purified stage of mind one becomes able to understand Kṛṣṇa consciousness.

In texts 8–10, the spiritual results of each recommended practice have been described. By thinking of Kṛṣṇa, as described in text 8, we will always live with Kṛṣṇa. By following the regulative principles of *bhakti,* as mentioned in text 9, we will develop our desire to attain Kṛṣṇa. By working for Kṛṣṇa, as described in text 10, we will come to the perfect stage. No result, however, has been mentioned for following the practice Kṛṣṇa recommends in text 11. The practice of giving up the fruits of work, unless those fruits are offered to Kṛṣṇa, is not in and of itself spiritual, and therefore it does not yield tangible fruit.

In text 12, the renunciation of the fruits of one's work *for Kṛṣṇa's service,* as described in text 10 – not simply the detached work described in text 11 – is placed in perspective with other less important practices for spiritual advancement.

12 If you cannot take to this practice, then engage yourself in the cultivation of knowledge. Better than knowledge, however, is meditation, and better than meditation is renunciation of the fruits of action, for by such renunciation one can attain peace of mind.

"If you cannot take to this practice" refers to the practice of *niṣkāma karma-yoga* described in text 10 (not to the practice of giving up all results of one's work for a good cause, described in text 11). "Knowledge" here refers to *brahma-jñāna,* knowledge of the soul as different from the body, and "meditation" suggests yogic meditation by which one will realize the Supersoul.

Thus these verses describe a sequence: text 8 – perfected devotional service, which means always remembering Kṛṣṇa; text 9 – devotional service in practice, or performing *sādhana-bhakti* and working for Kṛṣṇa as Kṛṣṇa desires (i.e., performing typical temple services); text 10 and 12 – *niṣkāma karma-yoga* or working with detachment and offering the fruits of that work to Kṛṣṇa. This stage awards one peace, *bhakti,* as described in "the peace formula" (Bg. 5.29).

Two other stages, which are lower than *niṣkāma karma-yoga,* are also mentioned in text 12: *yoga* and cultivating knowledge, or *brahma-jñāna.* Still lower than *brahma-jñāna,* and without a direct transcendental result, is the method mentioned in text 11: detached work without offering the fruits to Kṛṣṇa. (Kṛṣṇa has already explained in chapter five that by working in a detached fashion one attains *brahma-jñāna.*)

Thus Kṛṣṇa has delineated relative grades of spiritual processes and spiritual progress. Śrīla Prabhupāda has also explained these stages in his purport:

> In summary, to reach the Supreme Personality of Godhead, the highest goal, there are two processes: one process is by gradual development, and the other process is direct. Devotional service in Kṛṣṇa consciousness is the direct method, and the other method involves renouncing the fruits of one's activities [the stage in text 11]. Then one can come to the stage of knowledge, then to the stage of meditation, then to the stage of understanding the Supersoul, and then to the stage of the Supreme Personality of Godhead. One may take either the step-by-step process or the direct path. The direct process is not possible for everyone; therefore the indirect process is also good. It is, however, to be understood that the indirect process is not recommended for Arjuna, because he is already at the stage of loving devotional service to the Supreme Lord. It is for others, who are not at this stage; for them the gradual process of renunciation, knowledge, meditation, and realization of the Supersoul and Brahman should be followed. But as far as *Bhagavad-gītā* is concerned, it is the direct method that is stressed. Everyone is advised to take to the direct method and surrender unto the Supreme Personality of Godhead, Kṛṣṇa.

In the final verses in this chapter, Kṛṣṇa again comes to the point of pure devotional service. He describes thirty-five transcendental qualities possessed by His pure devotees, which make those devotees dear to Him.

13–14 One who is not envious but is a kind friend to all living entities, who does not think himself a proprietor and is free from false ego, who is equal in both happiness and distress, who is tolerant, always satisfied, self-controlled, and engaged in

devotional service with determination, his mind and intelligence fixed on Me – such a devotee of Mine is very dear to Me.

The last eight texts of this chapter (13–20) describe the internal symptoms of persons engaged in pure devotional service. The term *adveṣṭā,* or nonenvious, is exemplified when a devotee thinks in terms of his enemy – as Śrīla Baladeva Vidyābhūṣaṇa says – "This person hates me, and that is because of my own *prārabdha-karma* [matured reaction of *karma*]; as Kṛṣṇa is the ultimate controller, his hatred must have Kṛṣṇa's sanction."

15 He for whom no one is put into difficulty and who is not disturbed by anyone, who is equipoised in happiness and distress, fear and anxiety, is very dear to Me.

16 My devotee who is not dependent on the ordinary course of activities, who is pure, expert, without cares, free from all pains, and not striving for some result, is very dear to Me.

17 One who neither rejoices nor grieves, who neither laments nor desires, and who renounces both auspicious and inauspicious things – such a devotee is very dear to Me.

18–19 One who is equal to friends and enemies, who is equipoised in honor and dishonor, heat and cold, happiness and distress, fame and infamy, who is always free from contaminating association, always silent and satisfied with anything, who doesn't care for any residence, who is fixed in knowledge and who is engaged in devotional service – such a person is very dear to Me.

Śrīla Prabhupāda writes: "We may find some repetition in the descriptions of the qualifications of a devotee, but this is just to emphasize the fact that a devotee must acquire all these qualifications. Without good qualifications, one cannot be a pure devotee. *Harāv abhaktasya kuto mahad-guṇāḥ:* one who is not a devotee has no good qualification. One who wants to be recognized as a devotee should develop the good qualifications. Of course he does not extraneously endeavor to acquire these qualifications, but engagement in Kṛṣṇa consciousness and devotional service automatically helps him develop them."

20 Those who follow this imperishable path of devotional service and who completely engage themselves with faith, making Me the supreme goal, are very, very dear to Me.

Śrīla Viśvanātha Cakravartī Ṭhākura concludes this chapter: "These characteristics that arise in one from devotion and from peacefulness are not material qualities. This is in accordance with the statement 'Kṛṣṇa is satisfied only by devotion, never by material qualities.' The word 'but' (*tu*) in this verse indicates the introduction of a new idea. The devotees described up to this point have each perfectly cultivated one aspect of their personalities. Those mentioned in this verse, however, are desirous of perfecting all these qualities. Therefore, even during the stage of *sādhana,* they are superior to those on other paths even if those individuals have achieved the perfected stage of their paths. For this reason the word *atīva* ('extremely' or 'very, very') is used in this verse."

Śrīla Prabhupāda summarizes this chapter in his purport: "In this chapter, from verse 2 through the end . . . the Supreme Lord has explained the processes of transcendental service for approaching Him. Such processes are very dear to the Lord, and He accepts a person engaged in them. The question of who is better – one who is engaged in the path of impersonal Brahman or one who is engaged in the personal service of the Supreme Personality of Godhead – was raised by Arjuna, and the Lord replied to him so explicitly that there is no doubt that devotional service to the Personality of Godhead is the best of all processes of spiritual realization."

Chapter Thirteen

Nature, the Enjoyer, and Consciousness

In the first six chapters of *Bhagavad-gītā,* Kṛṣṇa discussed how *karma*, action on the platform of knowledge, leads to *bhakti.* In the second six chapters, Kṛṣṇa spoke directly of Himself and the glories of devotional service. In the third six chapters, beginning with chapter thirteen, Kṛṣṇa discusses how *jñāna* leads to *bhakti.*

Śrīla Prabhupāda introduces the topics of the final six chapters in his purport to texts 1–2: "Now, starting with the thirteenth chapter, how the living entity comes into contact with material nature and how he is delivered by the Supreme Lord through the different methods of fruitive activities, cultivation of knowledge, and the discharge of devotional service are explained. Although the living entity is completely different from the material body, he somehow becomes related. This also is explained."

Arjuna begins chapter thirteen by asking about six topics.

1–2 Arjuna said: O my dear Kṛṣṇa, I wish to know about prakṛti [nature], puruṣa [the enjoyer], and the field and the knower of the field, and of knowledge and the object of knowledge. The Supreme Personality of Godhead said: This body, O son of Kuntī, is called the field, and one who knows this body is called the knower of the field.

Arjuna requests knowledge about *prakṛti* (nature); *puruṣa* (the enjoyer); *kṣetra* (the field of activities); *kṣetra-jña* (the knower of the field of activities); *jñānam* (knowledge), and *jñeyam* (the object of knowledge).

Kṛṣṇa immediately begins to address Arjuna's third topic by identifying the body as the field (*kṣetra*). He also deals with the fourth topic by saying that the soul is the knower of the field (*kṣetra-jña*).

In texts 3–7, Kṛṣṇa will continue to explain the field of activities and the knower of the field. In text 3, He will also begin to explain knowledge, the fifth topic about which Arjuna inquired.

3 O scion of Bharata, you should understand that I am also the knower in all bodies, and to understand this body and its knower is called knowledge. That is My opinion.

As we hear Kṛṣṇa's answers in this chapter, we will learn how the living entity is brought into connection with his body and is entangled by it. The body, in this chapter, is often referred to as a *kṣetra,* a field. Just as different crops grow in a farmer's field according to the seeds he has planted, a living entity's happiness and distress similarly grow in his body – his field of activities – according to his previous actions. The living entity, as the *kṣetra-jña,* knows his own body, but Kṛṣṇa says that another *kṣetra-jña* knows all bodies. That *kṣetra-jña* is the Supersoul. A farmer, like the soul, knows all about his own field, but the king, like the Supersoul in everyone's heart, is the ultimate controller and knower of each and every field in his kingdom. In addition, the soul can only imperfectly know his own body; the Supersoul has complete and perfect knowledge of all bodies.

In this verse Kṛṣṇa has defined knowledge (*jñāna*) as knowing the body, the soul, and the Supersoul. He will complete His description of knowledge in texts 8–12 and 24–37 by explaining the process of achieving knowledge.

Śrīla Prabhupāda defines *jñāna* in his purport: "Perfect knowledge of the constitution of the body, the constitution of the individual soul, and the constitution of the Supersoul is known in terms of Vedic literature as *jñāna*. That is the opinion of Kṛṣṇa. To understand both the soul and the Supersoul as one yet distinct is knowledge. One who does not understand the field of activity and the knower of activity is not in perfect knowledge."

Kṛṣṇa already discussed this point in chapter five: The living entity's realization that "I am not this body" constitutes enlightenment. Such enlightenment, however, born of the mode of goodness, is insufficient for liberation. When his knowledge increases to include knowledge of the Supersoul, he becomes liberated. Thus to come to the *brahma-bhūta* (liberated) platform, one needs to know the Supersoul.

Śaṅkarācārya and other impersonalists have commented extensively on this verse. They say that the word *ca* means: "You should know that he who is the knower within the body is also (*ca*) Me," i.e., the soul is the same as the Supersoul. Were that true, however, Kṛṣṇa would be contradicting His own statements in chapter fifteen wherein He clearly makes distinctions between the soul and the Supersoul. If the soul and the Supersoul are factually one, as Māyāvādīs claim, how could one aspect of the "one," which is by definition undifferentiated, give knowledge to the other aspect of the "one"? How could the other aspect be lacking? How could something undifferentiated even possess an aspect? If both were "one," absolutely no differentiation (even in terms of knowing and not knowing) could exist.

Śrīla Prabhupāda also comments on *ca* in his purport: "The word *ca* is significant, for it indicates the total number of bodies. That is the opinion of Śrīla Baladeva Vidyābhūṣaṇa. Kṛṣṇa is the Supersoul present in each and every body apart from the individual soul. And Kṛṣṇa explicitly says here that the Supersoul is the controller of both the field of activities and the finite enjoyer."

Śrīla Viśvanātha Cakravartī Ṭhākura explains:

> This body, equipped with senses, is the facility for material contact and is the so-called field because it is the ground on which the tree of material existence grows. The *jīva* who knows the body is called the *kṣetra-jña*, both in his condition of bondage, wherein he identifies himself with the body (thinking in terms of "I" and "mine"), and in his liberated condition, in which he does not indentify with the body (or conceptions of "I" and "mine").
>
> Like a farmer, the *kṣetra-jña* is also the enjoyer of the fruits of the tree in his field, as described by the Personality of Godhead: "The village vultures eat one fruit of this tree, while the forest swans eat another. One who, by the grace of worshipable souls, understands this tree, composed of *māyā* and appearing in many forms, is an actual knower of the *Vedas*." This

verse means: Vultures, who live outside a village, are called vultures (*ghṛdhra*) because they "seize" [sense gratification]. They are like the conditioned *jīvas,* who eat one fruit of this tree – misery. Even if they attain heaven, their experience is ultimately miserable. The swans living in the forest, however, are like liberated *jīvas*. They eat the fruit of happiness. The complete enjoyment of liberation is derived from their experience.

Thus the one tree of material existence appears in many forms, as the means of attaining hell, heaven, and liberation. Because it is born from the Lord's external energy, it is called *māyā-mayam*. By the grace of the worshipable spiritual masters, one is made to understand this tree. Those who are in knowledge of the *kṣetra* and *kṣetra-jña* actually know the *Vedas.*

Śrīla Baladeva Vidyābhūṣaṇa explains: "This body is perceived by ignorant persons as different kinds of selves: 'I am a demigod,' 'I am a human,' 'I am stout' and so on. Nonetheless, one who knows that in all conditions (sleeping, sitting, etc.) the body is separate from the self and is the means of the self's enjoyment and liberation – that person, distinct as the knower of the body, which is his object of knowledge – is called the *kṣetra-jña* by experts in knowledge of the factual identity of the field and the knower of the field."

Kṛṣṇa continues to explain the field of activities and its knower in the next text.

4 Now please hear My brief description of this field of activity and how it is constituted, what its changes are, whence it is produced, who that knower of the field of activities is, and what his influences are.

Kṛṣṇa raises five points in this verse, which He will elaborate on later in this chapter: 1) how the body is constituted (explained in text 6); 2) what changes the body undergoes (explained in texts 7 and 20); 3) how, when, and where the body is produced (explained in texts 6, 21, and 22); 4) the identity of the knower of the field of activities (explained in texts 14–18 and 23), and 5) the influence of the knower (explained in texts 14–18).

Although Kṛṣṇa will discuss these five points and address the remaining topics from text 2, He says He will explain them only in brief because they are limitless topics. However, should Arjuna wish to know them in greater detail, Kṛṣṇa next tells Arjuna where such information can be found.

5 That knowledge of the field of activities and of the knower of activities is described by various sages in various Vedic writings. It is especially presented in Vedānta-sūtra with all reasoning as to cause and effect.

Although Kṛṣṇa has just said in text 3, "That is My opinion," and although He has already established His position as the Supreme Personality of Godhead, He nonetheless refers to two other authorities to substantiate His words. Kṛṣṇa, in the role of *guru,* thus presents corresponding references to *sādhu* and *śāstra*. Śrīla Prabhupāda states: "The Supreme Personality of Godhead, Kṛṣṇa, is the highest authority in explaining this knowledge. Still, as a matter of course, learned scholars and standard authorities always give evidence from previous authorities. Kṛṣṇa is explaining this most controversial point regarding the duality and nonduality of the soul and the Supersoul by referring to a scripture, the *Vedānta,* which is accepted as authority."

By quoting from the *Taittirīya Upaniṣad* of the *Yajur Veda,* Śrīla Prabhupāda confirms Kṛṣṇa's words that more details are available in the *Vedas*. There are basically two Vedic systems by which one progresses indirectly, without descending information, in realization. The second chapter of the *Taittirīya Upaniṣad,* which Śrīla Prabhupāda quotes in his purport, describes one of them. It is called *vyaṣṭi,* the system in which a person directs his meditation toward the self and thus seeks to understand the Absolute by considering himself a fragment of the Supreme. Analogously, one can study the nature of the entire ocean by scrutinizing a drop. The second indirect system is called *samaṣṭi,* in which one studies the entirety of the universe while considering it the body of the Supreme.

In the *vyaṣṭi* system, one observes, encasing the living entity's consciousness, five *kośas,* or sheaths: *anna-maya,* dependence on food for existence; *prāṇa-maya,* living symptoms and life forms; *jñāna-maya,* thinking, feeling, and willing; *vijñāna-maya,* distinguishing the mind and life symptoms from the self; and *ānanda-maya,* realization of the all-blissful nature. All five are progressively developed stages of subjective, individual consciousness (or self-concepts) and are also objective manifestations of the Lord's energy in which Brahman, the Absolute, or the greatest, is realized even if indirectly or relatively.

A mundane example of subjective consciousness that nevertheless has objective existence is one's relationship with his country of birth. A citizen does not create the concept of belonging to that country as its citizen; the country itself creates the category and the requirements of citizenship. Citizenship, therefore, exists independently as a reality outside of an individual. However, a human being who possesses the requirement of a specific type of subjectively experienced consciousness will identify with his country and consider himself Indian or American or Russian. Dogs, monkeys, birds, and so on do not possess the required subjective consciousness to identify themselves with their country of birth, though they certainly exist within that country. In the same way, the five *kośas* are both subjectively experienced stages of consciousness and objective energies – levels of Brahman realization – manifest by the Supreme.

One experiencing the *anna-maya* stage experiences a unifying oneness by viewing all as potential food. Such a consciousness makes no distinction between that which is alive and that which is not. It does not even possess any awareness of its own existence as separate from the existence of all else. Although this self-concept is the most basic form of consciousness, it is nevertheless also a manifestation of the Lord's energy.

When one comes to the stage of *prāṇa-maya,* his consciousness advances to an awareness of his own active life symptoms, and he identifies with them. His view of the external world is unified by the principle of maintaining his own survival. Materialistic human society, more or less, exists on this primitive level of realization. Again, as with all the *kośas,* this stage of consciousness is also the Lord's energy.

In *jñāna-maya,* one's self-concept expands to awareness of his own thinking, feeling, and willing. One's perception of reality is then based on and limited by that vision. Śrīla

Rāmanujācārya, however, explains that the *Taittirīya Upaniṣad* places on the *jñāna-maya* platform only those civilized human beings who follow Vedic culture. According to him, this is because one's perceptions and actions must be based on actual knowledge, Vedic knowledge, to qualify one for the platform of *jñāna-maya,* which is full of knowledge.

These first three stages refer to a living entity trapped in illusion – one who fully identifies with and is limited by his field of activities. In the fourth stage, the *vijñāna-maya* stage, the living entity realizes himself as eternal spirit, separate from his gross and subtle bodies. This is the platform of transcendental knowledge.

The Supreme Lord is known as *ānanda-maya,* full of bliss, and in this final stage of consciousness, one realizes and identifies himself as a servant of that supremely blissful Lord.

Thus the Lord expands His energy as the five *kośas* and provides levels of consciousness to the *kṣetra-jña,* the knower of a field of activities.

Śrīla Prabhupāda writes: "To enjoy His transcendental bliss, [the Supreme Lord] expands into *vijñāna-maya, prāṇa-maya, jñāna-maya,* and *anna-maya.* In the field of activities the living entity is considered to be the enjoyer, and different from him is the *ānanda-maya.* That means that if the living entity decides to enjoy in dovetailing himself with the *ānanda-maya,* then he becomes perfect. This is the real picture of the Supreme Lord as the supreme knower of the field, the living entity as the subordinate knower, and the nature of the field of activities. One has to search for this truth in the *Vedānta-sūtra,* or *Brahma-sūtra.*"

6–7 The five great elements, false ego, intelligence, the unmanifested, the ten senses and the mind, the five sense objects, desire, hatred, happiness, distress, the aggregate, the life symptoms, and convictions – all these are considered, in summary, to be the field of activities and its interactions.

Here Kṛṣṇa gives a more detailed explanation of the field of activities. Text 6 lists the five great elements, false ego, intelligence, the unmanifest, the ten senses, the mind, and the five sense objects – the twenty-four material elements. Text 7 describes seven qualities of the mind derived from the interactions of the twenty-four elements. These qualities are also within the realm of the living entity's field of activities.

Kṛṣṇa mentioned in text 4 that He would discuss the *vikāras,* the changes undergone by the body. Śrīla Prabhupāda mentions these changes in his purport: "The body is the representation of all these factors, and there are changes of the body, which are six in number: the body is born, it grows, it stays, it produces by-products, then it begins to decay, and at the last stage it vanishes. Therefore the field is a nonpermanent material thing. However the *kṣetra-jña,* the knower of the field, its proprietor, is different."

The field of activities for the conditioned soul can be compared to a playground in a backyard surrounded by a big fence. The child playing there has freedom to play as he wishes, but he cannot extend his activities beyond the allotted field. He is limited by the fence. Similarly, the living entity is limited by the interactions of his body, mind, and *karma*, which constitute his field of activities. An earthworm, for example, has a very small field of activities. He cannot read, write, jump, or run. He can simply crawl through the dirt, surface when it rains, and crawl back into the soil when the rain stops. A dog has a relatively larger field of activities, and a human being a still larger one. One's *kṣetra* is based on his *karma*.

A wealthy child will possess many toys to play with in his backyard, but he is still restricted by the fence. Although he may be proud of the scope of his playground and even think himself happy and free with his swing and toy car and sandbox, he is nevertheless absorbed only in an insignificant backyard. He knows nothing of life beyond the fence. Similarly, the living entity, according to the limitations of the body and mind he has received through his *karma,* cannot see beyond his limited field of activities.

Every living entity's *kṣetra* is arranged by his *karma,* through the agency of *māyā.* Kṛṣṇa therefore is not partial, because as the Supersoul, the knower of all *kṣetras,* He simply sanctions the awarding of each living entity's field of activities.

Kṛṣṇa next explains the process of knowledge – that process which helps the living entity transcend his insignificant and limited "backyard."

8–12 Humility; pridelessness; nonviolence; tolerance; simplicity; approaching a bona fide spiritual master; cleanliness; steadiness; self-control; renunciation of the objects of sense gratification; absence of false ego; the perception of the evil of birth, death, old age, and disease; detachment; freedom from entanglement with children, wife, home, and the rest; even-mindedness amid pleasant and unpleasant events; constant and unalloyed devotion to Me; aspiring to live in a solitary place; detachment from the general mass of people; accepting the importance of self-realization; and philosophical search for the Absolute Truth – all these I declare to be knowledge, and besides this whatever there may be is ignorance.

This is a continuation of Kṛṣṇa's explanation of knowledge. Kṛṣṇa has already defined knowledge as knowing the field and the two knowers of the field. These verses describe the process of obtaining *jñāna*. According to Śrīla Viśvanātha Cakravartī Ṭhākura, of the twenty items mentioned, seventeen apply to both the *jñānī* and the *bhakta*. The last two, accepting the importance of self-realization (*adyātma-jñāna-nityatvam*) and philosophical search for the Absolute Truth (*tattva-jñānārtha-darśanam*), are technically only for the *jñānī*. "Constant and unalloyed devotion to Me" is the sole quality specifically for the devotee. All other qualities come to a devotee who exclusively endeavors for constant, unalloyed devotion.

These twenty items include qualities like cleanliness, which if developed are favorable for spiritual advancement. They also include elements of the process of advancement, such as approaching a bona fide spiritual master and perceiving the evils of birth, death, disease, and old age. Integrated as a process, these items are the means of acquiring transcendental knowledge, or an accurate understanding of the body, the soul, and the Supersoul.

Therefore, taken as a process that carries one to transcendence, these twenty items have nothing to do with the field of activity and its interactions. Śrīla Prabhupāda explains the relationship between the process of knowledge and the field of activities: "This process of knowledge is sometimes misunderstood by less intelligent men as being the interaction of the field of activity. But actually this is the real process of knowledge. If one accepts this process, then the possibility of approaching the Absolute Truth exists. This is not the interaction of the twenty-four elements, as described before. This is actually the means to get out of the entanglement of those elements."

In the next set of verses (13–19) Kṛṣṇa addresses Arjuna's sixth topic: the object of knowledge.

13 I shall now explain the knowable, knowing which you will taste the eternal. Brahman, the spirit, beginningless and subordinate to Me, lies beyond the cause and effect of this material world.

The term "knowable" (*jñeyam*) used here signifies "the object of knowledge" about which Arjuna inquired in text 1. Śrīla Prabhupāda clearly mentions here that there are two knowable objects: "The Lord has explained the field of activities and the knower of the field. He has also explained the process of knowing the knower of the field of activities. Now He begins to explain the knowable, first the soul and then the Supersoul. By knowledge of the knower, both the soul and the Supersoul, one can relish the nectar of life."

Texts 14–18 will describe the Supersoul as the *jñeyam,* and this text, as Śrīla Prabhupāda explains, describes the first object of knoweldge, the soul: "The description of Brahman mentioned in this verse is in relation to the individual soul, and when the word Brahman is applied to the living entity, it is to be understood that he is *vijñāna-brahma* as opposed to *ānanda-brahma*. *Ānanda-brahma* is the Supreme Brahman Personality of Godhead." These terms, *ānanda* and *vijñāna,* refer to the discussion in text 5, where the terms *ānanda-maya* and *vijñāna-maya* were discussed.

In texts 14–18, lofty verses resembling the *Upaniṣads,* the Supersoul is described. These verses make it sound as though that which is knowable is the impersonal Brahman – until text 18, where Kṛṣṇa's actual meaning becomes apparent. Śrīla Prabhupāda, however, in each translation and purport, mercifully reveals Kṛṣṇa's intention: that these verses describe the Supersoul.

14 Everywhere are His hands and legs, His eyes, heads, and faces, and He has ears everywhere. In this way the Supersoul exists, pervading everything.

Śrīla Prabhupāda's purport strongly confirms that this verse, which refers to the all-pervading, describes the Supersoul, not the living entity. In his purport to *Śrīmad-Bhāgavatam* 2.2.1, however, Śrīla Prabhupāda describes that those who wish to understand this verse as referring to the living entity as all-pervading may properly do so: "The kingdom of God is unlimited; therefore the number of the assisting hands of the Lord is also unlimited. The *Bhagavad-gītā* (13.14) asserts that the Lord has His hands, legs, eyes, and mouths in every nook and corner of His creation. This means that the expansions of differentiated parts and parcels, called *jīvas* or living entities, are assisting hands of the Lord, and all of them are meant for rendering a particular pattern of service to the Lord."

15 The Supersoul is the original source of all senses, yet He is without senses. He is unattached, although He is the maintainer of all living beings. He transcends the modes of nature, and at the same time He is the master of all the modes of material nature.

16 The Supreme Truth exists outside and inside of all living beings, the moving and the nonmoving. Because He is subtle, He is beyond the power of the material senses to see or to know. Although far, far away, He is also near to all.

That Kṛṣṇa described the knowable in text 16 as *avijñeyam,* unknowable, indicates that the Supersoul cannot be understood by the material senses. Only by hearing with devotion from transcendental sources can He be understood.

17 Although the Supersoul appears to be divided among all beings, He is never divided. He is situated as one. Although He is the maintainer of every living entity, it is to be understood that He devours and develops all.

18 He is the source of light in all luminous objects. He is beyond the darkness of matter and is unmanifested. He is knowledge, He is the object of knowledge, and He is the goal of knowledge. He is situated in everyone's heart.

Finally, in text 18, Kṛṣṇa clearly reveals the identity of the one He has been describing. The *jñeyam* is the Supersoul, who is *hṛdi sarvasya,* within the heart of all. Śrīla Prabhupāda kindly informed us earlier in his translations and purports to verses 14, 15, and 17 that the supreme knowable object, who has been described as unknowable, is nevertheless situated in everyone's heart as Paramātmā. Śrīla Prabhupāda cites several verses from the *Śvetāśvatara Upaniṣad* to substantiate that these *Gītā* texts have been describing neither the living entity nor Brahman but the Supersoul.

Kṛṣṇa ends his explanation of the knowable by describing to Arjuna the qualifications of one able to understand these topics.

19 Thus the field of activities [the body], knowledge, and the knowable have been summarily described by Me. Only My devotees can understand this thoroughly and thus attain to My nature.

Kṛṣṇa uses the word *mad-bhakta* to indicate that only His devotees can understand this subject; others cannot. Śrīla Prabhupāda confirms this: "The Lord has described in summary the body, knowledge, and the knowable. This knowledge is of three things: the knower, the knowable, and the process of knowing. Combined, these are called *vijñāna,* or the science of knowledge. Perfect knowledge can be understood by the unalloyed devotees of the Lord directly. Others are unable to understand."

Later in his purport, Śrīla Prabhupāda provides a valuable summary of the difficult subjects described thus far in the chapter:

> Now, to summarize, one may understand that verses 6 and 7, beginning from *mahā-bhūtāni* and continuing through *cetanā dhṛtiḥ,* analyze the material elements and certain manifestations

of the symptoms of life. These combine to form the body, or the field of activities. And verses 8 through 12, from *amānitvam* through *tattva-jñānārtha-darśanam,* describe the process of knowledge for understanding both types of knower of the field of activities, namely the soul and the Supersoul.

Thus three items have been described: the field of activity (the body), the process of understanding, and both the soul and the Supersoul. It is especially described here that only the unalloyed devotees of the Lord can understand these three items clearly. So for these devotees *Bhagavad-gītā* is fully useful; it is they who can attain the supreme goal, the nature of the Supreme Lord, Kṛṣṇa. In other words, only devotees, and not others, can understand *Bhagavad-gītā* and derive the desired result.

The next set of verses (20–27) explain *prakṛti* and *puruṣa,* the first two topics about which Arjuna inquired.

20 Material nature and the living entities should be understood to be beginningless. Their transformations and the modes of matter are products of material nature.

Kṛṣṇa begins His explanation of how material nature (*prakṛti*) and the *puruṣas* combine (referring to the soul in texts 20–22 and 24, and to the Supersoul in text 23). Their union is described as *anādi,* beginningless. Speaking of this combination, Śrīla Prabhupāda explains in his purport: "Actually the living entity is originally the spiritual part and parcel of the Supreme Lord, but due to his rebellious nature, he is conditioned within material nature. It really does not matter how these living entities or superior entities of the Supreme Lord have come in contact with material nature. The Supreme Personality of Godhead knows, however, how and why this actually took place."

Both the living entity and the Lord are changeless and eternal. Only the material nature undergoes *vikāra,* transformation. Although the living entity remains unchanged, out of ignorance he identifies with the changes of his body.

The relationship between the living entity and the changes caused by material nature is elaborated on in the next verse.

21 Nature is said to be the cause of all material causes and effects, whereas the living entity is the cause of the various sufferings and enjoyments in this world.

This text again addresses the topic of the doer. The living entity is the cause of all his sufferings and enjoyments because he has illicitly embraced *māyā* with the desire to predominate and enjoy independently of Kṛṣṇa. He thus becomes entangled in material nature. Taking his *karma* into consideration, material nature then creates for him a field meant ultimately for suffering. This all takes place under the sanction of the actual *puruṣa,* the Supersoul. Therefore, although nature is the cause of the entire material manifestation, the living entity causes his own happiness and distress. Kṛṣṇa explains this point further in the next verse.

22 The living entity in material nature thus follows the ways of life, enjoying the three modes of nature. This is due to his association with that material nature. Thus he meets with good and evil amongst various species.

Puruṣaḥ prakṛti-stho hi, bhuṅkte prakṛti-jān guṇān/ kāraṇaṁ guṇa-saṅgo 'sya, sad-asad-yoni-janmasu. Kṛṣṇa is actually the only *puruṣa,* or predominating enjoyer. The *jīva,* in contrast, as described in Bg. 7.5, is His subordinate energy. Because of illusion, however, he is placed within the material energy (*puruṣaḥ prakṛti-stho hi*) to imagine himself a *puruṣa*. Thus incarcerated and suffering within matter, the *jīva* focuses his attempt (*bhuṅkte prakṛti-jān guṇān*) on the impossible: enjoying by exploiting creations of the *guṇās,* the modes of material nature. By his association with material nature while in an enjoying spirit (*kāraṇaṁ guṇa-saṅgo 'sya*), a *jīva* traps himself in the cycle of repeated birth and death (*sad-asad-yoni-janmasu*). Practically, by his attempt, the living entity "becomes" matter and experiences change – birth, death, old age, and disease – though he is changeless. Kṛṣṇa next describes the actual *puruṣa.*

23 Yet in this body there is another, a transcendental enjoyer, who is the Lord, the supreme proprietor, who exists as the overseer and permitter, and who is known as the Supersoul.

This verse describes the relationship between the Paramātmā and *jīvātmā*. In the language of this chapter, both are *kṣetra-jña*. Here the Supersoul is called *puruṣaḥ paraḥ,* the transcendental enjoyer. He is the overseer and permitter, and by His sanction the living entity may attempt to fulfill his desires to act as a *puruṣa*. Śrīla Prabhupāda explains:

> The fact is that every individual living entity is eternally part and parcel of the Supreme Lord, and both of them are very intimately related as friends. But the living entity has the tendency to reject the sanction of the Supreme Lord and act independently in an attempt to dominate nature, and because he has this tendency he is called the marginal energy of the Supreme Lord. The living entity can be situated either in the material energy or in the spiritual energy. As long as he is conditioned by the material energy, the Supreme Lord, as his friend, the Supersoul, stays with him just to get him to return to the spiritual energy. The Lord is always eager to take him back to the spiritual energy, but due to his minute independence the individual entity is continually rejecting the association of spiritual light. This misuse of independence is the cause of his material strife in the conditioned nature. The Lord, therefore, is always giving instruction from within and from without. From without He gives instructions as stated in *Bhagavad-gītā,* and from within He tries to convince the living entity that his activities in the material field are not conducive to real happiness. "Just give it up and turn your faith toward Me. Then you will be happy," He says. Thus the intelligent person who places his faith in the Paramātmā or the Supreme Personality of Godhead begins to advance toward a blissful eternal life of knowledge.

Kṛṣṇa confirms the result of truly understanding the relationship between the soul and the Supersoul in the following text.

24 One who understands this philosophy concerning material nature, the living entity and the interaction of the modes of nature is sure to attain liberation. He will not take birth here again, regardless of his present position.

Texts 24–26 describe the result of understanding this knowledge. Śrīla Prabhupāda explains in his purport: "Clear understanding of material nature, the Supersoul, the individual soul, and their interrelation makes one eligible to become liberated and turn to the spiritual atmosphere without being forced to return to this material nature."

Are there methods to gain liberation other than those just described?

25 Some perceive the Supersoul within themselves through meditation, others through the cultivation of knowledge, and still others through working without fruitive desires.

The Supersoul is the object of knowledge (*jñeyam*), and three different methods of perceiving Him are herein described. Meditation refers to an *aṣṭāṅga-yogī* meditating on Paramātmā. Cultivation of knowledge refers to a *sāṅkhya-yogī* practicing the instructions of Lord Kapila to know the Supersoul. Śrīla Baladeva Vidyābhūṣaṇa states that the practitioners of *sāṅkhya-yoga* have philosophy as their primary means and meditation as their secondary means. Working without fruitive desires refers to *niṣkāma karma-yoga*. Śrīla Baladeva Vidyābhūṣaṇa says that such persons may seek philosophical knowledge or meditate, but their primary means of understanding the Supersoul is detached work. Kṛṣṇa has extensively discussed all three paths in the first six chapters of the *Gītā*.

Can one advance if he cannot meditate, pursue *sāṅkhya,* or do *niṣkāma karma-yoga*?

26 Again there are those who, although not conversant in spiritual knowledge, begin to worship the Supreme Person upon hearing about Him from others. Because of their tendency to hear from authorities, they also transcend the path of birth and death.

Hearing with faith from authorities has great potency.

The final section of this chapter (texts 27–35) summarizes the information already presented and explains how to distinguish the *kṣetra* from the *kṣetra-jña*.

27 O chief of the Bhāratas, know that whatever you see in existence, both the moving and the nonmoving, is only a combination of the field of activities and the knower of the field.

Śrīla Baladeva Vidyābhūṣaṇa explains that *prakṛti* and the *jīva* have been united since time immemorial. Kṛṣṇa continues to describe their separate, individual existences in the next verse.

28 One who sees the Supersoul accompanying the individual soul in all bodies, and who understands that neither the soul nor the Supersoul within the destructible body is ever destroyed, actually sees.

29 One who sees the Supersoul equally present everywhere, in every living being, does not degrade himself by his mind. Thus he approaches the transcendental destination.

One should be neither disturbed nor envious. He must act properly and see the Supersoul – the ultimate sanctioning agent – present in all beings.

30 One who can see that all activities are performed by the body, which is created of material nature, and sees that the self does nothing, actually sees.

This verse explains further the knowledge given in text 21: "I, the soul, am the cause of various sufferings and enjoyments, but I do nothing; only material nature acts." For the purpose of engendering humility, it is stressed herein that the individual soul does nothing.

31 When a sensible man ceases to see different identities due to different material bodies and he sees how beings are expanded everywhere, he attains to the Brahman conception.

All bodies must one day cease to exist. Therefore, when we see many different individuals, we should stop seeing them as their fields of activity; the *kṣetra-jña* – both the soul and the Supersoul – have nothing to do with matter. That is Brahman vision.

What does a person with Brahman vision see?"

32 Those with the vision of eternity can see that the imperishable soul is transcendental, eternal, and beyond the modes of nature. Despite contact with the material body, O Arjuna, the soul neither does anything nor is entangled.

Kṛṣṇa states clearly that only the body changes. The soul is eternal and changeless.

As the soul is nevertheless within his body, does he combine with it?

33 The sky, due to its subtle nature, does not mix with anything, although it is all-pervading. Similarly, the soul situated in Brahman vision does not mix with the body, though situated in that body.

Kṛṣṇa answers by saying that matter and spirit do not mix.

34 O son of Bharata, as the sun alone illuminates all this universe, so does the living entity, one within the body, illuminate the entire body by consciousness.

Here Kṛṣṇa offers a second example to explain the point He just made in text 33. Finally, He gives a one-verse chapter summary.

35 Those who see with eyes of knowledge the difference between the body and the knower of the body, and can also understand the process of liberation from bondage in material nature, attain to the supreme goal.

As suggested by the chapter title, "Nature, the Enjoyer, and Consciousness," this chapter describes material nature, the Supersoul, and the living entity. Śrīla Prabhupāda sums up the chapter's main points in his purport:

> The purport of this thirteenth chapter is that one should know the distinction between the body, the owner of the body, and the Supersoul. One should recognize the process of liberation, as described in verses eight through twelve. Then one can go on to the supreme destination....

One can understand that this body is matter; it can be analyzed with its twenty-four elements. The body is the gross manifestation. And the subtle manifestation is the mind and psychological effects. And the symptoms of life are the interaction of these features. But over and above this, there is the soul, and there is also the Supersoul. The soul and the Supersoul are two. This material world is working by the conjunction of the soul and the twenty-four material elements. One who can see the constitution of the whole material manifestation as this combination of the soul and material elements and can also see the situation of the Supreme Soul becomes eligible for transfer to the spiritual world. These things are meant for contemplation and for realization, and one should have a complete understanding of this chapter with the help of the spiritual master.

Chapter Fourteen

The Three Modes of Material Nature

The key verse connecting chapter thirteen to chapter fourteen is Bg. 13.22. *Puruṣaḥ prakṛti-stho hi, bhuṅkte prakṛti-jān guṇān/ kāraṇaṁ guṇa-saṅgo 'sya, sad-asad-yoni-janmasu:* "The living entity in material nature thus follows the ways of life, enjoying the three modes of nature. This is due to his association with that material nature. Thus he meets with good and evil amongst various species."

Chapter thirteen described the conditioned soul as distinct from material nature yet entangled by it, trapped within his field of activities. Chapter fourteen reveals in detail how the living entity is limited and controlled, within his field, by the powerful shackles of material nature – the three modes – goodness, passion, and ignorance. At the end of chapter fourteen, Kṛṣṇa informs us how to attain freedom from these modes.

1 The Supreme Personality of Godhead said: Again I shall declare to you this supreme wisdom, the best of all knowledge, knowing which all the sages have attained the supreme perfection.

Kṛṣṇa uses the word *bhūyaḥ,* "again," to indicate that He will repeat the knowledge He mentioned in Bg. 13.22. How is this knowledge "the best of all"? Śrīla Baladeva Vidyābhūṣaṇa explains Kṛṣṇa's words: " 'Again I will speak a kind of knowledge different from what I have spoken so far. It deals specifically with the modes of nature. It is the best of all kinds of knowledge about the *prakṛti* and the *jīva,* and it resembles a distillation of yogurt from milk. Realizing this knowledge and meditating on it thoughtfully, all great sages attained, in this very world, correct perception of the Supreme Soul.' "

Śrīla Prabhupāda's purport introduces the subjects of this chapter and links them to chapter thirteen:

> From the seventh chapter to the end of the twelfth chapter, Śrī Kṛṣṇa in detail reveals the Absolute Truth, the Supreme Personality of Godhead. Now, the Lord Himself is further enlightening Arjuna. If one understands this chapter through the process of philosophical speculation, he will come to an understanding of devotional service. In the thirteenth chapter, it was clearly explained that by humbly developing knowledge one may possibly be freed from material entanglement. It has also been explained that it is due to association with the modes of nature that the living entity is entangled in this material world. Now, in this chapter, the Supreme Personality explains what those modes of nature are, how they act, how they bind, and how they give liberation. The knowledge explained in this chapter is proclaimed by the Supreme Lord to be superior to the knowledge given so far in other chapters. By understanding this knowledge, various great sages attained perfection and transferred to the spiritual world.

The proper use of intelligence is to understand śāstric truths. Usually, Śrīla Prabhupāda decries philosophical speculation because it is generally used as a process that attempts to uncover the Absolute Truth by one's limited intellectual strength. In his purport, however, Śrīla Prabhupāda invites readers to engage in philosophical speculation. Here, philosophical speculation refers to hearing from bona fide sources and then using one's intelligence to understand what has been heard.

In the next verse, Kṛṣṇa further glorifies the knowledge explained in this chapter.

2 By becoming fixed in this knowledge, one can attain to the transcendental nature like My own. Thus established, one is not born at the time of creation or disturbed at the time of dissolution.

Śrīla Baladeva Vidyābhūṣaṇa states that we attain this knowledge by worshiping the feet of our spiritual master.

After glorifying the knowledge that He is about to reveal, Kṛṣṇa begins to explain the relationship between material nature, the conditioned living entities, and Himself.

3 The total material substance, called Brahman, is the source of birth, and it is that Brahman that I impregnate, making possible the births of all living beings, O son of Bharata.

4 It should be understood that all species of life, O son of Kuntī, are made possible by birth in this material nature, and that I am the seed-giving father.

Kṛṣṇa now describes the soul's entanglement. He first identifies Himself as the source – the ultimate father – of all living entities. Śrīla Prabhupāda writes, "The purport is that the material world is impregnated with living entities, who come out in various forms at the time of creation according to their past deeds."

The placement of the souls under the control of material nature is next described.

5 Material nature consists of three modes – goodness, passion, and ignorance. When the eternal living entity comes in contact with nature, O mighty-armed Arjuna, he becomes conditioned by these modes.

The eternal living entity comes in contact with material nature and becomes conditioned by it. In other words, despite his desire for independent enjoyment, his existence is subject to strict control by the modes of material nature.

The fault which causes the soul's conditioned state certainly rests in his own independent desire. We cannot blame Kṛṣṇa any more than a criminal can blame a judge for his jail sentence.

We have misused our minute independence. Out of emnity toward Kṛṣṇa, we have rejected our consitutional position as His servitor. Therefore we had to come to the temporary, material world of illusion. All *jīvas* in the spiritual world willingly and lovingly keep Kṛṣṇa's service at the center of their consciousness. How, then, could we live there?

Once we come to the material world, we need to assume a false identity, a false ego. False ego, which is like a reflection of our true consciousness in matter, is the covering over the soul first supplied by material nature and is the juncture between our spiritual identity and our material existence. Any ego-identity in which we may imagine ourselves the central figure is acceptable to our perverse consciousness.

Based on that false ego, the elemental ingredients for both subtle and gross material bodies are generated. Based on such bodies, we become controlled by a specific combination of the modes of material nature and "naturally" become attracted to exploiting particular combinations of matter. Thus the soul, constitutionally Kṛṣṇa's eternal servant – full of bliss, knowledge, and eternity – becomes attracted to the material atmosphere and conditioned by it. He is then strictly controlled by the modes of material nature and experiences his self as if it were made of temporary matter.

Every inhabitant of the material world has earned his prison sentence, and all are bound by the ropes of material nature – with the three strands of goodness, passion, and ignorance twisted tight to give them strength.

The next group of verses describes the effects of each of the modes on the conditioned soul. Texts 6, 7, and 8, one after another, explain the ways in which goodness, passion and ignorance force a soul to experience his existence.

6 O sinless one, the mode of goodness, being purer than the others, is illuminating, and it frees one from all sinful reactions. Those situated in that mode become conditioned by a sense of happiness and knowledge.

Arjuna is addressed as *anagha,* sinless. The two sins of the mode of goodness are attachment to *sukha,* happiness, and *jñāna,* knowledge, but Arjuna is not bound by either. It is *attachment* to happiness and knowledge (not happiness and knowledge themselves) that binds the living entity in the mode of goodness. Such attachment breeds pride, and both attachment and pride are symptoms of the mode of passion. In other words, attachment to *jñāna* causes *ajñāna,* ignorance. As Śrīla Prabhupāda explains in his purport, "The difficulty here is that when a living entity is situated in the mode of goodness he becomes conditioned to feel that he is advanced in knowledge and is better than others. In this way he becomes conditioned."

7 The mode of passion is born of unlimited desires and longings, O son of Kuntī, and because of this the embodied living entity is bound to material fruitive actions.

In text 6, the word *nirmala,* "pure," was used. Here, *rāga,* which can mean "colored," is used. The person in the mode of passion sees everything colored by his unlimited desires, and he experiences *tṛṣṇā-saṅga,* a thirst or hankering for boundless material enjoyment. Because of his intense, multiple hankerings, he is always forced to engage in *karma-saṅga,* hard work.

As explained in Bg. 3.37, the mode of passion tends to degrade to ignorance.

8 O son of Bharata, know that the mode of darkness, born of ignorance, is the delusion of all embodied living entities. The results of this mode are madness, indolence, and sleep, which bind the conditioned soul.

In goodness we can work purely. In passion we at least produce fruits from our work that may be offered to Kṛṣṇa. Ignorance, however, produces nothing but deeper ignorance. *Sattva,* goodness, creates inactivity based on knowledge, but *tama,* ignorance, creates inactivity based on a lack of knowledge.

Śrīla Baladeva Vidyābhūṣaṇa comments: "The use of the word *tu* here indicates that ignorance is opposed to the other two modes. *Pramāda,* madness, opposes goodness; *ālasya,* indolence, opposes passion; and *nidrā,* sleep, opposes both goodness and passion."

Śrīla Prabhupāda describes the difference between goodness and ignorance in his purport: "The mode of ignorance is just the opposite of the mode of goodness. In the mode of goodness, by development of knowledge, one can understand what is what, but the mode of ignorance is just the opposite. Everyone under the spell of the mode of ignorance becomes mad, and a madman cannot understand what is what. Instead of making advancement, one becomes degraded."

Text 9 summarizes texts 6, 7, and 8.

9 O son of Bharata, the mode of goodness conditions one to happiness; passion conditions one to fruitive action; and ignorance, covering one's knowledge, binds one to madness.

When one is contaminated by goodness, he is too self-satisfied to follow the dictates of the Supersoul. When one is contaminated by the mode of passion, his desires speak too loudly and he cannot hear the voice of his dear friend, the Supersoul. If one is contaminated by the mode of ignorance, he is too inert, ignorant, and mad to hear the Supersoul. Thus the modes of nature condition the living entity and keep him satisfied in different encasements as he pursues pleasure in the material world.

Does one mode become predominant within a person? If so, how?

10 Sometimes the mode of goodness becomes prominent, defeating the modes of passion and ignorance, O son of Bharata. Sometimes the mode of passion defeats goodness and ignorance, and at other times ignorance defeats goodness and passion. In this way there is always competition for supremacy.

After describing the effects of the modes, Kṛṣṇa now tells Arjuna that the modes are not constant in their influence on the living entity. According to our *karma,* our work, our association, our choice of food, and so on, a particular mode becomes predominant within us.

Here Kṛṣṇa indicates the awkwardness of the eternal, nonchanging soul's predicament within this constantly changing world. Śrīla Prabhupāda therefore writes, "One who is actually intent on advancing in Kṛṣṇa consciousness has to transcend these three modes."

Texts 11–13 explain how the effects of the three modes of material nature are manifested.

11 The manifestations of the mode of goodness can be experienced when all the gates of the body are illuminated by knowledge.

12 O chief of the Bharatas, when there is an increase in the mode of passion the symptoms of great attachment, fruitive activity, intense endeavor, and uncontrollable desire and hankering develop.

13 When there is an increase in the mode of ignorance, O son of Kuru, darkness, inertia, madness, and illusion are manifested.

By studying these three texts we get an idea which modes of nature are affecting us. Often, different times of the day and various occurrences throughout the day place us under the control of one mode or another. The next two verses describe death in each of the modes of nature.

14 When one dies in the mode of goodness, he attains to the pure higher planets of the great sages.

15 When one dies in the mode of passion, he takes birth among those engaged in fruitive activities; and when one dies in the mode of ignorance, he takes birth in the animal kingdom.

The next three verses discuss the results of acting in each of the modes of nature.

16 The result of pious action is pure and is said to be in the mode of goodness. But action done in the mode of passion results in misery, and action performed in the mode of ignorance results in foolishness.

While developing our Kṛṣṇa consciousness we must attempt to perform our services in at least the mode of goodness. Service tinged by passion and ignorance adversely affects our consciousness. How can we aspiring devotees become purified enough to serve in goodness? Srila Prabhupāda explains the process:

> If one hears about Kṛṣṇa, or God, then gradually he becomes freed from the clutches of darkness and passion, and actually he then comes to the platform of goodness. And when he is perfectly in goodness, then this passion and ignorance and their by-products cannot touch him. *Tadā rajas-tamo-bhāvāḥ kāma-*

lobhādayaś ca ye: if we hear the *Bhāgavatam* and *Bhagavad-gītā* regularly, then we become free from the effects of the modes of ignorance and passion, gradually, though it takes time... but it is sure. The more you hear about Kṛṣṇa – Kṛṣṇa means His instruction or about Him, what He is – the more you become purified. So that is the test of how one has become purified. One purified from the base qualities of passion and ignorance is no more attacked by greediness and passion. When he is no more disturbed by these base qualities of passion and greediness, then he is happy. (From a discussion between Śrīla Prabhupāda and Hayagrīva on Socrates)

17 From the mode of goodness, real knowledge develops; from the mode of passion, greed develops; and from the mode of ignorance develop foolishness, madness, and illusion.

While text 16 describes the results of action in each of the three modes of nature, this text explains the intermediate causes of those results. Action in goodness results in knowledge, which brings about proper action resulting in purity. Action in passion produces misery because it is caused by unlimited desires and insatiable greed. Action in ignorance brings about madness and illusion, which cause one to act foolishly.

Śrīla Prabhupāda's purport stresses development of the mode of goodness: "Since the present civilization is not very congenial to the living entities, Kṛṣṇa consciousness is recommended. Through Kṛṣṇa consciousness, society will develop the mode of goodness. When the mode of goodness is developed, people will see things as they are. In the mode of ignorance, people are just like animals and cannot see things clearly.... In the mode of passion, people become greedy, and their hankering for sense enjoyment has no limit."

18 Those situated in the mode of goodness gradually go upward to the higher planets; those in the mode of passion live on the earthly planets; and those in the abominable mode of ignorance go down to the hellish worlds.

Two verbs are used in this verse to tell of the destinations of those who act in the modes of nature. *Gacchanti*, "go," is used twice to describe the destinations of those in goodness and those in ignorance. *Tiṣṭhanti,* "stay," indicates that those in passion stay on earth in their next life.

Varieties of activity and other factors, as Kṛṣṇa explains to Uddhava in the Eleventh Canto, affect how we are influenced by the modes of nature: *āgama,* which *śāstras* we hear; *āpaḥ,* the water we drink and the types of food we eat; *prajā,* our association; *deśa,* where we live; *kāla,* the time of the day; *karma,* our activities; *janma,* our conditioning from birth; *dhyāna,* our thoughts; *mantras,* what we chant; and *saṁskāras,* the *varṇāśrama* ceremonies we undergo, which begin with impregnation and end with burial.

Having described the all-pervasive control of the modes of nature, Kṛṣṇa tells us in the next and final section of this chapter how to transcend the modes and explains His own position in relation to them.

19 When one properly sees that in all activities no other performer is at work than these modes of nature and he knows the Supreme Lord, who is transcendental to all these modes, he attains My spiritual nature.

Kṛṣṇa here equates transcending the modes of material nature with liberation from the material world. The first step is to observe the modes working on us. Then, by observing the modes at work, we can understand that the modes, not we, are active, and that we are separate. In this way, we can come to understand that we are eternal living entities, separate from both our everyday activities and the modes.

The second step is to understand Kṛṣṇa's position. Although Kṛṣṇa appears to be acting within the material sphere, He is fully transcendental. Śrīla Prabhupāda writes: "A man in Kṛṣṇa consciousness is not controlled by the spell of the material modes of nature. It has already been stated in the seventh chapter [7.13–14] that one who has surrendered to Kṛṣṇa is relieved from the activities of material nature. For one who is able to see things as they are, the influence of material nature gradually ceases."

Kṛṣṇa next describes the results we can look forward to if we transcend the modes.

20 When the embodied being is able to transcend these three modes associated with the material body, he can become free from birth, death, old age, and their distresses and can enjoy nectar even in this life.

A person free from the modes of nature is freed from distress and enjoys life on the spiritual platform.

Next, Arjuna asks three questions about transcending the modes of nature. Kṛṣṇa gives His answers in texts 22–25.

21 Arjuna inquired: O my dear Lord, by which symptoms is one known who is transcendental to these three modes? What is his behavior? And how does he transcend the modes of nature?

Śrīla Baladeva Vidyābhūṣaṇa expands and rephrases the meanings of Arjuna's questions. Arjuna first asks what symptoms of transcendence will manifest in a person no longer affected by the modes. The question rephrased is, "How do we understand that someone has already transcended?" The second question – "What is his behavior?" – means, "Is his behavior regulated or enacted according to his own desire?" The third question asks: "By what practices does he achieve transcendence?"

Kṛṣṇa's answers to these questions continue until the end of the chapter.

22–25 The Supreme Personality of Godhead said: O son of Pāṇḍu, he who does not hate illumination, attachment and delusion when they are present or long for them when they disappear; who is unwavering and undisturbed through all these reactions of the material qualities, remaining neutral and transcendental, knowing that the modes alone are active; who is situated in the self and regards alike happiness and distress; who looks upon a lump of earth, a stone, and a piece of gold with an equal eye; who is equal toward the desirable and the undesirable; who is steady, situated equally well in praise and blame, honor and dishonor; who treats alike both friend and enemy; and who has renounced all material activities – such a person is said to have transcended the modes of nature.

Two of the questions are answered in these verses. The answer, primarily text 22, to the first question explains that a transcendentalist is neutral to the modes. He is free from hankering and envy, being indifferent to their pushings. Those are the symptoms of one unaffected by the modes. Śrīla Prabhupāda writes: "When one is conscious of the material body, he acts only for sense gratification, but when one transfers the consciousness to Kṛṣṇa, sense gratification automatically stops. One does not need this material body, and he does not need to accept the dictations of the material body. The qualities of the material modes in the body will act, but as spirit soul the self is aloof from such activities. How does he become aloof? He does not desire to enjoy the body, nor does he desire to get out of it. Thus transcendentally situated, the devotee becomes automatically free. He need not try to become free from the influence of the modes of material nature."

The next question – "What is such a person's behavior?" – is answered in texts 23–25. He is equally disposed and sees everything equally because he has realized that he has nothing to do with material existence. Such a person never acts whimsically. Rather, in full surrender to Kṛṣṇa and aloof from the modes, he executes his Kṛṣṇa conscious duties with fixed determination.

While the answers to both questions seem similar, there is a subtle difference. The *symptoms* (text 22) are perceivable only by the person himself, whereas the *behavior* (texts 23–25) is perceivable by others.

The basic point is the same: Through knowledge, we become detached from the pushings of the modes and liberated from this world.

Kṛṣṇa ends this chapter by discussing *bhakti,* the method of transcending, and He thus answers Arjuna's third question from text 21.

26 One who engages in full devotional service, unfailing in all circumstances, at once transcends the modes of material nature and thus comes to the level of Brahman.

While the process of knowledge just described (texts 22–25) gradually elevates one to the platform of equanimity, one engaged in full devotional service immediately and automatically transcends the modes of nature. The word *avyabhicāreṇa* implies having the tendency to render service to no one except Kṛṣṇa. Because the devotee is serving Kṛṣṇa exclusively, he has no opportunity to serve the modes. This is the direct process of transcendence. Therefore, he immediately reaches the Brahman platform, where the modes of material nature have no power over him. On that platform, which is fully spiritual and beyond the modes of nature, pure devotional service begins.

In his comment on text 2, Śrīla Baladeva Vidyābhūṣaṇa stated that this knowledge was attained "by worshiping the feet of our spiritual master." Why? Because development of a service mood, as opposed to an enjoying mood, shatters the glue that binds us to the material world. Thinking of ourselves as "my *guru's* servant" and fixing his order as our life and soul frees us from *māyā*. The modes may dictate a variety of allurements to us, but devotees surrendered to their *guru* follow the *guru's* instructions and do not heed the pushings of the modes. Their attitude of devotion and service, not merely the ability, like that of a *jñānī,* to discriminate between the modes and the pure soul, carries them to perfection.

Bhakti is for both the *sādhaka,* the practitioner, and the *siddha,* the perfect devotee. *Karmīs* and *jñānīs* must eventually give up their processes as they attain higher stages of consciousness, but one need never give up *bhakti.* Even *karmīs* and *jñānīs,* who do not desire the shelter of Kṛṣṇa's service as their ultimate goal, must take to devotional service in order to achieve the fruit of their processes.

Śrīla Prabhupāda further glorifies *bhakti:*

> This verse is a reply to Arjuna's third question: What is the means of attaining to the transcendental position? As explained before, the material world is acting under the spell of the modes of material nature. One should not be disturbed by the activities of the modes of nature; instead of putting his consciousness into such activities, he may transfer his consciousness to Kṛṣṇa activities. Kṛṣṇa activities are known as *bhakti-yoga* – always acting for Kṛṣṇa.…So if one engages himself in the service of Kṛṣṇa or His plenary expansions with unfailing determination, although these modes of material nature are very difficult to overcome,

> one can overcome them easily. This has already been explained in the seventh chapter. One who surrenders unto Kṛṣṇa at once surmounts the influence of the modes of material nature.

One may ask after reading text 26 why one in full devotional service will attain Brahman. After all, his desire is not Brahman realization but Kṛṣṇa's service. Kṛṣṇa therefore expands His answer for clarification and ends the chapter by describing His own relationship to Brahman. He thus again stresses *bhakti.*

27 And I am the basis of the impersonal Brahman, which is immortal, imperishable, and eternal and is the constitutional position of ultimate happiness.

Śrīla Śrīdhara Svāmī comments: "Kṛṣṇa is the concentrated form of Brahman, as the sun is the intensified form of light. Although Kṛṣṇa and Brahman are nondifferent, Kṛṣṇa is the support of Brahman. The completeness of Brahman is Kṛṣṇa."

Śrīla Viśvanātha Cakravartī Ṭhākura explains Kṛṣṇa's words: " 'Because everything is dependent on Me, if one worships Me with the desire for impersonal merging, he will merge into Brahman and attain the nature of Brahman.' "

Arjuna, too, has confirmed Kṛṣṇa as the *paraṁ brahma,* the supreme truth, the Personality of Godhead, in Bg. 10.13.

Brahman is the basic transcendental platform on which pure devotional service takes place. In Bg. 13.13 Kṛṣṇa said, "Brahman, the spirit, beginningless and subordinate to Me, lies beyond the cause and effect of this material world." This Brahman, which is the goal of the impersonalists, is subordinate to Kṛṣṇa, the Supreme Personality of Godhead, and it rests upon His existence.

Śrīla Prabhupāda writes about the importance of devotional service for the living entity:

> The living entity, although Brahman by nature, has the desire to lord it over the material world, and due to this he falls down....By engagement in devotional service in full Kṛṣṇa consciousness, he is immediately situated in the transcendental position, and his unlawful desire to control material nature is removed. Therefore the process of devotional service...should

> be practiced in the association of devotees. Gradually, by such association, by the influence of the spiritual master, one's material desire to dominate is removed, and one becomes firmly situated in the Lord's transcendental loving service. This method is prescribed from the twenty-second to the last verse of this chapter. Devotional service to the Lord is very simple: one should always engage in the service of the Lord, should eat the remnants of foodstuffs offered to the Deity, smell the flowers offered to the lotus feet of the Lord, see the places where the Lord had His transcendental pastimes, read of the different activities of the Lord, His reciprocation of love with His devotees, chant always the transcendental vibration Hare Kṛṣṇa, Hare Kṛṣṇa, Kṛṣṇa Kṛṣṇa, Hare Hare/ Hare Rāma, Hare Rāma, Rāma Rāma, Hare Hare, and observe the fasting days commemorating the appearances and disappearances of the Lord and His devotees.

In his purport to the opening verse of this chapter, Śrīla Prabhupāda stated that one could come to an understanding of devotional service by studying this chapter of *Bhagavad-gītā,* "The Three Modes of Material Nature," through "philosophical speculation." By applying our intelligence to understanding the nature of the modes' stringent control in the world, we will understand the power of the Supersoul, who controls those modes. Then, if we are free from envy, we will understand our insignificance and surrender to that controller.

Chapter Fifteen

The Yoga of the Supreme Person

Chapter fourteen described the modes of nature, those forces that simultaneously restrict and control a soul within his field of activities. Now Kṛṣṇa, using an allegory of an *aśvattha,* a banyan tree, describes the entire material world, with its varieties of fields of activities situated on higher and lower branches of that tree.

1 The Supreme Personality of Godhead said: It is said that there is an imperishable banyan tree that has its roots upward and its branches down and whose leaves are the Vedic hymns. One who knows this tree is the knower of the Vedas.

The banyan tree of the material world is upside down – roots up and branches down – because it only reflects reality, the reality of the spiritual world. Just as a reflection rests upon water, this tree rests upon the desire of the living entities.

As the branches of a real banyan tree produce offshoots that grow down into roots and further trunks, this reflected tree similarly has endlessly complicated, intertwined trunks, roots and branches. One can picture neither its beginning nor its end. A soul situated within the complexities of this incomprehensible tree remains trapped. All existence beyond the tree is forgotten, and he is fully enamored with the tastes of its fruits and berries.

Śrīla Viśvanātha Cakravartī Ṭhākura explains that the word *aśvattha* can also be understood as follows:

> "*Śva*" in *aśvattha* means "tomorrow." "*Aśva*" can thus mean "not tomorrow." "*Stha*" means "stay," and it becomes grammatically modified here to *ttha*. Thus *aśvattham* can be taken as "that which will not exist tomorrow." The material world

is *aśvattham,* not existing tomorrow – both for the devotees and the nondevotees. It won't exist tomorrow for the devotees because they will become liberated tomorrow and attain the spiritual world. The tree won't exist tomorrow for the nondevotees because everything they are attached to will cease to exist. Although their attachments will cease to exist tomorrow, the nondevotees' material existence is eternal, as indicated by the word *avyayam.*

Śrīla Prabhupāda further explains:

The entanglement of this material world is compared here to a banyan tree. For one who is engaged in fruitive activities, there is no end to the banyan tree. He wanders from one branch to another, to another, to another. The tree of this material world has no end, and for one who is attached to this tree, there is no possibility of liberation. . . .If one can understand this indestructible tree of illusion, then one can get out of it. This process of extrication should be understood. In the previous chapters it has been explained that there are many processes by which to get out of the material entanglement. And, up to the thirteenth chapter, we have seen that devotional service to the Supreme Lord is the best way. Now, the basic principle of devotional service is detachment from material activities and attachment to the transcendental service of the Lord. The process of breaking attachment to the material world is discussed in the beginning of this chapter.

2 The branches of this tree extend downward and upward, nourished by the three modes of material nature. The twigs are the objects of the senses. This tree also has roots going down, and these are bound to the fruitive actions of human society.

Depending upon which branch a living entity is located, he will possess a certain material body and a specific type of senses, and according to the combination of modes that influences that part of the tree, he will be attracted to particular "twigs," or sense objects. Thus the living entity, traveling from one birth to the next, from the higher branches of demigod life to the lower branches of animal life, seeks pleasure, but in fact attains only further entrapment in fruitive action and future deaths – *mūlāny anusantatāni karmānubandhīni*.

Śrīla Prabhupāda states in his purport, "This planet of human beings is considered the field of activities." This indicates that *karma* is accumulated only in human life. Knowing this, one who follows the *Vedas* can elevate himself within this tree.

Kṛṣṇa continues His allegory in the next two verses.

3–4 The real form of this tree cannot be perceived in this world. No one can understand where it ends, where it begins, or where its foundation is. But with determination one must cut down this strongly rooted tree with the weapon of detachment. Thereafter, one must seek that place from which, having gone, one never returns, and there surrender to that Supreme Personality of Godhead from whom everything began and from whom everything has extended since time immemorial.

Śrīla Viśvanātha Cakravartī Ṭhākura comments that philosophers have their own opinions about the nature of the world: "This world is real," "It is false," "It is eternal," and so on.

Because "the real form of this tree cannot be perceived," are we unable, out of our ignorance, to cut down the banyan tree of this material world? No. It *must* be cut down. This tree is so strongly rooted – *su-virūḍha-mūlam* – that it cannot be pulled down. The ax with which we must chop at it is made of detachment and renunciation and is sharpened by knowledge and discrimination. We must cut down this tree completely by full detachment lest our minds run again toward sense gratification.

Śrīla Prabhupāda describes both the processes of detachment and the attainment of the real "tree" in his purport:

> It is now clearly stated that the real form of this banyan tree cannot be understood in this material world. Since the root is upwards, the extension of the real tree is at the other end. When entangled with the material expansions of the tree, one cannot see how far the tree extends, nor can one see the beginning of this tree. Yet one has to find out the cause. . . .One has to search out that origin of this tree, the Supreme Personality of Godhead, through the association of persons who are in knowledge of that

> Supreme Personality of Godhead. Then by understanding one becomes gradually detached from this false reflection of reality, and by knowledge one can cut off the connection and actually become situated in the real tree.
>
> The word *asaṅga* is very important in this connection because the attachment for sense enjoyment and lording it over the material nature is very strong. Therefore one must learn detachment by discussion of spiritual science based on authoritative scriptures, and one must hear from persons who are actually in knowledge. As a result of such discussion in the association of devotees, one comes to the Supreme Personality of Godhead. Then the first thing one must do is surrender to Him....The Supreme Personality of Godhead, Kṛṣṇa, is the original root from whom everything has emanated. To gain favor of that Personality of Godhead, one has only to surrender, and this is a result of performing devotional service by hearing, chanting, etc.

Kṛṣṇa further describes the process of surrender and the qualities of those who do surrender and thereby attain the spiritual world.

5 Those who are free from false prestige, illusion, and false association, who understand the eternal, who are done with material lust, who are freed from the dualities of happiness and distress, and who, unbewildered, know how to surrender unto the Supreme Person attain to that eternal kingdom.

The process of surrender, as stressed in this verse, is highlighted by Śrīla Prabhupāda in his purport:

> The first qualification is that one should not be deluded by pride. Because the conditioned soul is puffed up, thinking himself the lord of material nature, it is very difficult for him to surrender unto the Supreme Personality of Godhead. One should know by the cultivation of real knowledge that he is not the lord of material nature; the Supreme Personality of Godhead is the Lord. When one is free from delusion caused by pride, he can begin the process of surrender....One has to get out of this false notion that human society is the proprietor of this world....And when one has an understanding of things as they

are, he becomes free from all dual conceptions such as happiness and distress, pleasure and pain. He becomes full in knowledge; then it is possible for him to surrender to the Supreme Personality of Godhead.

Kṛṣṇa now answers two questions: What is the nature of the place that a detached, surrendered soul will attain? If one goes there, does he come back?

6 That supreme abode of Mine is not illumined by the sun or moon, nor by fire or electricity. Those who reach it never return to this material world.

As He did in Bg. 8.20, Kṛṣṇa gives a brief description of the spiritual world. Śrīla Prabhupāda says we "should be captivated by this information" because if we are not, we will tend to be enamored with the objects of sense enjoyment and will endlessly transfer from one field of activity to another, jumping from branch to branch, in the cycle of *saṁsāra.*

7 The living entities in this conditioned world are My eternal fragmental parts. Due to conditioned life, they are struggling very hard with the six senses, which include the mind.

Just as Kṛṣṇa is eternal, Kṛṣṇa's fragmental, eternal parts – the living entities (*mama eva aṁśaḥ*) – are also certainly eternal. Kṛṣṇa's use of the word *sanātana* in this verse informs us that the living entity's eternality as an individual is not illusory as the Māyāvādīs claim. We are, individually, eternally part and parcel of Kṛṣṇa and belong only with Kṛṣṇa in His abode.

Now, however, all conditioned living entities are unnaturally captivated by *māyā,* and rather than achieving pleasure, they are forced to struggle and suffer even as they plan for their elusive future pleasures.

This verse hints at the mind's power to determine the living entity's future, and the next verse continues that thrust, explaining how, determined by his thoughts, a soul attains his next body.

8 The living entity in the material world carries his different conceptions of life from one body to another as the air carries aromas. Thus he takes one kind of body and again quits it to take another.

When the blowing wind passes over a fragrant rose garden, it acquires a sweet scent. Yet the air itself is not sweet; its sweetness is acquired. When that same air passes over sewage, its odor becomes vile. Again, the air's foul smell is not the actual scent of the air but rather the scent of that with which the air has come into contact. Similarly, although the soul is trapped in a gross body and subtle mind, he remains aloof from all his apparent qualities, whether he exhibits the fragrant mode of goodness or the foul mode of ignorance.

The quality of the mind, as explained in the following verse, attracts its next gross body, like a magnet attracts an iron nail.

9 The living entity, thus taking another gross body, obtains a certain type of ear, eye, tongue, nose, and sense of touch, which are grouped about the mind. He thus enjoys a particular set of sense objects.

After taking shelter of his mind's desires and obtaining his next body and senses, the living entity begins to exploit his specifically allotted sense objects.

Our particular body – its eyes, ears, tongue, nose, and all else – is formed around our mind's desires. If we desire to fly, to hang-glide, for example, why undergo the tribulation of artificially attaching ourselves to wings? If our life's pleasure is scuba diving, why go to the trouble of having to resurface to fill our air tanks? It's easier to become a fish. Based on the mind's desires, a gross body is generated with a particular facility for pleasure.

Kṛṣṇa will now answer the question of why people can't see this happening.

10 The foolish cannot understand how a living entity can quit his body, nor can they understand what sort of body he enjoys under the spell of the modes of nature. But one whose eyes are trained in knowledge can see all this.

Those who lack knowledge are *vimūḍhas.* They are blinded by unending attempts to enjoy their senses. Because they identify with the happiness and distress arising from the senses, they remain unable to distinguish matter from spirit. Their intense desire for bodily and mental pleasure has covered their ability to experience their own spiritual existence.

What is the cure for this ignorance? Kṛṣṇa says knowledge. Those "whose eyes are trained in knowledge" by hearing and learning *śāstra* can see. Lack of śāstric learning brings about the following result.

11 The endeavoring transcendentalists, who are situated in self-realization, can see all this clearly. But those whose minds are not developed and who are not situated in self-realization cannot see what is taking place, though they may try to.

Pure-hearted spiritualists see that the soul transmigrates. The blind who lack knowledge see nothing. Even one without knowledge, however, can see Kṛṣṇa in His opulent manifestations in matter and become attracted to Him.

12 The splendor of the sun, which dissipates the darkness of this whole world, comes from Me. And the splendor of the moon and the splendor of fire are also from Me.

13 I enter into each planet, and by My energy they stay in orbit. I become the moon and thereby supply the juice of life to all vegetables.

In text 6, Kṛṣṇa described the spiritual world as not needing sunlight, moonlight, fire, or electricity. In the material world, however, we need such things, and Kṛṣṇa says that He is their source. Although we conditioned souls, in our pride, acknowledge neither our dependence on Kṛṣṇa nor on those things produced by Him, we are nevertheless fully dependent on the sun, moon, and fire. Kṛṣṇa's choice of examples is therefore most excellent, because it is He who is maintaining us by providing our most basic necessities of life.

14 I am the fire of digestion in the bodies of all living entities, and I join with the air of life, outgoing and incoming, to digest the four kinds of foodstuff.

The potency of vegetables, so essential for strength, health, and the pleasures of our palate, is supplied by Kṛṣṇa. Yet even eating causes misery without the fire of digestion, which also comes from Kṛṣṇa. Again, we are fully dependent on Kṛṣṇa as our maintainer.

Kṛṣṇa completes His description of Himself as maintainer in the next verse.

15 I am seated in everyone's heart, and from Me come remembrance, knowledge, and forgetfulness. By all the Vedas, I am to be known. Indeed, I am the compiler of Vedānta, and I am the knower of the Vedas.

Śrīla Viśvanātha Cakravartī Ṭhākura further explains Kṛṣṇa's thoughts: "'Just as the fire of digestion is within the stomach, I am situated in the hearts of all moving and nonmoving beings as the principle of intelligence. Indeed, from Me – the intelligence principle – comes remembrance of things once experienced, forgetfulness, and perception born from contact of the senses with their objects.' Having thus described how He helps living entities in a bound condition, He next states, in the words beginning 'By all the *Vedas*,' how He helps them attain liberation."

Thus Kṛṣṇa serves each living entity from within his heart by activating remembrance, knowledge, and forgetfulness. If one were to remember each occurrence, especially the miseries experienced, throughout his unlimited births, he would be unable to function.

Śrīla Prabhupāda describes in his purport: "The *Vedas* give us direction by which to understand Kṛṣṇa and the process of realizing Him. The ultimate goal is the Supreme Personality of Godhead....By understanding Vedic literature one can understand his relationship with the Supreme Personality of Godhead, by performing the different processes one can approach Him, and at the end one can attain the supreme goal, who is no other than the Supreme Personality of Godhead."

Śrīla Prabhupāda's words clearly indicate *sambandha, abhidheya,* and *prayojana.* Texts 16–18 give knowledge of our relationship with Kṛṣṇa (*sambandha-jñāna*) and are also sometimes referred to as the *tri-slokī Gītā* for knowledge. Kṛṣṇa also, as "the knower of the *Vedas*" and "the compiler of *Vedānta,*" assists souls in these three verses in transcending material existence by summarizing the essence of the *Vedas,* which is the *Vedānta.*

Text 19 indicates *abhidheya-jñāna,* the process of attainment, and the final verse, 20, refers to *prayojana,* the goal.

16 There are two classes of beings, the fallible and the infallible. In the material world every living entity is fallible, and in the spiritual world every living entity is called infallible.

Śrīla Prabhupāda explains in his purport: "As already explained, the Lord in His incarnation as Vyāsadeva compiled the *Vedānta-sūtra.* Here the Lord is giving, in summary, the contents of the *Vedānta-sūtra.* He says that the living entities, who are innumerable, can be divided into two classes – the fallible and the infallible. The living entities are eternally separated parts and parcels of the Supreme Personality of Godhead. When they are in contact with the material world they are called *jīva-bhūta,* and the Sanskrit words given here, *kṣaraḥ sarvāṇi bhūtāni,* mean that they are fallible. Those who are in oneness with the Supreme Personality of Godhead, however, are called infallible."

This oneness with Kṛṣṇa of those infallible souls in the spiritual world is herein called *kūṭa-sthaḥ,* a oneness in desire. We are therefore required, as Kṛṣṇa said in texts 4 and 5, to be detached from the material world as Kṛṣṇa is detached, and, overcoming our desire for independent enjoyment, to surrender to Him.

17 Besides these two, there is the greatest living personality, the Supreme Soul, the imperishable Lord Himself, who has entered the three worlds and is maintaining them.

Śrīla Viśvanātha Cakravartī Ṭhākura comments that the word *tu* (but) used in *uttamaḥ puruṣas tv anyaḥ* distinguishes the

Supersoul, the supreme *puruṣa* mentioned in this verse, from the two other *puruṣas*, the fallible and the infallible, mentioned in text 16.

In addition, Kṛṣṇa now directly states what He has already described in texts 12–15: He is *bibhartā,* the maintainer of all living entities. Kṛṣṇa concludes His summary of *Vedānta* in the next verse.

18 Because I am transcendental, beyond both the fallible and the infallible, and because I am the greatest, I am celebrated both in the world and in the Vedas as that Supreme Person.

Kṛṣṇa, the Supreme Personality of Godhead, is different from all other living entities and is the source of both the Brahman and Paramātmā features of the Absolute Truth. Prabhupāda's purport explains: "No one can surpass the Supreme Personality of Godhead, Kṛṣṇa – neither the conditioned soul nor the liberated soul. He is therefore the greatest of personalities....the Supreme Personality is exhibiting and diffusing His spiritual effulgence, which is the ultimate illumination. That Supreme Personality also has a localized aspect as Paramātmā."

What are the activities of one who has assimilated the knowledge of the previous three verses, especially the knowledge that Kṛṣṇa is the Supreme Personality of Godhead?

19 Whoever knows Me as the Supreme Personality of Godhead, without doubting, is the knower of everything. He therefore engages himself in full devotional service to Me, O son of Bharata.

This knowledge is the true fruit of the *Vedas,* and one who knows it becomes *sarva-vit,* the knower of everything. Therefore, he performs pure devotional service.

20 This is the most confidential part of the Vedic scriptures, O sinless one, and it is disclosed now by Me. Whoever understands this will become wise, and his endeavors will know perfection.

This verse summarizes chapter fifteen. One who knows Kṛṣṇa as the Supreme serves Him with devotion, which awards both wisdom and perfection. What happens to one who doesn't serve Kṛṣṇa? As Prabhupāda explains in his purport, "... however intelligent he may be in the estimation of some common man, he is not perfectly intelligent."

Śrīla Prabhupāda also comments on the word *anagha* before summarizing the chapter:

> The word *anagha,* by which Arjuna is addressed, is significant. *Anagha,* O sinless one, means that unless one is free from all sinful reactions it is very difficult to understand Kṛṣṇa. One has to become free from all contamination, all sinful activities; then he can understand. But devotional service is so pure and potent that once one is engaged in devotional service he automatically comes to the stage of sinlessness.
>
> While one is performing devotional service in the association of pure devotees in full Kṛṣṇa consciousness, there are certain things which require to be vanquished altogether. The most important thing one has to surmount is weakness of the heart. The first falldown is caused by the desire to lord it over material nature. Thus one gives up the transcendental loving service of the Supreme Lord. The second weakness of the heart is that as one increases the propensity to lord it over material nature, he becomes attached to matter and the possession of matter. The problems of material existence are due to these weaknesses of the heart. In this chapter the first five verses describe the process of freeing oneself from these weaknesses of heart, and the rest of the chapter, from the sixth verse through the end, discusses *puruṣottama-yoga.*

As stated above, to understand *puruṣottama-yoga* we have to be sinless. Thus this chapter discusses breaking our material attachments and understanding Kṛṣṇa as the source of Brahman; as the maintainer, the Paramātmā; and as Bhagavān, the Supreme Personality of Godhead. Finally, knowing all this, one surrenders and becomes one with Him in desire and service. That is the conclusion of all *śāstra* – the *yoga* of the Supreme Person.

CHAPTER SIXTEEN

The Divine and Demoniac Natures

In describing the banyan tree of the material world, chapter fifteen discussed how the three modes of material nature combine to nourish the various branches of that tree. Chapters sixteen and seventeen describe the higher and lower branches on that tree. Kṛṣṇa thus begins this chapter by describing qualities that elevate us: those born of goodness.

1–3 The Supreme Personality of Godhead said: Fearlessness; purification of one's existence; cultivation of spiritual knowledge; charity; self-control; performance of sacrifice; study of the Vedas; austerity; simplicity; nonviolence; truthfulness; freedom from anger; renunciation; tranquility; aversion to faultfinding; compassion for all living entities; freedom from covetousness; gentleness; modesty; steady determination; vigor; forgiveness; fortitude; cleanliness; and freedom from envy and from the passion for honor – these transcendental qualities, O son of Bharata, belong to godly men endowed with divine nature.

Here Kṛṣṇa lists *sampadam daivīm:* twenty-six qualities of the divine nature. Śrīla Prabhupāda gradually introduces this chapter in his purport:

> In the beginning of the fifteenth chapter, the banyan tree of this material world was explained. The extra roots coming out of it were compared to the activities of the living entities, some auspicious, some inauspicious. In the ninth chapter, also, the *devas,* or godly, and the *asuras,* the ungodly, or demons, were explained. Now, according to Vedic rites, activities in the mode of goodness are considered auspicious for progress on the path of liberation, and such activities are known as *daivī prakṛti,* transcendental by nature. Those who are situated in the transcendental

> nature make progress on the path of liberation. For those who are acting in the modes of passion and ignorance, on the other hand, there is no possibility of liberation. Either they will have to remain in this material world as human beings, or they will descend among the species of animals or even lower life forms. In this sixteenth chapter the Lord explains both the transcendental nature and its attendant qualities and the demoniac nature and its qualities. He also explains the advantages and disadvantages of these qualities.

Śrīla Prabhupāda concludes his purport by reminding us to cultivate transcendental qualities, which, as he stated earlier, are born of activity in the mode of goodness: "All these twenty-six qualifications mentioned are transcendental qualities. They should be cultivated according to the different statuses of social and occupational order. The purport is that even though material conditions are miserable, if these qualities are developed by practice, by all classes of men, then gradually it is possible to rise to the highest platform of transcendental realization."

Kṛṣṇa now sketches the ignorant, demoniac nature, which He will further describe in texts 7–20.

4 Pride, arrogance, conceit, anger, harshness, and ignorance – these qualities belong to those of demoniac nature, O son of Pṛthā.

Śrīla Prabhupāda discusses in his purport to this verse each of these *sampadam āsurīm*, or six qualities of the demoniac nature:

> In this verse, the royal road to hell is described. The demoniac want to make a show of religion and advancement in spiritual science, although they do not follow the principles. They are always arrogant or proud in possessing some type of education or so much wealth. They desire to be worshiped by others, and demand respectability, although they do not command respect. Over trifles they become very angry and speak harshly, not gently. They do not know what should be done and what should not be done. They do everything whimsically, according to their own desire, and they do not recognize any authority.

> These demoniac qualities are taken on by them from the beginning of their bodies in the wombs of their mothers, and as they grow they manifest all these inauspicious qualities.

Kṛṣṇa next removes Arjuna's doubt about whether his own participation in the battle as a warrior – and therefore as a killer – will be due to possessing a demoniac temperament.

5 The transcendental qualities are conducive to liberation, whereas the demoniac qualities make for bondage. Do not worry, O son of Pāṇḍu, for you are born with the divine qualities.

Kṛṣṇa says to Arjuna, *mā śucaḥ:* "Do not worry." Śrīla Prabhupāda expands the point: "Lord Kṛṣṇa encouraged Arjuna by telling him that he was not born with demoniac qualities. His involvement in the fight was not demoniac, because he was considering the pros and cons. He was considering whether respectable persons such as Bhīṣma and Droṇa should be killed or not, so he was not acting under the influence of anger, false prestige, or harshness. Therefore he was not of the quality of the demons."

Even one with a demoniac nature can change his qualities in favorable association, because one's qualities develop according to one's association. By associating with those overwhelmed by lust, anger, and greed, we become lusty, angry, and greedy. Then again, we can develop perfect qualities by associating with the perfect: *guru, sādhu,* and *śāstra*.

In Melbourne, during his 1975 visit, Śrīla Prabhupāda was asked, "How can I become sincere?"

His answer: "How can you become a drunkard? If you want to become a drunkard, you associate with drunkards. If you want to become sincere, associate with these devotees. They are sincere."

6 O son of Pṛthā, in this world there are two kinds of created beings. One is called divine and the other demoniac. I have already explained to you at length the divine qualities. Now hear from Me of the demoniac.

Śrīla Prabhupāda states in his purport that the essential distinction between the divine and the demoniac is adhering to the Vedic literature: "The conditioned living entities are divided into two classes in this world. Those who are born with divine qualities follow a regulated life; that is to say they abide by the injunctions in scriptures and by the authorities. One should perform duties in the light of authoritative scripture. This mentality is called divine. One who does not follow the regulative principles as they are laid down in the scriptures and who acts according to his whims is called demoniac or asuric. There is no other criterion but obedience to the regulative principles of scriptures." Kṛṣṇa will Himself confirm this point at the end of the chapter.

After having briefly explained the demoniac nature in text 4, Kṛṣṇa will now explain it in detail in texts 7–20. Arjuna will thus see that he himself, as well as his fighting, is free of demoniac tendencies.

7 Those who are demoniac do not know what is to be done and what is not to be done. Neither cleanliness nor proper behavior nor truth is found in them.

Kṛṣṇa will later state directly that actions performed without proper discrimination between right and wrong are symptomatic of the mode of passion, a mode with which the demoniac are richly endowed: "O son of Pṛthā, that understanding which cannot distinguish between religion and irreligion, between action that should be done and action that should not be done, is in the mode of passion." (Bg. 18.31)

Because *śāstra* defines the difference between engagement in religious and irreligious life, it follows that those bereft of discrimination between proper and improper actions are also bereft of either faith in *śāstra* or a proper understanding of it. Thus the demoniac, rather than basing their actions on *śāstra,* base them on bodily consciousness. Therefore they act with little concern for truth or the welfare of others.

Even if a demon propounds a philosophy, its value is compared to the preaching of the vulture and the jackal. Once, a boy died, and his relatives, lamenting with great emotion, gathered around the body in preparation for the funeral ceremony.

Suddenly a jackal appeared, and with sweet words, began to glorify that which those present felt for the boy. He also began to speak of the boy's wonderful qualities and then requested those present to spend the precious hours until sunset (before which a body should be cremated) bathed in sweet remembrances of the boy. They could return in the morning to burn the body, he said.

Meanwhile, a vulture, after eyeing the situation from above, swooped down. He immediately began philosophically refuting the jackal's words. The vulture explained that the soul, the actual loved one in the body, had already departed, and that lamenting for a dead body was simply sentimental and foolish. The vulture then recommended that all present should become philosophically fixed in the difference between body and soul and should leave without further lamentation. In this way the vulture, who would feast on the body if the relatives left, spoke to defeat the jackal's argument. The jackal, being a creature of the night, planned to devour the body in the dark.

Regardless of the specific words spoken, the vulture, the jackal, and the demoniac speak philosophy only to achieve their selfish ends.

8 They say that this world is unreal, with no foundation, no God in control. They say it is produced of sex desire and has no cause other than lust.

The next ten verses (9–18) explain the abominable activities performed by those possessing this mentality.

9 Following such conclusions, the demoniac, who are lost to themselves and who have no intelligence, engage in unbeneficial, horrible works meant to destroy the world.

Śrīla Baladeva Vidyābhūṣaṇa comments: "The demoniac create philosophies to propound their personal opinions. By adhering to their philosophies, they destroy the whole world. Resorting to these philosophies, these persons of meager intelligence, who possess petty opinions, are 'lost to themselves' in the sense that they cannot perceive the actual distinction between the self, the body and other things. They are engaged in horrible work and devote themselves to malicious and cruel activities. By causing the world to deviate from the principles of spiritual life, they are the enemies of the world, and thus they exert their influence for the world's destruction."

Text 9 contains an often used term: *ugra-karma*, or painful, distressful, horrible, and atrocious activities. In his purport to this verse, Śrīla Prabhupāda offers animal-killing and nuclear weapons as examples of *ugra-karma,* and in his *Bhāgavatam* commentaries he offers other examples: technological advancement, slaughterhouses, breweries, cigarette factories, nightclubs, and large-scale industrial development and trade.

10 Taking shelter of insatiable lust and absorbed in the conceit of pride and false prestige, the demoniac, thus illusioned, are always sworn to unclean work, attracted by the impermanent.

11–12 They believe that to gratify the senses is the prime necessity of human civilization. Thus until the end of life their anxiety is immeasurable. Bound by a network of hundreds and thousands of desires and absorbed in lust and anger, they secure money by illegal means for sense gratification.

The demoniac have unlimited desires, and driven by those desires they are drowning in the ocean of sense gratification until the moment of death (*pralaya-antām*). The demoniac possess determination, but only for sense gratification. *Pāśa* means "rope." *Āśā-pāśa-śatair* means that they are caught in the net of attempting to satisfy their myriad desires. It is from the rope of their desires that they will one day hang.

The following texts describe their thoughts after they acquire money "by illegal means."

13–15 The demoniac person thinks: "So much wealth do I have today, and I will gain more according to my schemes. So much is mine now, and it will increase in the future, more and more. He is my enemy, and I have killed him, and my other enemies will also be killed. I am the lord of everything. I am the enjoyer. I am perfect, powerful, and happy. I am the richest

man, surrounded by aristocratic relatives. There is none so powerful and happy as I am. I shall perform sacrifices, I shall give some charity, and thus I shall rejoice." In this way, such persons are deluded by ignorance.

The demoniac think that all has been accomplished by their endeavor. The next verse explains their actual achievement.

16 Thus perplexed by various anxieties and bound by a network of illusions, they become too strongly attached to sense enjoyment and fall down into hell.

17 Self-complacent and always impudent, deluded by wealth and false prestige, they sometimes proudly perform sacrifices in name only, without following any rules or regulations.

18 Bewildered by false ego, strength, pride, lust, and anger, the demons become envious of the Supreme Personality of Godhead, who is situated in their own bodies and in the bodies of others, and blaspheme against the real religion.

Śrīla Prabhupāda mentions in his purport to text 18 that the demoniac envy not only the Lord but the Vedic scriptures. Śrīla Viśvanātha Cakravartī Ṭhākura comments that the demoniac also envy those who worship the Lord. Their envy takes the forms of being unable to tolerate a devotee's advancement and of seeing only a devotee's faults, despite his numerous good qualities.

The next two texts describe Kṛṣṇa's reciprocation with the demoniac.

19 Those who are envious and mischievous, who are the lowest among men, I perpetually cast into the ocean of material existence, into various demoniac species of life.

20 Attaining repeated birth amongst the species of demoniac life, O son of Kuntī, such persons can never approach Me. Gradually they sink down to the most abominable type of existence.

Śrīla Baladeva Vidyābhūṣaṇa comments:

> Arjuna may ask, "But, after many lifetimes, they should eventually receive Your mercy, by which they will be freed from their demoniac births."
>
> Lord Kṛṣṇa answers: "These foolish persons take birth in demoniac forms of life birth after birth. Failing to achieve Me, they descend to lower forms of life, even taking birth as dogs."
>
> In the phrase "failing to achieve Me," the word *eva,* "certainly," indicates: "There is no possibility of My mercy falling on them. It is even difficult for them to achieve a good form of life that would be a prerequisite to obtaining Me."
>
> The following question can then be raised: "But the Supreme Lord automatically has His every desire fulfilled. He can make even the unqualified qualified."
>
> The answer is: "Yes, He could, if He had such a desire. But actually He does not have even the seed of that desire. Thus the author of the *Vedānta-sūtra* has described the Lord's partiality in the *sūtra, vaiṣamya-nairghṇyena:* the Supreme seems to be unfair because of His partiality to some and His enmity toward others."

Śrīla Prabhupāda's writes strongly in his purport to text 20: "It is clearly stated that the demoniac people, life after life, are put into the wombs of similar demons, and, not achieving the mercy of the Supreme Lord, they go down and down, so that at last they achieve bodies like those of cats, dogs, and hogs. It is clearly stated that such demons have practically no chance of receiving the mercy of God at any stage of later life."

Birth after birth they suffer, especially by being born into lower species. Because such souls have no desire to get out of material existence, they don't. They don't want Kṛṣṇa's mercy, and He doesn't give it to them.

According to Śrīla Baladeva Vidyābhūṣaṇa, Arjuna now asks Kṛṣṇa: "People hearing this are going to want to give up these qualities. What can they do to accomplish this?" Kṛṣṇa answers this question, and in this way presents us with our own choice: either adopt demonic life and become degraded or reject it and obtain the supreme destination.

21 There are three gates leading to this hell – lust, anger, and greed. Every sane man should give these up, for they lead to the degradation of the soul.

Kṛṣṇa orders every sane person to give up lust, anger, and greed. Those qualities are so vicious that even one possessing a divine nature should fear them. For a man, a woman personifies *kāma,* lust, because she is able to gratify all his sense desires. When *kāma* is unsatisfied, *krodha,* anger, is born. Anger is very difficult to control.

Krodha appears only when our desires are checked, but what if we are able to satisfy our desires without hindrance? Do we then become peaceful? No. We are filled with *lobha,* greed. Greed gives birth to *moha,* illusion, and loss of discrimination. Next comes *mada,* the intoxication of pride. From the mixture of these five, envy, *matsara,* is able to manifest fully. Thus all these demoniac qualities are rooted in lust.

What results does their avoidance award?

22 The man who has escaped these three gates of hell, O son of Kuntī, performs acts conducive to self-realization and thus gradually attains the supreme destination.

Our choice is clear. Choosing to escape the banyan tree of the material world entails choosing to free ourselves from lust, anger, greed, illusion, pride, and envy. Yet contemporary civilization, being demoniac, explicitly encourages the cultivation of lust, anger, and greed.

Kṛṣṇa now offers two verses as conclusions to this chapter. First, using a negative statement, Kṛṣṇa directs us to bring our activities in line with *śāstra*. Kṛṣṇa then, through a positive statement, offers the same direction in the final verse of this chapter.

23 He who discards scriptural injunctions and acts according to his own whims attains neither perfection, nor happiness, nor the supreme destination.

Śrīla Prabhupāda's purport shows the connection between not following *śāstra* and acting in lust, anger, and greed: "As described before, the *śāstra-vidhi,* or the direction of the *śāstra,* is given to the different castes and orders of human society. Everyone is expected to follow these rules and regulations. If one does not follow them and acts whimsically according to his lust, greed, and desire, then he never will be perfect in his life. In other words, a man may theoretically know all these things, but if he does not apply them in his own life, then he is to be known as the lowest of mankind."

24 One should therefore understand what is duty and what is not duty by the regulations of the scriptures. Knowing such rules and regulations, one should act so that he may gradually be elevated.

One should properly use his human life to faithfully follow *śāstra;* to avoid lust, anger, and greed; and to at least gradually elevate himself toward Kṛṣṇa consciousness. Śrīla Prabhupāda's purport carries to a conclusion concepts that Kṛṣṇa has been developing in the past several chapters:

> In human society, aversion to the principles of understanding the Supreme Personality of Godhead is the cause of all falldowns. That is the greatest offense of human life. Therefore, *māyā,* the material energy of the Supreme Personality of Godhead, is always giving us trouble in the shape of the threefold miseries. This material energy is constituted of the three modes of material nature. One has to raise himself at least to the mode of goodness before the path to understanding the Supreme Lord can be opened. Without raising oneself to the standard of the mode of goodness, one remains in ignorance and passion, which are the cause of demoniac life. Those in the modes of passion and ignorance deride the scriptures, deride the holy man, and deride the proper understanding of the Supreme Personality of Godhead. They disobey the instructions of the spiritual master, and they do not care for the regulations of the scriptures. In spite of hearing the glories of devotional service, they are not attracted. Thus they manufacture their own way of elevation. These are some of the defects of human society which lead to the demoniac status of life. If, however,

one is able to be guided by a proper and bona fide spiritual master, who can lead one to the path of elevation, to the higher stage, then one's life becomes successful.

CHAPTER SEVENTEEN

The Divisions of Faith

Kṛṣṇa concluded chapter sixteen by establishing that those who follow *śāstra* are divine and those who do not are demoniac. Śrīla Baladeva Vidyābhūṣaṇa introduces chapter seventeen with Arjuna inquiring:

> You have described in the previous chapter that those who study the *Vedas,* follow their injunctions, try to understand their meaning, and have faith in their authority are *devas*. You have then described as *asuras* those who disregard the *Vedas* and act outside the scope of Vedic injunctions. Now I have a question: What is the position of those who have comprehended the difficult texts of the *Vedas,* both learning them by rote and understanding their meaning, but who – because of lack of diligence – abandon the Vedic injunctions and instead worship demigods and others with the kind of faith found in worldly conduct? What is their position relative to the above-ascertained distinctions between the *devas* and *asuras*? Please answer this, taking into consideration both their neglect of Vedic injunctions and their possession of sincere faith.

1 Arjuna inquired: O Kṛṣṇa, what is the situation of those who do not follow the principles of scripture but worship according to their own imagination? Are they in goodness, in passion, or in ignorance?

Arjuna would like to know where, on the banyan tree of the material world, are those who faithfully follow something other than *śāstra*.

Śrīla Prabhupāda's purport further expands the connections between chapters:

In the fourth chapter, thirty-ninth verse, it is said that a person faithful to a particular type of worship gradually becomes elevated to the stage of knowledge and attains the highest perfectional stage of peace and prosperity. In the sixteenth chapter, it is concluded that one who does not follow the principles laid down in the scriptures is called an *asura,* demon, and one who follows the scriptural injunctions faithfully is called a *deva,* or demigod. Now, if one, with faith, follows some rules which are not mentioned in the scriptural injunctions, what is his position? This doubt of Arjuna's is to be cleared by Kṛṣṇa. Are those who create some sort of God by selecting a human being and placing their faith in him worshiping in goodness, passion, or ignorance? Do such persons attain the perfectional stage of life? Is it possible for them to be situated in real knowledge and elevate themselves to the highest perfectional stage? Do those who do not follow the rules and regulations of the scriptures but who have faith in something and worship gods and demigods and men attain success in their effort? Arjuna is putting these questions to Kṛṣṇa.

2 The Supreme Personality of Godhead said: According to the modes of nature acquired by the embodied soul, one's faith can be of three kinds – in goodness, in passion, or in ignorance. Now hear about this.

3 O son of Bharata, according to one's existence under the various modes of nature, one evolves a particular kind of faith. The living being is said to be of a particular faith according to the modes he has acquired.

4 Men in the mode of goodness worship the demigods; those in the mode of passion worship the demons; and those in the mode of ignorance worship ghosts and spirits.

In his purport to text 3 Śrīla Prabhupāda explains the principle of faith:

> *Śraddhā,* or faith, originally comes out of the mode of goodness. One's faith may be in a demigod or some created God or some mental concoction. One's strong faith is supposed to

> be productive of works of material goodness. But in material conditional life, no works are completely purified. They are mixed. They are not in pure goodness. Pure goodness is transcendental; in purified goodness one can understand the real nature of the Supreme Personality of Godhead. As long as one's faith is not completely in purified goodness, the faith is subject to contamination by any of the modes of material nature. The contaminated modes of material nature expand to the heart. Therefore according to the position of the heart in contact with a particular mode of material nature, one's faith is established. It should be understood that if one's heart is in the mode of goodness his faith is also in the mode of goodness. If his heart is in the mode of passion, his faith is also in the mode of passion. And if his heart is in the mode of darkness, illusion, his faith is also thus contaminated. Thus we find different types of faith in this world, and there are different types of religions due to different types of faith. The real principle of religious faith is situated in the mode of pure goodness, but because the heart is tainted we find different types of religious principles. Thus according to different types of faith, there are different kinds of worship.

As mentioned in this purport, faith comes from the mode of pure goodness. It is manifest, however, according to the modes that dictate our nature. According to the modes that dominate a person, therefore, he will naturally become attracted to a specific object and method of worship.

Śrīla Baladeva Vidyābhūṣaṇa explains that texts 2–4 describe those who have given up *śāstra* out of laziness or because the required worship was troublesome, yet faithfully worship the demigods. Texts 5–6, in contrast, describe not those who have whimsically given up following *śāstra* but those who are against Vedic practices.

5–6 Those who undergo severe austerities and penances not recommended in the scriptures, performing them out of pride and egoism, who are impelled by lust and attachment, who are foolish and who torture the material elements of the body as well as the Supersoul dwelling within, are to be known as demons.

Śrīla Baladeva Vidyābhūṣaṇa comments:

> It has been stated in the previous chapter that those who are neglectful of Vedic authority (*veda-bāhya*) can never be delivered from their bad fate. Now this is corroborated in the two texts beginning *aśāstra-* [texts 5–6]. There are those who execute austerities, in defiance of the *Vedas,* which are enjoined in their own concocted scriptures, and are horrible and cause distress to other living beings. These people are characterized by hankering for sense gratification and by their stubborn insistence that "We can accomplish everything on our own." They abuse the physical elements that compose their bodies. They emaciate their bodies by unnecessary fasting and so on. By their neglect, they also torment Me, the Supersoul dwelling in their bodies. They are oblivious – devoid of understanding how to discriminate according to scripture. You should know such persons, who are outside the scope of Vedic authority, to be demons. Thus it is implied that the bad fate of such persons is unavoidable.
>
> What conclusion can we draw from this? Those who worship Yakṣas and Rākṣasas according to their natural faith may receive the potent mercy of Vedic authorities, and then, by developing some faith in the revealed scriptures, their demoniac nature may subside. But those who worship demigods are factually in the mode of goodness, so by the mercy of saintly association it will be easier for them to develop faith in scriptural authority.

While reading these descriptions of the effects of the modes of nature on a person's worship and activities – and the following descriptions of food, sacrifices, austerities, and charity – we naturally place ourselves and others into categories of goodness, passion, or ignorance.

Individuals are not, however, neatly influenced by only one mode. Rather, they are influenced by unique and individual combinations of modes. The three modes of nature are thus compared to colors: goodness to yellow, passion to red, and ignorance to blue. Nine colors are created by mixing each color with the remaining two colors. By again mixing each of those nine with the other eight colors, eighty-one varieties occur. We could continue mixing colors again and again until an unlimited palette of colors is created. Similarly, the three modes can be mixed into three, nine, and eighty-one combinations, or mixed again to form even more subtle combinations. Indeed, each conditioned soul acquires an individually tailored body and set of circumstances in the material world. At times, therefore, we find a person whose modes basically agree with ours, yet who is still different from us. Our modes may correspond with another's in terms of nine, or even eighty-one shadings, but the more subtle shadings of modes between individuals must certainly exist.

We can, however, usually judge the quality of a person's faith – the modes by which he is dominated – by observing whom he worships and especially his preferences in eating, as Kṛṣṇa will describe in the next four verses.

7 Even the food each person prefers is of three kinds, according to the three modes of material nature. The same is true of sacrifices, austerities, and charity. Now hear of the distinctions between them.

8 Foods dear to those in the mode of goodness increase the duration of life, purify one's existence, and give strength, health, happiness, and satisfaction. Such foods are juicy, fatty, wholesome, and pleasing to the heart.

9 Foods that are too bitter, too sour, salty, hot, pungent, dry, and burning are dear to those in the mode of passion. Such foods cause distress, misery, and disease.

10 Food prepared more than three hours before being eaten, food that is tasteless, decomposed, and putrid, and food consisting of remnants and untouchable things is dear to those in the mode of darkness.

Food in the mode of goodness is made with pure ingredients and cooked with purity. It is then served in a clean place by pure people.

Śrīla Viśvanātha Cakravartī Ṭhākura explains that in text 9, "distress" refers to the pain felt while eating foods in the mode of passion. "Misery" refers to the depression one feels after thus eating, and "disease" refers to the results yet to be felt.

The next three verses describe various sacrifices performed according to the modes of nature.

11 Of sacrifices, the sacrifice performed according to the directions of scripture, as a matter of duty, by those who desire no reward, is of the nature of goodness.

12 But the sacrifice performed for some material benefit, or for the sake of pride, O chief of the Bhāratas, you should know to be in the mode of passion.

13 Any sacrifice performed without regard for the directions of scripture, without distribution of prasāda [spiritual food], without chanting of Vedic hymns and remunerations to the priests, and without faith is considered to be in the mode of ignorance.

The next six verses explain austerities performed in the modes.

14 Austerity of the body consists in worship of the Supreme Lord, the brāhmaṇas, the spiritual master, and superiors like the father and mother, and in cleanliness, simplicity, celibacy, and nonviolence.

15 Austerity of speech consists in speaking words that are truthful, pleasing, beneficial, and not agitating to others, and also in regularly reciting Vedic literature.

16 And satisfaction, simplicity, gravity, self-control, and purification of one's existence are the austerities of the mind.

17 This threefold austerity, performed with transcendental faith by men not expecting material benefits but engaged only for the sake of the Supreme, is called austerity in goodness.

18 Penance performed out of pride and for the sake of gaining respect, honor, and worship is said to be in the mode of passion. It is neither stable nor permanent.

19 Penance performed out of foolishness, with self-torture or to destroy or injure others is said to be in the mode of ignorance.

Austerities can be performed, in order of progressive difficulty, with the body, speech, or mind. This was referred to in text 17 as the "threefold austerity." Each austerity can be performed in either goodness, passion, or ignorance. As an austerity of speech, we should not speak words that pierce others' hearts. We should speak the truth, but not the bitter truth. A difficult mental austerity is to always desire others' welfare.

20 Charity given out of duty, without expectation of return, at the proper time and place, and to a worthy person is considered to be in the mode of goodness.

21 But charity performed with the expectation of some return, or with a desire for fruitive results, or in a grudging mood, is said to be charity in the mode of passion.

22 And charity performed at an impure place, at an improper time, to unworthy persons, or without proper attention and respect is said to be in the mode of ignorance.

Up to this point, Kṛṣṇa has described how one can recognize the modes of material nature under which a person exists by the person's worship, food, austerity, sacrifice, and charity. All three modes and their combinations are defective and bind one to the material world. Now Kṛṣṇa will explain that all defects can be removed from every combination of the modes of material nature. How? By chanting *oṁ tat sat.*

23 From the beginning of creation, the three words oṁ tat sat were used to indicate the Supreme Absolute Truth. These three symbolic representations were used by brāhmaṇas while chanting the hymns of the Vedas and during sacrifices for the satisfaction of the Supreme.

In his purport to this verse, Śrīla Prabhupāda comments, "It has been explained that penance, sacrifice, charity, and foods are divided into three catagories: the modes of goodness, passion, and ignorance. But whether first class, second class, or third class...when they are aimed at the Supreme – *oṁ tat sat,* the Supreme Personality of Godhead, the eternal – they become means for spiritual elevation."

The chanting of *oṁ tat sat* – or any name of God – purifies all activities with which the chanting is combined, and thus Kṛṣṇa's powerful name should accompany all performance of *tapasya,* charity, and sacrifice to remove the discrepancies inherent in those activities and to ensure that the consciousness of all participants is elevated.

Śrīla Prabhupāda further states: "One who acts without following the regulations of the scriptures will not attain the Absolute Truth. He will get some temporary result, but not the ultimate end of life. The conclusion is that the performance of charity, sacrifice, and penance must be done in the mode of goodness. Performed in the mode of passion or ignorance, they are certainly inferior in quality." The *Vedas* therefore teach a gradual path of elevation: performing activities in goodness and avoiding activities in passion and ignorance.

Following the Vedic path of goodness, however, is not Kṛṣṇa's conclusion. His real desire is more direct and will be described in the following verses.

24 Therefore, transcendentalists undertaking performances of sacrifice, charity, and penance in accordance with scriptural regulations begin always with "oṁ," to attain the Supreme.

25 Without desiring fruitive results, one should perform various kinds of sacrifice, penance, and charity with the word 'tat.' The purpose of such transcendental activities is to get free from material entanglement.

26–27 The Absolute Truth is the objective of devotional sacrifice, and it is indicated by the word "sat." The performer of such sacrifice is also called "sat," as are all works of sacrifice, penance, and charity which, true to the absolute nature, are performed to please the Supreme Person, O son of Pṛthā.

In this chapter, Kṛṣṇa recommends that faithfully following *śāstra,* we perform worship, penances, sacrifices, austerities – and even eat – in the mode of goodness. All our activities, however, regardless of the mode of nature under which they are performed, should be aimed at pleasing the Supreme Lord. And those activities should be further purified and made still more auspicious by accompanying them with the chanting of the Lord's names *oṁ tat sat.*

In the 1950s Śrīla Prabhupāda even placed the words *oṁ tat sat* before his signature on letters. *Oṁ* is a name of Viṣṇu. *Tat* is chanted to achieve liberation. All activities performed for the Lord's pleasure are *sat,* eternal. Thus the process of devotional service is clearly stressed in these verses.

After hearing which activities are *sat,* one naturally wishes to know which activities are *asat.* Kṛṣṇa responds to this query in the final verse of this chapter.

28 Anything done as sacrifice, charity, or penance without faith in the Supreme, O son of Pṛthā, is impermanent. It is called 'asat' and is useless both in this life and the next.

Sacrifice, charity, and penance should all be performed for the pleasure of *oṁ tat sat,* the Absolute Truth; otherwise, these activities remain within the confines of the material world, bound by goodness, passion, and ignorance. The gradual process of elevation should be avoided, and Kṛṣṇa consciousness should be taken up directly. There is no need to elevate ourselves gradually on the banyan tree of the material world. Even if, because of our natures, we naturally have faith in one thing or another, we should hear transcendental literature from pure souls, transcend our faith born of the modes of nature, and establish our faith on the spiritual platform. In this way, we should cut off our attachment to matter and attain the spiritual world through pure devotional service.

Śrīla Prabhupāda summarizes chapter seventeen:

> Anything done without the transcendental objective – whether it be sacrifice, charity, or penance – is useless. Therefore in this verse it is declared that such activities are abominable. Everything should be done for the Supreme in Kṛṣṇa

consciousness. Without such faith, and without the proper guidance, there can never be any fruit. In all the Vedic scriptures, faith in the Supreme is advised. In the pursuit of all Vedic instructions, the ultimate goal is the understanding of Kṛṣṇa. No one can obtain success without following this principle. Therefore, the best course is to work from the very beginning in Kṛṣṇa consciousness under the guidance of a bona fide spiritual master. That is the way to make everything successful.

...The mode of goodness is better than the modes of passion and ignorance, but one who takes directly to Kṛṣṇa consciousness is transcendental to all three modes of material nature. Although there is a process of gradual elevation, if one, by the association of pure devotees, takes directly to Kṛṣṇa consciousness, that is the best way. And that is recommended in this chapter. To achieve success in this way, one must first find the proper spiritual master and receive training under his direction. Then one can achieve faith in the Supreme. When that faith matures, in course of time, it is called love of God. This love is the ultimate goal of the living entities. One should therefore take to Kṛṣṇa consciousness directly. That is the message of this seventeenth chapter.

Chapter Eighteen

The Perfection of Renunciation

Chapter eighteen summarizes the contents of the entire *Gītā*. As Śrīla Prabhupāda explains, "Actually the *Bhagavad-gītā* is finished in seventeen chapters. The eighteenth chapter is a supplementary summarization of the topics discussed before. In every chapter of *Bhagavad-gītā,* Lord Kṛṣṇa stresses that devotional service unto the Supreme Personality of Godhead is the ultimate goal of life. This same point is summarized in the eighteenth chapter as the most confidential path of knowledge.... As in the second chapter a synopsis of the whole subject matter was described, in the eighteenth chapter also the summary of all instruction is given."

Kṛṣṇa's summary begins with a review of the basic conclusion of the first six chapters: dutiful, detached work brings no reactions.

1 Arjuna said: O mighty-armed one, I wish to understand the purpose of renunciation [tyāga] and of the renounced order of life [sannyāsa], O killer of the Keśī demon, master of the senses.

What is the goal of renunciation and of the renounced order of life? Should one work while remaining detached from the fruit of work (*niṣkāma karma*) or should one renounce activities to perform *jñāna-yoga*? Śrīla Baladeva Vidyābhūṣaṇa comments on this verse as follows:

> Arjuna remained unclear as to the Lord's meaning when He used the word *sannyāsa* in statements such as, "When the embodied living being controls his nature and mentally renounces all actions, he resides happily..." (Bg. 5.13), and when He used the word *tyāga* in statements such as, "Abandoning all attachment

to the results of his activities..." (Bg. 4.20). Arjuna thus inquires in this verse, "Do the words *sannyāsa* and *tyāga* have completely different meanings, like the two words "mountain" and "tree," or do they have congruous meanings, like the words "Kuru" and "Pāṇḍava"? If the first case is true, then I want to know what the separate identities of *sannyāsa* and *tyāga* are. If the second case is true, then maybe there is some superficial, quasi-distinction between the two ideas and I would like to know what that is. O mighty-armed Kṛṣṇa, O Hṛṣīkeśa, because You are the impeller of the active functions of intelligence, You Yourself have brought about my doubt. O killer of Keśī, please destroy my doubt as you destroyed Keśī."

Śrīla Prabhupāda comments: "Arjuna wants to clarify the two distinct subject matters of *Bhagavad-gītā,* namely renunciation (*tyāga*) and the renounced order of life (*sannyāsa*). Thus he is asking the meaning of these two words." Kṛṣṇa's answer begins in text 2.

2 The Supreme Personality of Godhead said: The giving up of activities that are based on material desire is what great learned men call the renounced order of life [sannyāsa]. And giving up the results of all activities is what the wise call renunciation [tyāga].

Kṛṣṇa begins His answer by giving the opinion of the learned and wise, who say that *sannyāsa* and *tyāga* are different. According to them, *sannyāsa* refers to the renunciation of materially motivated activities, specifically *karma-kāṇḍa* activities. *Tyāga,* on the other hand, refers to the renunciation of the fruits of one's activities.

In the next verse Kṛṣṇa offers further opinions.

3 Some learned men declare that all kinds of fruitive activities should be given up as faulty, yet other sages maintain that acts of sacrifice, charity, and penance should never be abandoned.

Śrīla Viśvanātha Cakravartī Ṭhākura has explained that the first group mentioned refers to the followers of Sāṅkhya. Desiring to avoid the reactions that fruitive actions bring, they encourage renunciation of all fruitive activities, especially those based on *karma-kāṇḍa* and which have as their main fault violence toward animals during sacrifice. In the second part of text 3, the *karma-mīmāṁsīs'* opinion is given. They say that sacrifice, charity, and penance are prescribed in the *Vedas* and should therefore never be renounced. Because these activities are mentioned in *śāstra,* they say, no one should consider them faulty or violent.

Finally, Kṛṣṇa gives His own opinion.

4 O best of the Bhāratas, now hear My judgment about renunciation. O tiger among men, renunciation is declared in the scriptures to be of three kinds.

The three kinds of renunciation are based on the three modes of material nature. Kṛṣṇa will describe them in texts 7–12.

Arjuna inquired about the difference between *tyāga* and *sannyāsa,* and Kṛṣṇa, in reply, mentions three types of *tyāga.* The Lord will now continue with His definitive answer to Arjuna's inquiry.

5 Acts of sacrifice, charity and penance are not to be given up; they must be performed. Indeed, sacrifice, charity, and penance purify even the great souls.

Śrīla Baladeva Vidyābhūṣaṇa comments that just as fibers exist within the stem of a lotus, these three activities contain knowledge that purifies the heart and elevates one.

Kṛṣṇa's conclusion is positive advice: "Everyone should perform these activities." Perform them, purify your heart, and set a good example. The mood in which these three should be performed is described in the next verse.

6 All these activities should be performed without attachment or any expectation of result. They should be performed as a matter of duty, O son of Pṛthā. That is My final opinion.

Kṛṣṇa herein concludes His opinion. Because it is *His* opinion, it is superior to the other opinions Kṛṣṇa previously offered. Activity need not be given up, because activities in and of themselves cause no reactions. We obtain reactions from our activities if, out of false ego, we think, "I am the doer and the fruits are mine to enjoy." Therefore Kṛṣṇa is once again proclaiming the true standard of renunciation as detachment from the fruits of work while performing duty. Arjuna should fight dutifully, but in the mood of renunciation, detached from the battle's results.

In the next six verses (7–12), Kṛṣṇa will define *tyāga,* renunciation, according to the three modes of nature. Kṛṣṇa first describes renunciation in the mode of ignorance.

7 Prescribed duties should never be renounced. If one gives up his prescribed duties because of illusion, such renunciation is said to be in the mode of ignorance.

In this verse Kṛṣṇa uses and equates the words *tyāga* (*parityāga*) and *sannyāsa,* which indicates His answer to the question, "Are *sannyāsa* and *tyāga* the same or different?" Though some think they are different, Kṛṣṇa's opinion is that the renounced order of life and renunciation of the fruits of work are, in fact, exactly the same. Indeed, Śrīla Prabhupāda translates both words here as "renunciation."

Renouncing prescribed duties because of illusion results in further illusion. Kṛṣṇa next explains renunciation in the mode of passion.

8 Anyone who gives up prescribed duties as troublesome or out of fear of bodily discomfort is said to have renounced in the mode of passion. Such action never leads to the elevation of renunciation.

A person influenced by passion knows he should perform his duty with detachment, but he rejects those duties as troublesome. Yet such a person nevertheless may want spiritual benefit. Therefore he thinks, "Why should I work hard? I will become a *sādhu,* a *sannyāsī.*" Whether problems arise from our work, business or family, the mode of passion pushes us to avoid those difficulties rather than to face them in the mood Kṛṣṇa next explains.

9 O Arjuna, when one performs his prescribed duty only because it ought to be done, and renounces all material association and all attachment to the fruit, his renunciation is said to be in the mode of goodness.

This is the same "opinion" Kṛṣṇa expressed about sacrifice, charity, and penance in text 6: "All these activities should be performed without attachment or any expectation of result. They should be performed as a matter of duty." Knowledge is the result of such proper renunciation, or dutiful, detached work. Kṛṣṇa next describes the symptoms of proper renunciation.

10 The intelligent renouncer situated in the mode of goodness, neither hateful of inauspicious work nor attached to auspicious work, has no doubts about work.

A person in the mode of goodness is determined to act properly regardless of the forthcoming pleasures or pains. Śrīla Prabhupāda confirms this in his purport as the proper attitude for a devotee: "A person in Kṛṣṇa consciousness or in the mode of goodness does not hate anyone or anything which troubles his body. He does work in the proper place and at the proper time without fearing the troublesome effects of his duty. Such a person situated in transcendence should be understood to be most intelligent and beyond all doubts in his activities."

Can't one just renounce all work, both the auspicious and the inauspicious?

11 It is indeed impossible for an embodied being to give up all activities. But he who renounces the fruits of action is called one who has truly renounced.

Kṛṣṇa answers, *na hi:* "Most certainly never! Don't give up activities, but act as a *karma-phala-tyāgī* by giving up your attachment to all the fruit of your work." Śrīla Prabhupāda's purport underscores Kṛṣṇa's definition of a *sannyāsī:* "There are many members of the International Society for Krishna Consciousness who work very hard in their office or in the factory or some other place, and whatever they earn they give to the Society. Such elevated souls are actually *sannyāsīs* and are situated in the renounced order of life."

The results achieved after death by both the attached and the detached are explained next.

12 For one who is not renounced, the threefold fruits of action – desirable, undesirable, and mixed – accrue after death. But those who are in the renounced order of life have no such result to suffer or enjoy.

Those attached to sense enjoyment achieve varied results after death from the activities they have performed. In contrast, the *tyāgī* fixed in knowledge attains liberation. We should note that in this verse Kṛṣṇa has again used both words, *sannyāsa* and *tyāga,* to emphasize that they are synonymous. Thus Kṛṣṇa has again established that the superior method of becoming free from the reactions to work is *niṣkāma karma* – renouncing the fruits of work, not the work itself.

Śrīla Prabhupāda notes in his purport to text 13: "A question may be raised that since any activity performed must have some reaction, how is it that the person in Kṛṣṇa consciousness does not suffer or enjoy the reactions of work?" Kṛṣṇa will now answer this question.

After having summarized His teachings on *karma,* Kṛṣṇa now describes from the viewpoint of *jñāna* (which is the subject matter of the last six chapters) how it is possible to act and yet remain free from all reaction.

13 O mighty-armed Arjuna, according to the Vedānta there are five causes for the accomplishment of all action. Now learn of these from Me.

Kṛṣṇa cites *Vedānta* and begins His analysis of activity by discussing the five causes of action, the most important being the Supersoul. Kṛṣṇa offers this analysis to help us become detached from seeing ourselves as the doers of all and thereby becoming bound. Kṛṣṇa will carry His analysis further to the perfection of *jñāna:* knowledge of the Supersoul.

14 The place of action [the body], the performer, the various senses, the many different kinds of endeavor, and ultimately the Supersoul – these are the five factors of action.

The *adhiṣṭhānam,* or place of action, refers to the entire body, or that which is held up by the skeleton. The *kartā,* the performer, is ultimately the soul, who when absorbed in material consciousness, acts through false ego. The *karaṇam,* or instruments, are the parts of the body, the senses. The *ceṣṭā* is the overall endeavor of the senses. *Daivam,* the Supersoul, is the ultimate controller over all the other factors. He is the Paramātmā, the Lord of all within the material world.

To convince us that we are not the only doers, Kṛṣṇa stresses that these five factors are the true causes of action, the ultimate "supercause" being the Supersoul's sanction. Śrīla Baladeva Vidyābhūṣaṇa comments that we are doers – our activities do spring from our own free will – but our endeavor is not the independent cause of actions:

> If the *jīva's* being a doer is under the regulating control of the Supreme Lord, then we have to say that his activity does not proceed from his own will and that he is actually just like a stone or some other inert object. In that case, don't the injunctions and prohibitions of scripture become useless? The answer is, the *jīva* receives from the Supreme Lord a body and senses endowed with specific potencies, of which he then becomes the proprietor. Acquiring those potencies, the *jīva* exerts his free will and assumes control of his body and senses for the purpose of fulfilling karmic endeavors. The Supreme Lord, present within all these coverings, sanctions the *jīva's* activity and inspires him to act. In this way there is no contradiction between the Supreme's control and the *jīva's* having his own willpower to act or to refrain from acting.

15 Whatever right or wrong actions a man performs by body, mind, or speech is caused by these five factors.

Kṛṣṇa categorizes action into three: that performed with the body, mind, or words. Action in all three categories can be performed either according to śāstric injunctions or against them.

In either case, however, it is the Supersoul who ultimately sanctions all action. This is confirmed as follows.

16 Therefore one who thinks himself the only doer, not considering the five factors, is certainly not very intelligent and cannot see things as they are.

Thinking "By my power I have done it" keeps one bound in the material world. Therefore in this verse Kṛṣṇa uses the word *kevalam,* "only." "Only I have done it!" In chapter three, Kṛṣṇa referred to such thinking – *kartāham iti manyate* – as fit only for *vimūḍhas,* or asslike people. Then in chapter sixteen, He characterized such thinking – *īśvaro 'ham ahaṁ bhogī* – as demoniac. Here again, and this time quoting *Vedānta* as His authority, Kṛṣṇa points out the lack of intelligence and the foolishness inherent in thinking ourselves the controllers and doers: *paśyaty akṛta-buddhitvān na sa paśyati durmatiḥ.*

Kṛṣṇa, in the next verse contrasts such a foolish thinker with an intelligent person who possesses knowledge and is free from illusion.

17 One who is not motivated by false ego, whose intelligence is not entangled, though he kills men in this world, does not kill. Nor is he bound by his actions.

Text 16 stated that if we think of ourselves as doers, we will become bound. Here, not seeing ourselves as the doers is cited as the cause of liberation. This verse applies specifically to Arjuna, who is poised to fight on the battlefield. Again Kṛṣṇa is trying to incite Arjuna to fight, this time by using arguments based on *jñāna.* At the same time, Kṛṣṇa insists that Arjuna fight in the proper consciousness, as an act of surrender. Kṛṣṇa assures Arjuna that such fighting will bring no reactions.

Śrīla Prabhupāda expresses this point in his purport:

> In this verse the Lord informs Arjuna that the desire not to fight arises from false ego. Arjuna thought himself to be the doer of action, but he did not consider the supreme sanction within and

without. If one does not know that a supersanction is there, why should he act? But one who knows the instruments of work, himself as the worker, and the Supreme Lord as the supreme sanctioner is perfect in doing everything. Such a person is never in illusion. Personal activity and responsibility arise from false ego and godlessness, or a lack of Kṛṣṇa consciousness. Anyone who is acting in Kṛṣṇa consciousness under the direction of the Supersoul or the Supreme Personality of Godhead, even though killing, does not kill. Nor is he ever affected by the reaction of such killing. When a soldier kills under the command of a superior officer, he is not subject to be judged. But if a soldier kills on his own personal account, then he is certainly judged by a court of law.

18 Knowledge, the object of knowledge, and the knower are the three factors that motivate action; the senses, the work, and the doer are the three constituents of action.

Kṛṣṇa here uses two words, *jñānam* and *jñeyam,* knowledge and the object of knowledge (two of the six topics in chapter thirteen). This again indicates that chapter eighteen is a summary of the *Gītā.*

By elaborating on the motives and constituents of action, here in text 18, Kṛṣṇa finishes His summary of *jñāna.* In pursuing that topic, Kṛṣṇa will again describe the effects of the three modes of nature (as He did in chapters fourteen and seventeen) in the next series of verses, texts 19–40. He begins by confirming that even the motivators of action and the constituents of action are under the dictates of the modes of nature. He first speaks of knowledge (a motivator), action (a constituent), and the performer of action (a constituent).

19 According to the three different modes of material nature, there are three kinds of knowledge, action, and performer of action. Now hear of them from Me.

20 That knowledge by which one undivided spiritual nature is seen in all living entities, though they are divided into innumerable forms, you should understand to be in the mode of goodness.

21 That knowledge by which one sees that in every different body there is a different type of living entity you should understand to be in the mode of passion.

22 And that knowledge by which one is attached to one kind of work as the all in all, without knowledge of the truth, and which is very meager, is said to be in the mode of darkness.

23 That action which is regulated and which is performed without attachment, without love or hatred, and without desire for fruitive results is said to be in the mode of goodness.

Kṛṣṇa has already recommended that action be dutifully performed in the mode of goodness. In his purport to text 23, Śrīla Prabhupāda closely equates the mode of goodness with Kṛṣṇa consciousness: "Regulated occupational duties, as prescribed in the scriptures in terms of the different orders and divisions of society, performed without attachment or proprietary rights and therefore without any love or hatred, and performed in Kṛṣṇa consciousness for the satisfaction of the Supreme, without self-satisfaction or self-gratification, are called actions in the mode of goodness."

24 But action performed with great effort by one seeking to gratify his desires, and enacted from a sense of false ego, is called action in the mode of passion.

25 That action performed in illusion, in disregard of scriptural injunctions, and without concern for future bondage or for violence or distress caused to others is said to be in the mode of ignorance.

26 One who performs his duty without association with the modes of material nature, without false ego, with great determination and enthusiasm, and without wavering in success or failure is said to be a worker in the mode of goodness.

Śrīla Prabhupāda again equates spiritual consciousness and the mode of goodness in his purport: "A person in Kṛṣṇa consciousness is always transcendental to the material modes of nature.

He has no expectations for the result of the work entrusted to him, because he is above false ego and pride. Still, he is always enthusiastic till the completion of such work. He does not worry about the distress undertaken; he is always enthusiastic. He does not care for success or failure; he is equal in both distress and happiness. Such a worker is situated in the mode of goodness."

27 The worker who is attached to work and the fruits of work, desiring to enjoy those fruits, and who is greedy, always envious, impure, and moved by joy and sorrow, is said to be in the mode of passion.

28 The worker who is always engaged in work against the injunctions of the scripture, who is materialistic, obstinate, cheating, and expert in insulting others, and who is lazy, always morose, and procrastinating is said to be a worker in the mode of ignorance.

One who is not Kṛṣṇa conscious is forced to act by the modes of material nature. And as in our knowledge and work, so also in our understanding and determination.

29 O winner of wealth, now please listen as I tell you in detail of the different kinds of understanding and determination, according to the three modes of material nature.

30 O son of Pṛthā, that understanding by which one knows what ought to be done and what ought not to be done, what is to be feared and what is not to be feared, what is binding and what is liberating, is in the mode of goodness.

31 O son of Pṛthā, that understanding which cannot distinguish between religion and irreligion, between action that should be done and action that should not be done, is in the mode of passion.

32 That understanding which considers irreligion to be religion, and religion to be irreligion, under the spell of illusion and darkness, and strives always in the wrong direction, O Pārtha, is in the mode of ignorance.

33 O son of Pṛthā, that determination which is unbreakable, which is sustained with steadfastness by yoga practice, and which thus controls the activities of the mind, life, and senses is determination in the mode of goodness.

Buddhi, intelligence or understanding, is in the mode of goodness when it recognizes and engages in a religious act. *Dhṛti,* determination, is that which makes the intelligence firm in its decisions. Determination that prevents us from performing degrading actions is also in the mode of goodness.

34 But that determination by which one holds fast to fruitive results in religion, economic development, and sense gratification is of the nature of passion, O Arjuna.

35 And that determination which cannot go beyond dreaming, fearfulness, lamentation, moroseness, and illusion – such unintelligent determination, O son of Pṛthā, is in the mode of darkness.

Kṛṣṇa next describes happiness in each of the three modes.

36 O best of the Bhāratas, now please hear from Me about the three kinds of happiness by which the conditioned soul enjoys, and by which he sometimes comes to the end of all distress.

37 That which in the beginning may be just like poison but at the end is just like nectar and which awakens one to self-realization is said to be happiness in the mode of goodness.

As happiness in goodness entails giving up interest in sense objects, its "nectar" – unlike the happiness derived from the mode of passion – comes only after some time. To experience happiness in goodness requires practice, *sādhana,* and control of the mind and senses. In contrast, happiness derived from passion and ignorance is immediate and requires no practice.

38 That happiness which is derived from contact of the senses with their objects and which appears like nectar at first but poison at the end is said to be of the nature of passion.

Unlike happiness in the mode of goodness, which only *appears* as if it were poison, happiness in the mode of passion quickly turns to poison. Ultimately, happiness in the mode of passion impresses an increasing number of desires on our consciousness and thus forces us to take further births and deaths.

39 And that happiness which is blind to self-realization, which is delusion from beginning to end, and which arises from sleep, laziness, and illusion is said to be of the nature of ignorance.

Kṛṣṇa next offers a one-verse restatement of the verses He has just spoken, and thus He summarizes the influence of the modes of nature.

40 There is no being existing, either here or among the demigods in the higher planetary systems, which is freed from these three modes born of material nature.

All conditioned souls are controlled by the three modes of nature. As Śrīla Prabhupāda explains in his purports, the modes of material nature determine all activities – high, low, and in between – within every planetary system in the universe.

Kṛṣṇa is developing His summary of all the prior chapters. As a basic summary of the first six chapters He explained *karma* and how detached work frees us from material bondage. Next He summarized the third set of six chapters, the *jñāna* chapters, in which work free of reaction is explained from the viewpoint of *jñāna:* When the eternal soul accepts that he is not the doer and surrenders to the ultimate sanctioner of all activities, the Supersoul, no reactions are accrued by him. Kṛṣṇa concluded by explaining the actual doer in the material world: the three modes of material nature.

Kṛṣṇa will now describe the progressive journey through *karma* and *jñāna* to realization of the Supersoul. He will then reach the philosophical conclusion of *Bhagavad-gītā: bhakti,* in which the living entity not only realizes the Supersoul but surrenders to Him, Kṛṣṇa, the Supreme Personality of Godhead.

41 Brāhmaṇas, kṣatriyas, vaiśyas, and śūdras are distinguished by the qualities born of their own natures in accordance with the material modes, O chastiser of the enemy.

Next Kṛṣṇa explains the qualities of work for those in each of the four *varṇas*.

42 Peacefulness, self-control, austerity, purity, tolerance, honesty, knowledge, wisdom, and religiousness – these are the natural qualities by which the brāhmaṇas work.

A *brāhmaṇa's* work is to cultivate and teach these qualities.

43 Heroism, power, determination, resourcefulness, courage in battle, generosity, and leadership are the natural qualities of work for the kṣatriyas.

A *kṣatriya* must have *īśvara-bhāva,* the ability to control others, but he must use such power for the protection – not the exploitation – of the citizens.

44 Farming, cow protection, and business are the natural work for the vaiśyas, and for the śūdras there is labor and service to others.

45 By following his qualities of work, every man can become perfect. Now please hear from Me how this can be done.

One can reach perfection by performing those prescribed duties Kṛṣṇa mentioned in texts 42–44. In which way can one perform those duties to achieve this result?

46 By worship of the Lord, who is the source of all beings and who is all-pervading, a man can attain perfection through performing his own work.

Śrīla Prabhupāda elaborates on how one's work – although within the modes of material nature – can be practically turned into *bhakti* through *niṣkāma karma-yoga:*

Everyone should think that he is engaged in a particular type of occupation by Hṛṣīkeśa, the master of the senses. And by the result of the work in which one is engaged, the Supreme Personality of Godhead, Śrī Kṛṣṇa, should be worshiped. If one thinks always in this way, in full Kṛṣṇa consciousness, then, by the grace of the Lord, he becomes fully aware of everything. That is the perfection of life. The Lord says in *Bhagavad-gītā* (12.7), *teṣām ahaṁ samuddhartā.* The Supreme Lord Himself takes charge of delivering such a devotee. That is the highest perfection of life. In whatever occupation one may be engaged, if he serves the Supreme Lord he will achieve the highest perfection.

Śrīla Viśvanātha Cakravartī Ṭhākura says, "Worshiping Kṛṣṇa by one's own prescribed work, offering it to Him while thinking within one's mind, 'May my Lord be pleased by this work,' one attains to the perfection of real knowledge."

Śrīla Baladeva Vidyābhūṣaṇa raises the question, "What if one possesses the nature and qualities of work of one *varṇa,* but wishes to perform the work of a different *varṇa*?" Kṛṣṇa answers that question in the following text.

47 It is better to engage in one's own occupation, even though one may perform it imperfectly, than to accept another's occupation and perform it perfectly. Duties prescribed according to one's nature are never affected by sinful reactions.

48 Every endeavor is covered by some fault, just as fire is covered by smoke. Therefore one should not give up the work born of his nature, O son of Kuntī, even if such work is full of fault.

Śrīla Baladeva Vidyābhūṣaṇa comments: "Kṛṣṇa confirms that all prescribed duties, not only the work of a *kṣatriya,* contain faults, or 'smoke.' Even a *brāhmaṇa's* work has defects. One should therefore cleanse away the faulty part of one's duty by offering the duty to the Supreme Lord. And for the sake of self-realization one should serve – giving careful attention to that part of his duty which gives rise to knowledge."

Rather than renouncing the work born of one's nature, one should worship the Lord through his work. Detachment and devotion while working, not renunciation of the activity, will cancel the defects inherent in the work. Śrīla Prabhupāda's purport to text 47 concisely sums up the entire process: "Anything done for personal sense gratification is a cause of bondage. The conclusion is that everyone should be engaged according to the particular mode of nature he has acquired, and he should decide to work only to serve the supreme cause of the Supreme Lord."

Worshiping the Lord through our work elevates us in knowledge. Kṛṣṇa will now describe further steps up the *yoga* ladder.

49 One who is self-controlled and unattached and who disregards all material enjoyments can obtain, by practice of renunciation, the highest perfect stage of freedom from reaction.

50 O son of Kuntī, learn from Me how one who has achieved this perfection can attain to the supreme perfectional stage, Brahman, the stage of highest knowledge, by acting in the way I shall now summarize.

These verses refer to a *yogī* on the path of *jñāna-yoga* who has purified his consciousness through work and has thus already progressed upward from the stage of *karma* to the stage of *jñāna*. Śrīla Viśvanātha Cakravartī Ṭhākura, in his comment to text 49, explains: "It being the case that all work is covered with fault, the person on the first level of *sannyāsa* rejects the faulty aspects of work – namely, the mentality of being the doer and the expectation of profit. Thus in due course of time, he perfects his *sādhana*. After having ascended to the level of *yoga,* he gives up work itself. This is the second stage of *sannyāsa,* as described in this verse beginning *asakta-buddhiḥ sarvatra*."

Thus we can understand that a devotee who has worshiped the Lord by his work will not attain Brahman realization in the same way as does the *jñāna-yogī*. A devotee, after being purified by detached work, attains freedom from false ego and moves forward to realize and serve the Supreme Brahman.

The process practiced by an advanced *jñāna-yogī* to elevate him further is next described.

51–53 Being purified by his intelligence and controlling the mind with determination, giving up the objects of sense gratification, being freed from attachment and hatred, one who lives in a secluded place, who eats little, who controls his body, mind, and power of speech, who is always in trance and who is detached, free from false ego, false strength, false pride, lust, anger, and acceptance of material things, free from false proprietorship, and peaceful – such a person is certainly elevated to the position of self-realization.

Śrīla Prabhupāda mentions the result of a *yogī's* adherence to these practices in his purport: "Thus when he is completely free from false ego, he becomes nonattached to all material things, and that is the stage of self-realization of Brahman. That stage is called the *brahma-bhūta* stage."

Next Kṛṣṇa describes the *brahma-bhūta* platform.

54 One who is thus transcendentally situated at once realizes the Supreme Brahman and becomes fully joyful. He never laments nor desires to have anything. He is equally disposed toward every living entity. In that state he attains pure devotional service unto Me.

If the desire of the *jñāna-yogī* was to become one with Brahman, he will end his spiritual quest at that point. If, however, he was practicing *yoga* to attain Kṛṣṇa's service, or if he had obtained the fortune of associating with an exalted Vaiṣṇava and had had his desire changed from "becoming Brahman" to serving the Supreme Brahman, he would then naturally take to devotional service and progress further.

Śrīla Prabhupāda writes: "To the impersonalist, achieving the *brahma-bhūta* stage, becoming one with the Absolute, is the last word. But for the personalist, or pure devotee, one has to go still further, to become engaged in pure devotional service."

Śrīla Viśvanātha Cakravartī Ṭhākura writes:

> When one's superficial designations have dissipated, one becomes *brahma-bhūta* – of the nature of Brahman, or pure, uncovered spirit – because his contamination of the material

> modes is now finished. He becomes a satisfied soul, and then he no longer laments as before for what he loses, or hankers for what he has not obtained. That is because he no longer falsely identifies with his body and other material things. Like a child, He is equal to all beings, both the gentle and the wicked. This is because he no longer judges by externals. And then, when his *jñāna* has become extinguished, like a fire whose fuel is used up, he attains to eternal devotion for Me – in the form of hearing, chanting, and so on – which was already present within his *jñāna*. Because this *bhakti* is a function of My internal energy, it is distinct from *māyā's* energy and so is not dispelled even after both *avidyā* and *vidyā* are dispelled. Therefore this *bhakti* is *parā,* separate from and better than *jñāna,* and because it is separate from both *niṣkāma karma* and *jñāna,* it is exclusive (*kevala*).

The word "attains" (*labhate*) *bhakti* is used purposely here. Although *bhakti* was previously partly attained to allow for the achievement of liberation through the processes of *jñāna* and *vairāgya,* it wasn't clearly perceived, just as the Supersoul living in the heart is not clearly perceived. Therefore, instead of saying, "He performs devotional service," the Lord says, "He attains devotional service." It is just like a person keeping gold and gems in a mixture of beans. After the beans are removed, the gold and gems, which were already present, become separately available in their pure form (*kevala*).

What happens after attaining devotion?

55 One can understand Me as I am, as the Supreme Personality of Godhead, only by devotional service. And when one is in full consciousness of Me by such devotion, he can enter into the kingdom of God.

Śrīla Viśvanātha Cakravartī Ṭhākura comments:

> Having obtained that *bhakti,* what then does one achieve? This is answered with the introduction of a new idea in the verse beginning *bhaktyā* [text 55]. Only by *bhakti* does a *jñānī,* or one of the various kinds of devotees, factually understand Me. After all, I have said, "I am obtainable only by *bhakti*." This being the

case, the *jñānī* being discussed understands Me after the function of *vidyā* has stopped influencing him, and then he enters into Me in the sense of coming to experience the happiness of *sāyujya* (being merged into the existence of the body of the Lord).

... Some persons want to attain *sāyujya* without *bhakti* by *jñāna* alone. Imagining themselves to be *jñānīs,* their only success is the trouble they take. They are very contemptible. Others understand that without *bhakti* there can be no liberation, so they practice *jñāna* mixed with *bhakti.* But they consider the Personality of Godhead an illusory concept superimposed on *māyā* and think that the body of the Personality of Godhead is composed of the material modes. Therefore even when they achieve the culmination of *yoga,* those *jñānīs* who presume that they are liberated are still contemptible. Thus it is stated, "Each of the four social orders, headed by the *brāhmaṇas,* was born through different combinations of the modes of nature from the face, arms, thighs, and feet of the Supreme Lord in His universal form. Thus the four spiritual orders were also generated. If any of the members of the four *varṇas* and four *āśramas* fail to worship or intentionally disrespect the Personality of Godhead, who is the source of their own creation, they will fall down from their position into a hellish state of life." (*Bhāg*. 11.5.2–3)

... Factually, however, the nature of the Lord's humanlike form is *sac-cid-ānanda.* Its becoming visible is simply by the influence of the Lord's inconceivable mercy, as is stated in the *Nārāyaṇādhyātma:* "Although the Supreme Lord is always unmanifest, He becomes visible by His own energy. Without that energy, who could ever see that supreme master, the reservoir of all pleasure?"

Many thousands of *śruti* statements establish that the Supreme Lord's body is *sac-cid-ānanda:* "Displaying His *sac-cid-ānanda-vigraha,* He is sitting at the base of a desire tree in Vṛndāvana." "He takes His personal form, which is the same as the transcendental sound of the *Vedas*." Nonetheless, the contemptible *jñānīs* interpret other *śrutis,* such as, "Know *māyā* to be nature and the possessor of *māyā* to be the Supreme Lord" to mean that the Supreme Lord is also a false concept superimposed on *māyā*. In fact, however, the *māyā* the Lord is conjoined with is his personal, internal energy, which is also called *māyā*.

However, those who practice *jñāna* mixed with *bhakti,* while thinking that the personal form of the Supreme Lord is *sac-cid-ānanda,* gradually attain *bhakti* after the influences of *avidyā* and *vidyā* cease to act on them. They are *jīvan-muktas* and are of two types. Some of them perform devotional service for the sake of attaining *sāyujya*. These achieve transcendental realization of the Supreme Entity and *sāyujya* within that Supreme. They are certainly praiseworthy. The others are very fortunate souls. By some trick of fate they get the association of sober, pure devotees. By the influence of such devotees, they give up their desire for liberation. Like Śukadeva and others, they drown in the sweet taste of the mellows of devotional service. They are supremely praiseworthy.

In the last paragraph of his purport, Śrīla Prabhupāda explains:

> After attainment of the *brahma-bhūta* stage of freedom from material conceptions, devotional service begins by one's hearing about the Lord. When one hears about the Supreme Lord, automatically the *brahma-bhūta* stage develops and material contamination – greediness and lust for sense enjoyment – disappears. As lust and desires disappear from the heart of a devotee, he becomes more attached to the service of the Lord, and by such attachment he becomes free from material contamination. In that state of life he can understand the Supreme Lord.... After liberation the process of *bhakti,* or transcendental service, continues....Actual liberation is getting free from misconceptions of life.

Kṛṣṇa first spoke about elevation through *karma* and has just spoken about how a *jñāna-yogī* may advance to the highest perfection. Beginning here, and for the next eleven verses (56–66), Kṛṣṇa will speak directly about *bhakti*.

56 Though engaged in all kinds of activities, My pure devotee, under My protection, reaches the eternal and imperishable abode by My grace.

The Lord tells Arjuna that actions performed purely in Kṛṣṇa's service take place above the modes of nature, on the transcendental platform. If one does not work for Kṛṣṇa under Kṛṣṇa's direction, he will be forced to work under the dictation of the modes of nature. Inactivity is not an option.

Śrīla Prabhupāda's purport to this verse is sweet:

> The word *mad-vyapāśrayaḥ* means under the protection of the Supreme Lord. To be free from material contamination, a pure devotee acts under the direction of the Supreme Lord or His representative, the spiritual master. There is no time limitation for a pure devotee. He is always, twenty-four hours a day, one hundred percent engaged in activities under the direction of the Supreme Lord. To a devotee who is thus engaged in Kṛṣṇa consciousness the Lord is very, very kind. In spite of all difficulties, he is eventually placed in the transcendental abode, or Kṛṣṇaloka. He is guaranteed entrance there; there is no doubt about it. In that supreme abode, there is no change; everything is eternal, imperishable, and full of knowledge.

In this verse, Kṛṣṇa has used the words *mat prasādād avāpnoti śāśvataṁ padam avyayam* to state that by His grace a devotee attains His eternal, imperishable abode. In this regard, Śrīla Viśvanātha Cakravartī Ṭhākura gives the following dialogue between Kṛṣṇa and Arjuna:

> "A *sakāma* or *niṣkāma* devotee attains My eternal abode–Vaikuṇṭha, Mathurā, Dvārakā, or Ayodhyā."
>
> "But how do these various abodes persist at the time of total annihilation?"
>
> "My abode is infallible and does not undergo any loss even at the total annihilation of the universe. This is due to My inconceivable power."
>
> "But a *jñānī* comes to the stage of *naiṣkarmya* and achieves *sāyujya* only after many lifetimes of various austerities and only after all the material action of his senses has ceased. How is it, then, that the devotees attain Your eternal abode simply by taking shelter of You, even though they are still engaged in *karma* and still have material desires?"
>
> "By My grace this happens. You should understand that My mercy has inconceivable power."

What is the practical application of Kṛṣṇa's instructions for Arjuna?

57 In all activities just depend upon Me and work always under My protection. In such devotional service, be fully conscious of Me.

Śrīla Prabhupāda's purport to this verse is powerful, often quoted, and practical:

> When one acts in Kṛṣṇa consciousness, he does not act as the master of the world. Just like a servant, one should act fully under the direction of the Supreme Lord. A servant has no individual independence. He acts only on the order of the master. A servant acting on behalf of the supreme master is unaffected by profit and loss. He simply discharges his duty faithfully in terms of the order of the Lord. Now, one may argue that Arjuna was acting under the personal direction of Kṛṣṇa, but when Kṛṣṇa is not present how should one act? If one acts according to the direction of Kṛṣṇa in this book, as well as under the guidance of the representative of Kṛṣṇa, then the result will be the same. The Sanskrit word *mat-paraḥ* is very important in this verse. It indicates that one has no goal in life save and except acting in Kṛṣṇa consciousness just to satisfy Kṛṣṇa. And while working in that way, one should think of Kṛṣṇa only: "I have been appointed to discharge this particular duty by Kṛṣṇa." While acting in such a way, one naturally has to think of Kṛṣṇa. This is perfect Kṛṣṇa consciousness. One should, however, note that after doing something whimsically he should not offer the result to the Supreme Lord. That sort of duty is not in the devotional service of Kṛṣṇa consciousness. One should act according to the order of Kṛṣṇa. This is a very important point. That order of Kṛṣṇa comes through disciplic succession from the bona fide spiritual master. Therefore the spiritual master's order should be taken as the prime duty of life. If one gets a bona fide spiritual master and acts according to his direction, then one's perfection of life in Kṛṣṇa consciousness is guaranteed.

Śrīla Viśvanātha Cakravartī Ṭhākura describes Kṛṣṇa's instruction to Arjuna: " 'Offering all your activities, your *varṇāśrama* duties and your ordinary work to Me, you should be dedicated to Me. I should be your only goal and the whole purpose of Your life. In this way you should be renounced and without desires....Always fix your mind on Me, both while executing your duties and at other times as well. Always remember Me.' "

Śrīla Baladeva Vidyābhūṣaṇa adds: " 'Having Me as the only goal of your life, you should renounce, and offer all your prescribed work to Me, your master. Taking shelter of Me in *buddhi-yoga,* you should always think of Me while executing your duties.' "

What will be the result of following Kṛṣṇa's instructions? And of not following?

58 If you become conscious of Me, you will pass over all the obstacles of conditioned life by My grace. If, however, you do not work in such consciousness but act through false ego, not hearing Me, you will be lost.

What does Kṛṣṇa mean when He states that one acting through false ego, not hearing Him, will be lost?

59 If you do not act according to My direction and do not fight, then you will be falsely directed. By your nature, you will have to be engaged in warfare.

Śrīla Viśvanātha Cakravartī Ṭhākura adds more of Arjuna's and Kṛṣṇa's thoughts:

> "Well, it's true. For a *kṣatriya* like me, fighting is the supreme duty. But in this particular circumstance, I don't want to become involved because I fear the sinful reactions for killing family members."

In response, Kṛṣṇa, in a chastising mood, speaks this verse beginning *yad ahaṅkāram*. "Now you are not honoring My words, but later, because you are a great hero, your natural eagerness to fight will unavoidably manifest itself. Then, when you set out to kill Bhīṣma and the others on your own accord, I will laugh at you."

We should note Kṛṣṇa's words: Whether or not Arjuna surrenders to Kṛṣṇa, he will fight. Why, then, chapter after chapter, has Kṛṣṇa pushed Arjuna to fight? What was the necessity of Kṛṣṇa's offering numerous instructions?

Kṛṣṇa wanted Arjuna to fight in the proper consciousness – in Kṛṣṇa consciousness. Therefore He told Arjuna to surrender to Him and fight on His order with devotion. "Do it," Kṛṣṇa explained, "because I have already killed Bhīṣma, Karṇa, Droṇa – all these warriors." The armies have already been defeated, and the battle has already been won. Kṛṣṇa doesn't require Arjuna's martial skill for victory, but He wants Arjuna to act with devotion as His instrument. Arjuna's devotion will be expressed by fighting on the battlefield.

Śrīla Prabhupāda once explained during a 1974 morning walk in Los Angeles: "Somebody protested that 'Your Kṛṣṇa consciousness movement makes people dull,' but they have not seen the Vaiṣṇava. There were two fights in Indian history. One was between Rāma and Rāvaṇa and one was at Kurukṣetra. And the hero in both was a Vaiṣṇava. We are going to produce such Vaiṣṇavas, not these dull rascals, sitting down. We don't want these Vaiṣṇavas – sitting-down rascals. We want Arjuna or we want no one. That is a Vaiṣṇava."

Kṛṣṇa explains the point further in the next text.

60 Under illusion you are now declining to act according to My direction. But, compelled by the work born of your own nature, you will act all the same, O son of Kuntī.

Kṛṣṇa herein continues instructing all conditioned souls to surrender to Him because it is in their own interest. If we choose not to surrender to Kṛṣṇa, however, it does not mean that we will be able to remain independent. All – those who surrender and those who do not – are controlled. The difference is that the surrendered souls are controlled and protected by Kṛṣṇa, and the unsurrendered are forced to dance like marionettes, their strings pulled by illusion.

Ultimately, who is controlling illusion and rotating everyone through births and deaths on the wheel of *saṁsāra*?

61 The Supreme Lord is situated in everyone's heart, O Arjuna, and is directing the wanderings of all living entities, who are seated as on a machine, made of the material energy.

62 O scion of Bharata, surrender unto Him utterly. By His grace you will attain transcendental peace and the supreme and eternal abode.

The Lord has previously explained confidential knowledge about Brahman. Now He is explaining (as He will say in text 63) the "still more confidential" knowledge that we should surrender to the Supersoul situated in everyone's heart. Śrīla Prabhupāda points out in his purport to text 63: "The Lord has already explained to Arjuna the knowledge of *brahma-bhūta*. One who is in the *brahma-bhūta* condition is joyful; he never laments, nor does he desire anything. That is due to confidential knowledge. Kṛṣṇa also discloses knowledge of the Supersoul. This is also Brahman knowledge, knowledge of Brahman, but it is superior."

Śrīla Viśvanātha Cakravartī Ṭhākura writes: "Some say that taking shelter of the Supersoul as described here is meant only for worshipers of the Supersoul, whereas taking shelter of the Personality of Godhead is later going to be mentioned as appropriate for the worshipers of Godhead. Someone else, however, may say, 'The same Śrī Kṛṣṇa who is my worshipable Deity is also my spiritual master. He is teaching me *bhakti-yoga* and giving me helpful instructions that lead to the development of *bhakti-yoga*. I take shelter of Him. That same Kṛṣṇa is indeed the Supersoul within me. May He kindly impel me in all activities. I take shelter of Him.' Such a devotee constantly thinks in this fashion."

Śrīla Baladeva Vidyābhūṣaṇa explains Kṛṣṇa's words thus: "'You should in all ways take shelter of that Supreme Lord, the Supersoul, with the activities of your body and so on. You will achieve the supreme peace, characterized as release from all kinds of distress, and also the eternal abode, the personal residence of the Lord, glorified in such *śruti* statements as *tad viṣṇoḥ paramaṁ padam*. That Supreme Lord is none other than Me, your friend. This is proven by My previous statements, such as: "I am situated in everyone's heart." It is also proven by your agreement to this in your own statements made in accordance with the authority of Devarṣi Nārada and others, such as: "You are the Supreme Absolute Truth, the supreme abode," and by the empiric evidence of your vision of the universal form. Therefore you should follow My instructions.' "

Kṛṣṇa will now introduce the most confidential knowledge.

63 Thus I have explained to you knowledge still more confidential. Deliberate on this fully, and then do what you wish to do.

64 Because you are My very dear friend, I am speaking to you My supreme instruction, the most confidential knowledge of all. Hear this from Me, for it is for your benefit.

In text 64, the Lord has used the word *bhūyaḥ*, "again," to indicate He has already spoken this knowledge. Śrīla Prabhupāda explains where, why, and what Kṛṣṇa spoke previously: "The Lord has given Arjuna knowledge that is confidential (knowledge of Brahman) and still more confidential (knowledge of the Supersoul within everyone's heart), and now He is giving the most confidential part of knowledge: just surrender unto the Supreme Personality of Godhead. At the end of the ninth chapter He has said, *man-manāḥ:* 'Just always think of Me.' The same instruction is repeated here to stress the essence of the teachings of *Bhagavad-gītā*." Therefore chapter nine, which contains the verse beginning *man-manā bhava mad-bhakto,* is entitled "The Most Confidential Knowledge."

Śrīla Viśvanātha Cakravartī Ṭhākura has mentioned the following in his commentary on texts 63–64:

> Thus the six chapters teaching *jñāna* have reached their completion. These six chapters of the *śāstra, Śrī Gītā,* are jewels of spiritual education. They form part of a treasure chest containing the rarest secret of *bhakti*. The first six chapters dealing with *karma* form the golden, lower part of the chest, and the third six chapters dealing with *jñāna* form its gem-studded cover. The *bhakti* found within is the most precious treasure in the three worlds. It has the power to bring Śrī Kṛṣṇa under control. It

> shines brilliantly as the most excellent of precious jewels. The key to obtaining this jewel is the pair of verses on the cover of the treasure chest, the sacred sixty-four syllables beginning *man-manā bhava* [texts 65–66].

Seeing His dear friend Arjuna silently deliberating on the *Gītā-śāstra,* with its deep meanings, the Lord felt His heart melt like butter out of compassion and said, "My dear friend Arjuna, I will now speak the essence of this entire *śāstra.* You don't have to exert yourself any more with this troublesome deliberating."

65 Always think of Me, become My devotee, worship Me, and offer your homage unto Me. Thus you will come to Me without fail. I promise you this because you are My very dear friend.

As the most confidential knowledge, Kṛṣṇa reveals that Arjuna (and all others) should do four things. First, they should always think of Kṛṣṇa. Then they all should become devotees of Kṛṣṇa. Third, they should worship Kṛṣṇa, and fourth, they should offer Kṛṣṇa their obeisances and all their homage. In the second part of the verse, Kṛṣṇa reveals the result of practicing these four elements of devotional service.

Śrīla Prabhupāda's purport speaks for itself:

> The most confidential part of knowledge is that one should become a pure devotee of Kṛṣṇa and always think of Him and act for Him. One should not become an official meditator. Life should be so molded that one will always have the chance to think of Kṛṣṇa. One should always act in such a way that all his daily activities are in connection with Kṛṣṇa. He should arrange his life in such a way that throughout the twenty-four hours he cannot but think of Kṛṣṇa. And the Lord's promise is that anyone who is in such pure Kṛṣṇa consciousness will certainly return to the abode of Kṛṣṇa, where he will be engaged in the association of Kṛṣṇa face to face. This most confidential part of knowledge is spoken to Arjuna because he is the dear friend of Kṛṣṇa. Everyone who follows the path of Arjuna can become a dear friend to Kṛṣṇa and obtain the same perfection as Arjuna.

These words stress that one should concentrate his mind upon Kṛṣṇa – the very form with two hands carrying a flute, the bluish boy with a beautiful face and peacock feathers in His hair. There are descriptions of Kṛṣṇa found in the *Brahma-saṁhitā* and other literatures. One should fix his mind on this original form of Godhead, Kṛṣṇa. One should not even divert his attention to other forms of the Lord. The Lord has multi-forms as Viṣṇu, Nārāyaṇa, Rāma, Varāha, etc., but a devotee should concentrate his mind on the form that was present before Arjuna. Concentration of the mind on the form of Kṛṣṇa constitutes the most confidential part of knowledge, and this is disclosed to Arjuna because Arjuna is the most dear friend of Kṛṣṇa's.

Śrīla Viśvanātha Cakravartī Ṭhākura and Śrīla Baladeva Vidyābhūṣaṇa offer similar comments. Śrīla Viśvanātha Cakravartī Ṭhākura states:

"You will come to Me, achieve Me, so therefore offer your mind to Me. Or else offer your ears and other senses. Or else offer incense, flowers, and so on. I tell you truly that I will give you even My own self in exchange. You have no reason to doubt this."

The *Amara-koṣa* defines *satyam* as meaning "a vow" and "the true facts of a case." Yet Arjuna may reply, "But people born in Mathurā district always make vows. In every sentence they utter they use the word *satyam*."

Kṛṣṇa replies, "Then I say this. I make a solemn vow: 'You are dear to me!' And no one cheats someone who is dear to him."

Śrīla Baladeva Vidyābhūṣaṇa states:

"As explained before, if you develop the qualities of always thinking of Me and so on, you will certainly come to Me, who am your beloved friend Kṛṣṇa, the son of Devakī. I have qualities such as being dark blue like a blue lotus flower, and I appear in a human form. You will not go to some other form of Mine like the thousand-headed Puruṣa, the thumb-sized Supersoul, Lord Nṛsiṁha, or Lord Varāha. This is my vow, that in truth I will give you possession even of Myself, Your friend."

The *Nānārtha-varga* defines the word *satyam* as "a vow" and "the true facts of a case." Yet Arjuna replies, "But because You are from Mathurā, even Your having made a vow does not destroy my doubt."

To this the Lord responds, "Then I say this: You are very dear to Me, and the affectionate people of Mathurā do not deceive those who are dear to them, what to speak of deceiving one who is most dear. He to whom I am very dear is also very dear to Me. I cannot tolerate the absence of such a person, as I have already said in the words beginning *priyo hi* and so on. Therefore you should trust My words: 'You will indeed achieve Me.' "

One may doubt that he is able to take advantage of Kṛṣṇa's words and render the quality of pure devotional service that Kṛṣṇa has requested. Should he first undergo renunciation, austerities and vows to purify his heart so he will enhance his ability to surrender? Here is Kṛṣṇa's answer.

66 Abandon all varieties of religion and just surrender unto Me. I shall deliver you from all sinful reactions. Do not fear.

In his purport, Śrīla Prabhupāda glorifies full and immediate surrender to Kṛṣṇa's service as the process that will qualify us for that service: "[O]ne may think that unless he is free from all sinful reactions he cannot take to the surrendering process. To such doubts it is here said that even if one is not free from all sinful reactions, simply by the process of surrendering to Śrī Kṛṣṇa he is automatically freed. There is no need of strenuous effort to free oneself from sinful reactions. One should unhesitatingly accept Kṛṣṇa as the supreme savior of all living entities. With faith and love, one should surrender unto Him."

Later in his purport Śrīla Prabhupāda explains the uselessness of worry and hesitation: "The particular words used here, *mā śucaḥ,* 'Don't fear, don't hesitate, don't worry,' are very significant. One may be perplexed as to how one can give up all kinds of religious forms and simply surrender unto Kṛṣṇa, but such worry is useless."

Śrīla Viśvanātha Cakravartī Ṭhākura's commentary adds further drops of sweetness: "Kṛṣṇa says, 'Previously I told you that you did not have the qualification for the most excellent, unalloyed devotion to Me. At that time I said, "Whatever you do, whatever you eat..." and told you that your qualification was for *karma-miśra-bhakti*. Now, however, by My special mercy I have given you the qualification for unalloyed *bhakti*. I have violated My own rule that unalloyed devotion may be obtained only when, somehow or other, one receives the mercy of My pure devotee, just as I will violate My own promise while fighting with Bhīṣma.'"

Kṛṣṇa has just completed speaking the *Bhagavad-gītā*. What now should be done with the jewels of transcendental knowledge just spoken by Kṛṣṇa? Should they be kept secretly or distributed widely? If they should be distributed, who is qualified to receive them? What result comes to one who hears, studies, or preaches Kṛṣṇa's message?

67 This confidential knowledge may never be explained to those who are not austere, or devoted, or engaged in devotional service, nor to one who is envious of Me.

68 For one who explains this supreme secret to the devotees, pure devotional service is guaranteed, and at the end he will come back to Me.

69 There is no servant in this world more dear to Me than he, nor will there ever be one more dear.

70 And I declare that he who studies this sacred conversation of ours worships Me by his intelligence.

71 And one who listens with faith and without envy becomes free from sinful reactions and attains to the auspicious planets where the pious dwell.

Here are two excerpts from Śrīla Prabhupāda's purports:

> Generally it is advised that *Bhagavad-gītā* be discussed amongst the devotees only, for those who are not devotees will understand neither Kṛṣṇa nor *Bhagavad-gītā*....Anyone, however,

> who tries sincerely to present *Bhagavad-gītā* as it is will advance in devotional activities and reach the pure devotional state of life. As a result of such pure devotion, he is sure to go back home, back to Godhead. (Bg. 18.68)
>
> In the sixty-seventh verse of this chapter, the Lord explicitly forbade the *Gītā's* being spoken to those who are envious of the Lord. In other words, *Bhagavad-gītā* is for the devotees only. But it so happens that sometimes a devotee of the Lord will hold open class, and in that class not all the students are expected to be devotees. Why do such persons hold open class? It is explained here that although not everyone is a devotee, still there are many men who are not envious of Kṛṣṇa. They have faith in Him as the Supreme Personality of Godhead. If such persons hear from a bona fide devotee about the Lord, the result is that they become at once free from all sinful reactions and after that attain to the planetary system where all righteous persons are situated. Therefore simply by hearing *Bhagavad-gītā,* even a person who does not try to be a pure devotee attains the result of righteous activities. Thus a pure devotee of the Lord gives everyone a chance to become free from all sinful reactions and to become a devotee of the Lord. (Bg. 18.71)

Not only one who studies but one who even hears *Bhagavad-gītā,* as long as he hears without envy, is greatly benefited. Kṛṣṇa gives such preferential treatment to one who preaches *Bhagavad-gītā,* especially to those who preach to the devotees – or to anyone who will listen in proper consciousness. Therefore we should all hear, study, explain, and preach *Bhagavad-gītā* and become dear to Kṛṣṇa. Although we are most unqualified, Kṛṣṇa reserves special mercy for those who preach *Bhagavad-gītā:* "For one who explains this supreme secret to the devotees, pure devotional service is guaranteed. And at the end he will come back to Me. There is no servant in this world more dear to Me than he, nor will there ever be one more dear."

72 O son of Pṛthā, O conqueror of wealth, have you heard this with an attentive mind? And are your ignorance and illusions now dispelled?

Kṛṣṇa, the teacher, asks Arjuna, the student, "Have you understood? Have you heard properly?" Kṛṣṇa asks this because, out of affection for his surrendered student, He is prepared to explain the entire *Bhagavad-gītā* again.

73 Arjuna said: My dear Kṛṣṇa, O infallible one, my illusion is now gone. I have regained my memory by Your mercy. I am now firm and free from doubt and am prepared to act according to Your instructions.

Śrīla Prabhupāda's purport to *Śrīmad-Bhāgavatam* 2.4.19 explains: "In the beginning Arjuna placed himself as one of those who desire self-satisfaction, for he desired not to fight in the Battle of Kurukṣetra, but to make him desireless the Lord preached the *Bhagavad-gītā,* in which the ways of *karma-yoga, jñāna-yoga, haṭha-yoga,* and also *bhakti-yoga* were explained. Because Arjuna was without any pretension, he changed his decision and satisfied the Lord by agreeing to fight (*kariṣye vacanaṁ tava*), and thus he became desireless."

Śrīla Viśvanātha Cakravartī Ṭhākura adds the following exchange between Arjuna and Kṛṣṇa: "Arjuna replies, 'What more can I ask? Abandoning all *dharmas,* I approach You for shelter. I am now free from anxiety and have full trust in You. Henceforth, having taken full shelter of You, I will accept Your order as my *dharma*. You are the suitable bestower of shelter. I will no longer follow the *dharma* of my *āśrama* or the processes of *jñāna-yoga* and so on. From now on I will have nothing to do with any of those.' Then Kṛṣṇa says, 'My dear friend Arjuna, there remains a little work left in the matter of My relieving the earth of her burden, and I want to do this through you.'"

Thus addressed by the Lord, Arjuna took up his Gāṇḍīva bow and stood to fight.

74 Sañjaya said: Thus have I heard the conversation of two great souls, Kṛṣṇa and Arjuna. And so wonderful is that message that my hair is standing on end.

75 By the mercy of Vyāsa, I have heard these most confidential talks directly from the master of all mysticism, Kṛṣṇa, who was speaking personally to Arjuna.

76 O King, as I repeatedly recall this wondrous and holy dialogue between Kṛṣṇa and Arjuna, I take pleasure, being thrilled at every moment.

77 O King, as I remember the wonderful form of Lord Kṛṣṇa, I am struck with wonder more and more, and I rejoice again and again.

Here are three points from Śrīla Prabhupāda's purports to these verses. In his purport to text 75, Śrīla Prabhupāda explains that Sañjaya was able to hear and understand *Bhagavad-gītā* only by the mercy of his spiritual master, Śrīla Vyāsadeva. In his commentary on text 76, Śrīla Prabhupāda describes the perceivable result of Kṛṣṇa consciousness: "The result of Kṛṣṇa consciousness is that one becomes increasingly enlightened, and he enjoys life with a thrill, not only for some time, but at every moment." In text 77, Śrīla Prabhupāda says that Sañjaya enjoyed remembering "that wonderful [universal] form of Kṛṣṇa exhibited to Arjuna," and that by remembering it again and again, he "enjoyed it repeatedly."

Śrīla Viśvanātha Cakravartī Ṭhākura ends his commentary after text 73. He says: "I made a commentary on the following five verses, in which are found the essential purpose of the entire *Gītā*. But Lord Gaṇeśa sent his mouse-carrier to steal the two pages I had written. Not wanting to interfere, I have not rewritten those pages. Let Lord Gaṇeśa be pleased; obeisances to him. Thus I complete the *Sārārtha-varṣiṇī* commentary on *Śrīmad Bhagavad-gītā*. May it please the saintly devotees. May this sweet *Sārārtha-varṣiṇī*, "the commentary that rains down the essential meaning," give delight to the *cātaka* birds who are the Lord's devotees all over the world. And may its sweetness also shine in my own heart."

78 Wherever there is Kṛṣṇa, the master of all mystics, and wherever there is Arjuna, the supreme archer, there will also certainly be opulence, victory, extraordinary power, and morality. That is my opinion.

At the outset of *Bhagavad-gītā*, the blind King Dhṛtarāṣṭra was eager to hear Sañjaya's prediction of the outcome of the ensuing battle. Here is Sañjaya's answer: "Dhṛtarāṣṭra, give up hope. Victory belongs to the Pāṇḍavas because Kṛṣṇa favors their side."

Śrīla Baladeva Vidyābhūṣaṇa ends his *Gītā-bhūṣaṇa,* "the ornament of the *Bhagavad-gītā,*" with the following words: "Having obtained the boat of the Lord's desire, I have submerged myself in the sea of *Bhagavad-gītā,* where I have collected many very wonderful gems of its purports. Due to my great feelings of joy, I cannot raise myself out of this sea. I only hope that the cunning son of Nanda is pleased with me. I, Baladeva Vidyābhūṣaṇa, have with great effort compiled this commentary named *Śrī-gītā-bhūṣaṇa*. May the saintly devotees correct any faults it contains. They are always eager to taste the sweetness of pure love for Śrī Govinda, and their hearts are always melting with compassion."

Śrīla Prabhupāda sums up the message of the entire *Bhagavad-gītā* in the final paragraph of his Bhaktivedanta purports: "The living entity in his original position is pure spirit. He is just like an atomic particle of the Supreme Spirit. Thus Lord Kṛṣṇa may be compared to the sun, and the living entities to sunshine. Because the living entities are the marginal energy of Kṛṣṇa, they have a tendency to be in contact either with the material energy or with the spiritual energy. In other words, the living entity is situated between the two energies of the Lord, and because he belongs to the superior energy of the Lord, he has a particle of independence. By proper use of that independence he comes under the direct order of Kṛṣṇa. Thus he attains his normal condition in the pleasure-giving potency."

Appendixes

Appendix One

The Yoga Ladder: Ascending Step by Step to Perfection

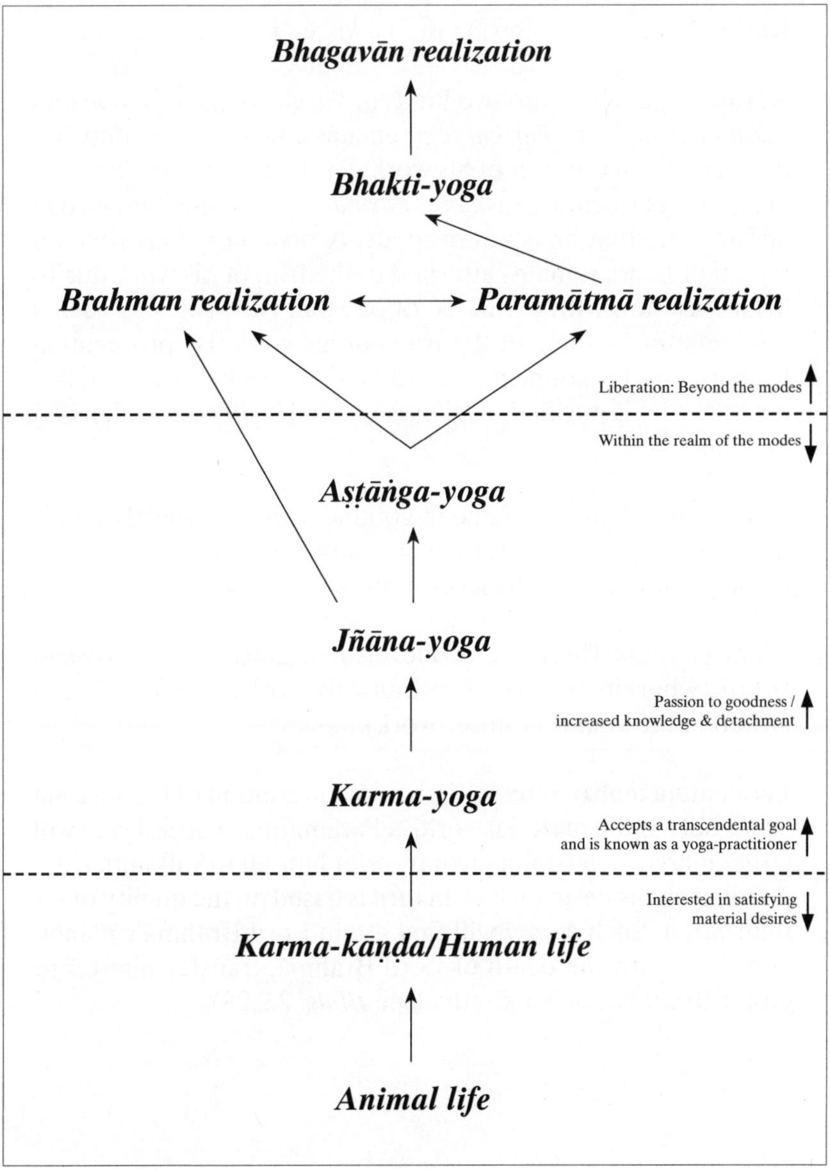

NOTES ON THE YOGA LADDER

Animal life: Those humans who do not follow *śāstra* to fulfill their material desires are considered as acting on the level of animals.

Karma-kāṇḍa: By following the *Vedas,* he may be elevated.

Karma-yoga: There are two kinds of *karma-yogīs: niṣkāma* and *sakāma.* A *niṣkāma karma-yogī* remains attached to his duty but detached from the fruit of his work. By detached work in goodness, one performing *niṣkāma karma-yoga* attains knowledge and realizes that he is not his body. A *sakāma karma-yogī,* on the other hand, remains attached to the fruit of his work due to his association with the mode of passion. Nevertheless, such a *yogī* renounces some of the fruits of his work. By prosecuting his duties and renouncing the fruits of his work, his knowledge increases, he is purified from passion, and he becomes elevated in goodness.

Jñāna-yoga: A *jñānī* is fixed in goodness and realizes that he is not his body but an eternal soul. Because he is fixed in goodness, he may renounce his prescribed duties.

Aṣṭāṅga-yoga: There are two levels in *aṣṭāṅga-yoga – yogaru-rukṣu* (wherein the *yogī* continues to work) and *yogārūḍha* (wherein the *yogī* renounces work).

Paramātmā realization: As Kṛṣṇa's manifestation of Paramātmā exists only in the material world, a Paramātmā-realized *yogī* will either merge with Brahman or transfer himself to Vaikuṇṭha, depending on his desire, which in turn is based on the quality of his realization. Such a *yogī* will first attain Lord Brahmā's planet, and then, with the death of Lord Brahmā, transfer himself to either Brahman or Vaikuṇṭha (see *Bhāg.* 2.2.28).

FURTHER NOTES

1) To achieve any realization, one needs at least some *bhakti.*

2) At any stage, if the practitioner gets the association of devotees, he can engage directly on the path of *bhakti.*

3) As one on the path of *bhakti* performs devotional service, he naturally goes through similar steps of purification as one on the step-by-step yoga ladder: his passion decreases and his goodness and transcendental knowledge increase. He becomes less attached to the fruits of his work and more attached to Kṛṣṇa's service. Thus a devotee may also be considered as practicing *sakāma* or *niṣkāma karma-yoga.*

4) In the *Bhagavad-gītā,* Kṛṣṇa many times recommends *bhakti-yoga* practiced on the *niṣkāma* level.

5) Kṛṣṇa's ultimate instructions are given at the end of the *Gītā* (18.65 and 18.66): pure *bhakti* begins when one surrenders and agrees to serve Kṛṣṇa with no desire other than to please the Lord.

6) One at any stage may transcend the modes through full surrender.

Appendix Two

The Yoga Ladder's Gradual Progression

The *Bhagavad-gītā's* first six chapters describe the *yoga* ladder, a progression by which a soul practicing spiritual life advances toward Kṛṣṇa. At the lowest rung of this ladder stands the person attached to worldly pleasures but following prescribed Vedic duties. This stage is described in chapter three, texts 10–16. By following duties prescribed by the *Vedas,* the beginner gradually gains knowledge of his eternal nature (described in chapter four), loses taste for the temporary, and continues to perform duties and sacrifices but with detachment. This mixing of work (*karma*) with knowledge (*jñāna*), or prescribed duties with detachment, is called *niṣkāma karma-yoga* (described in chapter five). The practice of *niṣkāma karma-yoga* leads to liberation from the bondage of the modes of nature, which causes the aspirant to realize the oneness of everything in existence. This is, of course, Kṛṣṇa's impersonal feature. At this point, the aspirant may legitimately renounce his prescribed duties for the full-time practice of *aṣṭāṅga-yoga* and realize the Paramātmā, the Supersoul, in everyone's heart (described in chapter six). The perfection of yoga practice is to be granted entrance into the kingdom of God through realization and worship of the Supreme Lord's personal feature, Bhagavān (stated in 6.47).

Further Considerations Regarding the Yoga Ladder

In general, as the *Bhagavad-gītā* describes, practices on the *yoga* ladder may be described as a progression from following *karma-kāṇḍa* to practicing *niṣkāma karma-yoga, aṣṭāṅga-yoga,* and finally *bhakti-yoga.* However, a person climbing these steps gradually may at any time step off his current rung on the ladder and maintain the realization he attained during his practice, forever remaining a *karmī, jñānī,* or *yogī*.

Additionally, the association of powerful devotees may radically alter the rung-by-rung progression to *bhakti*. Both *Śrīmad-Bhāgavatam* 11.20.11 and Śrīla Viśvanātha Cakravartī Ṭhākura's comment on it speak to this point:

> One who is situated in his prescribed duty, free from sinful activities and cleansed of material contamination, in this very life obtains transcendental knowledge or, by fortune, devotional service to Me.

Viśvanātha Cakravartī Ṭhākura writes: "What does this performer of *karma* attain? Situated on this planet, performing his duties, sinless because of performing *niṣkāma karma-yoga,* free from sin, pure in heart, he attains *jñāna* and liberation. If he unexpectedly attains association with persons practicing pure *bhakti* he attains pure *bhakti* to Me. Then he attains *prema*."

Śrīla Prabhupāda's *Bhagavad-gītā As It Is* serves as association with a great devotee, and throughout his translation and commentary Śrīla Prabhupāda directs the reader to bypass the circuitous, many-runged *yoga* ladder in favor of *bhakti,* or direct Kṛṣṇa consciousness. Although Śrīla Prabhupāda acknowledges the validity of the gradual path that leads to *bhakti,* he nevertheless points his readers directly to Kṛṣṇa and Kṛṣṇa's service in every one of his purports.[1]

I could present innumerable examples of this, but I have chosen just three – one each from chapters three, five, and six.

Bhagavad-gītā 3.11 essentially describes the "*karma-kāṇḍa*" rung of the *yoga* ladder, where one worships the demigods through Vedic sacrifices in order to attain worldly delights. Śrīla Prabhupāda comments: "Some of the *yajñas* are meant to satisfy particular demigods; but even in so doing, Lord Viṣṇu is worshiped in all *yajñas* as the chief beneficiary. It is stated

[1] Practitioners on the path of *bhakti* go through purifying stages of detachment similar to practitioners of the gradual path. But those on the path of *bhakti* are assisted and drawn upward by Kṛṣṇa's kind disposition and mercy.

also in the *Bhagavad-gītā* that Kṛṣṇa Himself is the beneficiary of all kinds of *yajñas: bhoktāraṁ yajña-tapasām.* Therefore, ultimate satisfaction of the *yajña-pati* is the chief purpose of all *yajñas.*"

Chapter five, text 3 stresses the performance of duties with detachment by one who has understood that the soul is different from the body: "One who neither hates nor desires the fruits of his activities is known to be always renounced. Such a person, free from all dualities, easily overcomes material bondage and is completely liberated, O mighty-armed Arjuna."

In his purport, Śrīla Prabhupāda points beyond dutiful, detached action to detached, Kṛṣṇa conscious action: "One who is fully in Kṛṣṇa consciousness is always a renouncer because he feels neither hatred nor desire for the results of his actions. Such a renouncer, dedicated to the transcendental loving service of the Lord, is fully qualified in knowledge because he knows his constitutional position in his relationship with Kṛṣṇa."

Indeed, Śrīla Prabhupāda's mode of presentation, which ignores *karma* and *jñāna* devoid of the fragrance of Kṛṣṇa's service, follows Kṛṣṇa's true desire (stated in 18.66), as it is described by Śrī Nārada Muni in *Śrīmad-Bhāgavatam* 1.5.12: "Knowledge of self-realization, even though free from all material affinity, does not look well if devoid of a conception of the Infallible [God]. What, then, is the use of fruitive activities, which are naturally painful from the very beginning and transient by nature, if they are not utilized for the devotional service of the Lord?"

Similarly, knowing that the goal of *yoga* is *bhakti* (6.47), in his purport to *Bhagavad-gītā* 6.31 Śrīla Prabhupāda points always and only to Kṛṣṇa's service when describing *yoga* and its purpose:

> A *yogī* who is practicing meditation on the Supersoul sees within himself the plenary portion of Kṛṣṇa as Viṣṇu – with four hands, holding conchshell, wheel, club, and lotus flower. The *yogī* should know that Viṣṇu is not different from Kṛṣṇa. Kṛṣṇa in this form of Supersoul is situated in everyone's heart....Nor is there a difference between a Kṛṣṇa conscious person always engaged in the transcendental loving service of Kṛṣṇa and a perfect *yogī* engaged in meditation on the Supersoul.

TWO BHAGAVAD-GĪTĀ CHAPTER TITLES

As stated earlier, the third chapter of the *Bhagavad-gītā,* "*Karma-yoga,*" describes the attainment of knowledge and detachment through working according to Vedic prescriptions. Chapter five, "*Karma-yoga,* Action in Kṛṣṇa Consciousness," describes the detached actions of one who has achieved transcendental knowledge. But because Śrīla Prabhupāda, knowing Kṛṣṇa's conclusive desire, directly points to *bhakti,* in the *Bhagavad-gītā* he often uses the term *karma-yoga* as a synonym for *bhakti-yoga.* An example from his purport to *Bhagavad-gītā* 2.51: "Service for the cause of the Lord is called *karma-yoga* or *buddhi-yoga,* or in plain words, devotional service to the Lord."

But knowing well the technical differences between the two in the frame of reference of the gradual path to *bhakti* via the *yoga* ladder, at other times Śrīla Prabhupāda classifies *karma-yoga* and *bhakti-yoga* as separate and on different levels – as he did in 1974 on a morning walk in Bombay:

Devotee 1: Pure *bhakti* and *karma-yoga* are considered to be exactly the same?
Prabhupāda: Pure *bhakti* is above *karma-yoga.*...Yes. Pure – pure devotion means *śravaṇaṁ kīrtanam … Śravaṇaṁ kīrtanaṁ viṣṇu-smaraṇaṁ pāda-sevanam* – that is pure *bhakti.*
Devotee 2: Does *karma-yoga* mean to exactly follow the *śāstras*?
Prabhupāda: *Karma-yoga* means *yat karoṣi yaj juhoṣi kuruṣva tat mad-arpaṇam.*
Devotee 3: Doing only for Kṛṣṇa.
Prabhupāda: Yes. That is *karma-yoga.*
Devotee 3: Which means?
Prabhupāda: "Whatever you do, the result give Me."
Devotee 1: To Kṛṣṇa.
Prabhupāda: Yes.
Devotee 2: So when one follows the nine activities of devotion purely, that is pure *bhakti.*
Prabhupāda: Yes.
Devotee 2: Then when he's following those nine activities, that's superior to *karma-yoga* – to follow those nine principles purely.
Prabhupāda: Yes.

CLARIFYING THE OVERLAPPING USE OF TERMS

These differing, contextualized, and overlapping definitions of the *yoga* ladder – of *karma-yoga* and *bhakti-yoga* – may confuse those seeking to understand the step-by-step progression of philosophical points in the *Bhagavad-gītā As It Is.* In *Surrender Unto Me,* therefore, to describe the *yoga* ladder, which emphasizes the direct practice of *bhakti-yoga* Śrīla Prabhupāda stressed, I have defined the ladder's rungs in specific, almost technical ways to highlight the distinctions between each step. In doing so, I hope to clarify the progression of stages of advancement toward pure devotional service.

DEFINING TERMS AS THEY ARE USED IN SURRENDER UNTO ME

Defining "karma-kāṇḍī" and "karmī"

A *karma-kāṇḍī* is a follower of the *karma-kāṇḍa* section of the Vedic literature. Such persons desire only attainments in the realm of matter and have no transcendental objective. In *Bhagavad-gītā* 9.21 Śrī Kṛṣṇa Himself minimizes the achievements of those who practice Vedic rituals for temporary enjoyment:

"When they have thus enjoyed vast heavenly sense pleasure and the results of their pious activities are exhausted, they return to this mortal planet again. Thus those who seek sense enjoyment by adhering to the principles of the three *Vedas* achieve only repeated birth and death."

He further criticizes them in *Bhagavad-gītā* 2.42, calling such Vedic followers *veda-vāda-ratāḥ,* "supposed followers of the *Vedas*": "Men of small knowledge are very much attached to the flowery words of the *Vedas,* which recommend various fruitive activities for elevation to heavenly planets, resultant good birth, power, and so forth. Being desirous of sense gratification and opulent life, they say that there is nothing more than this."

Śrīla Prabhupāda expands on Kṛṣṇa's words in his purport: "People in general are not very intelligent, and due to their ignorance they are most attached to the fruitive activities recommended in the *karma-kāṇḍa* portions of the *Vedas.* They do not want anything more than sense gratificatory proposals for enjoying life in heaven, where wine and women are available and material opulence is very common."

Following both Śrī Kṛṣṇa's and Śrīla Prabhupāda's mood, we have generalized this category of workers to include all workers (*karmīs*) whose endeavor is simply to enjoy the fruits of their labor, regardless of whether or not they are followers of the Vedic scriptures. As Śrīla Prabhupāda said to an interviewer: "The fruitive worker is like that. He is very busy in the office, and if you want to see him he will say, 'I am very busy.' So what is the result of your being so busy? He takes two pieces of toast and one cup of tea. And for this purpose you are so busy? He does not know why he is busy. In the account books he will find that the balance was one million dollars and now it has become two million. He is satisfied with that, but he will take only two pieces of toast and one cup of tea, and still he will work very hard. That is what is meant by *karmī.*"

Differentiating between a "karma-kāṇḍī" and a "karma-yogī"

Because *karmī* in the *Bhagavad-gītā* specifically refers to a follower of the fruitive, *karma-kāṇḍa* section of Vedic practices, strictly speaking, one can refer to any follower of Vedic *karma-kāṇḍa* sacrifices as a *karma-yogī*. Such a soul, regardless of his motives, will be elevated toward serving the Supreme because a follower of the *Vedas* receives the purifying effect of following Kṛṣṇa's words. But every "*karmī*" in the modern world gets this result. Still, even for a modern man, work detached from its fruit will purify him because of the power of detachment, which decreases passion and increases the influence of goodness:

> O chief of the Bhāratas, when there is an increase in the mode of passion the symptoms of great attachment, fruitive activity, intense endeavor, and uncontrollable desire and hankering develop. (14.12)

> The manifestation of the mode of goodness can be experienced when all the gates of the body are illuminated by knowledge. (14.11)

> From the mode of goodness, real knowledge develops; from the mode of passion, greed develops; and from the mode of ignorance develop foolishness, madness, and illusion. (14.17)

> When the living entity becomes strongly situated in the mode of goodness, then religious principles, characterized by devotional service to Me, become prominent. (*Bhāg.* 11.13.2)[2]

Vedic or non-Vedic, in *Bhāg.* 11.2.36, Kṛṣṇa Himself validates the efficacy of making offerings to Him in accordance with the particular nature one has acquired in conditioned life, whatever one does with body, words, mind, senses, intelligence, or purified consciousness one should offer to the Supreme, thinking, "This is for the pleasure of Lord Nārāyaṇa."

The BBT purport to that text quotes Śrīla Bhaktisiddhānta Sarasvatī Ṭhākura to indicate that those who make offerings to Kṛṣṇa are very different from ordinary *karmīs:* "Śrīla Bhaktisiddhānta Sarasvatī Ṭhākura has commented in this regard that a person who engages all the sensory activities of his body, mind, words, intelligence, ego, and consciousness in the service of the Supreme Lord cannot be considered to be on the same level as a *karmī* working for his personal sense gratification."

Śrīla Prabhupāda speaks in a similar way in his purport to *Bhagavad-gītā* 12.11: "It is also found that when one who is not even interested in the activities of Kṛṣṇa consciousness gives charity to some hospital or some other social institution, he gives up the hard-earned results of his activities. That is also recommended here because by the practice of giving up the fruits of one's activities one is sure to purify his mind gradually, and in that purified stage of mind one becomes able to understand Kṛṣṇa consciousness."

To differentiate "materialistic" *karma-kāṇḍīs* and other fruitive workers (*karmīs*) from those performing their prescribed

[2] Kṛṣṇa expands on this point in *Bhāg.* 11.13.1–7.

duties with a transcendental objective, including those spiritual aspirants who are not strictly following the Vedic formulas, we have used particular terms in *Surrender Unto Me*.

We have termed those with only material aspiration *karma-kāṇḍīs* or *karmīs*. To differentiate them from spiritual aspirants, we have termed the aspiring transcendentalist workers as *karma-yogīs,* or those attempting to transcend through work.

Śrīla Prabhupāda also defines *karma-yoga* like this when he distinguishes it from other *yoga* paths in his purport to *Bhagavad-gītā* 6.46: "When we speak of *yoga* we refer to linking our consciousness with the Supreme Absolute Truth. Such a process is named differently by various practitioners in terms of the particular method adopted. When the linking process is predominantly in fruitive activities it is called *karma-yoga,* when it is predominantly empirical it is called *jñāna-yoga,* and when it is predominantly in a devotional relationship with the Supreme Lord it is called *bhakti-yoga.*"

FURTHER DIVISIONS OF THE KARMA-YOGĪ

Karma-yoga can be divided into two categories based on the transcendental objective its practitioners aspire to achieve. Nondevotee *karma-yogīs* seek knowledge and impersonal liberation, and devotee *karma-yogīs* seek eternal service to the Supreme Lord. Both groups can be further divided:

a) Those whose work is motivated by the desire to attain at least some material results from their endeavors (*sakāma karma-yogīs*).

b) Those who are fully detached from the results of their work but remain attached to dutifully performing their work (*niṣkāma karma-yogīs*). Let's first describe *niṣkāma karma-yogīs.*

The nondevotee niṣkāma karma-yogī

The nondevotee *niṣkāma karma-yogīs* work only to fulfill the duties prescribed to them. They have no selfish, or fruitive, motives. Such detached workers accrue no good or bad reactions from their work.

One acting dutifully but with no desire to please Kṛṣṇa acts in the mode of goodness. The result of such detached action? Knowledge and, ultimately, liberation. As previously described in *Śrīmad-Bhāgavatam* 11.20.10–11, the nondevotee *niṣkāma karma-yogīs* can be transformed into devotee *niṣkāma karma-yogīs* through Vaiṣṇava association.

A nondevotee's practice of *niṣkāma karma-yoga* can therefore be understood as a step up the *yoga* ladder – a step toward further advancement in Kṛṣṇa consciousness.

The devotee niṣkāma karma-yogī

In *Bhagavad-gītā* 9.27 Kṛṣṇa prescribes a practical level at which Arjuna can perform devotional service: "Whatever you do, whatever you eat, whatever you offer or give away, and whatever austerities you perform – do that, O son of Kuntī, as an offering to Me."

In other words, perform your prescribed duty and, rather than being attached to the result of your work, offer it to Kṛṣṇa.

Differentiating between the devotee niṣkāma karma-yogī and a pure bhakti-yogī

In his comment on the above text, Śrīla Viśvanātha Cakravartī Ṭhākura defines the distinction between *niṣkāma karma-yoga* and pure devotional service (*ananya* or *kevala bhakti*): "*Ananya bhakti* doesn't mean that you perform an action and offer the results to the Lord. Rather, the action itself is offered to the Lord in surrender, simultaneous with its performance. This is mentioned by Prahlāda Mahārāja (*Bhāg*. 7.5.24): *iti puṁsārpitā viṣṇau bhaktiś cen nava-lakṣaṇā kriyeta bhagavaty addhā,* 'This *bhakti* of nine types offered to the Lord should be performed for the Lord.' Śrī Śrīdhara Svāmī has explained this *Śrīmad-Bhāgavatam* text as follows: 'In *ananya bhakti,* acts first offered to the Lord should be performed, rather than performing them first and offering them later.' Thus the present text is not included in *kevala* (pure) *bhakti,* since the acts are performed and then offered."

Śrīla Viśvanātha Cakravartī Ṭhākura later confirms this point in his comment on Bg. 18.66 when he speaks on behalf of Kṛṣṇa to explain Kṛṣṇa's point: "Previously I said that you were not qualified for *ananya bhakti,* the highest type of *bhakti,* but for *karma-miśra-bhakti* – 'Whatever you do, whatever you eat, whatever you offer or give away, and whatever austerities you perform – do that, O son of Kuntī, as an offering to Me.' "

Although Śrīla Baladeva Vidyābhūṣaṇa's explanation of *Bhagavad-gītā* 9.27 categorizes it as a householder's performance of pure devotional service – which differs from the category Śrīla Viśvanātha Cakravartī Ṭhākura gives the text – both *ācāryas* agree that the actual performance of one's duties and not only the offering of the results of one's work must be done for Kṛṣṇa's pleasure in order for those activities to be considered pure *bhakti.*

Śrīla Viśvanātha Cakravartī Ṭhākura uses the technical term *karma-jñāna-miśra-pradhani-bhūta-bhakti* for the type of *bhakti* Kṛṣṇa mentions in *Bhagavad-gītā* 9.27, in which (according to Śrīla Viśvanātha Cakravartī Ṭhākura) *bhakti* is the primary motivation but the offering not quite pure. As he further states in his commentary on text 9.27: "O Arjuna, because you cannot reject *karma, jñāna,* and other processes in your present state, and are not qualified for the supreme *bhakti,* and because you should not degrade yourself to perform the inferior *sakāma-bhakti,* you should perform *bhakti* with a slight mixture of *karma* and *jñāna,* but which is *niṣkāma.*"

This gradation of *bhakti* can also be termed *niṣkāma bhakti-yoga.* But to both clarify the gradual rungs on the *yoga* ladder and emphasize pure devotional service as the highest rung, *Surrender Unto Me* uses the term *niṣkāma karma-yoga* to mean the detached and full offering to Kṛṣṇa of the fruits of *karma* by one who has not yet surrendered his attachment to his specific work.

A DEVOTEE'S PERFORMANCE OF SAKĀMA KARMA-YOGA

Kṛṣṇa instructs Arjuna: "In the beginning of creation, the Lord of all creatures sent forth generations of men and demigods, along with sacrifices for Viṣṇu, and blessed them by saying, 'Be thou happy by this *yajña* [sacrifice] because its performance will bestow upon you everything desirable for living happily and achieving liberation.' " (3.10)

Practically speaking, Śrīla Viśvanātha Cakravartī Ṭhākura's comment on this text defines the practice of *karma-yoga* on the *sakāma* platform: "Therefore, one with an impure heart should perform actions without desire rather than give up action. Now, if you cannot be without desire in your actions, you should still perform actions offered to Viṣṇu, but *with* desire, and not give up actions completely. This is explained in seven verses.

"Long ago, along with *yajña,* Brahmā created the creatures qualified for offering to Viṣṇu and said, 'Increase more and more the population by this *dharma* or *yajña.* May this *yajña* bestow all desired enjoyment (*iṣṭa-kāma-dhuk*).' By this he indicated that they had material desires."

Again, devotees may practice *niṣkāma karma-yoga* by performing their prescribed duties with detachment and offering the fruits of their work to Kṛṣṇa, but they are not yet on the platform of pure devotional service. Similarly, stepping toward the rung of *niṣkāma karma-yoga,* less advanced devotees will perform their duties while offering Kṛṣṇa less than a complete tally of the fruits of their work. In other words, devotees at this level maintain material attachments. Although this level of devotional service is clearly inferior to a devotee's performance of both pure *bhakti* and *niṣkāma karma-yoga,* Śukadeva Gosvāmī also encourages those at this level of devotional service in *Bhāgavatam* 2.3.10: *akāmaḥ sarva-kāmo vā, mokṣa-kāma udāra-dhīḥ/ tīvreṇa bhakti-yogena, yajeta puruṣaṁ param,* "A person who has broader intelligence, whether he be full of all material desire, without any material desire, or desiring liberation, must by all means worship the supreme whole, the Personality of Godhead."

In his purport to this verse in the *Bhāgavatam* Śrīla Prabhupāda encourages everyone, regardless of whatever attachments or impurities they may have, to become purified by performing devotional service: "Everyone, whether an *akāma* or *sakāma* or *mokṣa-kāma,* should worship the Lord with great expedience. This implies that *bhakti-yoga* may be perfectly administered without any mixture of *karma* and *jñāna.* As the unmixed sun ray is very forceful and is therefore called *tīvra,* similarly unmixed *bhakti-yoga* of hearing, chanting, etc., may be performed by one and all regardless of inner motive."

As the existence of detached work implies the possibility of attached work, the existence *of niṣkāma bhakti* or *niṣkāma karma-yoga* implies the existence of *sakāma bhakti* or *sakāma karma-yoga.* In *Surrender Unto Me* we have defined these *sakāma* practitioners of *karma-yoga* as *sakāma karma-yogīs.*

A reference to *sakāma karma-yoga*, often referred to as *kāmya-karma,* can be found in *Bhagavad-gītā* 18.2 as well as in Śrīla Prabhupāda's purport to that text. It is also mentioned in Śrīla Viśvanātha Cakravartī Ṭhākura's *Gītā* commentary on texts 2.41, 2.42, 2.49, 2.50 and in Baladeva Vidyābhūṣaṇa's *Gītā* commentary on texts 2.31, 2.40, 2.41, 2.45, and 2.49. Śrīla Jīva Gosvāmī's *Krama-sandarbha* and Śrīla Viśvanātha Cakravartī Ṭhākura's commentary on *Śrīmad-Bhāgavatam* 1.5.12 also mention *sakāma karma,* which we describe as *sakāma karma-yoga,* or *karma-yoga* performed by one who is still *sakāma* and not *niṣkāma.*

A SUMMARY OF TERMS USED TO DESCRIBE THE PROGRESSION TO PURE BHAKTI

In *Surrender Unto Me* we have used the term *karma-kāṇḍī* to refer to a *karmī,* one who performs the duties he has been prescribed by the *Vedas* but who has no transcendental objective. We have also used the term to refer to any worker with no transcendental objective.

Surrender Unto Me describes two kinds of *karma-yogīs,* the nondevotee and the devotee *karma-yogī.* Each can practice on two levels.

A *sakāma karma-yogī* practices at the stage where he only partially renounces the fruits of his work.

One fully detached from the fruits of his work but who remains attached to the work itself is called, in this book, a *niṣkāma karma-yogī.*

And, we call a devotee practicing pure devotional service a *bhakti-yogī.*

Ultimately, as Rūpa Gosvāmī describes, it is the practice of pure devotional service that awards *prema-bhakti,* love of Kṛṣṇa.

Appendix Three

Śrīla Prabhupāda's Comments on the Bhagavad-gītā Chapters

Chapter One

The very beginning of the *Bhagavad-gītā,* the first chapter, is more or less an introduction to the rest of the book. (9.1)

Chapter Two

This chapter instructs us in self-realization by an analytical study of the material body and the spirit soul, as explained by the supreme authority, Lord Śrī Kṛṣṇa. This realization is possible when one works without attachment to fruitive results and is situated in the fixed conception of the real self. (2.1)

Śrīla Bhaktivinoda Ṭhākura has summarized this second chapter of the *Bhagavad-gītā* as being the contents for the whole text. In the *Bhagavad-gītā,* the subject matters are *karma-yoga, jñāna-yoga,* and *bhakti-yoga*. In the second chapter *karma-yoga* and *jñāna-yoga* have been clearly discussed, and a glimpse of *bhakti-yoga* has also been given, as the contents for the complete text. (2.72)

The Supreme Personality of Godhead Śrī Kṛṣṇa has very elaborately described the constitution of the soul in the second chapter, with a view to delivering His intimate friend Arjuna from the ocean of material grief. And the path of realization has been recommended: *buddhi-yoga* or Kṛṣṇa consciousness. (3.1)

In the second chapter, as a prelude to the *Bhagavad-gītā,* many different paths were explained, such as *sāṅkhya-yoga, buddhi-yoga*, control of the senses by intelligence, work without fruitive desire, and the position of the neophyte. This was all presented unsystematically. A more organized outline of the path would be necessary for action and understanding. (3.2)

In the second chapter, preliminary knowledge of the soul and its entanglement in the material body were explained. How to get out of this material encagement by *buddhi-yoga,* or devotional service was also explained therein. (5.1)

In the second chapter of the *Bhagavad-gītā,* the Supreme Lord explained that a living entity is not the material body; he is a spiritual spark. And the Absolute Truth is the spiritual whole. (12.1)

CHAPTER THREE

...Lord Kṛṣṇa elaborately explained *karma-yoga,* or work in Kṛṣṇa consciousness, in this third chapter. (3.1)

This third chapter of the *Bhagavad-gītā* is conclusively directive to Kṛṣṇa consciousness by knowing oneself as the eternal servitor of the Supreme Personality of Godhead, without considering impersonal voidness the ultimate end. In the material existence of life, one is certainly influenced by propensities for lust and desire for dominating the resources of material nature. Desire for overlording and for sense gratification is the greatest enemy of the conditioned soul; but by the strength of Kṛṣṇa consciousness, one can control the material senses, the mind, and the intelligence. One may not give up work and prescribed duties all of a sudden; but by gradually developing Kṛṣṇa consciousness, one can be situated in a transcendental position without being influenced by the material senses and the mind – by steady intelligence directed toward one's pure identity. This is the sum total of this chapter. (3.43)

In the third chapter, it was explained that a person who is situated on the platform of knowledge no longer has any duties to perform. (5.1)

CHAPTER FOUR

In the fourth chapter the Lord told Arjuna that all kinds of sacrificial work culminate in knowledge. However, at the end of the fourth chapter, the Lord advised Arjuna to wake up and fight, being situated in perfect knowledge. Therefore, by simultaneously stressing the importance of both work in devotion and inaction in knowledge, Kṛṣṇa has perplexed Arjuna and confused his determination. (5.1)

CHAPTER FIVE

In this fifth chapter of the *Bhagavad-gītā,* the Lord says that work in devotional service is better than dry mental speculation. Devotional service is easier than the latter because, being transcendental in nature, it frees one from reaction. (5.1)

This fifth chapter is a practical explanation of Kṛṣṇa consciousness, generally known as *karma-yoga.* The question of mental speculation as to how *karma-yoga* can give liberation is answered herewith. To work in Kṛṣṇa consciousness is to work with the complete knowledge of the Lord as the predominator. Such work is not different from transcendental knowledge. Direct Kṛṣṇa consciousness is *bhakti-yoga,* and *jñāna-yoga* is a path leading to *bhakti-yoga.* Kṛṣṇa consciousness means to work in full knowledge of one's relationship with the Supreme Absolute, and the perfection of this consciousness is full knowledge of Kṛṣṇa, or the Supreme Personality of Godhead. (5.29)

CHAPTER SIX

In this chapter the Lord explains that the process of the eightfold *yoga* system is a means to control the mind and the senses. However, this is very difficult for people in general to perform, especially in the Age of Kali. Although the eightfold *yoga* system is recommended in this chapter, the Lord emphasizes that the process of *karma-yoga,* or acting in Kṛṣṇa consciousness, is better. (6.1)

CHAPTER SEVEN

In this seventh chapter of *Bhagavad-gītā,* the nature of Kṛṣṇa consciousness is fully described. Kṛṣṇa is full in all opulences, and how He manifests such opulences is described herein. Also, four kinds of fortunate people who become attached to Kṛṣṇa and four kinds of unfortunate people who never take to Kṛṣṇa are described in this chapter. (7.1)

This seventh chapter particularly explains how one can become a fully Kṛṣṇa conscious person....Many subjects have been discussed in this chapter: the man in distress, the inquisitive man, the man in want of material necessities, knowledge of Brahman, knowledge of Paramātmā, liberation from birth, death, and diseases, and worship of the Supreme Lord. (7.30)

In the seventh chapter we have already discussed the opulent potency of the Supreme Personality of Godhead, His different energies, the inferior and superior natures, and all this material manifestation. (9.1)

In the seventh chapter [Kṛṣṇa] spoke of the living entity as being part and parcel of the supreme whole and recommended that he transfer his attention fully to the whole. (12.1)

CHAPTER EIGHT

In this chapter Lord Kṛṣṇa answers different questions from Arjuna, beginning with "What is Brahman?" The Lord also explains *karma* (fruitive activities), devotional service and *yoga* principles, and devotional service in its pure form. (8.1)

This verse [8.28] is the summation of the seventh and eighth chapters, which particularly deal with Kṛṣṇa consciousness and devotional service. (8.28)

... [I]n the eighth chapter it was said that anyone who thinks of Kṛṣṇa at the time of quitting his body is at once transferred to the spiritual sky, to the abode of Kṛṣṇa. (12.1)

CHAPTER NINE

[T]he matters which are described in the ninth chapter deal with unalloyed, pure devotion. Therefore this is called most confidential....Now in chapter nine the glories of the Lord will be delineated. (9.1)

CHAPTER TEN

Now in this chapter [Kṛṣṇa] explains His specific opulences to Arjuna....He tells Arjuna about His manifestations and various opulences. (10.1)

Devotional service and worship of Kṛṣṇa are very clearly indicated in this chapter in verses eight through eleven. That is the way of pure devotional service. How one can attain the highest devotional perfection of association with the Supreme Personality of Godhead has been thoroughly explained in this chapter. (10.42)

CHAPTER ELEVEN

This chapter reveals Kṛṣṇa as the cause of all causes. (11.1)

One should understand, therefore, that the purport of this eleventh chapter is that the form of Kṛṣṇa is essential and supreme. (11.55)

CHAPTER TWELVE

In this chapter, from verse 2 through the end – from *mayy āveśya mano ye mām* ("fixing the mind on Me") through *ye tu dharmāmṛtam idam* ("this religion of eternal engagement") – the Supreme Lord has explained the processes of transcendental service for approaching Him. Such processes are very dear to the Lord, and He accepts a person engaged in them. (12.20)

CHAPTER THIRTEEN

The purport of this thirteenth chapter is that one should know the distinction between the body, the owner of the body, and the Supersoul. One should recognize the process of liberation, as described in verses eight through twelve. Then one can go on to the supreme destination. (13.35)

In the thirteenth chapter, it was clearly explained that by humbly developing knowledge one may possibly be freed from material entanglement. It has also been explained that it is due to association with the modes of nature that the living entity is entangled in this material world. (14.1)

CHAPTER FOURTEEN

If one understands this chapter through the process of philosophical speculation, he will come to an understanding of devotional service. (14.1)

Now, in this chapter, the Supreme Personality explains what those modes of nature are, how they act, how they bind, and how they give liberation. The knowledge explained in this chapter is proclaimed by the Supreme Lord to be superior to the knowledge given so far in other chapters. By understanding this knowledge, various great sages attained perfection and transferred to the spiritual world. The Lord now explains the same knowledge in a better way. This knowledge is far, far superior to all other processes of knowledge thus far explained, and knowing this many attained perfection. Thus it is expected that one who understands this fourteenth chapter will attain perfection. (14.1)

In chapter fourteen the contamination of all kinds of processes by material nature is described. Only devotional service is described as purely transcendental. (15.6)

CHAPTER FIFTEEN

It is explained in this chapter that the purpose of Vedic study is to understand Kṛṣṇa. (15.1)

In the previous chapters it has been explained that there are many processes by which to get out of the material entanglement. And, up to the thirteenth chapter, we have seen that devotional service to the Supreme Lord is the best way. Now, the basic principle of devotional service is detachment from material activities and attachment to the transcendental service of the Lord. The process of breaking attachment to the material world is discussed in the beginning this chapter. (15.1)

In this chapter the first five verses describe the process of freeing oneself from these weaknesses of heart, and the rest of the chapter, from the sixth verse through the end, discusses *puruṣottama-yoga*. (15.20)

CHAPTER SIXTEEN

In the beginning of the fifteenth chapter, the banyan tree of this material world was explained. The extra roots coming out of it were compared to the activities of the living entities, some auspicious, some inauspicious....In this sixteenth chapter the

Lord explains both the transcendental nature and its attendant qualities and the demoniac nature and its qualities. He also explains the advantages and disadvantages of these qualities. (16.1–3)

CHAPTER SEVENTEEN

Although there is a process of gradual elevation, if one, by the association of pure devotees, takes directly to Kṛṣṇa consciousness, that is the best way. And that is recommended in this chapter. To achieve success in this way, one must first find the proper spiritual master and receive training under his direction. Then one can achieve faith in the Supreme. When that faith matures, in course of time, it is called love of God. This love is the ultimate goal of the living entities. One should therefore take to Kṛṣṇa consciousness directly. That is the message of this seventeenth chapter. (17.28)

CHAPTER EIGHTEEN

The eighteenth chapter is a supplementary summarization of the topics discussed before. In every chapter of the *Bhagavad-gītā,* Lord Kṛṣṇa stresses that devotional service unto the Supreme Personality of Godhead is the ultimate goal of life. This same point is summarized in the eighteenth chapter as the most confidential path of knowledge. (18.1)

As in the second chapter a synopsis of the whole subject matter was described, in the eighteenth chapter also the summary of all instruction is given. (18.1)

Appendix Four

Śrīla Prabhupāda's Comments on the Three Divisions of the Bhagavad-gītā

Division One: Chapters 1–6

In the first six chapters of the *Bhagavad-gītā,* the living entity has been described as nonmaterial spirit soul capable of elevating himself to self-realization by different types of *yogas*. (7.1)

In the first six chapters of the *Bhagavad-gītā* the knower of the body (the living entity) and the position by which he can understand the Supreme Lord are described. (13.1–2)

In the first six chapters, stress was given to devotional service: *yogīnam api sarveṣām*... Of all *yogīs* or transcendentalists, one who always thinks of Me within himself is best." (18.1)

Division Two: Chapters 7–12

In the middle six chapters of the *Bhagavad-gītā* the Supreme Personality of Godhead and the relationship between the individual soul and the Supersoul in regard to devotional service are described. The superior position of the Supreme Personality of Godhead and the subordinate position of the individual soul are definitely defined in these chapters. The living entities are subordinate under all circumstances, but in their forgetfulness they are suffering. When enlightened by pious activities, they approach the Supreme Lord in different capacities – as the distressed, those in want of money, the inquisitive, and those in search of knowledge. That is also described. (13.1–2)

In the next six chapters, pure devotional service and its nature and activity were discussed. (18.1)

The words *idaṁ viditvā* indicate that one should understand the instructions given by Śrī Kṛṣṇa in this chapter and the seventh chapter of *Bhagavad-gītā*. One should try to understand these chapters not by scholarship or mental speculation but by hearing them in association with devotees. Chapters six through twelve are the essence of the *Bhagavad-gītā*. The first six and the last six chapters are like coverings for the middle six chapters, which are especially protected by the Lord. If one is fortunate enough to understand the *Bhagavad-gītā* – especially these middle six chapters – in the association of devotees, then his life at once becomes glorified beyond all penances, sacrifices, charities, speculations, etc., for one can achieve all the results of these activities simply by Kṛṣṇa consciousness. (8.28)

Previously, beginning with the seventh chapter, the Lord has already explained His different energies and how they are acting. Now in this chapter He explains His specific opulences to Arjuna. In the previous chapter He has clearly explained His different energies to establish devotion in firm conviction. Again in this chapter He tells Arjuna about His manifestations and various opulences. (10.1)

DIVISION THREE: CHAPTERS 13–18

Now, starting with the thirteenth chapter, how the living entity comes into contact with material nature and how he is delivered by the Supreme Lord through the different methods of fruitive activities, cultivation of knowledge, and the discharge of devotional service are explained. Although the living entity is completely different from the material body, he somehow becomes related. This also is explained. (13.1–2)

In the third six chapters, knowledge, renunciation, the activities of material nature and transcendental nature, and devotional service were described. It was concluded that all acts should be performed in conjunction with the Supreme Lord, represented by the words *oṁ tat sat,* which indicate Viṣṇu, the Supreme Person. The third part of the *Bhagavad-gītā* has shown that devotional service, and nothing else, is the ultimate purpose of life. This has been established by citing past *ācāryas* and the *Brahma-sūtra,* the *Vedānta-sūtra.* Certain impersonalists consider themselves to have a monopoly on the knowledge of *Vedānta-sūtra,* but actually the *Vedānta-sūtra* is meant for understanding devotional service, for the Lord Himself is the composer of the *Vedānta-sūtra* and He is its knower. That is described in the fifteenth chapter. In every scripture, every *Veda,* devotional service is the objective. That is explained in the *Bhagavad-gītā.* (18.1)

Appendix Five

A Summary of the Bhagavad-gītā

The *Bhagavad-gītā* opens with blind King Dhṛtarāṣṭra requesting his secretary, Sañjaya, to narrate the battle between his sons, the Kauravas, and their cousins, the Pāṇḍavas. Lord Kṛṣṇa, the Supreme Personality of Godhead, out of affection for His devotee, the Pāṇḍava prince Arjuna, has agreed to drive his chariot. As Arjuna takes up his bow and prepares to fight, he sees the sons of Dhṛtarāṣṭra drawn in military array and requests infallible Kṛṣṇa to draw his chariot between the two fighting forces. There, in the midst of both armies, Arjuna's mind reels as he foresees the imminent death of his teacher, relatives, and friends. He throws down his bow and arrows and decides not to fight.

In chapter one and at the beginning of chapter two Arjuna presents his arguments for refusing to fight. Basically, he fears the sinful reactions of killing. But after Arjuna surrenders to Lord Kṛṣṇa and requests the Lord to instruct him, the Lord begins countering Arjuna's objections. First, Kṛṣṇa analytically explains that no killing can actually take place because the eternal soul never dies. Kṛṣṇa then explains that fighting in His service is transcendental and will bring no sinful reaction. Kṛṣṇa also explains the *Vedas'* purpose as being the gradual elevation of souls to Kṛṣṇa consciousness. Kṛṣṇa thus encourages Arjuna to remain fixed in His service – to fight – and ignore the mind's desires.

As Kṛṣṇa's explanations why Arjuna should fight were only a summary, and since Kṛṣṇa glorifies both *buddhi-yoga,* intelligence used in spiritual advancement of knowledge (2.45, 2.49–50), and *karma,* work (2.47–48, 2.50), Arjuna becomes confused and wishes to use Kṛṣṇa's instruction to perform *buddhi-yoga* as an excuse to retire from the battlefield for a life of contemplation. Arjuna therefore opens chapter three by asking Kṛṣṇa why He is encouraging fighting if intelligence is better than fruitive work.

Kṛṣṇa then explains *karma-yoga,* reaction-free devotional work, and clears up Arjuna's mistaken idea that all work is fruitive and leads to bondage. Kṛṣṇa explains that Arjuna should fight, for avoiding sinful reactions through devotional work is better than attempting to escape reactions through renouncing work. Kṛṣṇa also instructs Arjuna to fight to set the proper example of duty. Kṛṣṇa therefore tells Arjuna to fight, but with knowledge and detachment (3.29–30), without falling victim to his own attractions and aversions.

Then, in answer to Arjuna's question on the cause of a soul's being impelled to improper action or neglect of duty, Kṛṣṇa names the enemy: lust. He recommends Arjuna regulate his senses, become fixed in his pure identity as a servant of Kṛṣṇa, and thereby avoid lust's control. With spiritual strength and deliberate intelligence, he should conquer that forceful and sinful enemy, lust.

Since in chapter three Kṛṣṇa has recommended that Arjuna fight in full knowledge of Him (3.30), the Lord, in chapter four, explains different aspects of transcendental knowledge. First, Kṛṣṇa explains attaining knowledge through the disciplic succession. Then after successively explaining His own appearance and mission, the Lord explains His devotional service as the goal of all sacrifices. (Kṛṣṇa had already referred to the importance of performing *yajña,* sacrifice, in 3.9–16.) Next, Kṛṣṇa explains the soul's relationship with Him as eternally His part and parcel, which must be learned by approaching a bona fide spiritual master. Chapter four ends with Kṛṣṇa glorifying transcendental knowledge and requesting Arjuna to arm himself with this knowledge – which burns all sinful reactions to ashes – and fight!

After Arjuna has been impressed with the importance of both work (which requires activity) and seeking knowledge (which tends to be inactive), Arjuna is perplexed. His determination is confused, and he sees fighting and knowledge as contradictory. Therefore Arjuna opens chapter five by asking Kṛṣṇa to definitively explain whether the renunciation of work (speculation, *sāṅkhya, jñāna,* inaction-in-knowledge) or work in devotion is superior. Kṛṣṇa answers that one who is detached from his work's results is the one who is truly renounced. Such a person knows that while the body acts, he, the soul, actually does nothing. Arjuna should, therefore, do his duty and steadily act for the satisfaction of Kṛṣṇa. Impartially viewing the external world, he should reside in his body aloof from bodily activities. By fixing his consciousness on the Supreme and knowing that Kṛṣṇa is the true enjoyer, the goal of sacrifice and austerity, and the Lord of all planets, he, the pure soul, will find true peace beyond this material world.

In the first five chapters Kṛṣṇa has explained *buddhi-yoga,* working with the consciousness focused on Kṛṣṇa without fruitive desires. The Lord has also explained *sāṅkhya, karma-yoga,* and *jñāna-yoga* as processes to obtain liberation and as stepping stones to Kṛṣṇa consciousness. At the end of the fifth chapter (5.27–28) and continuing on to the sixth chapter (wherein Kṛṣṇa explains practical points for a *yogī*), Kṛṣṇa explains *dhyāna-yoga,* concluding that *dhyāna,* or meditation on Kṛṣṇa, is the goal of meditation.

Kṛṣṇa begins the sixth chapter by explaining that the neophyte *yogī* engages in fruitive sitting postures while the advanced *yogī,* the true *sannyāsī,* works without attachment. Such a *yogī* liberates himself and is not degraded by his mind's activities. Carefully controlling his mind, body, and self in Kṛṣṇa's service, the *yogī* strictly practices *dhyāna-yoga* in a secluded place. Fixing his mind on the self and on Kṛṣṇa, he attains transcendental happiness in the kingdom of God. Arjuna then points out that the main difficulty in practicing *yoga* is controlling the mind. Kṛṣṇa responds by saying that one can overcome the obstinate mind through constant practice and determination. In responding to Arjuna's query about the fate of an unsuccessful *yogī,* Kṛṣṇa answers that one unsuccessful in his practice will still take birth in a family of wise transcendentalists and automatically become attracted to yogic principles. Kṛṣṇa finally states in the last two verses of the chapter that the *yogī* is greater than the ascetic, the *jñānī,* and the *karmī.* And the greatest of all *yogīs* is he who always thinks of Kṛṣṇa and with great faith worships Him in loving service.

Knowing Kṛṣṇa's instruction at the end of chapter six, one should initiate his practice of *yoga* from the point of concentrating the mind on Kṛṣṇa. Chapter seven thus opens with Kṛṣṇa explaining knowledge of Himself and His opulent energies. Thus Arjuna can fully worship Kṛṣṇa, as described at the end of chapter six, and think of Him with devotion as he fights.

Kṛṣṇa first explains that He is the Supreme Truth and that everything in existence is a combination of His material and spiritual energies. He is the active principle within all and is all-pervasive through His diverse material and spiritual energies. Because the modes of nature, which emanate from Kṛṣṇa (and which do not affect Him), control the world's activities, only those who surrender to Kṛṣṇa can cross beyond these modes to know Him. Four kinds of impious souls never surrender to Kṛṣṇa, while four kinds of pious souls do. Kṛṣṇa also covers Himself from the impersonalists, who are less intelligent, and from those who surrender to demigods. But those who are truly pious, the undeluded, serve Kṛṣṇa with determination and practice their devotional service on the Brahman platform, which is the goal of the impersonalists. Those souls who know Kṛṣṇa as the governor of the material manifestation, the demigods, and sacrifice, can know and understand Kṛṣṇa – even at the time of death.

Chapter eight begins with Arjuna asking Kṛṣṇa about Brahman, *karma,* the demigods, the material world, and knowing Him at the time of death. Kṛṣṇa briefly answers Arjuna's first five questions and then begins explaining in detail how to know Him at the time of death. Since one attains what one remembers at the time of death, if one remembers Kṛṣṇa, one goes to Him. Kṛṣṇa then explains how He can be constantly thought of as the transcendental person who knows everything, as the oldest, the controller, the smallest, and the maintainer. Thus by practicing *yoga* and remembering Him, Kṛṣṇa explains, one will go to the eternal spiritual world and never again return to this temporary, miserable material world. After describing the different yogic ways in which one may leave this world, Kṛṣṇa advises Arjuna not to worry about other paths – either Vedic study, *yoga,* austerities, sacrifices, charity, *jñāna,* or *karma* – for the results of all these will be obtained through performing devotional service. And in the end, such a *yogī* in devotion reaches the supreme eternal abode.

After Kṛṣṇa answers Arjuna's questions in chapter eight, He continues speaking, in chapter nine, the knowledge about

Himself that He had begun explaining in chapter seven. Kṛṣṇa prefaces chapter nine by stating that the knowledge He will now reveal is most confidential, for it is about His actual position, which only the nonenvious and faithful can understand. Kṛṣṇa continues explaining that although independent and aloof, He pervades, creates, and annihilates the entire cosmos through His material energy. Those *mahātmās* who know Kṛṣṇa as the Supreme Personality of Godhead take shelter of Him and serve Him as the only enjoyer and the supreme object of worship.

Kṛṣṇa then explains the fortunate position of such devotees. If one worships Kṛṣṇa, Kṛṣṇa cares for him, compensates for his deficiencies, and preserves his strengths. And all Kṛṣṇa asks for is an offering of a leaf, a flower, or some water – if it is offered with devotion. Thus His devotee comes to Him. Even if a devotee unintentionally commits a horrendous act, he will be rectified, for Kṛṣṇa promises that His devotee will never perish.

In chapters seven and nine, Kṛṣṇa has explained knowledge of His energies. In chapter ten, Kṛṣṇa explains His opulences more specifically and thereby reveals Himself as the Supreme Personality of Godhead, the source of all. Kṛṣṇa also tells how His pure devotees know that He is the unborn Supreme Lord, the source of all sages, the source of the material and spiritual worlds, and the source of all qualities and attitudes. Thus pure and wise devotees worship Kṛṣṇa, converse about Him, and with thoughts dwelling in Him, undeluded and free from sin, they engage in His service. Out of compassion, Kṛṣṇa, within their hearts, destroys any remaining ignorance. After hearing of Kṛṣṇa's opulences, Arjuna confirms Kṛṣṇa as the Supreme Lord by quoting authorities, and explains that only Kṛṣṇa can truly know Himself. Kṛṣṇa then tells of His divine manifestations within this world – as the Supersoul, the ocean, the Himalayas – which merely indicate His limitless opulences, for a single fragment of Kṛṣṇa's energy pervades and supports this entire universe!

Arjuna, although acknowledging that Kṛṣṇa in the two-armed form that he now sees before him is Supreme, still requests Kṛṣṇa to reveal His all-pervading universal form that supports the universe. Thus, in chapter eleven, Kṛṣṇa proves Himself the Supreme Lord, and He establishes the criterion that anyone who claims to be God must also show a universal form. Kṛṣṇa reveals to Arjuna His wondrous, effulgent, all-expansive form, and Arjuna sees all soldiers on both sides dying within it. Kṛṣṇa explains His form as time, the destroyer of all the worlds, and requests that Arjuna, knowing in advance of the inevitable deaths of all the warriors, become His instrument. In answer to Arjuna's fearful prayers, Kṛṣṇa first shows His four-armed form before again returning to His original two-armed form. Kṛṣṇa then states that this two-armed form can be seen only by pure devotees, and such pure devotees, working for Kṛṣṇa, free from desire for fruitive activities, making Kṛṣṇa the supreme goal of their lives, certainly come to Him.

In chapter twelve, Arjuna, after witnessing Kṛṣṇa's awesome universal form, wishes to confirm his own position as a devotee, the highest worshiper of the Supreme. He thus asks whether worshiping Kṛṣṇa through devotional service or worshiping the impersonal is superior. Kṛṣṇa immediately responds, saying that one engaged in His personal service is the topmost. One should therefore engage in Kṛṣṇa's service and fix his mind solely on Kṛṣṇa. If that cannot be done, one should follow the rules and regulations of *bhakti-yoga,* which purify one, so he is able to do so later. Kṛṣṇa then describes other processes that eventually lead to His pure devotional service.

The qualities that endear a devotee to Kṛṣṇa, such as equality in both happiness and distress, independence from the ordinary course of activities, satisfaction, and the faithful following of the path of devotional service, are also mentioned as part of the process of worshiping Kṛṣṇa in devotional service.

Arjuna opens chapter thirteen inquiring about the field of activities and the knower of that field. Kṛṣṇa answers that the conditioned soul's body and the body's interactions with the material world are his limited field of activities. By understanding the difference between the body, the soul, and the Supersoul, and by following the process of knowledge, the soul can transcend dualities, realize his eternal subordination to Kṛṣṇa, and attain the supreme destination.

The thirteenth chapter clearly explains that by humbly developing knowledge one can become freed from material entanglement. It also explains that the living entity's entanglement within the material world is due to his association with the modes of material nature (13.20–22). In chapter fourteen, the Supreme Personality explains in detail the three modes – goodness, passion, and ignorance – as the forces that bind and control all conditioned souls within this world. A soul can, however, transcend these modes through devotional service. (All other processes are contaminated by the modes.) Thus the limitations imposed by his field of activities can be overthrown, and the soul can be elevated to the Brahman platform, the constitutional position of purity and happiness – a platform of which Kṛṣṇa is the basis.

As one must be detached from the modes and their results in order to be attached to the service of the Lord, Kṛṣṇa describes in chapter fifteen the process of freeing oneself from matter's grip. He begins by comparing the material world to a gigantic, upside-down banyan tree, inviting Arjuna to detach himself from it through surrender. Thus the soul can end his transmigrations and return to Him in the spiritual world.

Although the foolish cannot understand that the soul transmigrates from one body to another according to the mind's desires, transcendentalists see this clearly. The foolish can learn to see properly by knowing Kṛṣṇa as the splendor of the sun, moon, and fire; as the one keeping the planets in orbit and making vegetables succulent; as the fire of digestion; as the Paramātmā in everyone's heart; as the giver of remembrance, knowledge, and forgetfulness; and as the goal of the *Vedas* and the compiler of *Vedānta*. Kṛṣṇa reveals that knowing Him as the Supreme Personality of Godhead and engaging in His service is the ultimate purpose of the *Vedānta* and the most confidential part of the *Vedas*.

In chapter fifteen, auspicious, elevating activities are described as part of the banyan tree. In chapter sixteen, after mentioning twenty-six godly qualities, Kṛṣṇa explains the demoniac nature, which degrades the soul through arrogant, ignorant and conceited pursuits of sense gratification and power.

Kṛṣṇa explains the demoniac mentality as follows: The demoniac think the world is unreal and produced only of sex desire. Taking shelter of lust, they think of sense gratification as the goal of life and scheme to illegally increase their wealth. While plotting to kill their enemies, they think themselves powerful and happy, and surrounded by their relatives, they use sacrifices and charity only to further increase their happiness. Perplexed by illusory anxieties, bewildered by complacency, impudency, and wealth, and envying the Supersoul within their own bodies and within the bodies of others, demons blaspheme real religion. These mischievous, lowest of men are repeatedly cast by Kṛṣṇa into demoniac species and gradually sink to the most abominable forms of existence.

Kṛṣṇa ends the chapter by explaining that because lust, anger, and greed are the beginning of demoniac life, all sane men should give them up and understand their duty by faithfully following the scriptures.

Kṛṣṇa concludes chapter sixteen by declaring that the ultimate difference between the divine and the demonic is that the divine follow the scriptures while the demons do not. At the beginning of chapter seventeen, Arjuna inquires more about those who don't follow scriptures but who worship according to their imagination. Kṛṣṇa answers by describing how the combination of the modes of material nature that control a particular person will dictate his faith, worship, eating, sacrifices, charity, and austerity. The chapter ends with Kṛṣṇa explaining the syllables *oṁ tat sat* and how these syllables indicate that any sacrifice, austerity, or charity dictated by the modes and performed without devotional service is useless in this life and the next. One should therefore directly take to Kṛṣṇa's service in Kṛṣṇa consciousness.

The entire *Bhagavad-gītā* is concluded in seventeen chapters, and in the eighteenth chapter, Kṛṣṇa reviews the knowledge already presented. In this chapter Kṛṣṇa concludes, as He has done throughout the *Bhagavad-gītā,* that one should practice devotional service, Kṛṣṇa consciousness.

Since Arjuna's basic reason to renounce his duty of fighting was fear of sinful reaction, Kṛṣṇa explains true renunciation and how to transcend sinful reactions through 1) becoming renounced from the fruits of activities, 2) abiding by the order of the Supersoul, and 3) worshiping the Lord with the fruit of one's work by acting either as a *brāhmaṇa, kṣatriya, vaiśya,* or *śūdra* according to one's mode of nature. (Each leads Arjuna to fight.) Thus one can achieve the self-realized position of *brahma-bhūta* and from that position, detached from all material things, one can practice pure devotional service.

Kṛṣṇa can be known only through surrendering to Him in devotional service, and by this direct process – free from *karma* or *jñāna* – Arjuna need not fear any sinful reactions. Under Kṛṣṇa's protection, such a pure devotee will reach Kṛṣṇaloka. Kṛṣṇa instructs Arjuna that he should surrender to the Supreme Lord within his heart and thus attain peace in the supreme, eternal abode. The most confidential knowledge is then explained by Kṛṣṇa: "Become My devotee, always think of Me, act for Me, worship Me, and offer all homage unto Me. Surrender unto Me alone. Do not fear sinful reactions."

After hearing the instructions of Śrī Kṛṣṇa, Arjuna is fixed and ready to fight. Sañjaya, after narrating this conversation to Dhṛtarāṣṭra, ecstatically thinks of the wondrous universal form of Kṛṣṇa and predicts victory for Arjuna, the supreme archer, for he is surrendered to Kṛṣṇa, the master of all mystics.

Appendix Six

Outline of the Bhagavad-gītā

Chapter One

A. Introduction (1.1–1.27)

Both armies have lined up on the battlefield and are prepared to fight.

B. Arjuna's doubts (1.28–1.42)

Arjuna explains his reasons for wishing not to fight.

Chapter Two

A. More doubts (2.1–2.10)

Arjuna gives more reasons for not fighting, but surrenders to Kṛṣṇa.

B. Jñāna (2.11–2.30)

Kṛṣṇa's first instructions (*jñāna*): The soul can never die; the body can never be saved.

C. Karma-kāṇḍa (2.31–2.38)

Kṛṣṇa next explains working in *karma-kāṇḍa* consciousness: material gains (heaven or a kingdom) from fighting and material losses (infamy and sin) from not fighting.

D. Buddhi-yoga [Niṣkāma karma] (2.39–2.53)

Kṛṣṇa explains *buddhi-yoga* (*niṣkāma karma*), wherein one works (*karma*) with knowledge (*jñāna*) and is thus detached from the fruits of his work.

E. Samādhi (2.54–2.72)

By working in *buddhi-yoga,* one attains material detachment and the equipoised platform of liberation called *samādhi.*

CONNECTION BETWEEN CHAPTERS 2 & 3

In the previous chapter, Kṛṣṇa told Arjuna to keep all abominable activities far distant by *buddhi-yoga.* Taking the meaning of *buddhi* as intelligence, Kṛṣṇa's order would mean that Arjuna, by using his intelligence, should avoid all abominable activities and not fight. Yet, thinks Arjuna, Kṛṣṇa is still urging me to fight! Thus chapter three opens with Arjuna requesting Kṛṣṇa to clarify His apparently contradictory instructions.

CHAPTER THREE

A. Renunciation or work? (3.1–3.2)

Arjuna inquires whether it is better to be situated in knowledge or to work, as if the two were opposed to one another.

B. Niṣkāma karma-yoga (3.3–3.9)

Kṛṣṇa recommends *niṣkāma karma-yoga,* work combined with knowledge and detachment. The fruit of that work should be offered for the satisfaction of Viṣṇu. *Niṣkāma karma-yoga* allows the soul, who is active by nature, to be purified through his detached activities.

C. From karma-kāṇḍa to karma-yoga (3.10–3.16)

If one cannot perform detached, dutiful work, it is better to follow the *karma-kāṇḍa* section of the *Vedas.* But one should do these Vedic duties, which prescribe sacrifices, for Kṛṣṇa's pleasure.

D. Niṣkāma karma to set the correct example (3.17–3.35)

Dutifully acting without attachment sets the correct example for others, who, being less advanced, need the proper example of following prescribed śāstric duties.

E. Beware of lust and anger (3.36–3.43)

Lust and anger, or passion and ignorance, foil one's performance of duty. Thus one incurs sin. The senses must be regulated and the intelligence strengthened to control lust.

CONNECTION BETWEEN CHAPTERS 3 & 4

In chapter three, we have just heard that lust covers knowledge and that ignorance (lack of knowledge) binds us with attachments. Dutiful, detached work has been recommended to attain transcendental knowledge. Thus after emphasizing transcendental knowledge, Kṛṣṇa opens chapter four by explaining how transcendental knowledge is received.

CHAPTER FOUR

A. Transcendental knowledge about Kṛṣṇa (4.1–4.10)

Transcendental knowledge about Kṛṣṇa received by disciplic succession reveals the truth about Kṛṣṇa's form, birth, and activities. One who knows these truths and thus takes shelter of Kṛṣṇa becomes purified and attains Kṛṣṇa.

B. Applying transcendental knowledge (4.11–4.15)

Although Kṛṣṇa sanctions the awarding of the fruits of everyone's work, Kṛṣṇa Himself is neutral and awards those fruits according to the living entity's desires and *karma.* One who understands Kṛṣṇa in this way remains free from material bondage.

C. Understanding karma on the platform of jñāna (4.16–4.24)

By applying transcendental knowledge, one can perform detached actions in Kṛṣṇa's service. These actions are *akarma,* actions without reactions, and are on the absolute platform. Thus Kṛṣṇa explains how *karma* can be seen as *jñāna.*

D. Sacrifices lead to transcendental knowledge (4.25–4.33)

The fruit of all kinds of Vedic sacrifices is transcendental knowledge, which leads to liberation and ultimately to pure devotional service.

E. Conclusion (4.34–4.42)

Because acting on the transcendental knowledge received through the disciplic succession destroys the sinful reactions to all work, one should do his duty fixed in transcendental knowledge.

CONNECTION BETWEEN CHAPTERS 4 & 5

In explaining transcendental knowledge to Arjuna, Kṛṣṇa has

glorified *jñāna* (4.16–18) and spoken of action in inaction and inaction in action. In text 41, Kṛṣṇa glorified both *jñāna* and renunciation. But in text 42, Kṛṣṇa again orders Arjuna to fight. Therefore chapter five opens with a question by Arjuna that is similar to the one he asked at the beginning of chapter three: "Which is better, work or renunciation of work?" Kṛṣṇa will answer Arjuna's question and will explain the process of achieving liberation through *karma-yoga* in greater depth than He did in chapter three.

CHAPTER FIVE

A. Niṣkāma karma-yoga is easier than renouncing work (5.1–5.6)

Arjuna again asks whether renouncing work is superior to working with detachment. Kṛṣṇa replies that both are equal in the sense that both are means to the same goal. But Kṛṣṇa emphasizes working with detachment as easier and superior.

B. The performance of niṣkāma karma-yoga (5.7–5.12)

One performing *niṣkāma karma-yoga* identifies neither with his body nor the activities that his body performs. Through his detached actions, he is freed from the reactions of his activities.

C. Knowledge: The three doers (5.13–5.16)

The living being (doer No. 1) who knows that all bodily activities are automatically carried out by the modes of material nature (doer No. 2), after those activities are sanctioned by the Supersoul (doer No. 3), attains enlightenment through that knowledge.

D. Liberation: Focusing on the Supersoul (5.17–5.26)

One who, in knowledge, devotionally fixes his consciousness on the Supersoul and remains materially equipoised, attains liberation in the near future.

E. Liberation: Aṣṭāṅga-yoga previewed (5.27–5.28)

One achieves the same liberation through the practice of *aṣṭāṅga-yoga.*

F. Peace on the platform of liberation (5.29)

A person in full consciousness of Kṛṣṇa attains liberation from the pangs of material miseries.

CONNECTION BETWEEN CHAPTERS 5 & 6

In chapter five, Kṛṣṇa has explained how to achieve liberation through *niṣkāma karma-yoga,* and at the chapter's end, He explained how to achieve that same liberation through *aṣṭāṅga-yoga.* Now Kṛṣṇa will describe in greater detail the process of *aṣṭāṅga-yoga.*

CHAPTER SIX

A. Advancing in yoga through detached work (6.1–6.4)

Aṣṭāṅga-yogīs, like *niṣkāma karma-yogīs,* engage in detached work to advance.

B. Yogārūḍha stage: Giving up work (6.5–6.9)

When a *yogī's* mental control reaches the stage of regarding well-wishers, the envious, the pious, and sinners equally, he may then give up even *niṣkāma karma-yoga.*

C. Further stages in the practice of yoga (6.10–6.32)

Kṛṣṇa describes the practices of *aṣṭāṅga-yoga* and its results: *yogārūḍha* (the perfectional stage) and ultimately the vision of the Supersoul.

D. Necessity of controlling the turbulent mind (6.33–6.36)

Although control of the mind is undoubtedly difficult, it is nevertheless essential and obtainable only by constant practice and detachment.

E. The destination of the unsuccessful yogī (6.37–6.45)

Unsuccessful transcendentalists obtain either heavenly enjoyment followed by an aristocratic birth (if they are slightly advanced) or birth in a family of wise transcendentalists that brings them immediate further training (if they are more advanced).

F. The topmost yogī (6.46–6.47)

Yogīs are greater than empiricists, fruitive workers, and

ascetics. And of all *yogīs,* those who with full faith always think of Kṛṣṇa and render transcendental loving service to Him are the highest of all.

CONNECTION BETWEEN CHAPTERS 6 & 7

Kṛṣṇa has explained in chapter six that the *yogī* most intimately united with Him is *mad-gatenāntar-ātmanā,* thinking of Him from within. Kṛṣṇa, in chapter seven, begins to explain how to become *mad-gatenāntar-ātmanā.*

CHAPTER SEVEN

A. Knowing Kṛṣṇa by hearing about Him (7.1–7.3)

Kṛṣṇa requests Arjuna to hear of both His material and spiritual energies, and He declares that the transcendentalist who succeeds in truly knowing Him is most rare.

B. Knowing Kṛṣṇa's material and spiritual energies (7.4–7.12)

Kṛṣṇa, as the source of both matter and spirit, can be seen in the world when we view all existence as a combination of Kṛṣṇa's material and spiritual energies. He is also the active essence of everything, and although Kṛṣṇa is not under His energies, the three modes, all else in material existence is manifested by combinations of goodness, passion, and ignorance.

C. Kṛṣṇa controls the modes – so surrender (7.13–7.14)

Those who surrender to Kṛṣṇa, the controller of the modes, will cross beyond the delusion caused by the three modes and come to know Him.

D. The impious never surrender; the pious do (7.15–7.19)

Four kinds of men never surrender, and four kinds do. Of those who surrender, the *jñānī* who has no material desires is both the best and the rarest.

E. Surrender to demigods and impersonalism (7.20–7.25)

Those who surrender to the demigods and those who are impersonalists have no knowledge of Kṛṣṇa and thus, in their foolishness, do not surrender to Him.

F. Bewilderment – and freedom by knowing Kṛṣṇa (7.26–7.30)

The living entity's bewilderment is caused by *māyā's* forcing him to see dualities; his freedom is caused by devotional service, which places him beyond those dualities. Thus by being conscious of Kṛṣṇa in devotional service one can know Him even at the time of death.

CONNECTION BETWEEN CHAPTERS 7 & 8

Kṛṣṇa, at the end of chapter seven, mentioned several difficult terms. Arjuna now questions Kṛṣṇa about what he has just heard.

CHAPTER EIGHT

A. Kṛṣṇa's answers to Arjuna's questions (8.1–8.4)

Arjuna asks Kṛṣṇa about Kṛṣṇa's words in the last two verses of chapter seven: Brahman, *adhyātma, karma, adhibhūta, adhidaiva, adhiyajña,* and how those in devotional service can know Him at the time of death. Kṛṣṇa briefly answers as follows:

1) Brahman is the indestructible living entity.

2) *Adhyātma* is the living entity's nature, which is to serve.

3) *Karma* is that activity and its reactions that cause the development of a material body.

4) *Adhibhūta* is the ever-changing material manifestation.

5) He who presides over all the demigods and their planets is the *adhidaiva,* the universal form of the Lord.

6) Kṛṣṇa, as the Supersoul, is within everyone's heart and is *adhiyajña,* the Lord of all sacrifices.

B. Remembering Kṛṣṇa at the time of death (8.5–8.8)

Since one attains whatever one remembers at the time of death, Kṛṣṇa recommends that Arjuna undeviatingly meditate on Him, dedicate his activities to Him, and thus attain Him.

C. Remembering Kṛṣṇa (8.9–8.13)

By meditating on Kṛṣṇa and His qualities, or by practicing *yoga-miśra-bhakti*, one can think of the Supreme Personality of Godhead when quitting the body and reach the spiritual planets.

D. Pure devotional service (8.14–8.16)

One who undeviatingly remembers Kṛṣṇa easily attains the Lord's abode, far from this miserable material world, because of constantly engaging in devotional service.

E. Comparing the material and spiritual worlds (8.17–8.22)

The material world, long-lasting as it seems, is continually being created and destroyed. Beyond this ocean of creation and destruction is Kṛṣṇa's eternal abode, wherein He is present, and which is attainable only by unalloyed devotion to Him.

F. The supremacy of pure devotion in attaining Kṛṣṇa (8.23–8.28)

To attain Kṛṣṇa's abode, *yogīs* must pass from this world according to mystic formulas. Devotees need only remain fixed in devotion.

CONNECTION BETWEEN CHAPTERS 8 & 9

In the eighth chapter, Kṛṣṇa has explained that the *ananya* devotee surpasses the path of light and darkness. Now Kṛṣṇa will explain how to become such a devotee.

CHAPTER NINE

A. Hearing – qualifications and disqualifications (9.1–9.3)

The nonenvious and faithful will attain Kṛṣṇa by hearing this most confidential knowledge about Him. Faithlessness forces one to take birth and death.

B. Aiśvarya-jñāna: Kṛṣṇa's relationship to the world (9.4–9.10)

Kṛṣṇa pervades, creates, and annihilates the entire cosmos through His material energy. Although Kṛṣṇa is the supreme director, the material world nevertheless moves independently, and Kṛṣṇa thus remains neutral and detached.

C. Fools neglect bhakti; the divine don't (9.11–9.25)

Fools who think Kṛṣṇa's form is ordinary are defeated in their endeavors (11–12); *mahātmās* who know that Kṛṣṇa possesses a transcendental form take shelter of Him and worship Him (13–14). Actually, all who take shelter of a conception of the Supreme and worship it, are ultimately worshiping Kṛṣṇa, but they worship Him indirectly. These are of three types:

1) *Ekatvena* – the monist, the lowest, worships himself as one with the Supreme (11–12).

2) *Viśvato-mukham* – a worshiper of the material, universal form is the best (16–19).

3) *Pṛthakvena* – a demigod worshiper, is higher than the *ekatvena* (20–25).

D. The glories of devotional service to Kṛṣṇa (9.26–9.34)

One who worships Kṛṣṇa with devotion – or even offers Him the fruits of his work – becomes freed from reactions and comes to Kṛṣṇa. The worship is simple and the result super-excellent. (26–28)

Kṛṣṇa shows favoritism to His devotee. Kṛṣṇa considers a devotee saintly, even if he's committed a horrible act, and He quickly rectifies the devotee. (29–31)

All are purified by devotional service. By thinking of Kṛṣṇa, offering Him obeisances, and becoming absorbed in Him, one will go back to Godhead, regardless of his position. (32–34)

CONNECTION BETWEEN CHAPTERS 9 & 10

Especially at the end of chapter nine, Kṛṣṇa has described devotional service. To help generate further devotion in His devotee, Kṛṣṇa now explains His opulences.

CHAPTER TEN

A. Understanding Kṛṣṇa's unknowability, one serves Him (10.1–10.7)

Kṛṣṇa describes that His origin is impossible to understand, for He is the source of all. (A creation cannot independently understand its own source.) One who understands this serves Kṛṣṇa with devotion.

B. The Catur-ślokī Gītā (10.8–10.11)

Kṛṣṇa describes the opulence of His position as the source of all, the eagerness of His devotees to love and serve Him, and His own reciprocation with that eagerness. The essence of the *Gītā* is stated in four verses:

1) All of Kṛṣṇa's opulences are summarized in text 8. By knowing these opulences as the Lord's, one can attain the realizations of texts 9, 10, and 11.

2) Knowing Kṛṣṇa as the source of all, the devotees cannot maintain their lives without Him. They thus worship Him with the great desire described in text 9.

3) Kṛṣṇa's reciprocation with such devotees is described in text 10.

4) The devotee's real intelligence, which overcomes the ignorance caked on his heart by millions of births, is awarded by Kṛṣṇa as described in text 11. The Lord enters His devotee's heart just as a bee enters a lotus flower.

C. Arjuna accepts Kṛṣṇa's position and asks to hear more of His opulences (10.12–10.18)

Arjuna refers to previous authorities and confirms that Kṛṣṇa is the Supreme Personality of Godhead. He then prays to Kṛṣṇa to know more of His glories so he can always think of Him and remember Him; otherwise, as He stated earlier, Kṛṣṇa will remain unknowable.

D. Kṛṣṇa's opulences (10.19–10.42)

In response to Arjuna's request, Kṛṣṇa describes the most prominent among His limitless, all-pervading opulences. After naming eighty-two opulences, Kṛṣṇa summarizes by explaining that these opulences simply *indicate* His glory, for He pervades and supports the entire universe with a mere fragment of His total potency.

CONNECTION BETWEEN CHAPTERS 10 & 11

After hearing Kṛṣṇa say in chapter ten that He pervades and supports the entire universe, Arjuna wishes to see that all-pervasive form of the Lord.

CHAPTER ELEVEN

A. Arjuna's request and Kṛṣṇa's description of His universal form (11.1–11.8)

Arjuna, although acknowledging that the two-armed form of Kṛṣṇa is Supreme, requests Kṛṣṇa to show him the all-pervading, universal form of which Kṛṣṇa spoke in chapter ten. Kṛṣṇa first describes His universal form and then bestows on Arjuna the vision necessary to see it.

B. Sañjaya's description of Arjuna's vision (11.9–11.31)

Sañjaya describes that Kṛṣṇa bestows on Arjuna the necessary vision. Arjuna then beholds Kṛṣṇa's universal form with astonishment, and he hesitatingly begins to describe what he sees. Arjuna first sees all existence, immeasurable, with great radiance, in one place within this form (14–19). Second, Arjuna sees Kṛṣṇa's frightening, all-destructive *kāla-rūpa,* or form of time. Arjuna asks this form, "What is your mission? Who are you?" (20–31)

C. "Time I am. Become my instrument" (11.32–11.34)

Kṛṣṇa answers, "Time I am, the destroyer of the world. The great warriors on both sides are already slain by My plan. You can be but an instrument. Arise and fight!"

D. Arjuna's prayers (11.35–11.46)

Arjuna, trembling, prays to the universal form. He also begs Kṛṣṇa's forgiveness for having previously, in ignorance, treated the Lord as his friend. Arjuna then fearfully requests Kṛṣṇa to again reveal His two-armed form as the Supreme Personality of Godhead.

E. Only pure devotees see Kṛṣṇa's two-armed form (11.47–11.55)

At Arjuna's request, Kṛṣṇa withdraws His universal form (47–48). He then first shows Arjuna His four-armed form (49–50), and finally His two-armed form (50–51). Kṛṣṇa's most wonderful form, His two-armed form, can be directly seen only through pure, undivided devotional service. (52–55)

CONNECTION BETWEEN CHAPTERS 11 & 12

After hearing of the Lord's inestimable impersonal opulences, Arjuna again wants to hear about devotion and to clarify his own position as a devotee, who works for Kṛṣṇa, as opposed to a *jñānī*, who renounces work.

CHAPTER TWELVE

A. Bhakti is superior to impersonalism (12.1–12.7)

A worshiper of the impersonal is less perfect and undergoes more difficulty than one who worships Kṛṣṇa with great faith and fixed attention. The path of devotion is recommended not only because it is easier to follow, but also because Kṛṣṇa Himself personally takes charge of delivering His devotee.

*B. Progressive stages of devotion (12.8–12.12)**

1) One lives in Kṛṣṇa by continuously fixing one's mind and intelligence on Him. (8)
2) One practices the regulative principles of *bhakti-yoga* to increase one's desire and ability to remember and obtain Kṛṣṇa. (9)
3) One surrenders one's work to Kṛṣṇa. (10)
4) One cultivates meditation or knowledge. (12)

C. Qualities that endear one to Kṛṣṇa (12.13–12.20)

Possessing divine qualities makes one dear to Kṛṣṇa, and anyone who faithfully follows the path of devotional service, making Kṛṣṇa the supreme goal, is very dear to Him.

CONNECTION BETWEEN CHAPTERS 12 & 13

Kṛṣṇa has promised in Bg. 12.7 to redeem His devotees. Now, to that end, He will declare the knowledge needed to elevate His devotees from the material world.

CHAPTER THIRTEEN

A. Arjuna's six questions (13.1)

Arjuna asks Kṛṣṇa to explain six topics: 1) *prakṛti* (nature), 2) *puruṣa* (the enjoyer), 3) *kṣetra* (the field of activities), 4)

* Verse 12.11 is not included as a progressive stage of devotion because surrendering one's work to a mundane cause does not bring a result in relationship to *bhakti*.

kṣetra-jña (the knower of the field), 5) *jñāna* (knowledge and the process of knowing), 6) *jñeya* (the object of knowledge).

B. Kṛṣṇa explains the field of activities and the knower of the field (topics 3, 4, and 5) (13.2–13.7)

Kṛṣṇa explains the field of activities as the body, by which the soul engages in his allotted sphere of activities within the material world. Kṛṣṇa also explains that the soul, the knower of the field, has knowledge only of his own field of activities. Kṛṣṇa Himself, however, as the Supersoul, is the knower of all the fields of activity of all living entities. To know the field and its knowers is called knowledge.

C. Kṛṣṇa further explains the process of knowledge and liberation (topic 5) (13.8–13.12)

Those activities by which a soul obtains knowledge beyond the limitations of his field of activities – and thus transcends his field – is called the process of knowledge.

D. Kṛṣṇa explains the object of knowledge (topic 6) (13.13–13.19)

The soul can know the Supersoul, who is the ultimate object of knowledge. Only devotees can understand the field of activities (the body), the process of knowledge, and both the soul and the Supersoul.

E. Kṛṣṇa explains prakṛti, puruṣa and their union (topics 1 and 2) (13.20–13.26)

1) *Prakṛti, puruṣa* (the *"jīva,"* or *kṣetra-jña*) and their union: Material nature causes all material changes and effects, and the living entity meets with good and bad according to the qualities he has acquired due to his association with material nature (20–22).

Paramātmā puruṣa (*kṣetra-jña*): The Supersoul exists within all bodies as the overseer, the permitter, and the supreme proprietor (23).

Result: One who understands *prakṛti (kṣetra), puruṣa (kṣetra-jña jīva/kṣetra-jña* Supersoul), and their interactions attains liberation from birth in the material world. Other methods of obtaining liberation are *jñāna, aṣṭāṅga,* and *karma.* (25–26)

F. Jñāna-cakṣus: the vision of knowledge (13.27–13.35)

Those who see the distinction between the body, its owner, and the Supersoul, and who recognize the process of liberation, can attain the supreme goal. (35)

CONNECTION BETWEEN CHAPTERS 13 & 14

Kṛṣṇa in chapter thirteen has explained that the living entity is trapped in his field of activities. Kṛṣṇa will now explain the nature of the trap – how he is controlled by the modes of material nature within that field. In other words, the knowledge explained briefly in Bg. 13.22 will now be expanded.

CHAPTER FOURTEEN

A. The liberation and conditioning of living entities (14.1–14.4)

After glorifying the knowledge that He will now speak, Kṛṣṇa explains that by Him, the Supreme Lord, the material energy is impregnated with the living entities.

B. The modes bind the pure soul (14.5–14.9)

Kṛṣṇa then explains that the eternal living entity connects with the material energy through conditioning by the three modes of material nature. The mode of goodness conditions one to happiness, passion to fruitive activities, and ignorance to madness.

C. Recognizing a mode's supremacy (14.10–14.13)

The modes compete with one another for supremacy in an individual. Knowledge manifests from goodness; from passion manifests attachment, uncontrollable desire, and intense endeavor; and from ignorance comes inactivity and madness.

D. Acting and dying within the modes (14.14–14.18)

Both the results of one's actions and the results after one's death are predominated by a specific mode of nature and thus bring about certain results.

E. Transcending the modes (14.19–14.27)

One transcends all three modes by knowing that all in this

world takes place under the modes and by understanding that Kṛṣṇa's activities are transcendental to the modes. Kṛṣṇa explains that one can transcend the modes by engaging unfailingly in full devotional service. One will then come to the Brahman platform, of which Kṛṣṇa is the source.

CONNECTION BETWEEN CHAPTERS 14 & 15

Kṛṣṇa described at the end of chapter fourteen that one transcends the modes through devotional service. But to attain devotion to Him, one needs detachment from the material world. Kṛṣṇa begins chapter fifteen by explaining the need for detachment with a metaphor that compares the material world to an *aśvattha,* a banyan tree. Then Kṛṣṇa describes *puruṣottama-yoga* in texts 6–20.

CHAPTER FIFTEEN

A. Becoming detached from the material world (15.1–15.5)

One should detach himself from the material world, which is a reflection of the spiritual world, and one should surrender to Kṛṣṇa and attain that spiritual world.

B. Transmigration (15.6–15.11)

One's goal should be to leave the material world and return to the spiritual world. Although all living entities are eternally part and parcel of Kṛṣṇa, they now struggle from body to body searching for pleasure. Transcendentalists see this clearly, but blind materialists cannot.

C. Kṛṣṇa's position as our maintainer (15.12–15.15)

Knowing Kṛṣṇa's opulent position as our maintainer on both the cosmic and personal levels – and His position as the compiler of *Vedānta* and knower of the *Vedas* – should attract us to Him.

D. The tri-ślokī Gītā of knowledge: A summary of the Vedas and the Vedānta (15.16–15.18)

1) Conditioned living entities are fallible. Living entities in harmony with the Lord's desire are infallible (16).

2) Beyond both the fallible and the infallible is the transcendental Supreme Person, the Supersoul, who maintains

the three worlds (17).

3) Kṛṣṇa is celebrated both in this world and the *Vedas* as that Supreme Person, the Supersoul (18).

E. Knowing Kṛṣṇa means knowing everything (15.19–15.20)

Whoever knows Kṛṣṇa's position knows everything, and he engages Himself in Kṛṣṇa's service. Knowing this most confidential part of the Vedic scriptures makes one wise and brings perfection to his endeavors.

CONNECTION BETWEEN CHAPTERS 15 & 16

Chapter fifteen described the banyan tree of the material world. The modes of material nature nourish both the upper, auspicious, divine branches of the tree and the lower, demoniac branches. In the sixteenth chapter, Kṛṣṇa first explains the divine qualities that elevate one on the tree and lead ultimately to liberation. He will explain in detail the demoniac qualities and the mentality which drives one lower on the tree and ultimately to hell.

CHAPTER SIXTEEN

A. Transcendental and demoniac qualities (16.1–16.6)

Kṛṣṇa first mentions twenty-six divine qualities and then describes six demoniac qualities.

B. The demoniac nature (16.7–16.20)

To assure Arjuna that he possesses divine not demoniac qualities, Kṛṣṇa further describes the activities, mentality, and qualities of one who has demoniac tendencies. Kṛṣṇa casts these mischievous demons into repeated births in demoniac, abominable species.

C. The choice: escaping to the supreme destination (16.21–16.24)

The three gates leading to the soul's degradation and his entanglement in a demoniac mentality are lust, anger, and greed. Every sane man should give these up, act for purification and attain the supreme destination. (21–22) This means that instead of acting controlled by lust, anger and greed, one should act in accordance with *śāstra*. (23–24)

CONNECTION BETWEEN CHAPTERS 16 & 17

In chapter sixteen, Kṛṣṇa has established that faithful followers of *śāstra* are divine and that the faithless are demoniac. But into which category does a man fit who follows with faith something other than *śāstra*? Is he in goodness, passion, or ignorance?

CHAPTER SEVENTEEN

A. The modes determine one's faith and one's worship (17.1–17.7)

Arjuna inquires about the situation of one who worships, but not according to *śāstra*. Kṛṣṇa replies that one who doesn't follow *śāstra* worships according to the faith dictated by his acquired modes of material nature.

B. Foods in the modes (17.8–17.10)

The easiest way to discover a person's situation under the modes is by observing what food he eats. Kṛṣṇa thus first describes foods in goodness, passion, and ignorance.

C. Sacrifices in the modes (17.11–17.13)

Sacrifices can also be performed in the modes: dutifully (goodness), fruitively (passion), or unfaithfully (ignorance).

D. Austerity in the modes (17.14–17.19)

Austerities can be of the body, speech, and mind. Each of these austerities can be performed in goodness, passion, or ignorance.

E. Charity in the modes (17.20–17.22)

Charity can also be performed in goodness, passion, or ignorance. The results will differ.

F. The conclusion: oṁ tat sat (17. 23–17.28)

All activities are contaminated by the modes, and those defects can be offset by acting, even if within the modes of nature, in Kṛṣṇa's service: *oṁ tat sat.* The conclusion is that when sacrifice, penance, and austerity are performed without faith in the Supreme – without a transcendental goal

– they are useless both in this life and the next.

CONNECTION BETWEEN CHAPTERS 17 & 18

To emphasize the goal of surrender to Kṛṣṇa, the essence of the previous chapters is taught in the final chapter. Kṛṣṇa begins His summary of all He has previously spoken by reiterating His prescription that Arjuna renounce the fruits of work, not work itself.

CHAPTER EIGHTEEN

A. Summary of chapters 1–6: karma section (18.1–18.12)

A true *sannyāsī* does not renounce his activities but is detached from their fruits. Thus Kṛṣṇa concludes that the renounced order of life (*sannyāsa*) and renunciation of the fruits of action (*tyāga*) are the same. To perform work in this way is renunciation in the mode of goodness.

B. Summary of chapters 13–18: jñāna section (18.13–18.18)

To help us perform activities without becoming bound, Kṛṣṇa cites *Vedānta* and analyzes activities as comprised of five factors. The most prominent of these factors is the Supersoul. One who acts under the direction of the Supersoul is unaffected by reactions to his actions.

Summary of the Yoga Ladder (C-H)

Karma

C. The modes control all activities (18.19–18.40)

One's work according to the five factors mentioned above is dictated by the three modes of material nature. This includes one's knowledge (19–22), one's actions (23–26), one's performance of action (27–28), one's understandings (29–32), one's determination (33–35), and one's happiness (36–39). All activities within the universe are thus controlled by the three modes of material nature.

Sakāma to niṣkāma karma-yoga

D. Freedom from reaction by occupational work (18.41–18.48)

Although all work is controlled by the modes, one can

nevertheless become free from the reactions of work by acting as a *brāhmaṇa, kṣatriya, vaiśya,* or *śūdra* in *niṣkāma karma-yoga* while worshiping the Lord through that work.

From niṣkāma through liberation to devotional service

E. Confidential knowledge: from reaction-free work through jñāna-yoga to the Brahman platform and pure devotional service (18.49–18.55)

One practicing *niṣkāma karma-yoga,* detached work, attains goodness and the knowledge that he is not his body. He finally attains the Brahman platform. By serving Kṛṣṇa on this platform, with devotion, one reaches the kingdom of God.

F. Working in pure devotional service (18.56–18.60)

One on the platform of devotion should work under the order of the Lord, fully depending on Him and being fully conscious of Him. One will thus be free from the control of the modes of material nature.

G. More confidential knowledge: surrender to the Supersoul (18.61–18.63)

More confidential knowledge than the knowledge that one is spirit soul is knowledge that one should surrender to the Supersoul.

H. The most confidential knowledge of all: become a pure devotee of Kṛṣṇa (18.64–18.66)

Always think of Kṛṣṇa, become Kṛṣṇa's devotee, worship Kṛṣṇa, offer all homage unto Kṛṣṇa, and thus come to Kṛṣṇa. Surrender to Kṛṣṇa; do not fear sinful reactions.

I. Preaching and studying the Bhagavad-gītā (18.67–18.71)

For one who explains this knowledge of the *Bhagavad-gītā* to austere, nonenvious devotees, pure devotional service is guaranteed. Those who study the *Bhagavad-gītā* worship Kṛṣṇa with their intelligence, and faithful and nonenvious hearers become free from sinful reactions.

J. Arjuna is firmly fixed (18.72–18.73)

After hearing the *Bhagavad-gītā,* Arjuna is fixed and determined to act according to Kṛṣṇa's instructions.

K. Sañjaya's predictions (18.74–18.78)
Sañjaya ecstatically thinks of the wondrous form of Kṛṣṇa and predicts victory for Arjuna, the supreme archer, and Kṛṣṇa, the master of all mystics.

Appendix Seven

Answering Two Questions on the Bhagavad-gītā Verses 12.9–12

In this appendix I attempt to answer two questions about my understanding of verses 12.9–12 and the presentation of the progression found in them. Of all the sections in the *Bhagavad-gītā,* I have found these verses especially difficult to connect. Indeed, each *ācārya* has described and explained Kṛṣṇa's words in his own way. Because of this, I have basically limited my comments to the understanding I have gathered from Śrīla Prabhupāda's translations and purports.

QUESTION: After reading the first paragraph of the comment to text 10:

> The previous two verses dealt primarily with engaging our mind, the chief of the internal senses, on Kṛṣṇa. This verse, a stage lower, directs our external senses in Kṛṣṇa's service as a means of further advancement. Even if we are unable to think of Kṛṣṇa through absorption in His devotional service, either in perfection or in practice, we can make progress by working for Him. This platform is called *karma-yoga.*

Someone could ask, "Doesn't text 9 deal primarily with *vaidhi-bhakti* or *sādhana-bhakti,* including 'working,' i.e., doing practical things for Kṛṣṇa, and doesn't text 10 describe the work for Kṛṣṇa performed by those unable to follow the rules of devotional service?"

ANSWER: When Śrīla Prabhupāda, in his purport to text 10, speaks about being unable to follow the rules, one may infer that he is referring to an inability to follow the four rules that qualify one for initiation. However, in his purport to text 9, Śrīla

Prabhupāda described the rules and regulations about which he is speaking – the basic activities of *sādhana-bhakti:* "To practice the regulative principles of *bhakti-yoga* one should, under the guidance of an expert spiritual master, follow certain principles: one should rise early in the morning, take bath, enter the temple and offer prayers, and chant Hare Kṛṣṇa, then collect flowers to offer to the Deity, cook foodstuffs to offer to the Deity, take *prasāda,* and so on. There are various rules and regulations which one should follow. And one should constantly hear the *Bhagavad-gītā* and *Śrīmad-Bhāgavatam* from pure devotees. This practice can help anyone rise to the level of love of God, and then he is sure of his progress into the spiritual kingdom of God. This practice of *bhakti-yoga,* under the rules and regulations, with the direction of a spiritual master, will surely bring one to the stage of love of God."

In text 8, Kṛṣṇa describes one who has already achieved attachment to Him and full absorption in Him, and text 9 describes the activities – the rules and regulations – by which one may achieve that result. Text 10, the discussion about the inability to follow "the regulative principles of *bhakti-yoga,*" seems, again, to be referring to the principles of engagement described in text 9, which is a specific level of activity or service to Kṛṣṇa. In text 10, Kṛṣṇa is clearly describing a devotee who serves on a lesser level, the level of *karma-yoga,* and Śrīla Prabhupāda, in his purport, details the services offered by devotees practicing on the levels of either *niṣkāma karma-yoga* or *sakāma karma-yoga*. The result of such service is elevation in Kṛṣṇa consciousness.

A way to distinguish between the type of activities Kṛṣṇa recommends in text 9 and the type of activities Kṛṣṇa recommends in text 10 is to note the differences in relation to how the mind is engaged. Those engagements described in text 9 directly engage the mind in Kṛṣṇa's service and those mentioned in text 10 only indirectly engage the mind. Thus the activities of text 9 are superior. In text 10, which describes *karma-yoga,* the devotee offers to Kṛṣṇa the fruit of the work he is already doing. That is the description given in Śrīla Prabhupāda's purport. Thus in text 10 I comment: "The previous two verses dealt primarily with engaging our mind, the chief of the internal senses, on Kṛṣṇa. This verse, a stage lower, directs our external senses in Kṛṣṇa's service as a means of further advancement. Even if we are unable to think of Kṛṣṇa through absorption in His devotional service, either in perfection or in practice, we can make progress by working for Him. This platform is called *karma-yoga*."

QUESTION: After reading the first sentence of the comment to text 12,

> "If you cannot take to this practice" refers to the practice of *karma-yoga* described in text 10…

Someone could ask, "Don't the words, 'If you cannot take to this practice' in text 12 clearly refer to being unable to follow the principles mentioned in text 9?"

ANSWER: One can easily reach this conclusion because of the first sentence in Śrīla Prabhupāda's purport to text 12: "As mentioned in the previous verses, there are two kinds of devotional service: the way of regulative principles and the way of full attachment in love to the Supreme Personality of Godhead. For those who are actually not able to follow the principles of Kṛṣṇa consciousness it is better to cultivate knowledge, because by knowledge one can be able to understand his real position."

Two problems arise if we accept that the words of text 12, "If you cannot take to this practice," refer to text 9. First, Kṛṣṇa would be more or less negating His own words in text 10, which instructed Arjuna that if he could not perform the activities described in text 9, the direct practices of Kṛṣṇa consciousness, then he should follow the instructions in text 10 and practice *karma-yoga*. By accepting Kṛṣṇa's words in text 12, "If you cannot take to this practice," to refer to text 9, however, we would accept Kṛṣṇa as saying, "If you cannot follow the direct practices of Kṛṣṇa consciousness, then cultivate knowledge, which will lead upward."

The second (and similar) problem is that such an instruction would also contradict the second paragraph in Śrīla Prabhupāda's purport to text 12, in which he divides the path into two: direct (focusing on Kṛṣṇa as the goal) and indirect (not focusing directly on Kṛṣṇa as the goal, but focusing on nondevotional renunciation of the fruits of work, the cultivation of knowledge of Brahman or meditation on the Supersoul). Why would Kṛṣṇa be advising that a soul be thrust from the direct path to the indirect path when He has already mentioned *karma-yoga* in text 10, an alternative which is also on the direct path?

My conclusion, therefore, is that Kṛṣṇa's words in text 12, "If you cannot follow..." refer to being unable to work for Kṛṣṇa, or unable to practice *karma-yoga* as He instructed in text 10. The entire progression thus makes sense.

Still, a problem, arises. By accepting my conclusion, the first two sentences of Śrīla Prabhupāda's purport to text 12 then become difficult to understand. Those sentences are: "As mentioned in the previous verses, there are two kinds of devotional service: the way of regulative principles and the way of full attachment in love to the Supreme Personality of Godhead. For those who are actually not able to follow the principles of Kṛṣṇa consciousness it is better to cultivate knowledge, because by knowledge one can be able to understand his real position."

To reconcile all of the above, I take it that the engagements Kṛṣṇa describes in text 10, those of *karma-yoga,* actually do fall within the realm of *vaidhi-bhakti* – the way of regulative principles. Or, at the very least, the *karma-yogī* is not resentful of the regulative principles and works sincerely, as Prabhupāda writes in his purport to Bg. 3.31, "without consideration of defeat and hopelessness." With this mood, "he will surely be promoted to the stage of pure Kṛṣṇa consciousness." That is the practical view. Many devotees fall into the category of text 10. Not accepting this view, such devotees might renounce the practice of *niṣkāma karma-yoga* or *sakāma karma-yoga* as described by Kṛṣṇa in text 10 and begin cultivating knowledge of Brahman.

Thus, accepting Kṛṣṇa's words in text 12, "If you cannot take to this practice" as referring to *karma-yoga* as described in text 10, the progression, as Śrīla Prabhupāda has described it in the second paragraph of his purport and as I have described it in my comment, remains intact.

INDEX

A

B

C

D

Dāmodara-līlā, 207
Death
  dishonor worse than, 35–36
  fruitive desires, 44
  Kṛṣṇa and, 189, 216, 218
  lamentation, 26, 28
  preparations for, 164, 171–72, 176–77
  time of, 52, 169–170
Defection, 5–6
Demigods
  Kṛṣṇa Lord of, 121
  Kṛṣṇa not understood by, 148, 206, 208, 236
  Kṛṣṇa source of, 164, 208, 260
  liberation and, 176–77
  universal form, 94, 228
Demigods, worship of
  as agents of Lord, 94
  indirect worship of Kṛṣṇa, 168–69, 192
  material desires, 84–85, 159
  results of, 41, 62–63, 159–61, 190, 193
  as Supreme Lord, 189
  See also Karma-kāṇḍa; Sacrifices
Demoniac nature, 155, 298–304
Demons
  activity of, 300–304
  austerities of, 311–12
  qualities of, 298–99, 305
  scripture and, 300, 303, 305–6, 309–10
  surrender to Kṛṣṇa, 155–56
  See also Duṣkṛtinas
Desires
  analogies, 51, 107
  desirelessness, 60–61, 173, 350
  devotional service, 83–85, 293, 339
Desires (*continued*)
  mode of passion, 275, 277
  responsibility, 114–15
  See also Lust
Detachment
  acting with, 44–45, 59, 106
  attachment to Kṛṣṇa and, 108
  banyan tree, 287–88
  devotional service, 39, 140
  by hearing, 288
  material entanglement, 316
  purification by, 110–11
  sinful reactions, 44–45, 90–91, 110
  See also Attachment; *Karma-yoga, niṣkāma;* Prescribed duty; Renunciation
Determination
  fighting for Kṛṣṇa, 37
  modes of nature, 328, 330
  one-pointed intelligence, 40–41, 45
  protection due to, 197, 198
  in service, 163–64, 188, 191, 248, 281–82
  yoga, 134–35, 335
Devas, 297, 309. *See also* Demigods
Devotees
  Bhagavad-gītā and, 348–49
  blasphemy of, 303
  dear to Kṛṣṇa, 247–49
  dependence on Kṛṣṇa, 340
  desirelessness, 60, 61
  difficulties, 241–42
  fearlessness, 195
  fighting by, 342
  four types of, 159
  happiness and distress, 47
  jñāna-miśra, 157–58
  Kṛṣṇa provides for, 211
  Kṛṣṇa appears for, 82
  Kṛṣṇa's reciprocation with, 10, 184, 195–97, 207, 211–12

G

J

K

L

M

N

O

P

T

W